THE

SOCIALIST REGISTER 1980

THE
SOCIALIST REGISTER
1980

EDITED BY

RALPH MILIBAND

and

JOHN SAVILLE

THE MERLIN PRESS
LONDON

First published in 1980
by the Merlin Press Ltd.
3 Manchester Road,
London, E.14.

SBN 085036 266 0 cl
085036 267 9 pbk
Printed in Great Britain by
Whitstable Litho Ltd., Whitstable, Kent

TABLE OF CONTENTS

PREFACE

The essays in this seventeenth volume of the *Socialist Register* deal with many different topics: but they share a concern to probe from independent socialist positions some of the main issues and problems which confront the Left in the world today. One of the Editors attempts to tackle the questions posed to socialists by Soviet intervention in Afghanistan, the Vietnamese intervention in Kampuchea, and other such enterprises; and we hope that this discussion will be continued in future volumes of the *Register*. John Palmer discusses the economic crisis of world capitalism and the challenges which it poses to the Left; and S.M. Miller outlines the likely points of tension in the eighties, in the United States and elsewhere. This article, and the following one by Stanley Aronowitz on the labour movement and the Left in the United States, are a necessary reminder that the American Left is part of American reality, and that its condition and prospects are a matter of crucial concern to socialists everywhere else. Jane Jenson, from her own personal experience, provides an illuminating account of the French Communist Party's encounter with feminism; and at a time of great controversy in the Labour Party, John Saville reassesses the personality and politics of Hugh Gaitskell. John Saul explains the background of Robert Mugabe's electoral victory in Zimbabwe and Susanne Mueller contributes an original and challenging account of the Tanzanian experience. Fred Block's essay pursues an important theme in the discussion of the theory of the state, namely the question of the state's autonomy; and Laurence Harris, in the light of some recent books on the welfare state, asks pertinent questions about the state's role in this and other spheres. The essay from Hungary by György Bence and János Kis is an important document on the state of Marxism in Hungary. Finally, Peter Worsley contributes a searching critique of Immanuel Wallerstein's influential work *The Modern World-System*.

Of our contributors, John Palmer is European Correspondant of the London *Guardian*. S.M. Miller is Professor of Sociology at Boston University and Stanley Aronowitz is Professor of Sociology at the University of California, Santa Cruz. Jane Jenson teaches Political Science at Carleton University, Ottawa, and John Saul is at Atkinson College, York University, Toronto. Susanne Mueller is at the African Studies Centre of Boston University, and Fred Block is in the Sociology Department of the University of Pennsylvania. Laurence Harris is Senior Lecturer in Economics at the Open University and Peter Worsley is Professor of

Sociology at the University of Manchester. As the Introduction to their essay indicates, György Bence and János Kis are at present deprived by the Hungarian authorities of any form of scholarly employment. We are grateful to our contributors for their help but, as usual, wish to stress that the views expressed by any of the contributors to this volume are not necessarily shared by the others, or by the Editors. We are also grateful for their cooperation and help to Martin Eve and David Musson of Merlin Press.

We very much welcome suggestions from readers as to the kind of material we should be publishing; and we are always glad to consider offers of contributions. All correspondence and material should be addressed to Merlin Press.

July 1980   R.M.
                                                                                                       J.S.

THE

SOCIALIST REGISTER 1980

MILITARY INTERVENTION
AND SOCIALIST INTERNATIONALISM*

Ralph Miliband

1

Soviet military action in Afghanistan has once again served to underline the need for socialists to clarify their positions on the issue of military intervention by the USSR and other Communist states in other countries—including of course intervention against other Communist states. Before the USSR's intervention in Afghanistan, there was Vietnam's intervention in Kampuchea and its overthrow of the Pol Pot regime; and there was also China's intervention in Vietnam. Before that, there was Cuba's intervention in Angola and also in Ethiopia. Other instances from the less recent past readily come to mind—for instance Soviet intervention in Czechoslovakia in 1968 and in Hungary in 1956; and so on back to the overthrow by the Red Army of the Menshevik regime in Georgia in 1921 and its abortive march on Warsaw in 1920.

These very different episodes—or at least some of them—have raised much more difficult questions for socialists than does American and other Western military intervention all over the world. Insofar as such Western intervention has been intended to shore up reactionary regimes against revolutionary movements of very diverse kinds, socialists have had no problem in opposing it. But Russian, Chinese, Vietnamese and Cuban military intervention has produced no such easy unanimity on the left. On the contrary, it has generated great uncertainty, confusion and division; and it has commonly led to the adoption of positions which are not based on any obvious socialist principle but rather on antecedent sympathies or antipathies, according to which a particular intervention is approved or condemned. Empirical justification comes later; and given sufficient selectivity and a strong will to believe, it comes quite easily.

That there should be much uncertainty and confusion over military intervention by Communist states is not surprising: the issues, for socialists, are often full of difficulties and dilemmas. To recognise that this is so is perhaps the first rule to be followed in discussing them. But the

---

*An early version of this article was presented to a private seminar in London in May of this year. The discussion that followed was very helpful and I am grateful to the participants.

1

difficulties and dilemmas make it all the more necessary to clarify the principles on which judgments are made. This is what the present article tries to do.

2

It may be best to begin with the one set of conditions in which military intervention poses no problem in terms of socialist principles. This is where a more or less progressive government (the use of the formula will be justified presently), enjoying a large measure of popular support, is seeking to repel a counter-revolutionary internal movement, in conditions of civil war or approximating to civil war; or where such a government is seeking to repel a military attack from abroad which is clearly designed to overthrow it. Both internal and external attack may of course be combined. Military help to a threatened government is obviously justified in such circumstances in terms of socialist internationalism. What precise form the help should take must remain for the requesting government to decide, just as states being asked for help must take many different considerations into account, including the larger international implications of the giving of help, particularly if it is to assume the form of military intervention.

Even in these circumstances, it is crucial that the requesting government should remain in charge, and that it should not surrender its destinies to another power, however friendly. This may raise problems, even serious problems, for instance of military command, or of strategic decision-making. But to the greatest possible extent, the requesting government must remain in charge and seek to preserve ultimate sovereignty; otherwise, there is a great danger that military intervention will soon come to bear a disturbing resemblance to military domination and even occupation.

The classic case of justified external military help is (or perhaps more accurately should have been) that of the Spanish Civil War, where a liberal-left government was faced with a military rebellion of fascist inspiration, backed by Fascist Italy and Nazi Germany. The International Brigade that was then formed, mostly at Communist initiative, was the most remarkable example of international socialist solidarity and of 'proletarian internationalism' in history. And for all the many foul features of Soviet help to the Spanish Republic, that help also falls under the rubric of international solidarity. What was wrong with Soviet intervention is that there was not enough of it; and that one of the forms it took was the liquidation of large numbers of anti-Stalinists who were fighting for the Republic.

Another more recent example is that of Cuban intervention in Angola. Whether initially prompted by the USSR or not, Cuban military intervention there was clearly justified on the criteria advanced earlier. For it contributed to the survival of a revolutionary government just emerging from a long anti-colonial war against Portugal, enjoying a large measure of popular support, and faced with internal enemies backed by South Africa, the United States, Zaire, China, and so on.[1] In the same line of thought, Soviet and Chinese help to Vietnam was similarly justified, and there would have been every justification, in principle, for more such intervention, had the Vietnamese asked for it—although larger considerations of war and peace would obviously have had to be taken into account.

I have referred here to 'more or less progressive' governments and regimes, and use this formula in order to take some necessary distance from the rhetoric which is the usual accompaniment of discussions of intervention, where the regime which is being helped tends to be accorded every conceivable socialist virtue and is painted in the most brilliant colours. Yet, such governments are not, and in the circumstances cannot be, as pure and praiseworthy as they are said to be by their internal spokesmen and external apologists. Whatever they may say about themselves, and whatever may be said on their behalf, the conditions in which they have come to power and in which they function, are bound to affect adversely—often very adversely—the 'socialism' which they proclaim. One of the many blights which Stalinism cast on socialist thinking was the habit—indeed the requirement—to view favoured regimes (beginning with Stalin's own) as unblemished examples of socialist construction; and the habit at least did not die with Stalin. The craving to believe is very strong; but it surely ought to be resisted. Governments do not have to be perfect in order to be supported—and *critical* support is the most that *any* government ought to be accorded. The legitimacy of intervention does not rest on the (always illusory) socialist perfection of the government that is being supported: it rests rather on a judgment that its survival is in peril; and that, for all its imperfections and shortcomings, it deserves to survive, because of the hopes it offers and because of the reactionary nature of the forces which are threatening its survival.

A second set of conditions is where a movement of opposition or liberation, with a substantial measure of support, is waging a military struggle, from its own liberated bases, against an authoritarian and reactionary regime representing landed, commercial and financial oligarchies, foreign concerns, multi-national corporations, and backed by the United States and other Western powers. It is worth stressing that such governments and regimes *have* ever since World War II enjoyed the backing of the United States and other Western powers because, however repressive and corrupt they may be, they are part of the Free World, meaning in effect the Free Enterprise world. This being the case, defending these regimes against their own people is an intrinsic part of the logic of imperialism. This logic requires such defence for a number of different but related reasons: as long as they are part of the Free World, they are available for the operations of free enterprise; they may also have strategic importance; and they may have resources—oil, uranium, etc.—which enhance their value to their protectors. The overthrow of reactionary and repressive regimes by popular movements, of whatever kind, is therefore unacceptable or at least unwelcome, because all the advantages which these governments offer to imperialism risk being extinguished; and there is also the risk that successor regimes may be sympathetic to Communist powers, or that they will at least be made less easy to handle than hitherto; and their success in achieving power in any case strengthens the anti-imperialist cause. The coming into being of successor regimes may not always be prevented; but in that case, they must be subverted and coopted back into the Western camp.

Clearly, movements of opposition and liberation require and deserve international socialist solidarity and support. But military intervention is a different matter: and as a matter of fact, such movements very seldom ask for it. The reason for this is obvious, namely that, if they did, they would run the very grave risk of being swamped and taken over by the intervening power, or at least of losing effective control over the struggle they are conducting; and its leaders would at the same time be bound to incur the accusation of being puppets or agents of that power. Liberation struggles, however inspired and whatever they call themselves, have almost by definition a strong nationalist ingredient. Very often, the movement is impelled by the will to rid the country of a regime which has brought it into dependence on another state: all other aims, including the achievement of economic, social, and cultural advances, are seen to pass through the achievement of national independence or statehood. Given this, acceptance of foreign protection by way of foreign military intervention cuts across this national—and nationalist—emphasis, or at least runs the very great risk of doing so. This is presumably why leaders of liberation and guerilla movements do not usually seek military aid beyond the supply of weapons, or training assistance, or military advisers.

Governments are a different matter. For they can at least claim sovereign authority, and are therefore better able to control the foreign intervention they require and may ask for. A group of revolutionaries in the field is likely to find such control more difficult to achieve. Also, the intervening power, being by definition 'friendly', is likely to be more inhibited in its relations with a formally independent government, able to claim sovereign authority, than with a revolutionary movement. But even in the case of governments, the risk of being swamped, of being taken over, or of suffering a serious reduction of authority, may be considerable, and is bound to weigh in the calculations which government leaders must make whether to invoke external military help or not.

The third set of conditions is the one the left has most commonly had to confront, and which it has found the most difficult. This is where military intervention has occurred without it being requested by a government enjoying any measure of popular support, or indeed by anyone at all except some individuals without authority (Hungary, 1956; Afghanistan, 1979); or where military intervention has occurred *against* a government enjoying a large measure of popular support, and at the behest of some individuals again without authority or support (Czechoslovakia, 1968). A rather different case which falls however within the same spectrum is that of Vietnam's intervention in Kampuchea: what might be called a frontier war between the two countries was taken further by Vietnam, to the point of overthrowing the Pol Pot regime and installing another regime in Phnom Penh, acceptable to the Vietnamese. The military intervention of China against Vietnam is of a different order, and must be treated separately.

In such cases as Hungary, Czechoslovakia, Kampuchea and Afghanistan, the claim that foreign armies had some legitimate ground for intervention because they were 'invited' to come in is evidently spurious; and it is only in bad faith that it can be advanced. But this is not of course the only ground on which intervention is defended. It is in fact defended on one or other of three different grounds (or on all three), each of which requires consideration: unlike the claim about intervention being 'invited', these other arguments raise precisely the issues which socialists have to confront.

One such argument is that, in case after case, there existed a grave and imminent threat of counter-revolution, backed by Western imperialism and indeed instigated by it, against a socialist regime and its revolutionary achievements. Even in Czechoslovakia in 1968, it was claimed, and still is, that whatever the intentions of Alexander Dubçek and the Czech Government might have been, there was a clear and immediate threat of 'things getting out of control', of the 'restoration of capitalism', or 'counter-revolution', of Czechoslovakia pulling out of the Warsaw Pact, and so on.

Such claims cannot by definition be conclusively proved or disproved, which is why it is possible for endless controversy to go on about them, without anyone's positions being much affected either way. It may be that a better way to proceed is to ask first of all what some of the key terms—notably counter-revolution—actually mean in this context. Misunderstanding of what the argument is about may thereby be avoided. For some, 'counter-revolution' is more or less synonymous with the replacement of a government wholly subservient to the USSR by a government not thus subservient. But this—typically Stalinist—definition is clearly not adequate. When Tito broke with Moscow in 1948, Communist parties everywhere—not to speak of the Soviet government—denounced him as an 'authentic Fascist' and as, in the terminology of the French Communist Party at the time, a 'Hitlero-Trotskyist', who was indeed leading a counter-revolution. Without a doubt, if Russian armies had intervened in Yugoslavia then, had succeeded in overthrowing Tito, and had installed a 'pro-Soviet' government in Belgrade, there would have been many to say that the Soviet Union had rescued the Yugoslav people from counter-revolution. This should perhaps serve to induce some caution in the making of statements about what would have happened in this country or that if the Russians had not intervened. For whatever else may be said about Tito's rule after 1948, it can hardly be said that he pushed through a 'counter-revolution' in Yugoslavia; and it is now said that the denunciation of him as a 'Fascist', 'counter-revolutionary', 'agent of the West', etc., were part of the history of Stalinist aberrations and are best forgotten. But the aberrations ought not to be forgotten, for they have important lessons to teach, and there is much evidence that the danger of repeating these aberrations or similar ones is still very much alive. Less dramatically than Yugoslavia by far, Rumania has managed to achieve a considerable degree of independence from the USSR in regard to both internal but particularly external affairs (which does not prevent the regime from being as repressive as any in Eastern Europe); but no one has so far claimed that President Ceacescu has engineered a 'counter-revolution' in his country.

Properly speaking, a counter-revolution may be said to have occurred when a regime of the left, Communist or not, has been overthrown (or for that matter replaced by legal means) and where the successor regime pushes through a series of economic, social and political measures designed to assure or restore the power, property and privileges of landlords, capitalists and other segments of the ruling class who have been threatened with dispossession or who have actually been dispossessed by the regime which the counter-revolution has replaced. This involves the return to landlords and capitalists of their land and factories and banks, and of property in general, where it has been taken from them. It also involves the re-affirmation of their power and preponderance by the suppression of the defence organisations of the subordinate classes—parties, trade unions, cooperatives, clubs and associations. It further involves the suppression or drastic curtailment of civil rights; the physical suppression of opposition leaders, of agitators, subversives and enemies of the state; and the political restructuring of the state in authoritarian directions.

Many counter-revolutions of this kind have occurred throughout Europe since 1918, sometimes against a newly-implanted Communist regime, but also against non-Communist left ones, or even against liberal and conservative ones when they were thought to be inadequate in opposing the left: Hungary in 1919, Italy in 1921 and after, Germany in 1933, Spain in 1936, France with the Vichy regime in 1940, and outside Europe Chile in 1973 are examples of such counter-revolutions and the list could easily be stretched out. It is not essential for a revolution actually to have occurred for a counter-revolution to be mounted: the apparent illogicality is purely in the semantics, not in the reality.

If counter-revolution is taken to involve the sort of changes which have been mentioned here, it would seem reasonable to say that in none of the cases where Soviet armies have intervened since World War II, with the doubtful exception of Afghanistan, has there been a clear and compelling threat of counter-revolution. As noted earlier, this is not susceptible to proof; but neither in the case of Hungary in 1956 nor certainly of Czechoslovakia in 1968, to take two major instances of Soviet intervention, is there evidence that counter-revolution was about to succeed, or likely eventually to succeed. Of course, there were, particularly in Hungary, people who had counter-revolutionary intentions: but that is obviously not the same thing. Nor is it my argument that the Communist monopoly of power would have been maintained intact in either country: on the contrary, it would have been loosened, and the process had already gone some way in Czechoslovakia. In both countries, there might well have come into being a coalition regime in which the Communist Party would not have been assured of an automatic preponderance; and other such variations can easily be conceived. The point is that, whatever may be thought of these possibilities, they cannot, on any reasonable assessment, be equated with 'counter-revolution', or anything like it.

This must be taken a little further. Had the processes at work in Hungary and Czechoslovakia not been crushed out of existence by military intervention, it is likely that there would have occurred a measure of 'liberalisation' of economic life in both countries—something like the New Economic Policy which Lenin and the Bolsheviks were forced to adopt in the Soviet Union in 1921, with a greater emphasis on the market and a redevelopment of artisan and small scale enterprise in manufacturing, retail trade, and so on. The evocation of such 'liberalisation' in economic activity tends to generate the cry of 'Restoration of Capitalism' among many purists. But this is a misconception. For the 'commanding heights' of the economy would have remained in the public sector, and the public sector would have remained massively predominant. It would surely have been exceedingly difficult to unscramble long-nationalised property and to restore factories, mines, land, etc., to their former owners. And there is one measure of 'liberalisation' which would have been of enormous socialist significance, namely the restoration of the right to strike. Purists make much too little of the grievous dereliction, in socialist terms, which the suppression of that right in Communist regimes represents. Not only would the reaffirmation of the right to strike have been proper in itself: it would also have strengthened the credentials of the regime in the eyes of the working class, and made all the less likely the 'restoration of capitalism'. Moreover, this reaffirmation would have been one element among many to mark the loosening of the grip of the monopolistic state over civil society; other such elements would have included the reaffirmation of a whole range of civil rights suppressed earlier. And there would also have occurred a substantial and possibly a major reorientation of the foreign relations of both countries; and this raises the question of Soviet 'security', which will be discussed presently. Tito's foreign policy, it may be said here, may well afford an example of what might have been the most likely course of events in this realm.

The fundamental question which socialists have to confront is not whether the kind of regime that would have emerged from the convulsions of 1956 and 1968 would have been the most absolutely desirable; but whether it would have been a worse alternative than the imposition by Russian arms of a regime altogether lacking in popular support and whose most distinctive characteristic is the tight monopoly of power exercised by a Communist leadership acceptable to Moscow. I suggest that the answer—again leaving out for the moment the question of Soviet 'security'—is that, in socialist terms, it would not have been a worse alternative. The reason for saying so is simply that there can be no good socialist warrant for the imposition by foreign arms of a 'socialist' regime which the overwhelming majority of people resent and reject.

This is no more than the affirmation of a principle akin to that of national self-determination. 'Self-determination' means the right to national independence, expressed by independent statehood. It is a very old principle to which most if not all strands of the socialist movement have always declared allegiance. Admittedly, there was a current of thought in the international socialist movement, most notably represented by Rosa Luxemburg, which rejected the 'slogan' of self-determination on the ground that it diverted the proletariat from its real revolutionary tasks; and Luxemburg continued to hold this view after 1917. But even she said in 1915 that 'socialism gives to every people the right of independence and the freedom of independent control of its own destinies'.[2] In effect, she believed that self-determination could not be achieved under capitalism, and that to seek it was a diversion from the main task; but she also believed that socialism would make self-determination possible and that it was indeed a fundamental right. So did the Bolshevik leaders believe this, with some qualifications other than those advanced by Luxemburg. They very reasonably held that, while self-determination could not be denied to a people who wanted it, and could particularly not be denied by the revolutionaries of an 'oppressor' nation like Czarist Russia, it was not incumbent upon them to press it upon people who were content with regional autonomy or federal arrangements. The Bolsheviks' own most important saving clause, however, was that the demand for self-determination must not run counter to the larger requirements of the class struggle, nationally and internationally. Even though they had recognised Georgia's more or less independent status in May 1920, they cast aside its Menshevik Government by military action in February 1921 and brought Georgia back into the Soviet fold. In due course, what had been a saving clause became a convenient excuse. From the early years of the Bolshevik

Revolution until some such time as 1956, there was one centre—Moscow—to decide for the world Communist movement what was in the best interests of the class struggle on a global scale; and this made it possible for the Soviet leaders to interpret the principle of self-determination—and any other principle—as they willed.

Military intervention need not formally deny national self-determination expressed as statehood. The Soviet Union did not incorporate Hungary in 1956 or Czechoslovakia in 1968, and thereby bring to an end their independent existence as states. But military intervention, under the 'doctrine', of 'limited national sovereignty', does turn this statehood into a largely formal thing, by ensuring that a government wholly subservient to the intervening power is installed in the given country. Even this is a lot better than incorporation and the end of statehood: but it does deprive statehood of a substantial part of its meaning. The principle of self-determination is not unduly stretched by the inclusion within it of the right of the people or of a majority of the people not to have a regime imposed upon them by a foreign power. Such imposition does constitute a drastic infringement of the principle of self-determination, which may here be taken to mean popular self-determination. It would be unrealistic to stipulate that under no circumstances of any kind must that principle ever be infringed. But the onus is on those who defend the infringement to show on what other principle the infringement was justified in any particular case; and the point does hold that it is only in the direst and most extreme circumstances that it could ever be justified.

There are many different ways—and not only by military intervention—in which the imposition of unpopular rule can occur. One such way is by the extension of help to reactionary and repressive regimes in order to enable them to defeat popular pressure and resistance; and the United States and its allies have engaged in such imposition on numerous occasions since the end of World War II.[3] It is in Cold War propaganda and apologetics that the Soviet Union and other Communist powers are the only ones to have imposed unwanted regimes upon other countries. But this does not negate the fact that Communist powers *have* engaged in such enterprises.

I have argued that the threat of counter-revolution was not a proper justification for military intervention in the cases of Hungary and Czechoslovakia. But what of Afghanistan? Here is a country where a revolutionary coup brought to power in April 1978 a leftwing government with strong Russian connections and sympathies. The leader of the new regime, Nur Mohammad Taraki, was himself overthrown and killed when he tried, in September 1979, to get rid of his Prime Minister, Hafizullah Amin. Amin took over but was in turn removed and executed at the end of December 1979, and replaced by Babrak Karmal. The removal of Amin and his replacement by Karmal was obviously instigated by the Soviet Union, which also marched into Afghanistan to provide military backing for him.

In Afghanistan as in Hungary and Czechoslovakia, the notion that the Russians were 'invited' in by any kind of legitimate authority is so absurd as not to require discussion. On the other hand, the question of counter-revolution in Afghanistan does require it. The regime that came into being in April 1978 had declared itself to be a revolutionary one, intent upon the thorough transformation of the country in socialist directions. In immediate terms, this meant setting in motion a number of greatly-needed reforms—some measures of land reform, improvements in the position of women, some attempts at alleviating an over 90% illiteracy rate, the grant-ing of cultural rights to national minorities, and the cancellation of debts owed by peasants to richer farmers and landlords.

From the first, the government confronted stubborn resistance and was itself undermined by acute internal dissension and factional struggles of a long-standing nature. It never had more than a very slender basis of support, concentrated in Kabul, and probably numbering no more than a few thousand people in a country of nearly seventeen million, of whom some two and a half million are town dwellers and the rest country dwellers, with a substantial number of nomads. By all accounts, the Taraki regime was fiercely repressive and thousands of people were imprisoned and many executed. This further reduced the government's base of support and fed the strength of its opponents, some of whom were supported by Iran, Pakistan, the United States and China. From the beginning of 1979 if not earlier, the Russians played an important role in the country's government and administration, and also in the military struggle against opposition forces. At the end of 1979, this turned into full scale military suppression, or attempted suppression, and this has since then assumed larger proportions.

In the case of the military interventions in Hungary and Czechoslovakia, it could be argued that Russian arms were safeguarding the economic, social and political transformations which had been brought about by the regimes which had come into being some ten years earlier in the Hungarian case and twenty years earlier in the Czech one. As I have said earlier, this argument, based on the threat of counter-revolution, is unconvincing. But even this justification is lacking in the case of Afghanistan. For the regime was new, had achieved very little, was exceedingly weak (except in the repression of those of its opponents it could reach) and did not appear to have any serious measure of popular support. There was no revolution to save in Afghanistan, only a government that proclaimed its revolutionary intentions but had extremely poor revolutionary prospects. The chances are that no government in Afghanistan resting on so slender a base as the Taraki and Amin regime could hope to achieve much; and that it would only be able to maintain itself—if at all—by continued repression and the help of foreign arms.

Here too, the question of alternatives has to be posed. It is of course convenient to argue that *no* alternative to Babrak Karmal existed save the blackest kind of reactionary regime, allied to the United States, Pakistan and China. This seems very unlikely. No doubt, there would have been much turmoil if the Russians had not intervened. Probably, the People's Democratic Party of Afghanistan (PDPA), or rather its leaders, would have lost the monopoly of power which they achieved with the coup of April 1978. The chances are that they would have had to share power with 'outside' elements by way of a coalition; and that there would have occurred a loosening of ties with the USSR.

No option of this sort appears to have been explored, either by the leaders of the PDPA or by the Russians. The reason for this is twofold: first, because it would precisely have meant the relinquishing of monopolistic power by the PDPA leaders, which was a difficult and risky enterprise that they were naturally loath to consider; and secondly because the Soviet Union feared that a loosening of power by the PDPA leadership would indeed have meant the erosion and possibly the end of their preponderant influence in a country which had come to be in their 'sphere of influence' and control. This, incidentally, would have restored a situation which had prevailed in the years preceding the coup of 1978, when Afghanistan under the rule of Mohammed Daud was the terrain of intense competition between the United States (via Iran) and the USSR. The coup of 1978 was in this sense a major victory for the USSR, which it was not prepared to see jeopardised by an attempted widening of the base of the regime. The question of security, which will be taken up presently, was obviously an important consideration. But the larger question, encompassing that of security, is that the end of monopolistic power in Afghanistan would have appeared to be a retreat of Soviet power, for which the only parallel or precedent is Tito's 'rebellion' against Stalin in 1948. The Soviet leaders were not prepared to risk such a retreat. Instead, they opted for the installation of a puppet regime backed by military force. It is possible that such a regime can be maintained by military force. But it seems more likely that the Russians themselves will be compelled to engineer some kind of compromise solution, since the present situation involves them in a war of pacification which, in the nature of the terrain and the opposition (and the help which the opposition will be able to get from outside), they cannot conclusively win. But however this may turn out, the fact remains that the military intervention altogether lacks legitimacy and has strengthened rather than weakened the forces of counter-revolution in Afghanistan.

3

'Preventing counter-revolution' and 'saving the revolution' is one argument which leads many socialists to accept the legitimacy of military intervention in such cases as Hungary or Czechoslovakia or Afghanistan. A second, closely related argument, is not usually stated explicitly but exercises a powerful attraction and goes as follows: the revolution may or may not have been supported by a majority of the people, or even by a substantial minority. But even if it was not, it did happen; and it must therefore be maintained at all costs and if necessary by force of foreign arms, not only because the alternative is counter-revolution, or because an alternative poses a threat to Soviet security, but also because *in due course* the people will come to see the advantages of the regime which the revolution installed. They will come to accept the regime and to support it. Early progress towards 'socialism' will thus have been made more or less against the will of the people. But given the advantages of the system and what it will do for the people, later progress will be made on the basis of popular support. In this sense, what military intervention is doing is to give the revolution a breathing space and to make possible its later consolidation and successes. Military intervention buys time for the revolution and could even be said to be an extreme form of 'substitutism', with foreign armies rather than the party 'substituting' themselves for the will of the proletariat and allied classes. Of course, 'substitutism' is a deformation. It runs counter to the Marxist 'scenario' for a socialist revolution, or at least to Marx's view of it; and it also runs counter to Lenin's view of the party as being closely linked to, even though separate from, the working class, and as requiring a large measure of popular support to make a revolution. But, the argument goes on, circumstances impose hard choices, particularly in an international context of implacable hostility to the revolutionary cause; and theory has to be adapted to the requirements of real life, without self-defeating and dogmatic adherence to frozen formulas; and so on.

The trouble with the argument is not only that it contradicts Marx's 'scenario' for a socialist revolution, or Lenin's: this is hardly a conclusive objection. The trouble is rather that the projection on which the argument is based is exceedingly dubious and has in fact been shown by experience to date to be wrong.

The crucial factor here is popular support, or rather lack of popular support. The revolution which is being saved by foreign arms is one which the large—usually the overwhelming—majority of the people, including of course the working class and peasants, oppose: it is precisely because of this opposition that foreign military intervention occurs. But the intervention itself constitutes a further condemnation of the regime which depends upon it, and further adds to its already great unpopularity; and it also further alienates the mass of the people from the 'socialism' which the regime and its foreign backers claim to represent and uphold. Military intervention also fuels a powerful nationalist sentiment, itself fostered by antagonism to the regime, and nationalist sentiment is further exacerbated when intervention is carried out by the armies of a country which is viewed by the mass of the people as a secular enemy and predator, whose government is believed to be furthering traditional aims of national agrandisement and domination. An obvious case in point is Poland; and it probably applies also to Vietnam in Kampuchea. Whether the belief is justified or not is not very material: it is deeply held.

These are very heavy burdens for a regime to bear, in terms of its minimal legitimation. Some regimes in Eastern Europe have borne the burdens more easily than others. But nowhere has a Communist regime imposed by foreign arms upon a hostile population been able to acquire massive popular legitimation. The reasons for this include foreign intervention but go well beyond it.

Almost by definition, a regime imposed upon a hostile population by foreign arms (or for that matter without the help of foreign arms) will be strongly repressive: opposition must be put down, civil rights must be denied, and civic life must be severely controlled, and thereby impoverished. This also deeply affects economic life and activity. The regime requires the cooperation of the working class, the peasantry, and the producers in general. But the working class, officially prevented from freely expressing its demands and grievances, and from using the one weapon which is most readily and immediately available to it, namely the right to strike, fights back by non-cooperation at work and everywhere else. Other classes and strata, also alienated and unable to express themselves, do the same. The result is resistance or at best indifference, inefficiency and corruption. Poor performance and non-cooperation aggravate economic difficulties; and these in turn enhance popular dissatisfaction.

In this perspective, the notion that these regimes can eventually come to enjoy a large and growing measure of popular support must appear illusory. For not only are they deeply marked by their dependence on foreign intervention for survival (and for the most part by their origin in foreign intervention); but also by the essential nature of the regimes which military intervention (or the threat of foreign intervention) serves to maintain. The point is that the regimes in question are not simply monopolistic and repressive from temporary necessity and transient adverse circumstances, but by their very structure. I mean by this that they are based on a view of 'socialism' as *requiring* the existence of one 'leading' party whose leaders do exercise monopolistic power; and monopolistic power by definition means the exclusion from power of everyone else, and also the deprivation of rights—speech, association, publication—which are essential for the exercise of power or at least pressure and which are so to speak the oxygen of civil society. To speak of this as a 'Soviet-type' regime is at one level inaccurate, since the rule of the soviets was intended to establish the opposite of concentrated and monopolistic power. But history has associated this monopolistic form of regime with the Soviet Union; and it is therefore convenient to refer to it as a 'Soviet-type' regime. Its early form was the largely unintended product of the circumstances of the Bolshevik Revolution; but it was perfected, with every deliberate intention, by Stalin. All Communist regimes which have come into being since World War II bear this stamp. Some of them are less repressive than others, with the extent of the repressiveness varying not only from country to country but over time within countries. But they are all monopolistic regimes, not excluding Yugoslavia.

Much confusion is engendered by the discussion of these regimes as 'transitional', meaning in effect 'transitional' from capitalism to socialism. Most notably, Trotskyist discussion, which has ever since Trotsky's *The Revolution Betrayed* of 1936 most probingly sought to advance the Marxist analysis of Soviet-type regimes, has also fostered much confusion about them by insisting that they were 'workers' states'; albeit 'bureaucratically deformed'; and that they were 'transitional' between capitalism and socialism. The main reason why this thesis is maintained is of course that in these regimes the private ownership of the means of production has been replaced by state ownership and control. Given this, it is argued, to my mind rightly, that the societies in question are no longer 'capitalist'; and that the description of them as 'state capitalist' does not fit any better. However, they are not 'socialist' either—hence the label 'deformed' or 'degenerate workers' states'. But this label is also defective, not only because they are obviously *not* 'workers' states', of any description, but also because the label is intended to suggest or imply that, for all their bureaucratic deformations, they are *on the way* to being socialist, in a process which, though it will not be painless, has been rendered inevitable by the abolition of the private ownership and control of the main means of production. This needs to be questioned.

The abolition of the private ownership and control of the main means of production is indeed a gigantic step; and it may be said to constitute an essential feature of a socialist society. But it is now very generally agreed that it is not a sufficient condition for the establishment of such a society. Even when this is readily acknowledged, however, it is also often believed that, given the 'base' which is provided by a predominant public economic sector, all other major features of a socialist society—notably democratic and egalitarian forms in economic, social and political life—must sooner or later follow. But this is much too simple and 'economistic' a reading of the 'base-superstructure' model; and an experience which is now sufficiently ample to be convincing shows that a predominantly (or for that matter an exclusively) public economic 'base' does not necessarily produce anything like democratic and egalitarian forms in economic, social and political life, or anything like a 'socialist consciousness' which would prepare the ground for them. On the contrary, such a 'base' may well produce markedly undemocratic and inegalitarian 'superstructures', with a strongly repressive state, a relatedly impoverished civic life, and general indifference and cynicism concerning the 'social good'. To be credible, the notion of 'transitionality' would need to point towards some degree of progress towards socialism in terms of socialist consciousness; for it is absurd to speak of any kind of socialism which does not involve at least popular support for it. But it would surely be rash to claim that the *idea* of socialism (never mind the actual regime) is more securely legitimated in Poland in 1980 than it was in 1970 or 1960 or 1950.

It may be that the picture is more favourable in other countries in Central and Eastern Europe, or in the USSR; but nowhere in Soviet-type societies does there appear to have occurred the *spread* of socialist consciousness which an 'economistic' reading of the 'base-superstructure' model as applied to these societies would suggest or imply. In other words, there is no good reason to think that the regimes in question, because of their public sector 'base', are likely to flower into legitimated socialist democracies, enjoying a large and growing measure of popular support, with a base of genuine popular power, and therefore able to dispense with their vast apparatus of repression and their abrogation of civic rights. On the contrary, and however varied the degree of repression which they experience at any given moment, they are all imprisoned in a very hard mould: not surprisingly, the people in charge, who exercise monopolistic power, have no wish to change in any fundamental way the system which gives them that power, and which they believe to be the only one capable of defending 'socialism'; and the forces making for *socialist* change are generally speaking weak.

On this view, the notion of Soviet-type societies as 'transitional' ones is misleading, illusory, and even vacuous. It is much more helpful to a proper assessment of these societies and their regimes to see them as specific systems, with their own particular mode of production and their own social and political structures. They lack an agreed label: but that does not detract from their reality or from their specificity. They are not capitalist systems. But they are also very far distant from anything that could be called socialism. The term is largely meaningless if it does not include a fundamental recasting of the 'relations of production' and the 'relations of life' in general in democratic and egalitarian directions: and this clearly requires the institutionalisation of the means whereby this can be achieved, or at least striven for. Merely to say this, in relation to Soviet-type societies, is to indicate how great is the distance which separates them from socialism, and how inappropriate it is to apply the notion of 'transition' to them. In the only terms that are ultimately decisive, namely in terms of the generation of socialist consciousness among the people, capitalist societies are at least as 'transitional' as Soviet-type ones.

This is in no way to suggest that these regimes do not have some very considerable achievements to their credit in the economic, social, and cultural-scientific spheres, or that they are not capable of further achievements. Nor is it to underestimate the enormous obstacles placed in their path by economic backwardness and imperialist hostility. Again, it is hardly necessary to say that there are any number of regimes in the world, strongly supported and greatly lauded by the Western powers, which are infinitely worse for their own people than Soviet-type regimes. But none of this turns the latter into socialist ones.

The relevance of these considerations to the question of military intervention as a form of 'substitutism' is obvious. The 'substitutist' argument is that these socialist regimes need time to establish themselves, and must be defended against 'counter-revolutionary' pressure against them. But these are *not* socialist regimes; and what they need to become socialist is not simply time but a fundamental transformation in their whole mode of being. In some of the most dramatic cases of military intervention in the post-war decades—Hungary, Czechoslovakia—this is precisely what a large part of of what is called 'counter-revolutionary' pressure was intended to achieve; and it is precisely what military intervention was intended to prevent. In other words, military intervention did not occur to save 'socialism', but to save monopolistic regimes that are not socialist or 'on the way' to socialism.

4

A subsidiary argument, which has sometimes been used to justify some military interventions, notably the Vietnamese intervention in Kampuchea, may be considered at this point. This is the argument that, whatever may be said against military intervention in most cases, it is defensible in some exceptional cases, namely in the case of particularly tyrannical and murderous regimes, for instance the regime of Idi Amin in Uganda and of Pol Pot in Kampuchea. Idi Amin, it will be recalled, sent Ugandan troops into Tanzania and occupied a substantial area of border territory; and Tanzanian troops did not merely push Ugandan troops back into Uganda but went on to occupy the country and overthrow Amin. Similarly in regard to Vietnam's overthrow of Pol Pot, the Vietnamese claimed that they were faced with repeated and large-scale incursions by Cambodian troops into Vietnam; and the horrifying nature of the Pol Pot regime, it has been claimed on behalf of Vietnam, as well as imperative security considerations (of which more presently), justified Vietnam's decision to march to Phnom Penh and to make an end of the Pol Pot regime.

The argument is obviously attractive: one cannot but breathe a sigh of relief when an exceptionally vicious tyranny is overthrown. But attractive though the argument is, it is also dangerous. For who is to decide, and on what criteria, that a regime has become sufficiently tyrannical to justify overthrow by military intervention? There is no good answer to this sort of question; and acceptance of the legitimacy of military intervention on the ground of the exceptionally tyrannical nature of a regime opens the way to even more military adventurism, predatoriness, conquest and subjugation than is already rife in the world today.

The rejection of military intervention on this score is not meant to claim immunity and protection for tyrannical regimes. Nor does it. For there are other forms of intervention than military ones: for instance economic pressure by way of sanctions, boycott and even blockade. Tyrannical regimes make opposition extremely difficult: but they do not make it impossible. And the point is to help internal opposition rather than engage in military 'substitutism'. As noted earlier, there are rare and extreme circumstances where nothing else may be possible—for instance the war against Nazism. Hitler's Third Reich was not only a tyranny. Nor was it merely guilty of border incursions against other states. It was quite clearly bent on war and the subjugation of Europe. But neither Uganda nor Kampuchea are in this order of circumstances. In socialist terms, the overthrow of a regime from outside, by military intervention, and without any measure of popular involvement, must always be an exceedingly doubtful enterprise, of the very last resort.

5

'Security' is perhaps the reason most commonly invoked to justify military intervention. In the case of Afghanistan, for instance, it has been said that the country has a 1,000 mile border with the USSR, that it is in its 'sphere of influence', and that the USSR could not therefore accept a regime in Kabul that was hostile to it, and liable to come under American influence. The same argument was used, *inter alia,* to defend military intervention in Hungary in 1956 and in Czechoslovakia in 1968; and it has been used to justify Vietnam's overthrow of the Pol Pot regime in Kampuchea.

In considering this argument, much confusion may be avoided if a clear distinction is made between two essentially different propositions. The first of these is that it is useful and desirable for any given country to have uncontentious, cooperative and friendly neighbours. This is indisputable. The second proposition is that the requirements of security do not only make it useful and desirable for this or that country to have such neighbours, but essential, to the point, where possible, of justifying military intervention when the requirements threaten to be no longer met. I think that this second proposition is dangerous and unacceptable from a socialist standpoint, and that it rests on shortsighted and mistaken calculations.

In the case of Afghanistan, it is worth repeating that the USSR found no difficulty in accommodating itself, before the coup of April 1978, to not having a preponderant influence there, and that the alleged security problem did not then appear in the least critical. It has been said that the USSR intervened at the end of 1979 because it feared a Khomeini-style revolution (or counter-revolution), which would have had a subversive effect on the Muslem populations of the USSR living in proximity to Afghanistan. But there is no evidence that such a revolution/counter-revolution was brewing in Afghanistan, or that the Russians were concerned with possible contagion. In short, security may well have been a consideration in the decision to intervene: but it is unlikely to have been decisive and compelling. As I have suggested earlier, there is a better explanation, namely the Soviet leadership's determination not to accept a loosening of the control it had been able to acquire since the coup of April 1978. Such a loosening of control would have represented a definite setback for them, and was unacceptable for a mixture of reasons—prestige, security, fear of repercussions, and so on.

In any case, security by virtue of occupation, and the maintenance of power of a puppet regime must be set against a number of contrary considerations. One of these is the fierce hostility which military intervention generates and the nationalist upsurge it produces. 'Security' is here turned into a mockery by the massive unpopularity of the occupier and his puppet government; and it is further degraded by the war of pacification which has been forced upon the Soviet Union, with all its attendant horrors. What kind of security is this?

The same question may be asked in regard to other countries upon which an unwanted regime has been imposed, for instance Poland. The Soviet Union believed at the end of World War II that a subservient regime in Warsaw was essential to its security. But here too, 'security' is turned into its opposite by the implacable hostility which a Soviet-imposed regime engendered and by the consequent inability of that regime to achieve a genuine measure of legitimation.

As against this, the argument is counterposed that the international context and the hostility of the United States and other Western powers at the end of World War II forced the USSR into the policies it pursued in Eastern Europe: faced with this hostility, it had no option but to create a *cordon sanitaire* for itself, and to prevent its erstwhile allies from using Eastern Europe as a potential advanced base against the USSR. This required the establishment of friendly regimes; and the only regimes that could be trusted to be truly 'friendly' were regimes firmly under Communist control. Soviet security required no less, particularly after the Cold War had got properly under way.

The argument not only leaves out of account the hostility engendered by the external imposition of a Communist regime, particularly one of a Stalinist kind: it also ignores other possibilities, such as are suggested by the case of Finland. 'Finlandisation' is often used by Cold War propagandists to suggest a state of virtual subjection to the USSR. But this is inaccurate.

It means in fact what the Finns describe as 'active neutrality'; and it involves the acceptance of powerful constraints upon the country's external policies. But Finland has remained internally independent. No country could be geographically more important to Soviet 'security'. But Stalin, no doubt influenced by the experience of the Soviet-Finnish war of 1939-40, decided in 1945 not to try and foist a Communist-controlled regime upon Finland, which had fought on the German side and had a long record of bitter enmity to the USSR and Communism. It does not seem unreasonable to suggest that Soviet security would have been at least as well served—to put it no higher—if the same kind of arrangements that were made in regard to Finland had been made in regard to Eastern Europe. Nor is it immediately obvious, on the grounds advanced earlier, that the cause of *socialism* has been better served and is further advanced in Eastern Europe than it is in Finland.

The major dimension which the argument from 'security' tends to ignore is that of popular support; and the question of popular support does not only relate to the countries concerned, but more widely. 'Revisionist' historians in the United States have been perfectly right to claim that there were very powerful forces in the United States and in Western Europe at the end of World War II which were determined to replace a shaky and conflict-ridden war-time alliance with the Russians by outright antagonism. But there were also masses of people in the United States, not least in the ranks of American labour, who appreciated the immense contribution which the Soviet armies had made to the defeat of Germany, and who wanted friendship with the USSR; and there were even more such people in West European labour movements, and beyond labour movements. It is possible that these sentiments would not have prevailed against the barrage of anti-Soviet and anti-Communist propaganda that was launched after 1945 by reactionary forces backed by vast resources and influence. But the least that can be said about this is that these forces would not have had such an easy time of it, and would not have been able to mount such a powerful crusade, had not the Russians given that crusade valuable ammunition by the manner of the settlement which they imposed in Eastern Europe in the post-war years. That settlement was totally Stalinist in inspiration and character; and it was a typical Stalinist perspective which interpreted 'security' in the narrowest and most constricted terms, and which recklessly underestimated the impact of Stalinist infamies on working class and other opinion in Western countries. The search for 'security', interpreted as the establishment of 'reliable' governments and regimes in what Stalin regarded as strategic areas, produced the strengthening of the very forces whose policies posed the major external threat to Soviet security; and the weakening of those forces in capitalist countries, notably their labour movements, which were most likely to oppose anti-Soviet and 'hardline' policies. The same is true of

Soviet military intervention in Afghanistan: this has obviously provided a very powerful reinforcement to the worst reactionaries in the Western camp.

Security considerations have also been invoked to justify the Vietnamese intervention in Kampuchea and its overthrow of the Pol Pot regime. It has been said that, with Chinese encouragement, the Cambodians mounted massive incursions into Vietnamese territory, which were intended to 'destabilise' Vietnam: 'the attacks from Cambodia threatened the whole process of peaceful unification and the integrity of the revolution in the South'.[4] Nothing less would therefore do than the overthrow of the Pol Pot regime.

This is a weak case. Border incidents opposing Kampuchea to Vietnam had occurred long before the Pol Pot regime came to power; and the later incursions were part of a pattern of deteriorating relations for which the Pol Pot regime cannot be held to be the sole culprit. The two regimes had maintained more or less 'normal' relations for some two and a half years after their victory in April 1975—it was only later that Vietnam discovered that the Kampuchean leadership was made up of 'fascists', and vice-versa. Not only is it inherently implausible to suggest that the over-throw of the Pol Pot regime was the only possible course open to the Vietnamese: it is also by no means certain that their security had thereby been much enhanced. No doubt, a pliant regime now exists in Phnom Penh. But it lacks legitimacy and requires the support of a Vietnamese army of occupation. The enterprise has reinforced secular suspicions of Vietnamese designs upon Kampuchea. Like the Russians in Afghanistan, the Vietnamese have been drawn into a permanent struggle with Kampuchean guerillas, with the usual accompaniment of repression and the killing of innocent civilians. The invasion has also weakened Vietnam's international position, and strengthened reactionary forces in the region and beyond. Here too, it does not seem unreasonable to ask 'What kind of security is this?'

It has also been said that the conflict between Vietnam and Kampuchea is only an expression of the wider Sino-Soviet conflict. If so, it is difficult to see how the invasion of Kampuchea and its occupation helps the Vietnamese to cope with the dangers the Chinese pose to them. A hostile Kampuchean regime, allied to China, has been eliminated, but at very considerable cost. And this elimination leaves the main threat precisely where it was. The Chinese launched a major attack upon Vietnam after the latter invaded Kampuchea, in order to 'teach Vietnam a lesson', to quote the infamous justification invoked for the action by Deng Xiaoping and others. Thousands upon thousands of soldiers, Chinese and Vietnamese, as well as civilians—men, women and children—have died to satisfy the Chinese leaders' pedagogic ambitions. The Chinese armies were repelled.

But Chinese hostility endures, and has hardly been diminished by the Vietnamese enterprises in Kampuchea.

It was in relation to American military strategists that C. Wright Mills coined the phrase 'crackpot realism'. But it applies as well to the leadership of Soviet-type regimes, so the record amply suggests. 'Crackpot realism' is here sustained by a narrow, Stalinist, interpretation of 'security' according to which what matters is territory not people. But the strategies which proceed from this not only tend to defeat their own purposes; they also have much larger implications for war and peace.

6

The USSR is not subject to the logic of imperialism; and the charge that it is bent on territorial conquest to the point of 'world conquest' is no more than reactionary ideological warfare. But the USSR does seek 'security', and its interpretation of the concept has led it, and continues to lead it, to seek the defence, consolidation, and, wherever possible, the extension of its 'sphere of influence', particularly but not exclusively in areas which it regards as being of strategic importance. This search for security has one specific feature which is of extreme importance, namely that it is best served when traditional structures in the countries concerned are revolutionised. This is why Soviet help is readily extended to revolutionary movements in the Third World: revolutionary strivings there and the Soviet search for security are roughly congruent. On the other hand, such movements and strivings are opposed by the United States and other Western powers. This is the fundamental source of tension and conflict in the world today: it is somewhere here that 'Sarajevo' is located.

It is obvious that an immense 'mutation', of global dimensions, is now proceeding. The Brandt Commission Report is quite right to stress the terrible poverty in which most countries of the Third World are plunged. However, it is not the poverty which is new, but the revolutionary stirrings in these countries. This is surely one of the most remarkable and inspiring features of the present epoch. For everywhere in the world, and in areas where passivity and resignation in the face of poverty and oppression have tended to be the rule, with only episodic outbursts of rebellion, there is now sustained resistance and struggle, both against local oppressors and their foreign backers and paymasters.

Quite certainly, this will continue to develop in the eighties and beyond. The movements concerned are ideologically very varied; but they are all nationalist and, to a greater or lesser extent, on the left. It must be taken for granted that the United States and other Western powers will seek to counter these movements and to prevent revolutionary upheavals (at least outside Soviet-type and Soviet-oriented regimes); or, if such upheavals do occur, that they will try to ensure that the new regimes, whatever they call themselves, do remain firmly in the 'Western' orbit. The means to be used for the purpose will differ greatly, according to circumstances, and range from economic pressure to military intervention. Conversely, it may also be taken for granted that many movements struggling for their country's independence from imperialist oppression and for social renovation, and that many regimes born of these movements successes, will seek help from the Soviet Union, in the form of economic assistance, or military material, or technical and military advisers, and so on; and that the Soviet Union will answer such calls for help, as a means of weakening Western influence and extending its own, in the hope of thereby strengthening its security.

Whatever the Soviet Union's motives may be, the help it accords to revolutionary movements and regimes is something that socialists cannot but welcome and support. The Cuban regime is now a repressive dictatorship of the Soviet-type model. But in comparison with other regimes in the Third World—many of them murderous dictatorships of an incomparably worse kind, yet completely supported by the United States and other capitalist powers—it is also a progressive regime. The point about it, and about other such regimes, is precisely that they have these two sides—a progressive side as well as a repressive one. Apologists only highlight the first, detractors the second, but both are part of one and the same reality. It is wrong, in a socialist perspective, to ignore the dark side of the Cuban regime; but it would be equally wrong, from the same perspective, not to acknowledge and welcome the help from the USSR which has kept Cuba afloat. Soviet help is by no means given everywhere in a good cause; and there can be no socialist justification whatever for an unqualified endorsement of its policies in their or any other area. But where it does help serve progressive purposes, it has to be supported.

In terms of impact on the international scene, however, and quite apart from the question of socialist principle which has been discussed here, there is an enormous difference between help solicited by and given to revolutionary movements and regimes, and military intervention designed to maintain or instal a deeply unpopular, unwanted and repressive regime. Even 'ordinary' help to revolutionary movements and regimes produces Western accusations of interference, subversion, expansionism, etc.; and it naturally comes up against American and other endeavours in 'counter-insurgency'. Even here, there are many possibilities for escalation of international tension and for the occurrence of explosive 'incidents'. But this is nevertheless very different from the impact produced by actual military intervention, even when that intervention occurs in a country like Afghanistan, which had already come earlier into the Soviet 'sphere of influence'. If it should occur outside that 'sphere of influence', in any circumstances, it must push the world to the brink of war, and quite conceivably over the brink.

The world of the eighties is in any case bound to be uniquely dangerous, not because of Soviet 'expansionism', but because there are certain to be many terrains on which the 'super-powers' will find themselves directly or indirectly engaged in competition and conflict. Independently of the Soviet Union or anybody else, revolutionary movements in the Third World and elsewhere will continue their efforts to destroy the local and international web of backwardness and oppression in which their countries are enmeshed; and some of these upheavals at least will occur in countries of high 'strategic' importance—for instance Pakistan, Thailand, the Phillipines, countries in Latin America, Saudi Arabia, the Gulf States, South Africa and other countries in Africa. The gigantic paradox of the epoch is that these upheavals, which spell hope for oppressed peoples, are also fraught with great perils of clash and confrontation between one 'super-power' bent on 'counter-insurgency' and the other bent on 'security'.

Nor will the process of radical change, or at least the attempt to effect radical change, be confined to the Third World. It would be extremely surprising if one country or other of the 'Soviet bloc' did not experience the kind of upheaval that has episodically been known there. Hungary 1956 and Czechoslovakia 1968 are much more likely to be repeated than not. And it is also very likely that the pressure, now so greatly slackened, for radical changes in Western capitalist countries, will grow again, in the shadow of economic crisis. But this means that there will be innumerable opportunities in the coming years for clash and confrontation between the United States and the USSR. Revolutionary stirrings and 'super-power' strivings here come together in a dangerously explosive package.

Military intervention, as in Afghanistan, adds to the danger; and opposing such intervention is therefore all the more necessary. Socialists have in the past been, and often are still now, inhibited in voicing opposition to unacceptable actions by the Soviet Union and other Soviet-type regimes by the very legitimate fear of finding their voice merged in that of a loud reactionary chorus. But it should be possible for socialist opposition to be voiced in its own terms, on its own premises, and with its own concerns: what this requires, among other things, is that it should be coupled with the insistence, which opposition to Soviet actions should never be allowed to dim, that the fundamental source of tension and danger lies in the determination of the United States and other capitalist powers to stem and reverse the tide of revolutionary change in the world.

NOTES

1. On the other hand, the Cubans had no business helping Ethiopia against Somalia, and their intervention in the conflict between the two countries is a very different matter from that in Angola. The point gains particular force by reference to the fact that Ethiopia is seeking to crush a legitimate movement of independence, namely the Eritrean one. Eritrea was annexed to Ethiopia

by a purely arbitrary act of defiance of the United Nations. The country does not 'belong' to Ethiopia and is entitled to independence.

2. R. Luxemburg, The Junius Pamphlet: The Crisis in the German Social Democracy, in M.-A. Waters, Ed., *Rosa Luxemburg Speaks* (New York, 1970) p. 304.

3. For some recent documentation, see N. Chomsky and E.S. Herman, *The Washington Connection and Third World Fascism* and *After the Cataclysm. Post War Indochina and the Reconstruction of Imperial Ideology,* these being Vol. I and II of *The Political Economy of Human Rights,* Spokesman Press, Nottingham, 1979.

4. A. Barnett, 'Inter-Communist Conflicts and Vietnam', in *Marxism Today,* August 1979, pp. 247-8.

ECONOMIC CRISIS

John Palmer

The word 'crisis' is one of the most overworked in the socialist dictionary. It has come to convey less and less with the passing of the years. But it is difficult to avoid using the term to describe the present economic and political conjuncture in Britain. That is to say it is difficult to see how the problems of the British economy can be resolved without either a fundamental change in the system or in the political assumptions about the system shared by both governments and organised labour since the 1930s.

In purely economic terms the crisis of British capitalism is all too obvious. Economic output is actually falling, and falling further and faster than we have experienced since the end of the Second World War. Unemployment is heading towards two million and the debate among conventional economic forecasters is how far it will go towards three million in the next year or two.

In the meantime inflation shows a stubborn resistance to all known remedies. This is leaving monetarists as baffled now as Keynesians have been for the last few years. Even if inflation comes down in the immediate future to under 20 per cent a year, very few economists expect it to regain single figures for as far ahead as anyone can, with profit, attempt to forecast. If there are differences of prediction between the different economic forecasting bodies such as the National Institute, the London Business School, the Cambridge Economic Policy Group—and the Treasury itself—they concern the precise admixture of gloom as between catastrophic inflation, unemployment, growth, new investment and the balance of trade. The gloom remains a constant.

But if it can be accepted that the economic situation is serious enough to be described as a 'crisis'—what kind of a crisis is it? Is it essentially a short term, perhaps cyclical combination of problems, essentially peculiar to Britain? Is it something which is more the product of ideologically anachronistic monetarist government (or governments) than of any failure of the system as such?

Alternatively, is the crisis essentially international and one which, whatever its immediate, conjunctural features, betrays a more profound and longer term 'impasse' into which the economic system has fallen and out of which it is unlikely to recover without either social revolution or dramatic changes in the political super-structure, including, perhaps, in some western countries, abandonment not only of the post-war socio-political consensus but even democracy itself?

The kind of answers given to these questions are bound to influence the political response of the Left to the present situation. If the crisis is essentially short term, or cyclical or essentially 'British' or a mere product of mistaken government policies—then it can be assumed that there is life left in the old, reformist dog. Conversely if the crisis is 'structural', a response which is limited to the horizons of 'pure and simple trade unionism' or is predicated on the possibility of a Keynesian reformist solution, may prove disastrously mistaken.

Just as there are markedly different species of political and economic 'reformism' so it would be a mistake to make an amalgam of all types of economic catastrophism which are current at present. The belief that the system is doomed is by no means limited to Marxists. In one form or another it is shared by the more extreme theorists of the Club of Rome and those who see a planetary economy increasingly starved of natural resources and doomed to a future of 'nil growth' or something remarkably like it. Such an apocalyptic view owes nothing to any analysis of the capitalist mode of production itself and is anyway increasingly challenged by the facts. There is a problem of ecologically balanced and resource-conscious development to which socialists have been inadequately sensitive. Such development abjures nuclear power in favour of alternative—socially and ecologically more acceptable—energy forms. But there is no reason to suppose that with responsible planning and utilisation the world's natural resources are running out. Indeed some of the more alarmist accounts of resource scarcity have been commercially self-interested—there is evidence, for instance, that the oil companies are deliberately understating the international actual and potential reserves of carbon fuels. Club of Rome alarmism about natural resource scarcity actually legitimises nil economic growth and trade union passivity.

Allowing for the moment that there is an economic crisis in Britain, is there also an international crisis? Remarkably little attention has been devoted to the world aspect of the present economic situation by conventional, mostly Keynesian economists, even by the more radical Keynesians who advise the Labour Left. It is difficult to avoid the conclusion that this is a political phenomenon. Ideologically, Labour Left Keynesians are firm believers in the notion of 'socialism in one country' and central to their parliamentary strategy for the transformation of Britain is the belief that organised labour in Britain can not only break with the established political and economic order in international political isolation, but proceed to build an alternative economic order in continuing isolation.

The essentially 'nationalist' perspective of the Labour Left (and its

Communist Party allies) inspires the demand for import controls. These form an essential foundation of the Alternative Economic Strategy. However, import controls really only make economic sense if either a) the world economy is expanding and the other capitalist states can afford to shrug off British protectionism or b) import controls are part of a comprehensive socialisation of British industry, including sweeping state control of the banks and import/export houses. Neither assumption seems justified by the facts.

Most available evidence suggests that there is a nascent but rapidly maturing international economic crisis. The conjunctural situation is striking. We appear already to have entered another economic recession not only in the United States, but in much of Western Europe and in Japan as well. The latest forecasts coming out of the Paris headquarters of the Organisation for Economic Cooperation and Development (the so-called 'club' of the richest capitalist economies) are gloomy indeed. They call for an average OECD growth rate of between 0 and 1 per cent (against 3½ per cent last year and an average of around 5 per cent in the past fifteen years) with unemployment everywhere approaching forty year records.

At the same time the OECD foresees annual inflation rates averaging 10 per cent and still rising at the end of this year. Thanks to the succession of oil price increases in the past twelve months, the collective balance of payments deficit with the OPEC member states will now exceed $55 billion in 1980. At the very least the latest international recession will be longer and deeper than any since 1945, including the downturn which followed the quadrupling of oil prices in 1973.

Once again the new recession will continue to be burdened with a high inflation rate. Rapid inflation adds to the prevailing lack of confidence in the future by capitalists, makes them less 'risk' minded and impedes the restructuring of the system (that is to say the switch from low-profit sectors to potentially higher-profit sectors) which is the *sine qua non* of any sustained recovery from recession. To the extent that slumps perform a 'useful' purpose for capitalism—in that they encourage the identification of new growth points and encourage the switch of investment and employment accordingly—simultaneous inflation and recession tend to lead to 'unhealthy', abortive periods of recovery which are shortlived precisely because they have not been accompanied by the scale of restructuring really needed.

This is, however, much more than a conjunctural problem. The pattern in recent years has been one of longer and more socially costly periods of economic recession followed by shorter, increasingly inflationary periods of recovery. The recent cycle of recessions both reflects and, at the same time has considerably exacerbated, what is the most alarming symptom of capitalist decline—the steady fall in the rate of return on invested capital. The figures for the declining rate of profit are open to a variety of interpretations and anyway differ from country to country. But the decline in the rate of return on invested capital in manufacturing as well as the decline in the *share* of profits of total output is unmistakeable.

Very often this decline in the rate of profit—extremely marked in the case of Britain and the United States but a subject of concern in most of the developed capitalist economies in the Northern hemisphere—is associated with a precipitate decline in the rate of new investment. But the decline in investment is at least as much the consequence, as the cause, of the fall in the rate of profit. Something of the same phenomenon—viewed from a different angle—can be seen in the remarkable decline in the rate of growth of productivity in many of the older industrialised economies.

Again, the decline in the rate of growth of output—measured variously in relation to investment or the growth in incomes—is simultaneously a cause and an effect of the fall in profitability. There is a tendency on the Left to dismiss talk—much of it emanating naturally from Tory and right-wing Labour monetarists—of a profits crisis. There is also dispute on the Left as to whether—if at all—workers are responsible for this decline in profitability. The fact is that the *primary* reasons for the long-term decline in profitability lie quite outside the workers' responsibility and have to do with a whole range of unpredicted (indeed unpredictable) changes in the international market leading to anarchic investment and production decisions made by individual capitalist firms and industries blind to the impact of their decisions on their fellows.

This said, the extent to which workers and their trade unions are successful in defending the real value of their wages and in defending their jobs must contribute to the total crisis. Wage demands do affect the rate of profit in particular enterprises while the more workers are able to keep threatened jobs, or factories, or whole industries in existence, the more their actions necessarily impede that restructuring of industry which is a precondition to economic recovery *within capitalism*. To exclude workers' actions from any analysis of the overall capitalist crisis is to mystify the economic system and to resort to the politics of 'conspiracy theory'. One form this takes, even on the far Left in Britain, is the belief that always and at all times the capitalists are in a better shape than they claim. Paradoxically, such 'militancy' encourages reformism both by diverting attention from the roots of the crisis in the *system as a system* and by disarming trade unionists when the employers can convincingly display that the profits cupboard is actually bare.

In the older, 'Northern' industrialised economies the profitability crisis has generated the inflation/unemployment epidemic which has undermined confidence in traditional Keynesian, state-interventionist, demand-management economics. This has opened up the ideological space in the system to make possible the monetarist revival. But as the cyclic recession starts to bite and preoccupy politicians and decision makers—even at the expense of concern about inflation—monetarism comes under challenge.

The choice before governments like Mrs. Thatcher's is to pursue their monetarism to the furthest logical conclusions demanded by the situation or risk potential political disaster by retreat and a 'U-turn' back to intervention. But to pursue monetarism to its furthest extremes requires a belief that the power of the trade union movement has been decisively broken and that it is incapable of mounting any counter attack in defence of jobs, conditions and work-place organisation.

The evidence thus far suggests that the trade union movement in Western Europe (particularly in Britain) has been badly shaken and ideologically disarmed by the impact of the monetarist offensive. But it is far from having been defeated let alone destroyed. By and large money wages are keeping within spitting distance of inflation—thus preventing any significant restoration of profit margins in threatened enterprises and industries. The defence of jobs has been signally less successful but we are still a very long way from the wholesale closures of entire industries needed if the re-structuring of British and European capitalism is to proceed.

Given this uncertain balance of industrial power between the trade unions on the one side, and the employers and the Government on the other, the trend will be for the employers to turn on the Government. The worse the profits squeeze becomes the more we can expect the pressure for state intervention to grow—to cut taxes and interest rates and, if necessary, to mount rescue operations of the type that led to the Heath Government 'nationalising' Rolls Royce, Alfred Herbert and so many others in the early 1970s.

The other factor undermining monetarism is its inability to show results within its own terms of reference. The key index for British monetarists has been the Public Sector Borrowing Requirement since this, in current conditions, determines how much the state has to resort to the printing press and thus fuel inflation. But the combination of inflation and recession itself will tend to boost the PSBR—both by cutting government fiscal revenue and increasing state spending on unemployment and social security. It is very difficult to see how the Government can make the off-setting cuts in state spending to compensate since the resulting unemployment and economic deflation will itself tend to push the PSBR up again.

The pressure for a 'U-turn' is, therefore, fuelled both by the immediate profits and potential bankruptcy crises and also by a loss of intellectual faith in monetarism by the employers and Establishment commentators as it is seen not to produce the goods. But periods of intervention only 'buy' shorter and shorter periods of relief for the British economy. To the extent that the restructuring of the economy is delayed by intervention (and its traditional allies—reflation and incomes policy) the ground is laid for worse inflation and deeper recession thereafter. The net result is that the state sector is left with a bigger and bigger first aid department carrying a financing load which the 'productive' and profitable sectors of the economy are too weak to sustain without a further erosion of profitability and a further exacerbation of inflation.

There is an additional exogenous factor which is tending to deepen periods of recession and restrict periods of upturn. The steady rise in the real cost of oil is important for two reasons. Firstly it transfers economic resources from the oil consumers to the producers—that is to say from economies with a marked ability to absorb capital and those with obvious socially and politically limited ability to absorb and employ oil surpluses.

The result of the mismatch between the OPEC surpluses and their re-employment in the world economy is clear even if the exact measurement of that mismatch is difficult. The best estimate is a loss of about one to two per cent in world economic growth and a rather faster loss of growth in world trade. True, the international banks are flush with oil money (for the OPEC oil states have not devised any way of dispensing with the recycling role of the banks). But the banks have to have regard for the profitability and 'security' of their investments. Demand for OPEC surplus funds is most marked on behalf of third world, non-oil-producing, developing countries where profitability and even security of investment is most in question. This gap between the funds available in the international financial system and their re-employment represents a net 'deflationary' leak from the world economy.

The picture looks somewhat different from the standpoint of a third group of countries—the newly-industrialised nations (NICs). Their very existence represents a challenge to socialist theory which predicted that none of the ex-colonial developing countries would make it to the degree of industrialisation and economic growth witnessed in South Korea, Taiwan, Singapore, Brazil or Mexico. They are rapidly moving from dependence on the cheap labour-intensive heavy industries to more sophisticated, high technology industries.

The very existence of the NICs—following on the trail blazed by Japan—has added an exacerbating element to the structural problems of world capitalism. These countries are typically adding to international productive capacity in precisely those industries which are most marked by profit and productivity declines in Western Europe and North America. Sometimes—though not always—it is the same multinationals which are expanding modern steel works or motor plants or shipbuilding yards. But the result is the same to put those industries in the older core countries of the capitalist world under even greater competitive pressure than they would otherwise be.

Of course this process is ridden with serious risks for the capitalist classes in those newly-industrialised countries—and for the multinationals with whom they are so often partnered. It is difficult for them to borrow the capital needed to fuel the rate of economic expansion set in train by their industrialisation. They are typically authoritarian dictatorships without the advantages in terms of political stability of 'normal' democratic safety valves. That makes the system vulnerable to even limited economic and social discontent as witness recently South Korea. A re-awakening labour movement in these countries poses a potentially deadly political threat which, in the older capitalist states, could be at least partially defused by reform possibilities within existing parliamentary and trade union politics. Even so, the economic 'miracle' of their industrialisation and international super-competitiveness is impressive, and destabilising for the world system.

We are witnessing—on a world scale—a partial restructuring of international capitalism in sectors that are crucial to employment—away from the older centres of industrial development to a highly selective—but geographically dispersed—penumbra of rapidly industrialising economies. From the point of view of capitalism as a *world system* this process makes a great deal of sense; indeed it is difficult to imagine a future of sustained growth for the world system unless there is some episodic re-allocation of resources, reflecting changes in the international division of labour. It is what happened in Western Europe after the 19th century rise to industrial predominance of Britain and—in the years between and just after the Second World War—between Western Europe and the United States.

This is, however, not how the process is viewed from the standpoint of Western European or North American capitalism. This is partly a question of the potential scale of the restructuring of the world system which is now taking place. Take the steel industry for example. All the current projections about the rate at which modern, highly-advanced new steel-making capacity is being developed outside Western Europe and the US suggests that—even if there were no prospect of a lengthy economic recession—there is no way the bulk of steel making in these areas can return to profitability.

The outlook is similar for textiles and shipbuilding, while a similar nemesis may be awaiting industries as diverse as motors, electrical and electronics and important sectors of engineering. What recession in the older capitalist economies means is that the vulnerability of these industries to decline and obsolescence accelerates.

There is no way in which the Governments of Western Europe can allow the scale of destruction to their traditional, national industries required as a result of changes in world productive capacity. Of course some restructuring is under way and is directly responsible for much of the present epidemic of unemployment in the EEC countries. But measured by the needs of the world system, these changes are taking place too little—and too late.

The reluctance of West European capitalism to make the scale of switch in its industrial base called for, has another important effect. It involves the national states in increasing the direct and indirect, hidden and open subsidies to 'inefficient', unprofitable industries. The scale of state support for its declining industries, particularly in the state sector, is a major factor pushing government expenditure upwards and thus feeds the dramatic growth in national money supply.

State subsidy for the unprofitable industrial sectors is a necessity imposed on governments not primarily because of the political and social consequences of seeing these industries disappear. It is also because their collapse would push into unprofitability a further layer of industries which supply or are otherwise dependent on the loss-making sectors.

According to the pure gospel of monetarism, the wholesale abandonment of loss making should be followed by the appearance of alternative, potentially profitable enterprises. Indeed the classical function of slump in capitalist economies is to lay the basis for these new industries by clearing out the loss-making 'deadwood' and—in the process—driving down the cost of labour to the point where its re-employment becomes profitable.

The gospel bore greater relevance to reality in times past, when wage movements responded more directly to changes in the labour market and when the impact of the market among predominantly small independent firms made price competition particularly important. It is still truer of the United States than it is of Western Europe. But in all the older industrialised capitalist economies the growth of giant multinational firms whose pricing policies are determined by much wider factors than the state of internal market competition and the growth of big trade unions capable of defending real wage levels at a time of falling employment and profits, have made the link between monetary restraint, recession and reduced inflation much more problematic.

The giant firms tend to price up in times of recession in an attempt to generate the cash flow needed to finance investment, promotion and the very high level of fixed costs with which they are typically faced. No doubt there is a level of unemployment which would undermine the wage-bargaining strength of organised labour, but in countries such as Britain, it is almost certainly at levels where the bulk of British industry would, by definition, have already disappeared.

It might be argued that if it takes such a radical degree of de-industrialisation to break the wage/price spiral at the cost of organised labour, the employers and the government will, in the end, have no option but to pursue their policies to that point. Maybe. But that end is still some way off in terms of the political risks which even a Thatcher Tory government will be prepared to take in the interim.

Then there is the fact that British capitalism's political strength is related to its industrial base. Of course that base has to prove itself reasonably 'healthy' but no base at all is worse than a sickly base when it comes to governments attempting to wield political influence in international trade or other negotiations.

There is no way in which the vacuum created by the wholesale disappearance of the bulk of traditional British industry will be filled by new, smaller enterprises. For a start, there simply are not enough infant capitalists—nor have there been for a couple of generations—precisely because of the crushing size of British industrial giants. That is not to say there are not and will not be marginal, profitable sectors and markets for the petty capitalists to exploit; but they can in no way compensate for the vast enterprises they would replace either in terms of employment generated or in terms of international industrial muscle power. The 'enterprise' zones to be created in the decaying inner cities will only give birth to fly-by-night sweat shops or existing firms which will move in from regions where they are still subject to normal taxation, as well as wage and environment regulations. The net addition to employment and industrial capacity will be minimal.

This might—indeed this *would* eventually change if wage levels could be driven low enough in the major industries. But the immediate effect of a big cut in real wages would be to depress the overall level of effective demand and thus productive activity in the economy as a whole. Since this is the objective of government and employer policy in virtually every other industrial country the result of such a 'Dutch auction' in wage cutting would simply be to drive down production and employment even further but without restoring to any one national capitalism a sufficiently decisive cost and profit advantage to encourage it to reverse the trend and begin to expand investment and output.

All these observations are open to qualification. The last recession did produce a slight cut in real wages and this was followed—after 1976—by a partial and shortlived industrial recovery. But the fact is that the system comes out of each recession with a higher—not a lower—residual level of inflation and with the trend in industrial productivity and profitability still pointing firmly downwards. All of which forces the state back into 'industrial intervention'—in other words to having to prop up and subsidise an even wider swathe of industries than before.

Is the downward spiral inevitable? Clearly not if an answer could be found to persistent inflation, progressively deeper recessions, declining industrial innovation in the older core economies. It would also help if the major world economic powers could agree on a coherent international monetary system which automatically recycled available funds to where they could be most profitably and most *securely* invested. But for as long as the wholesale collapse of the traditional, heavy industries in the core capitalist countries is unacceptable in political terms, there can be no consistent anti-inflationary monetary policy. For as long as there is political compulsion to 'support' loss-making industries on anything like the present scale, massive budget deficits are inevitable.

Of course closures and bankruptcies do take place and will take place on a much larger scale in the present recession than in any previous post-war recession. But there is no way that any government, including Thatcher's, can see its way to abandoning wholesale the car, machine tool, textile, electronic or heavy engineering industries. Worse still the closures and redundancies that do take place—in other words the partial re-structuring which is under way—has signally failed to reduce real wages to the point where profitable and sustained re-expansion can begin again. Unless some ruling class somewhere can inflict a truly massive defeat on its labour force it will not be able to take advantage of what restructuring is taking place.

To say that there cannot be sustained and reasonably non-inflationary growth in the present circumstances is not to say that no growth can occur. A monetary 'U-turn' by the Tory Government or a simultaneous turn to reflation by the OECD governments as a whole would purchase some period of growth. Indeed such an option is bound to look increasingly attractive as unemployment mounts and election dates near.

But recent experience suggests that the monetarists are right when they say that reflation in conditions of declining productivity and profitability will only induce a still greater inflation. In the case of relatively 'open' economies such as Britain's this can also be relied on to lead to vastly increased import dependence—thus accelerating the indirect de-industrialisation of the British economy.

Inevitably in this situation, the appeal of the import controllers—particularly the more sophisticated versions proposed by the Cambridge Economic Policy Group—is bound to grow. In theory, it should be possible for the British government to negotiate the right to impose across the board—non-discriminatory—import tariffs and quotas against a faster growth of output and demand in the UK. In theory, again, such a trade-off might enable other countries actually to end up selling more to Britain than if deflation and de-industrialisation are allowed to take their toll on real demand. It is true that there is no more effective way of controlling imports than through deflation and slump.

The response of the British Left to the prospect of import controls has been confused. The Labour and Communist Party Left see import controls as some amazing short cut to the development of a non-capitalist economy. Actually, the imposition of such controls would actually increase the control of the 'capitalist state' over the economy as a whole—a quasi-corporatist development which would immensely underpin pressure for control of wages and even direction of labour.

On the other hand the opposition to import controls by sections of the revolutionary far Left sounds like nothing more than a left-wing defence of Manchester free trade school economics. It is one thing to oppose greater control and direction of the economy by a bourgeois state. It is quite another thing to object to import controls because they hit other countries. This is an inevitable by-product of any kind of state control of foreign trade. Is it seriously imagined that such control of foreign trade (albeit as part of the socialist transformation of industry) would not 'discriminate against imports in any transition short of the development of international socialist planning of the world economy?'

In point of fact, the kind of import controls which would be taken by a Tory or Labour government would be bound to lead to retaliation. Even if, in theory, no one need suffer a decline in absolute trade levels, such controls would lead to a re-allocation of the international balance of trade; and this at a time when the industrialised economies as a whole have a collective balance of payments deficit with the oil-producing states.

Even the non-selective controls favoured by the Cambridge group defy the rules of the Common Market, GATT and the IMF. At a time when hidden and open protectionist pressures are on the increase throughout the capitalist world, this is probably enough to rule them out on any scale for a conventional Tory or Labour Government. It might not be enough to prevent a 'Left Labour' Government setting out down this path. But such would be the international reaction—aided and abetted by all those sectors of private industry at home who would stand to lose out in any trade—that even a Left Labour Government would be faced with some awkward choices very quickly.

It would either have to retreat precipitately at the first warning shot across its bows by the EEC, IMF or whoever. Alternatively it would have to replace private and corporate control of the economy with its own control—and at a pace which might exceed the political support of its electoral base. It is one thing to win power on the basis of a programme of wholesale socialisation, it is quite another to be forced to such a policy piecemeal and in response to events outside the government's own control.

There is one other possibility for securing some renewed expansion in the economic system—rearmament. Rearmament in the late 1940s and 1950s did contribute to the achievement of the longest period of stable growth in the history of capitalism. That was partly because expenditure in the arms sector underpinned employment and wage incomes. But also partly because military research and development was crucial in force-feeding capital investment in the newer technological industries—a process which helped sustain productivity and profitability levels even given the pressures of protracted full employment.

No one in their senses would suggest that Carter, or Thatcher or who-ever, would boost arms spending *simply* to boost output, employment, investment and technological innovation. But they are well aware that higher spending on war preparation does, in the short term, have these effects. It is true that the 'benefits' of higher arms spending on the economy are notoriously difficult to quantify. They were certainly far greater and more obvious during the last Cold War arms drive which began just before the Korean War in the early 1950s.

At that time—and even more so in the immediate period before the Second World War—there was a complementarity between productive and destructive industry. Typically the arms industries and civil industry had similar degrees of capital intensiveness and technological input. There was a discernible 'spin off' for every 'war dollar' spent in terms of jobs created and, more importantly, new technological innovation brought into the value-creating, strictly capitalist sector of the economy.

Today, every dollar spent (even allowing for inflation) purchases less sustained employment and less technological innovation. That is because the arms sector has become so highly specialised. Thirty years ago the skills and technologies needed to make tanks differed little from those needed to make tractors; or military and civil aircraft. However in the era of the multi-war-head nuclear missile there is only a very limited civil sector which can expect to benefit from getting its research and develop- ment on the cheap through state-financed arms spending.

There is evidence to suggest that inflation was kept relatively low, even during periods of prolonged full employment and rising real wages in the 1940s, 1950s and early 1960s, because exceptionally rapid technological innovation—obtained 'on the cheap' by capitalist industry as a result of state-financed military R and D—kept production costs down and sustained both productivity and profitability. As the arms sector veered away on a course of its own (including its space programme offshoots) from the generality of industry, this bonus for keeping inflation in check during periods of full employment gradually diminished.

Any gain in terms of employment, productive investment, or higher output achieved through a big increase in arms spending now is likely to be transient. It is likely to be more than outweighed by a worsening of inflation. And that is to ignore the political and social repercussions when it becomes appreciated that governments are increasing public spending on nuclear missiles, chemical warfare and the arms sector generally, while cutting back on education, health and social services.

A more attractive option is what has come to be called the 'Brandt Commission strategy' named after the recent report on relations between the industrialised and developing countries. The Brandt Report called for a radically new international economic and trading order. It was inspired by a form of global Keynesianism, involving the deliberate transfer of resources from the rich to the poor countries in order to bring the poorer countries into the global economic system and thus generate the market demand for the industrially advanced goods and services which the older capitalist countries can produce.

There are several obvious snags with the Brandt strategy. The first is that it would require a truly massive transfer of resources—involving increased aid, improved terms of trade, debt relief and support for the export prices of raw material exporting countries. This could only be achieved by an international operation. But not all the advanced capitalist countries are under the same compulsion to invest in this way today in order to promote the benefits of increased world trade and prosperity tomorrow.

The very competitive relationships between the different capitalist economies makes it very difficult for them to reach a common view on what needs to be done, on what scale and by what means, to close the global development gap. The result tends to be that the rich capitalist countries reach agreement only at the level of the lowest common denominators and offer only minimal transfers of resources through official development aid and other means. And the rich countries make even this conditional on their continuing freedom to take back from the poorer countries—through repatriated profits and loan repayments—much more than they transfer in aid of all kinds.

The simple fact is that the private flow of investment far exceeds official aid. And private investment is increasingly concentrated on that handful of developing countries which has an outside chance of achieving economic take-off. To make matters worse, investment in those countries tends to flow into precisely those industries where the older capitalist countries have most excess capacity and are least competitive. In that sense the appearance of the NICs has exacerbated the world wide problem of industrial overcapacity and is adding another depressing factor to the international rate of profit—the ultimate motor and dynamic of economic growth.

For all of this, the short-term trade cycle has not been abolished. At the time of writing, we appear to be on the verge of a new downturn. The effects of this downturn will be difficult to separate from the consequences of the world-wide structural disequilibrium of international capitalism. Secondary factors such as the rapid rise in the relative price of oil or the precariously fragile stability of the international banking system could even threaten something dangerously like collapse.

A more likely perspective is that the world economy does go into a new cyclical downturn; that governments do eventually make the dreaded 'U' turn back to some species of Keynesian demand management. This can be expected to lead to a weak and hesitant recovery beginning perhaps sometime in 1981 or 1982. There is no reason to think that this recovery will not, in its turn, give way quickly to yet another and more serious downturn by the middle of the decade with inflation and monetary policy as far beyond control as they are now.

This perspective is bound to be affected by Britain's North Sea oil reserves. Indeed to listen to some Keynesians, they see this asset and the government revenue it will generate over the next few years as about the only chance for financing a return to expansionist economic policies.

There is no denying the importance of North Sea oil. Even according to the latest, more sober estimates of the Government energy 'Brown Book', self sufficiency in oil will be achieved—for a period of about a decade—in the next year. Exchequer revenue which totalled £2.2 billion last year could rise to £10 billions annually over the next few years in spite of the slower rate of exploitation. This is, of course, due to the dramatic and continuing rise in the real price of oil internationally.

It is no easy matter to calculate the overall economic effects of North Sea oil. For a start its impact must be put in the context of higher international oil prices generally. Britain's economic fortunes are still going to be more dependent on the growth of overseas industrial markets than on oil revenues directly. Yet the higher OPEC prices are pushing overseas markets into a steep decline. The loss of 'national income' from this contraction seems likely to be greater than the direct boost to national income from oil sales.

Oil sales will almost certainly mean that the British balance of trade and overall balance of payments will move into an even bigger surplus than might be expected during a period of recession. The effects of this will be to push up the international exchange value of sterling on world currency markets even further than it has already gone. In theory this relentless rise in the value of the pound could be offset by major reductions in interest rates. Some interest rate cuts must be expected in the coming months, but it seems most unlikely that the reductions can go far enough to offset the upward pressure of oil money attracted to sterling if only because inflation is going to remain in double figures and it is difficult seeing any establishment government—let alone Mrs Thatcher's—pushing down the real cost of money by very much.

As has been clearly established in recent months, the high and rising value of sterling is accelerating the slump in industrial profitability and—added to the recession—it is speeding up the process of bankruptcy and de-industrialisation. Yet, thanks to North Sea oil, there is little the government can do about it; foreign exchange controls on the outward movement of capital have had little effect and it is difficult to see what can be done to halt or reverse the flow of 'hot money' to London for as long as oil assures a strong balance of payments, particularly at a time when other international currencies can be expected to lose value more rapidly than sterling.

There remains the question of exchequer revenue. At the very least domestic public oil income should reduce the Public Sector Borrowing Requirement—a key financial index particularly for a government which gives top priority to monetary control policies. On the other hand, as outlined earlier, recession (particularly protracted stagnation in output) combined with protracted unemployment and continuing trade union resistance to big reduction in real wage levels, all suggest that the PSBR will be under simultaneous upward pressure.

Even so there are bound to be increased government resources provided by oil which would be available for either improved social expenditure or making a start to the refurbishing of bankrupt British industry. But money is not enough for governments of the present type. Indeed the evidence suggests that it is not lack of funds which has impeded industrial investment and modernisation in recent years but lack of profitable or (within the relatively short timescale favoured by British capitalists) potentially profitable investment opportunities (witness the Wilson report on City finance markets). Without a drastic restoration of profitability it is difficult to see even the riches of the North Sea doing more than marginally slowing the relative rate of decline of British industry in relation to the world system.

Such a situation cannot continue indefinitely. The political tolerance of the middle class to debilitating periods of inflation and speculative growth followed by protracted periods of recession and decline is limited. If Thatcher's strategy fails, there may well be a polarisation of opinion in the middle classes. Some may be tempted by a Labour Government (even one which by virtue of its 'left' programme and the left-wing records of some of its leaders enjoyed some authority with trade unionists). Others may be tempted to play with the extreme Right or quasi-authoritarian figures who promise the smack of firm government. There should be a market for salon conspirators and organisers of businessmen's governments in the aftermath of a Thatcher defeat.

Further speculation as to different political options has little value. The question that begs answering is what will be the response of the Labour movement to any development remotely on the lines suggested above. Here trade union militancy is already seen not to be enough. Trade union militants do not live by industrial bread alone. The famine of socialist politics on the shop floor has directly fed the demoralisation and partial undermining of the shop steward movement. A link between trade union resistance to attacks on jobs, living standards and shop floor organisation, on the one hand, and a socialist vision of a practical, humane, alternative economic order, can halt the draft to the right in the trade unions.

Such a link will not be forged by the mere recital of old and favourite—(or new and unorthodox)—programmatic formulae. The gap between the particular on the shop floor or trade union branch and the general—in terms of an alternative socialist order—is too great to be credible. There have to be steps in between. It is a sense of the need for these intermediary steps which has inspired those trade unionists who have tried to work out a strategy based on 'alternative production'. Without some understanding and acceptance by rank and file trade unionists of the possible alternatives for running society—which means, in practice, practical alternatives for *this* industry, in *this* place at *this* time—any fight back in the trade union movement will have an episodic, defensive and self-defeating character.

Only a fool would fail to realise the weaknesses of the socialist movement in Britain today. The Left is paying the price for office-seeking (whether in Parliament or the trade unions) at the expense of securing a real, mass base. But there is also evidence of a loss of faith in the 'status quo', and a related loss of confidence in the expertise and authority of those in power (a function of political disillusion and failure by successive governments). There is also a much narrower educational and cultural gap between rulers and ruled, managers and managed, (a function of the mass media as much as the post-war schooling system). Among socialists, there is greater realisation that the world is a small place whose problems require world-wide solutions. Another is the widespread adoption of non-capitalist cultural values illustrated, for example, by the numbers of school leavers who prefer social service employment to managerial careers.

A socialist strategy which embraces agitation and propaganda for 'alternative production plans' offers no guarantee that the credibility gap which has opened up between socialists and the mass of even organised workers will be quickly or easily bridged. That would be to ignore the roots of ruling-class ideology in the ranks of organised labour (racism, sexism, nationalism etc.). But it does offer one important way of closing the gap between what workers perceive as the reality of the present economic situation (unprofitability, decline in demand, uneconomic working etc.) and a perspective which links trade union defence of jobs and conditions to a perspective of how else industry could be organised.

In one important sense the agitation for the replacement of market criteria in production with those based on social need actually cuts with the grain. It is perceived widely to 'make sense'. It is also a means of combatting the real fears of bureaucratic control (remote officialdom laying down what will be produced and how in the now totally discredited Soviet model). It is one of the living links between day-to-day struggles against closures, redundancies and public spending cuts and a system of planned production for social need under democratic workers' control.

It also cuts with the grain in another less direct sense. In a growing number of ways the British economy is already 'post-capitalist', in the sense that purely market considerations are less and less central to production and investment decisions. Government control and state intervention is here to stay and everyone knows it. The logic of the market place IS giving way to a variety of other considerations. There is some truth in the Keith Joseph complaint that there are too many obstacles in the way of the capitalist entrepreneur in Britain today for the market system to work as it should. The 'obstacles' have been erected partly by working-class pressure (minimum wage legislation, regional planning, consumer protection) and partly by the capitalist state for its own interests (preservation of loss-making prestige industries, arms spending, etc.).

Central to the Thatcher strategy is the belief that the clock can be turned back and the dynamic of the market place restored. It is a dubious prospect and one that does not command the wholehearted support of the Tory Party, the CBI or the bulk of the economic establishment. If there is a reaction away from 'monetarism', it may well be towards a kind of Tory corporatism (incomes policy etc.) which will actually weaken the play of purely market forces still further.

Thatcherism does seem, on this view, to be a temporary deviation on Britain's road to some kind of state capitalism. But a state capitalism which occurs through gradual social and economic change and not one created in the aftermath of a failed socialist revolution or the imposition of authoritarian rule from outside (as in eastern Europe) is unlikely to command the active loyalty of working people.

At present the political pendulum is set firmly to the right. But a determined socialist strategy, which attempts to link reaction to the present crisis (unemployment, social services, wages etc.) to the working-out of detailed alternative production plans covering the major industries (and by definition the major trade unions) could provide the ideological impetus to renewed advances by the Left.

There will be no shortage of critics pointing to the dangers of such an approach. There are those who see any concern with alternative planning as 'reformist' and, worse, encouraging class collaboration by militants and active trade unionists. Such dangers do exist. It would be surprising if some employers would not be tempted to try and divert any demands for 'alternative production plans' into safer waters. Indeed in most other countries, the ideas and suggestions of the work force about new products, processes and changes in work practices, are already treated more seriously than in Britain.

Fears that trade unionists will be turned en masse into collective entrepreneurs to replace the discredited marketing managers, investment bankers and the like is a fantasy. The point about alternative planning is not that there are lots of market-place winners which capitalist managements are too dim to see and exploit. It is that the market place is 'too marginal' today to give birth to those new products and processes which offer the possibility of reasonably guaranteed employment for the bulk of the industrial labour force.

The experience of the Lucas Aerospace experiment, still very much the lone pioneer in this area, was that the potential alternative production grew out of calculations about *social need*. What is needed throughout British industry today is an elementary census on what kind of social needs exist which are not satisfied and are unlikely to be satisfied by traditional market place, capitalist enterprise but which could be satisfied by existing work forces and (with modest chances in the first instance) existing plant and machinery.

It should go without saying that any general acceptance by the trade union movement of a 'Lucas-type' strategy would immediately raise the question of the state and state power. For alternative production planning on any scale requires that working people have control of the banks, responsibility for the financing of investment—in other words have control of the levers of state power.

It would also be an additional means of raising all the issues surrounding public spending cuts. To talk about production for social need is to talk about ways in which 'productive' industry should be serving the needs— among other things—of health, welfare and education. It is to develop a socialist perspective in which the social services are not seen as a 'drain on resources' but as part and parcel of the process by which society will add to its wealth-creating potential.

In the short-run it offers the possibility of trade unionists in the social services discussing with trade unionists in manufacturing industry about how their interests are actually and should increasingly be, interlinked. Why should not social service workers present industrial trade unionists with ideas about the equipment which they need and which they are denied at present?

Of course in the immediate future, at best, such an approach is really only meaningful as part of the battle of 'ideas' which forms such an important terrain over which the class struggle is fought today. But even the most elementary trade unionism requires some kind of political context in contemporary conditions, when 'national interest'—'economic realities' and a hundred and one other concepts which seek to limit the industrial and political options before working people are being deployed with such vigour and, it must be admitted, success by government and employers.

The Left cannot allow the arguments about what is 'practical' and 'realistic' to be coopted by the other side. To do so is to assist the process of de-politicisation in the broad labour movement which has made possible the retreats and the Tory counter-offensive of the recent past. An alternative politics cannot, of course, be proscribed independently of the actual struggle of trade unionists in particular industries. But the general approach can be canvassed and encouraged by the Left with profit.

What this means is transitional politics. There is no more reason to believe that ultimatist slogans or maximalist demands carry any more conviction among the mass of working people today than they did fifty years ago. That is not to say that the scope for reformist politics in the labour movement is exhausted. It is not. But in today's conditions of semi-permanent economic crisis the consistent reformist is obliged to reject the institutional limits of reformism or acquiesce in the counter-reformism which has increasingly been the hallmark of recent Labour governments.

What then of internationalism? The circumstances of the Left and the labour movements in the older capitalist economies is not so very different to those of the British Left and trade unions. Most of them are some way down the path of de-industrialisation on which Britain has been a trail blazer.

Internationalist politics at the moment is a question more of propaganda than of anything else. But surely it is possible for Left to speak unto Left about national economic and industrial strategy. Surely it is possible to air demands for international trade planning by countries with like-minded socialist governments to begin to arrest economic and industrial decline. This would mean, in the first instance, 'a European policy' for industries such as steel, shipbuilding, textiles, which are obviously facing similar crises.

If the Left fails to project its alternative strategy in an internationalist context, it will be all the more vulnerable to a nationalist, rightist backlash if the Tories lurch from pure monetarism to a 'little England' corporatist strategy. That is why mere anti-Common Marketism is not enough—indeed in and for itself it is another glaring ideological gap in the Left's political armoury.

Of course to speak about a socialist 'European' strategy is itself unacceptably abstract. What it means, in the first instance, is the exchange of experience and analysis on the Left in Europe. Secondly, it implies agreement on at least an outline socialist programme which conceives of the socialist reorganisation of society on a European basis. This would imply the application, on a European basis, of a planned international division of labour but one based on the principle of production for social need. It might involve, in the interim (and it could be a protracted interim) to a world-wide socialism, a confederation of socialist states in Europe. In the here and now it would mean the coordination of trade union struggles against unemployment, austerity, falling living standards, but in the context of a Europe-wide struggle for a different social and political order.

Even to put this down in black and white is to invite the charge of utopianism. But might it not be more 'practical' in a situation where purely reformist, national political perspectives simply do not carry credibility with a larger and larger number of militants? Of course to win the advanced guard of industrial militants to such a programme is not to win the mass of the British, let alone the European working class. But it is the essential first step. In a prolonged period of economic crisis, with sections of the middle class turning sharply to the right (and, in so doing influencing the climate of 'public opinion' which so largely shapes popular working-class attitudes) and with the present lurch back to Cold War stances between the nuclear blocs, the time is surely overdue for the Left to come to terms with its declining influence and prepare the political ground for a counter-offensive?

'THE EIGHTIES AND THE LEFT: AN AMERICAN VIEW*

S.M. Miller

The 80s start in an unusual way, unlike the beginnings of the 60s and 70s. Shocks, enormous uncertainties, trouble are expected. Of course, turmoil and surprises marked the two previous decades: the unrest of 1968 and the emergence of OPEC were not minor occurrences. Other decades or eras have begun with false confidence about what would occur in the next years. A few had an air of change about them. But deep disturbances were largely unanticipated. By contrast, all agree that great if unclear difficulties will characterise the 80s.

This unease is important of itself as well as reflecting the visible piling up of problems and a highly unsettled world. The sense of uncertainty is the dominant beginning context, clouding judgements, making economists more cautious than is their wont, leading to rapid and great swings in public opinion. In this situation, the Left experiences great difficulties because it does not know how to orient itself to a world uncertain, wanting to avoid that recurrent Left delusion of apocalyptic predictions but suspecting that upheavals, turmoil and radical changes may emerge.

The widespread, disturbing uncertainty of the present calls for avoiding rigid directions of action. Rather, enormous flexibility and sensitivity will be necessary; they require an interpretation of what might be the basic lines of development of the 80s. Much of this essay is certain to appear commonplace; putting issues together in one loose framework—even if the theoretical scaffolding is absent—is its potential contribution. While the essay concentrates on the experience of the United States and to a lesser extent, of the United Kingdom, some contentions may apply to other countries as well. In any case what happens to the US will influence strongly many other nations. But the 80s will be experienced and interpreted very differently by Asians or Africans or South Americans or even Italians or the French. I apologise in advance for its US-centre bias.

Thinking About the Future

How to think about the future? Predictions about the future mainly rely on three approaches. One method utilises a crystal ball where the

---

*I appreciate the help of Donald Tomaskovic-Devey and the comments of Ralph Miliband and Michael Useem.

courageous or foolhardy peer into the dim future and predict events which are far from visible at the present time. For the Marxist, the emphasis is upon contradictions, or, in the language of functional sociology, structural strain and poor articulation within and between the economy and the state. Some Marxists manifest an unfortunate proclivity to see capitalist decline as inevitably unfolding because of contradictions. Few counter-vailing forces are discerned, even though Marx emphasised such tendencies. Deductions are made largely from Marxist economic analysis. 'Accidents' have little role in this perspective. This mode of analysis is a form of radical functionalism.

The dotted line approach to prediction plots the already exhibited trends and projects them into the future with the same, increasing, or lower rates of change. Simple-minded predictions can lead us into the technological determinist absurdities of Herman Kahn in an early period of his intellectual peregrination when he centred on the unfolding of projectable tendencies or the insurgency of inexorable trends rather than on the tension of political and economic difficulties. A more complicated view transmutes straight-line projections by covertly employing standards that affect fore-casting. Thus, how we view the 80s will be a refraction of how we view the 70s. Just as the needs of the 70s coloured and shaped interpretations of the 60s, the needs of the 80s will colour how we think about the 70s and how we think of the 70s should affect the 80s. For example, if the notion prevails that the US has been too weak and vacillating on the international scene, a widespread view at the beginning of 1980, a more forceful and adventurous foreign policy is likely in the 80s. If it is believed that Americans have not tried enough to conserve energy and to lower their standard of living to deal with problems, then the likelihood is that coercive ways will be adopted to lower standards of living. What becomes the received wisdom about what went wrong in the past affects what is done at a later time. If generals fight the last war, politicians and economists fight what they interpret as the mistakes of recent elections and policies. Old policies never die; they are reborn as their antithesis.

An important question in the projection approach to predictions is what unit of time should be projected? Should one only look at the 70s and try to ascertain what developments in the 80s would perhaps be accentuated? Should we look at the period from the 60s to the end of the 70s? Or are decades not useful periods for structuring thinking? Or should the post-war period since 1945 be the centre of our concern in inter-pretation? Or should a longer time period serve as the base of the projections? Since I think current domestic changes break with much of the policy of governments in the post-World War II period, this longer period has my attention.

One can be critical of the projections-of-the-past approach without necessarily embracing the crystal ball. A third way of guessing at the future is much more constrained than either approach and is disdained by most Marxists. The argument here is that the long-run and the middle-run are largely shaped by short runs. Rather than focussing on dominant trends or tendencies or utilising a crystal ball, this orientation stresses that short run activities and consequences shape what in retrospect turns out to be the middle-run or long-run. One variant of this approach denies that one can predict very far into the future because short-run incidents pile on each other and affect in unpredictable ways following events. In a less limited variant it is possible to discern underlying significant tendencies while recognising that the long-run structures the way these tendencies are specifically manifested and modified as well as what their consequences may be. Radical thinkers underplay both variants because they stress the importance of the short-run. Although this essay concentrates on longer-term tendencies, I believe that it is always important to pay attention to the exigencies of the moment, the short-run pressures, accidents and events which build up into longer-term effects.[1]

The stress on long-term forces rather than events contributes to economic determinism or radical functionalism. What specifically happens is regarded as so structured by particular long-term strains, contradictions or processes that no alternative or offsetting action can operate. In the radical functionalist approach, which was quite popular for a period, a frequent assertion is that 'It is no accident that. . .' In a highly differentiated society like the US, accidents and the unanticipated often occur and 'the system' is loosely articulated so that what happens in one part of society may be insulated from other parts. In highly dynamic, complex, differentiated societies, interactions are not always simple, direct, determined or invariant. In thinking, then, about the future, it is important to move away from one of the errors of the 70s—an overly-deterministic radical functionalism.

What Happened in the Seventies?

The 70s were characterised by extraordinary economic difficulties. Inflation hit; unemployment increased. An economic experience, new at least in the post-war capitalist world, appeared—that of stagflation, rising prices with economic decline. Unsettled and unsettling economic conditions are likely to prevail in much of the 80s.

Confidence in the state's ability to handle economic and social difficulties weakened during the 70s. Corruption became more visible, especially in the United States. This decline in both legitimacy and belief in the competence of the state is likely to continue. The state is going to be increasingly directed toward handling the problems of the day and will find it very difficult to be effective.

Although the private economy performed poorly, public esteem for business, at least in the USA, did not decline rapidly as criticism of government deepened and spread.

Left groups have had a mixed record, certainly not the large successes which disturbed economic conditions are expected to produce. While they succeeded in some local actions in both countries and have been able to mobilise sizeable groupings in the USA on particular issues such as the Equal Rights Amendment (for women), environmental abuse and occupational safety, they have not had much influence on macro-economic decisions. Indeed, at the end of the decade, economic policy had moved to a pro-business course which heavily penalised workers and the poor. In the United States the anti-war movement had some effect but it has not fully understood the nature of that effect. For example, the anger at the Cambodian 'incursion' probably limited the activities that Nixon and Kissinger intended to pursue.

The overall picture at least in the United States is of a largely unfocussed left and a record of limited successes. The outstanding actions were the growth of feminist, environmental and energy groupings but such single interest organisations do not always follow left policies and do not generally work in concert.

Mood as Content

The profound sense of uncertainty as the 80s begin is extensive: Peace or war; short- or long-run inflation and/or deflation, some measure of domestic tranquillity or rebellious public outbursts? The feeling is not only generally pessimistic—things will get worse—but also of a great loss of confidence in the political and administrative capacity of government to clear away the dark clouds.

Under what circumstances does uncertainty grow? When there is a sense that great changes are occurring which are not fully shaped or visible; when the response of governments to change and threat is affected by many domestic and foreign considerations which run in competing directions; when institutionalised political activity seems little or simplistically related to important issues; when the possibility of an environmental disaster, whether of earthquake, nuclear or chemical origins, is high even if the likelihood of any particular upheaval in any particular locality is low; when disturbing and important events can occur in so many places and in so many ways e.g., shutoff of Mideast oil supplies or the bankruptcy of financially over-extended non-OPEC Third World nations.

In such circumstances the sense of control over personal destiny and confidence in the efficacy of national action wither. In itself, the un-certainty is a significant economic, political and psychological circumstance. It can be an ominous political sign, inviting quick solutions through military action. Or it can cause great and rapid swings in popular opinion so that national figures can swiftly gain and lose support for their actions. *Mood becomes content as well as context.* A search for stability, order, tradition and efficiency can become attractive catch-words regardless of their coerciveness or emptiness. A time of uncertainty can be a dangerous age searching for the chimera of order and confidence or it can be a period where creativity is high, imagination unencumbered and political movements bloom as difficult circumstances demand new and bold measures. This uncertainty demands a non-deterministic outlook. What happens will be to some extent shaped by what left groups do.

But certainly not completely. This essay centres on the possible consequences of heterogenity among nations and within nations, on 'outside the nation'/'inside the nation' struggles. Not only is US hegemony declining but the interests of capitalist nations are more clearly conflictful and tense. Within many nations what is the national interest is increasingly an unsettled and unsettling issue, particularly as the interests of internationally-oriented enterprises and smaller firms more sharply collide. Of course, struggle among and within nations is nothing new. What is new is that the world 'system' is in difficulty and that many nations at the same time are forced to confront the question, about which there is much disagreement, of how to deal with their acutely growing problems of declining political consensus and severe economic difficulties. Since domestic economic problems deeply involve world economic and political relations, the outside-inside struggles interweave more strongly than in many other eras.

To a major extent the issue is what is 'the national interest?' At one level, that is the abiding issue raised by radical movements. At another level, it is one that radical movements elucidate poorly. This period of uncertainty will force left groups to clarify their perspectives or decline even further.

Some left writers seem to argue that American national economic interests are those of the multinational corporations. What is necessary for the multinationals is what is necessary for the American capitalist economy. This view, of course, is what the multinationals in all capitalist nations assert—not heeding their interests will plunge the nation into economic ruin. That seeming convergence does not make this left analysis *ipso facto* misleading but it should cause rethinking of the proposition or at least to differentiate it more sharply from the self-serving propaganda of the multinationals, their paid hacks and uncritical economists who follow the Pied Piper of the market. Nor does this analysis provide lines of action, at least in the short-run, for building support for alternative lines of development.

THE INTERNATIONAL SCENE

In this section relations among capitalist nations are first discussed, then US-USSR relations, and finally some Third World issues.

Tensions among Capitalist Nations

After the 1957 launching of Sputnik which demonstrated that the Soviet Union's surprising technological capacity rivalled that of the United States, the American historian William Appleman Williams published an article on the implications of the Soviet Union's becoming the first nation in space exploration. While the article disappointed, the title did not. It was prophetic: 'The American Century, 1946-56.' The United States and the world are struggling to live through that decline in American hegemony and the response to it of the USA, the USSR, and the rest of the world.

The erosion is occurring over a long period and will continue perhaps for a longer time. The decline in American supremacy does not necessarily mean that Soviet dominance is growing.[2] Nor is the decline steady and continuous. At times US power may grow or its decline may slow while in other periods it may speed up. The long-term decline is clear: nonetheless, attention must be paid to the current efforts to rebuild American domination through adventurous actions and to its attaining of temporary hegemonic influence.

The contracting of American economic supremacy is revealed in these items: in 1945, the United States produced perhaps a half of the total output of capitalist countries; in 1980, perhaps a third.[3] The US dollar is in grave difficulty as the world reserve currency and the US can no longer force the rest of the world to accept its export deficit.

The defeat in Vietnam is the most obvious military manifestation of US decline. More important perhaps was the development of OPEC, the ending of the era of low energy prices and the inflationary pressures and threats of shortages that the oil producers have created. The new energy era requires deep-seated changes in the capitalist west.

In the period of US dominance, it appeared that most capitalist nations had similar economic and political interests: the promotion of economic growth, the expansion of foreign trade, the maintaining of cheap raw material prices, stable exchange rates, the mobility of capital, the increasing scope of government as economic regulator, the expansion of welfare state policies to produce domestic consensus. As the 80s begin, not only have domestic disagreements intensified in many countries but the apparent mutuality of interest among capitalist nations is breaking up. US capitalist allies are not always willing to follow the American lead, e.g., in the response to the Iranian hostages issue, exemplifying the continuing diminution of US dominance over the capitalist world as well as over the Third World.

The emergence of West Germany and Japan as great economic powers has led some important business-political leaders to develop the Trilateral Commission to foster cooperation, joint action and joint sharing of burdens among the capitalist Big Three. Trilateralism is still largely symbolic but it is a significant indication that the United States is no longer the controlling power of even the capitalist world.

Can the United States, West Germany and Japan work together and concert their policies to yield joint benefit? That goal is extremely difficult to achieve as US pressures to reduce imports from Japan attest. As John Maynard Keynes pointed out in *The General Theory of Employment, Interest and Money* (1936), nations with less than full employment have great difficulty permitting imports which might further increase unemployment levels. The recurrent economic difficulties of the US and other capitalist nations will likely intensify the conflicts among the Big Three as each strives to maintain domestic employment.

One important way that the United States maintains a trilateral attitude with West Germany and Japan is in serving as the Hessians for them. In the American rebellion against Britain, the latter hired Hessian troops to do some of the fighting. Similarly, but on a much grander and leading scale, the United States serves as 'the shield' protecting Western Europe and Japan from the 'Soviet menace', providing not only a counter threat of nuclear weaponry but also sizeable ground forces for and leadership of the NATO forces. West Germany and Japan can, consequently, keep their military expenditures at a low level. As the American economy falters, American military activity makes trilateralism attractive and bolsters the weakened political significance of the United States. If the Cold War wanes or the economic price of trilateralism becomes too great for West Germany and Japan, then the subdued competition among the Big Three is likely to come to the fore.[4]

Trilateralism in the sense of shared, coordinate costs and actions among the Big Three with continuing American 'leadership' but with a more decisive role for the other two, is not likely to be realised. Great tensions exist among the Big Three. The Soviet Union may attempt to play on these tensions in order to reduce US domination; anti-Americanism may grow; the US may try to force West Germany and Japan to heed American directives by strong economic and military manoeuvres. The breakup of trilateralism would be a severe blow to the US.

The difficulties will be compounded by conflict between the Big Three and the other capitalist nations. The heterogeneity among the capitalist nations makes it difficult for Trilateral 'coordination' to reconcile successfully the interests of the Big Three with the other capitalist nations. A weaker, less successful capitalist set of nations—Britain, Italy, the Southern tier of Europe—will likely find the policies of the Big Three difficult to accept. Their needs call for increasing protection against imports, the lowering of food prices (in contrast to European Community policies), the planned development of particular industries, world economic growth to sustain employment levels, and a sizeable public sector for domestic tranquillity.

The heterogeneity of the capitalist world is widened by the recent emergence of satellite capitalist or export platform nations.[5] The Hong Kongs, Taiwans, South Koreas, Singapores, and even larger countries like Brazil are becoming the locale of manufacturing firms whose capital and control come from the larger capitalist countries. In a reversal of classic Leninist imperialism of providing the markets for the manufactured products of the colonial powers, these satellite capitalisms are producing manufactured goods to be sold in the colonial nations.

Cheap labour, low regulation, and special tax incentives, conspire to attract manufacturing from the established capitalist nations to these new industrial bases with their difficult mixes of industrialised cities and still large rural bases.

The effect in the older capitalist nations, especially the US, has been devastating. Whole regions are being deindustrialised as industries (or sections of them) move out or decline and are restarted in the satellite nations. The rationale is that the market, in this case the world market, must prevail and that over the long run the older capitalist nations will expand in the new high-technology fields and thereby provide employment as well as right the balance of payments.

This is a very contestable proposition. More likely is high, continuing levels of unemployment which will further undermine the effort to maintain free trade and the mobility of capital.

If the export of capital to or the import of products from the satellite capitalist nations is curtailed by the larger capitalist nations, the former will be in great economic and political difficulties. New regimes may emerge which may be more concerned with national internal develop- ments. Even without the pressure of external constraints on capital and exports, the uneven development within these satellites is likely to result in turmoil in the coming decade. Since Western investments are heavy in these nations, the possibilities of intervention are considerable.

The economic growth of the 60s and 70s involved an enormous expansion of trade among nations and the emergence of new trading nations, especially the satellite capitalist nations. It is highly questionable whether many capitalist countries can have an effective domestic policy that meets economic and political needs and still be so heavily involved in foreign trade. Among the Big Three, West Germany has been the most successful because of the willingness of German workers to accept slow increases in their wages in order to curb inflation and improve German competitiveness. Japan is already undergoing strains because of internal pressures for wage increases and social improvements. The US is having the greatest difficulties in maintaining or developing an effective competitive stance in many fields, most notably at this time automobile production. The weaker capitalist nations are suffering and the satellite capitalist nations may be in difficulty.[6]

A continuation of a heavy engagement in and expansion of foreign trade will strain increasingly the internal economics and politics of most capitalist nations. The obvious capitalist need is for some way of regulating world trade. Multinational banks and corporations fear, however, that any restraint on free movement will spread and adversely affect them. Consequently, there will be great debate in many countries, obviously the US, over protectionism, selective controls, quotas, and the like. While the Cambridge Economic Policy Group has made a case, surprisingly scanty at this point, for selectivity in imports and capital outflow for the UK, in other nations, again the US, a left approach and analysis are lacking. Piecemeal protectionism, as in steel and auto, are encouraged by particular unions but a broad-scale analysis of the problems of foreign trade remains to be done. Foreign trade will be a prime economic and political issue of the 80s; left groups are unprepared to deal with it, analytically or politically. Some unions are setting policy by supporting the regulation of foreign trade and investment but the long-run interests of workers are not being examined. My view is that the great expansion of trade is unsettling and requires some selectivity to make internal economic policy work. I will come back to the issue in the domestic section.

In sum, the capitalist nations have diverse and competing interests as the American umbrella suffers wide rips. Trilateralism seeks to mend the tears among the Big Three while OECD attempts to sew together all the main capitalist countries. The struggle over developing and maintaining each country's national economic interest in the context of the vast and strained world economic network will be a pronounced feature of the 80s. Leading business interest groups and most orthodox economists have a simple solution to free trade. The alternative in the current scene is piecemeal protectionism as visible problems of one industry or another emerge. Some left writers have been obsessed with the 'world economic system' but have so far failed to consider it as a basic issue of left political education and action. This is partly because of the mechanical interpretation of world economic activities and the neglect of conflict among and within the capitalist nations.

The US-USSR Rivalry[7]
In mid-1980 Cold War II has supplanted quasi-detente. US and USSR tensions are high at the beginning of the decade. They may abate during the next years; indeed, it is likely that at least the first half of the 80s will experience recurrent manoeuvres about a new rapprochment. Such efforts, however, are not certain to lead to a detente-like state; nor do they mean that military and political confrontation will be avoided for such pressures can be important elements in negotiations. A tense period is likely to continue to corrode international relations and to dominate domestic economics and politics.

Cold War II, as it is developing, differs in important respects from

Cold War I, the period roughly from the Berlin crisis of 1947 to the Berlin Wall.

First, the US-USSR rivalry clearly shifted in the 60s and 70s from its 1950s centring in both Western and Eastern Europe. Few now expect Soviet troops to swoop through Germany to France; Berlin is no longer the sticking point that it was in the 50s when the two Germanies had not worked out a modus vivendi. The US acceptance of the Soviet invasion of Czechoslovakia definitely marked what was already clear, that the US had no intention of 'rollback' Soviet hegemony over Eastern Europe (although Yugoslavia may be a contested terrain). The emergence of Eurocommunism, especially in Italy where the Communist Party is openly critical of many Soviet foreign interventions, has toppled the belief in monolithic Communism and the 'fifth column' fear of communist parties in Western Europe.

The scene of struggle is in the Third World. Vietnam, Ethiopia, Iran, Afghanistan have been the locale of recent military and/or political strife between the US and USSR (with China heavily involved against Soviet influence in Southeast Asia). The Korean War, of course, was the beginning of the shift of contention away from Europe, but the almost complete displacement of rivalry to the Asian and African perimeters in recent years is striking.

Vietnam with US forces and Afghanistan with Soviet troops have been the only two situations where the two big powers have directly and openly committed their own troops to battle in the Third World. Fighting through proxies is often difficult and may lead the two big powers to use increasingly their own troops. If the US and USSR directly involve themselves in Third World battles, tensions will grow mightily.

In Europe, then, the spheres of influence and power have been rather well demarcated and observed. In the Third World that is far from the case. The big powers will seek to take advantage of internal conflicts among Third World nations and the sporadic conflicts among them. That is where the great dangers are. In most of the Third World, the economic stakes for the big two are not very great.[8] This is particularly true for the USSR. The main, glaring disturbing exception is, of course, the Middle East. That is where the major jockeying for power between the US and USSR will occur. While nuclear war is unlikely between the US and USSR, many other kinds of battles could occur.

Second, the smouldering USSR-China dispute may emerge into warfare, particularly if the US plays 'the China card' and encourages China to battle against the Soviet Union or if the USSR preemptively responds to that threat. The present Chinese leadership is unlikely to engage in provocative action but Soviet military strength is stretched as long as the Chinese-USSR border seems a threatening zone to both sides. The Soviet Union might play 'the American card' against China by negotiating a close detente with the US, but that appears unlikely. The general point is that China is important in US-USSR relations and its role is changeable.

Third, both US and USSR have trouble with their Allies. At least Japan, West Germany and France are reluctant to follow what often seem to them to be adventurous US policies, especially when they learn of them after the fact. The possibilities of foreign policy splits within the capitalist nation are considerable and will grow if the US pursues the adventurous and aggressive policies many of its leading politicians advocate. An independent foreign policy line, in somewhat disguised form, may develop.

The Eastern European nations are in growing economic difficulties, particularly as the USSR's oil prices approximate those of the world market. These strains will debilitate further the political legitimacy of the governments. The Soviet foreign policy lead may be opposed if troops or a lowering of the standard of living are imposed.

Fourth, neither the USA nor the USSR are in a good position for expanding military expenditures. In the US, economic growth is ebbing and inflation is a recurrent danger, which would be fed by rising military outlays. The Soviet Union is having difficulty in maintaining or improving living standards and achieving efficient production. The economic and political price of rapidly increasing military expenses will be high for both sides.

The prospect that the US cannot economically afford big, new military activity without reducing the standard of living is only beginning to be sensed. But it is becoming recognised and may become an active political force in US-USSR tensions. Some would argue that military adventurism is a way of taking an unsettled citizenry's mind off its domestic troubles. But that tactic is unlikely today to contribute to the health of the state or the economy. External aggression by the US government may engender domestic hostility.

A major cost of war or near-war is that most nations can only pay attention to one major problem at a time. If the US engages in intense and expensive military posturing, its ability to deal effectively with its mounting economic and social problems will decline further. The same is probably true of the USSR.

Fifth, US foreign policy and American public attitudes are in an extremely fluid and frequently dangerous state. Although often jingoistic, there is also a tendency to draw back from the policy outburst. President Carter's ridiculous characterisation of the Soviet invasion of Afghanistan as producing the worst crisis since World War II did not receive the full measure of jeering that it deserved. Indeed, there was an instantaneous heating up of war emotions. But notice two things. First, the resulting measures against the USSR were extremely weak—the limitations on materials to be exported from the US (but not its allies), the boycott of the Moscow Olympics and the effort to obtain Congressional approval for very limited draft registration. These puny measures indicate the limits of American power. Second, the Afghan crisis rapidly receded in public interest and detente-like murmurs again appeared.

I do not want to minimise American warmongering but it is a 'sometime thing', frequently offset over time by a great desire to avoid war. Policy-makers also have to consider the possibilities and damage of confrontational resistance to a full scale draft and to serving in an unpopular shooting war abroad.

These considerations lead me to the conclusion that the US and USSR will engage in turbulent manoeuvring, making an unstable environment for other nations, and exacting heavy costs in Third World nations which become proxy battlefields. In the past the US and USSR have largely been out of phase in their desires for relaxation of tensions, curbing of new armaments and the like. When the two have had somewhat similar phases, some progress of relaxation has occurred. Domestic economic needs may push both powers to a more common phase during the 80s.

Western Europe could play an important role if it develops a position more independent from the US than in the past. Signs of this move exist in 1980. Whether this tendency will grow depends on Western Europeans' estimate of their need for American Hessians. In any case, many groups in Western Europe, not only leftists, are likely to have room for advocating new policies.

Unfortunately, left groups in most nations do not have a well-developed position about the US-USSR struggle. For example, left groupings in the US have an ambiguous relationship to the Cold War and the Soviet Union. On the one hand, they denounce American military expenditures, imperialism, intervention and hegemony as not only undemocratic but also as unsettling the world scene and producing a major war threat. It is not difficult (and certainly not unpopular in left circles) to be critical of the United States. What to make of the Soviet Union? One can have no doubts about denouncing intervention in Czechoslovakia or Afghanistan but what are the implications of Soviet power moves for detente and easing the Cold War? To take a completely American perspective—can the attack on military expenditures rest with a denunciation of the wastefulness and inefficiency of these enormous outlays? What is a reasonable military force for the US? What concessions, compromises or sacrifices should be made for detente—or rejected? What are the national interests of the USSR that other nations should accept as legitimate? What is the American (or Soviet) 'national interest' in Third World nations, if any? If unilateral disarmament is not an adequate answer to the Cold War and the nuclear bomb, is absolute non-involvement in the Third World an adequate position?

Certainly these are disturbing formulations but a left striving for wide and deep political support and for a useful and continuing detente has to face such issues and evolve a broad intellectually and politically responsive position on how the Cold War might wane and US-USSR relations move into a phase less damaging to the two powers and less destructive to the Third World.

Left groups do not have a rich intellectual heritage to draw from in thinking through these issues. Rather, they have frequently resorted to a simple-minded economic determinism in analysing international relations. That approach certainly helps although not completely to understand relations with oil-rich nations (remember US policy on Israel); much of what occurs elsewhere in the world is, however, not basically related to access to important raw materials. Strategically placed geographic areas are important even if offering little in the way of economic resources. Notions of systems threats, balance of power, spheres of influence—which have a political and sometimes more long-range orientation—can have considerable impact on international relations. The complicated 80s will require this broader understanding.

A useful and continuing detente requires an outlook on international relations which may differ importantly from the US and USSR positions. Two decades ago the Polish foreign Minister Rapacki advocated attractive policies to diminish military threats in Central Europe. They did not receive the support from Western Europe nations that they deserved (although they foreshadowed some later developments). In the 80s, proposals of similar merit are likely to emerge. While the left generally has not wielded great influence on foreign relations, it can help some Western European nations move towards a more independent policy which would cool tensions.

The Third Worlds

The Third World is increasingly differentiated. The situation of the oil-rich nations is far different from those of the Sahels, the countries at desperate levels with few prospects of improvements. In between, are nations with sizeable manufacturing industries coupled with enormous poverty in both their rural and urban areas. Their industrial achievements are not sufficiently recognised, partly because the most common indicator of growth, Gross National Product per capita, is a poor measure in nations with high birth rates. The internal tensions in these countries are considerable, as the expanding manufacturing sectors do not eliminate poverty but may aggravate it.

Aggravating the internal tensions is the difficult international economic situation of many Third World countries. The dependency of the newly-industrialising sectors of Third World countries upon a buoyant and expanding world market for their goods becomes painfully clear in times of world economic stagnation. These nations depend on external markets. When there are world economic contractions, they cannot fall back upon a large domestic market for their manufactured goods.

As the 80s begin, many of these nations are further imperilled by enormous international debt burdens. As their economic conditions worsen, repayment of this debt is unlikely. The bankers' national governments (primarily US-based banks are involved) or the International Monetary Fund will undoubtedly step in to save the banks in case of major defaults. The added price to the Third World countries will be the imposition of the typical IMF-deflationary policies which promote internal political strains. In addition the private loans that have financed substantial portions of Third World oil imports will no doubt be curtailed as the riskiness of their position becomes apparent. Again reduced domestic consumption can only lead to social and political unrest in these countries.

Some orthodox writers have outlined the shared future of the developing and developed countries. The latter will shed their older manufacturing industries, ranging from textiles to television, and will invest in Third World nations' capacities to produce cheaply commodities which are a large part of the West's consumption standards. The high-technology industries built around computers and automation will become the economic base of the developed countries as they shift to a new stage of industrial production. To a limited extent this process can be seen in the growth of satellite capitalist nations or export platforms discussed earlier. But the process has certainly not been even or effective. Union resistance to de-industrialisation of regions and sectors of the older capitalist economies is likely to grow as unemployment rises. Continuing Western investment is not assured. Capitalist investment in the Third World will go where the return is greatest so that individual Third World 'success' at this form of industrialisation depends upon competing with each other by keeping taxes and wages low. The result will again be political and social unrest within both the winners and losers. Some of the satellite capitalist nations will fade as other Third World nations underbid them. In any case new waves of manufacturing investment do not guarantee domestic peace in the Third World.

The Third World will be forced to join the capitalist nations on the economic roller coaster. What will be their response? Can the longer-time common interests of the Third World nations be marshalled into effective coalitions? Can raw materials producers organise price-fixing cartels as the OPEC nations have? Can the Third World organise to force a new inter-national economic order on the rest of the world? So far, only limited political success has been achieved. A deep, prolonged recession in the capitalist nations will further undermine the economic strength of any potential Third World producer cartels. The US and other capitalist nations will no doubt oppose new producer cartels more aggressively and effectively than they did the OPEC initiatives.

The Third World might organise against the economic and political intervention of the capitalist West and/or the Soviet Union. Regional alliances, although not effective as yet in Latin America and presently impossible in South Asia, have had success in Africa. In particular, the organising of African states around the Rhodesia/Zimbabwe civil war seems to have been the crucial factor in securing a just and relatively peaceful transition to black rule. Whether this form of political alliance will be successful again and in different circumstances is uncertain. Regional cooperation rather than cut-throat competition for Western investment among Third World control over their own development.

The more likely development strategy is, however, the persistence of the nationalistic and competitive economic and political alignments in the Third World. Given the economic exigencies discussed above, the immediate future of many Third World nations is bleak. Internal political and social strains will no doubt multiply. The struggle over political power will almost inevitably follow from the economic hardship that most Third World nations, and certainly those who compete unsuccessfully for Western investment, are likely to experience. As in the past, the tendency in many Third World countries will be the emergence of left-oriented insurgency movements, with varying levels of mass support, facing opposition by local and international capitalist powers. Frequently the unsettled domestic situation in many Third World nations will make it difficult for those on the left to decide which internal group to support. The US-USSR rivalry will complicate the line-up and outlooks of domestic groups.

The impact of many of these movements will be affected by US foreign policy which is presently in disarray. Old cold-warriors who favour direct military intervention are struggling against the new breed of foreign policy experts who advocate a more balanced approach. The recent events in Nicaragua and El Salvador highlight this shift in US foreign policy. In Nicaragua, after many years of supporting a cruel and unpopular government, the US withdrew its financial and political support of the Somoza regime when it appeared inevitable that the coalition of leftist insurgents were going to win control. Again, in El Salvador the US recently thwarted a rightist coup and demanded that the ruling government instituted land and banking reform (albeit of unknown consequences) rather than allow that nation to follow the path just trod in Nicaragua. US foreign policy incorporates (at least for a moment) the realisation that one can not simply fight, whether directly or through surrogates, ones 'enemies' to the death but must also pull out and cut losses when defeat seems inevitable. This was the lesson learned too late from the Vietnam experience. Intervention is not as easily accepted or as effectively pursued as it was in the 50s.

The United States can be counted on to continue through surrogates to oppose most left insurgencies, but it seems less likely to commit itself to prolonged military interventions. 'Surgical strikes', such as the failed attempt to free the hostages in Iran, will most likely be attempted by the

US in times of political need. Whether or not the first few of these 'cowboy and indian' manoeuvres are definable as 'successes' will influence the future of American military intervention in the Third World.

The Re-Capitalisation Turn

The post-World War II era has ended. Economic growth and an expanding social sector were pursued in the period from the 1950s to the early 1970s. Keynesian demand management through monetary and fiscal policies aimed at stimulating and regulating the economy while versions of William Beveridge's welfare state provided expanding public programmes so that the 'social wage' became an important part of individuals' 'command over resources over time', Richard Titmuss's well-known phrase.

A new social ideology is being developed in both the US and Great Britain. It is a drastic turn from growth with welfare statism; it seeks to restructure the economy. Its goal is 'the re-capitalisation of capitalism'[9] and includes (1) decreasing the importance of the public sector relative to the private—re-capitalisation in the political-economic sense of private enterprise becoming relatively more important as the public social sector declines; (2) promoting investment in the private sector, hopefully in the export manufacturing sectors, by increasing savings and thereby investment through lowered taxation on the well-to-do and corporations—re-capitalisation in the physical capital sense of increased and more productive capacity. These aims are being pursued while strong inflationary pressures are curbed by slowing economic growth.

Coupled with re-capitalisation are the objectives of (a) reducing regulations of businesses that assertedly interfere with productivity and competition (e.g., occupational safety requirements for factories; governmental regulation of airlines) and (b) over time, containing the rise in real wages in order to promote the greater competitiveness of American and British exports in world markets and to reduce the attractiveness of imports which undersell domestic goods.

With the strong and continuing pressure of inflation, re-capitalisation is also offered as a way of dealing with this threat. Increasing investment will increase productivity which will lead to lower costs per unit of production which will result in lower prices. This orientation is now termed 'supply-side economics' in contrast to 'the demand-side economics' of Keynesianism. It is presented as though oligopoly did not exist and prices were set by an automatic competitive market now damaged by governmentally steamed-up demand outstripping capacities to supply goods and as though Keynesianism in practice had not provided major reductions in taxation to stimulate investment.

The re-capitalisation strategy underlies the break with the Keynesian-

Beveridge, New Deal liberal, right-wing social-democratic hope which prevailed in post-World War II Britain and America. The expectation was that Keynesian demand management would increase the economic pie and produce 'full' or high-level employment. This enlarged economic pie would provide bigger slices to all while financing through taxation an expanding public social sector—the 'welfare state'—which would be used to improve the position of those at the bottom and would provide a 'social wage packet' or inlay of social services and cash transfers that would benefit the working and middle classes.

This marriage of Keynes and Beveridge was aimed at keeping the social peace through expanded consumption. It generally succeeded, even if very spottedly. Living standards did advance for a great many; government expanded schooling, pensions, housing; the relative numbers in abject poverty were probably reduced. It also greatly extended the role of government, made important changes in the functioning of enterprises as taxation affected business policies. On the other hand, it did not decrease many inequalities and produced new ones.

'Capitalism with a human face'—'You never had it so good', the Macmillan slogan of 1959: 'the peaceful revolution' as some propagandists termed it—was an important political force. It provided the source of legitimacy for post-war capitalism: everyone was to benefit and perhaps the poor most of all, as in John Kennedy's imagery the rising tide (of economic growth) lifted all boats (including, it was believed, the leaky vessels of the poor). Capitalism was no longer raw in tooth and claw, chewing up its wage-slaves in dark, satanic mills. It was shiny, hopeful, and improving the conditions of most. Keynesianism assumed a successful economic performance; Beveridge, a caring society.

This political-economic outlook had an important innings. While Britain had a less successful post-World War II capitalism than the US, West Germany, Japan, France, living standards did advance even in the UK. But social peace was not fully achieved. In the 60s, the United States experienced racial upheaval; Britain has known many strikes at national and local levels. In the main, however, the social democratic-liberal strategy was effective. The disturbances like those of May 1968 in France did not deeply or persistently push policies from their course.

Now, the social democratic strategy is in great difficulty and business leaders and many economists have convinced political leaders that re-capitalisation with deflation or slowed growth is the appropriate course to eradicate obstinate inflation and to improve gloomy long-term economic prospects. The theme is that slowed growth, even if it results in immediate decline in living standards, is necessary to combat inflation; high-level un-employment must be borne indeed instigated by government at times, if inflation is to be tamed. High profits through reduced taxation and contained wage rises are necessary to induce investment and thereby enhance industrial productivity. The anti-inflation campaign requires that governmental expenditures be lowered to match lower tax revenues; reduced public services are the necessary consequence. The implicit social compact of the post-war era built around the Keynes-Beveridge strategy is, at least for a long period, ended.

The anti-inflation actions are not restricted to draconian measures of deflation. They are linked to a policy of increasing productivity in industry through the re-privatisation of the Gross National Product, i.e., a reduction in the percentage of GNP that flows through government. The language that is beginning to be used is that of 're-investment', new physical capacity in industry. Physical investment in private concerns is to be stimulated in order to improve productivity and international competitiveness. What is implied is the expansion of capitalism, the private control of economic activity with the multi-national enterprises and banks having precedence. A great economic-political-social change is under way.

The 80s starts then with an effort to rekindle capitalism by burdening vast sections of the population through slowed increases in real wages, rising unemployment, and reductions in public services and transfers. What will be the economic and political course of these policies during the decade? The likelihood is that the stop-go actions that Britain suffered in the 60s and 70s will characterise both countries as sporadic political resistance and economic difficulties make longer-term policies difficult to maintain.

Major difficulties will surround the issue of unfettering or deregulating enterprise and economic activity. The theme is that government is incompetent and that the market can better achieve needed investments, improvements in productivity, expansion of exports, and containment of inflation. This policy is unlikely to sail smoothly to its destination.

The re-capitalisation strategy emerges in a period when strong inflationary pressures exist. The need then is for curbing inflation while re-structuring the economy. The achievement of either goal would be a great feat; a combined achievement requires extraordinary luck, economic skill and political acquiescence.

Decreasing taxation on corporations and the well-to-do in order to increase profits and savings in the hope of increasing productive investment is likely to have other results than those claimed for it. Rather than promoting investment in manufacturing, less useful economic activity will result. Heavy speculation (as in the real estate boom of Britain), unproductive investment in sectors other than manufacturing, and the flow of capital to more profitable foreign locales is likely to be the result if the movement of capital is not restricted.

Since such outward flows thwart the aim of increased domestic investment and productivity, there will be sizeable pressures to regulate trade— to promote exports and to discourage imports and capital outflow. The conflicting desires of different business and banking groups will collide and make policy difficult to keep on course.

One of the basic contradictions in the re-capitalisation strategy is that it is presented in the mood of the less regulation the better, let the market work its magic. This outlook wins broad-scale support which withers if only some particular industries benefit. But the needs of the current situation call for selectivity, increasing prospects for exports in specific industries with high export promise. The threats of speculation, capital out-flow and imports and the need to develop industries with dim short-run but good long-term prospects require the channelling of investment funds and curbs on imports.

In the 80s a two-fold struggle will take place, (a) between selectivity and specific subsidies and across-the-board non-selectivity, non-interfering incentives and (b) between selective import controls and 'free trade'. To protect domestic industry from imports raises prices but it also maintains domestic firms and jobs, at least in the short run. To impose tariffs or quotas runs the danger of retaliation by other countries which would threaten exports and the ability of banks, increasingly international, to move their capital as they wish. But without controls or subsidies, some industries will wither; potentially important industries might not grow.

A reluctant, slow movement towards selectivity during the decade will occur as across-the-board solutions prove ineffective. The left position on these difficult issues is always troubled and will be increasingly so in the decade. The left as well as labour unions lacks a coherent view of how to move within capitalism to a situation that furthers the position of workers and the poor without entrenching capitalist institutional formations and mentalities.

A second set of contradictions involves the wage bargain or class struggle. For central to the re-capitalisation/anti-inflationary/pro-export efforts is the containment of real wage increases. A variety of measures are in place or in prospect: a high, continuing level of unemployment 'disciplines' union leaders and members and bends them to accept lower increases. Low growth resulting from restrictions on the money supply forces employers to refuse wage increases; governmental restrictions (or withdrawal of protection) will make union organising and negotiating more difficult; low minimum wage requirements will not push up wage rates from the bottom, the willingness of corporations to sustain lengthy strikes will have long-term discouraging effects on unions in general.

The re-capitalisation strategy may encounter a further set of difficulties arising from the interests of the non-multinational corporations. Un-fortunately, left analyses have not been helpful in understanding the heterogeneity of corporations. Many Marxists speak of 'capital' as though it were an actor. This anthropomorphising obscures the important point that specific factions (not fractions) of capital are moved in particular ways by particular entrepreneurs and managers. This differentiation in the control over kinds and levels of capital is very important.

Again, to act as though the capitalist economy were dominated by the 1,000 largest enterprises and to consign the rest of American firms to a weak 'competitive capitalist sector' is to underestimate the significance for investment, employment and politics of what are important firms outside the top 1,000. Recent Marxist analyses have been obsessed with the multinational corporation and have obscured political and economic currents.

The re-capitalisation/anti-inflationary approach is presented as though it were of benefit to all enterprises. But not all firms benefit from free trade for many are endangered by imports or are unlikely to be successful exporters. Further, low growth to conquer inflation means that many medium-size and small businesses will suffer and be extinguished for they do not have the resources to play for the long haul as do larger firms.

One possibility in the 80s is that the interests of small- and medium-sized businesses and those of businesses in particular sectors may diverge from important elements of the re-capitalisation/anti-inflationary strategy. That is already evident in the efforts to restrict imports in several sectors. If the interests of particular types of businesses conflict increasingly with the dictates of the re-capitalisation/anti-inflationary strategy, which will primarily benefit the larger corporations; if the former organise to press for changes—a big if, no doubt—then there may be possibilities of joint action to push for more expansionary policies, which would result in higher levels of employment as a by-product of survival of these firms.[10]

Not to be ignored in this examination of the possible unravelling of the economic strategy which is being put in place in Britain and the United States is the financial instability of banks and corporations. The largest American banks now make more than half their profits from abroad. As John McKinlay and Don Devey have pointed out, they are heavily invested in Third World countries which have faint prospects of repayment. The banker-as-conservative-gentleman probably never widely existed; today, it is clear that bankers are rash speculators, inventing new ways to manufacture money, damning the risks involved. Central banks would try to prevent bank failures but a sudden and broad collapse of the speculative mania in a fragile situation could overturn policies and destabilise some capitalist economies. Although that statement does not imply a 1929 depression with a 20 per cent unemployment rate; it does point to the susceptibility to pressure of many capitalist economies and the difficulty of maintaining a consistent economic policy.

A second possible event for the United States is interruption in the flow of oil from the Middle East or big jumps in its price. Although the US is slowing its rate of growth in consumption of oil and may develop other energy sources, for some years its foreign oil dependence will remain heavy. Military intervention in the Middle East may cut the flow of oil or a swift surge of oil prices may rekindle a brutal inflation.

Over time, the anti-inflationary concern will lead to controls over prices and wages, overturning the 'free market' approach. In addition to the problems of oil supply and prices oligopolistic pricing by larger sections of industry pushes up prices. Obviously, wage push would press prices (if that vaunted productivity increase did not offset increases in labour costs). Also of significance is the response of politicians to popular pressure by stimulating the economy to reduce unemployment, increase incomes and improve re-election possibilities.

Political Responses

The discussion so far has underplayed the importance of politics, stressing rather economic structures and forces. The success of the re-capitalisation/anti-inflationary policies largely depends on their political acceptability. On that score, they start the decade with impressive gains.

First is the widespread acceptance of the contention that improvements in the standard of living must be sacrificed if the performance of the economy is to be improved. In the United States, the recognition of the end of an era of cheap energy has led to the politically important characterisation of the 80s and beyond as 'an age of scarcity'. In this difficult time of 'limits', another catch phrase, less must be accepted. Lowered standards of living or, at least, a lower growth in living standards than in the past, are in the offing. Expectations are being lowered.

This analysis is presented frequently as a radical one, particularly but not exclusively by those who are attracted to counter-cultural leftism and new styles of living. Having less will lead people, it is asserted, to live more simply, basically and profoundly. In a reversal of classical Marxism, scarcity rather than abundance will lead to positive transformation. This view does not deal with whose living standards are not to rise, how the decisions will be made, how the burden of re-structuring is to be shared and other distributive and power questions which in part characterise a radical analysis. The motif that 'there is nothing wrong with America that lowered expectations cannot solve' is increasingly accepted and cushions reactions to policies which will produce high unemployment, lower real income, reductions in public services and the like. The engineering of consent has moved frightfully fast. Conservative and neo-conservative thought is having a fete in the US, to some extent created by the mass media. American liberalism and right-wing social democracy are in eclipse as a new ideological hegemony sweeps through and conservative thought gains academic respectability as the higher wisdom and more practicable advice.

An important element of conservative ideology is that governments, especially the national government, are incompetent, wasteful and over-extended. Both liberals and Left have an inadequate reply to this contention. The final section will discuss this issue.

Left groups do not seem to have an answer to the difficulties of the present period. They lack a politically attractive, economically viable, short-run economic orientation. That statement does not imply that the Left has to offer a detailed set of specific policies. But to gain support it has to seem able to grapple with important issues. Mrs. Thatcher is undoubtedly wrong about how to deal with inflation but she offers a way. The Left, at least in the US, seems weak and fumbling on the inflation issue. Those on the Left who offer controls as the solution are confronted by strong arguments about their ineffectiveness and the bungling of government. Weak left and liberal responses to such contentions are not likely to win support.

The issue is not only inflation but more deep-seated difficulties of left and liberal-social democratic economic analyses and policy lines. The Keynesian schema, at both analytical and policy levels, is in disarray, weakening the persuasiveness of liberal-right-wing-social democratic recommendations. Marxian economic analyses were built around developments in 19th Century (British) capitalism and have lacked specificity and immediacy. The orientation is to criticise establishment policy rather than to offer serious alternatives to them. The call to nationalisation of industries lacks broad appeal and does not deal with important issues of inflation. Some changes, however, are occurring. In Britain, more than the US, some more basic or radical shorter-run economic policy analysis is occurring, but it is not comprehensive. The need is for shorter- or medium-run policies which move in transformational directions and build support, no easy task.

The glimmers of a shorter- or medium-term orientation are becoming evident: equitable price-wage-profits controls coupled with, rather than as a substitute for, monetary controls; controls over imports and capital outflow, coupled with a world-wide effort to reduce the unsettling effect of high reliance on international trade; supervision of investment to ensure development of particular sectors, moving away from stimulating aggregate savings and investment to selective expansion of those sectors which could serve longer-range economic growth and employment; worker involvement in decision-making in large enterprises coupled with work redesign. In general, the move will be towards affecting not only the level of GNP but its content and the way that it is produced. In effect, what will be developing is a radical supply-side economics, a restructuring of industry and macro-micro policies, to rival the conservative approach to generally higher profits, unselective investment and productivity.

It will take time for this approach to develop technically and politically. At least the first half of the 80s is likely to see the working class and poor heavily burdened by the re-capitalisation/anti-inflationary policies. The 'but' is that the present ideological hegemony of many conservative formulations could be swept aside by reactions to the effects of these policies.

Lowered standards of life, disappointed hopes, high unemployment especially of minority youth, may lead to strong reactions. The social policies of unemployment insurance, job training, public assistance or supplementary benefits are social stabilisers. How effective they will be in cooling discontent is uncertain: as the 80s wear on, they may be curtailed and provide less of a floor for economic losers or a political safeguard against violence and unrest, the confrontational elements of non-electoral political activity. The likelihood is that the state will pursue efforts to adjust social policies so as to accommodate temporarily electoral or confrontational pressures. If economic policies are somewhat successful, there is more room for accommodation and less likelihood of strong opposition. The amount of resistance to the losses suffered by many groups, then, is uncertain.

Strong reactions to events and more general anger may result in turmoil in the 80s. 'Long, hot summers', resistance by blacks and Hispanics, may occur in many American cities. Britain may also experience urban strife, particularly if the police pressure minority groups. An important new possibility is that high and continuing unemployment rates among whites as well as minorities may lead to confrontational actions. Most important perhaps for the US is the possibility of debilitating labour strikes.

While the possibilities of disturbances and turbulence are great, the likelihood is that they will be sporadic and confined, producing minor changes. One reason for limited outbursts is that conservative governments and political climates make it clear that the payoff to reduce rebellious activities will not be very satisfying. In a subtle way, this atmosphere reduces the likelihood of a spark setting off an angry night. Second, minority localities that have experienced destruction as a result of rioting seldom—or at least in the US—have a similar second experience in the next years. If this generalisation holds, then the number of localities in which the containment of unrest fails will be importantly limited. Third, police and political sophistication in defusing or delineating outbursts have grown.

These three reasons indicate a limited number and scope of rebellions. The other issue is whether the response to rebellion will produce significant changes in the conditions of turbulent populations. A reason for doubting that significant change will occur is that the outbursts are local and unfocussed. While underlying issues may involve basic discrimination, poverty, and unemployment, the trigger for the rebellion is usually immediate and local, e.g., specific acts of police brutality. Not much has to be done to mute anger, particularly since no far-reaching demands are enunciated and rebellious communities are not organised to continue struggling on basic issues. If anger persists on a national basis, mild placatory acts by government, e.g., increased expenditures on public assistance or low-paid temporary public jobs, may calm the turmoil. In the absence of a compelling issue and political centre, such social cushions are not only likely to defuse tensions but to split local support for resistance. Governments still have a lot of room for manoeuvre.

Unless new tactics and new balances between 'spontaneous' acts of rebellion and effective continuing organisational forms emerge and unless repressive actions result in events which mobilise large numbers, the 80s will be characterised in retrospect as largely exhibiting troubled acquiescence rather than disequilibrating rebellious events.[11]

A more significant area of unrest may be strikes and plant sabotage. One strand of US business is willing to go to the brink and confront unions, asking them to give up gains that they have won over the years. Other firms are less willing to face the threat of long strikes. The likelihood is of difficult, bloody strikes in the early part of the decade and then a business-union accord premised on a lower level of expectations by unions and their members.

In both Britain and the United States the key to the economic policies being set out to deal with inflation and restructuring depends on the willingness of the underlying populations to live with them for a long period. Intense labour strife and popular discontent would interfere with the working out of these policies. Dealing with these pressures while striving to maintain re-capitalisation strategies will be the dominant political motif of the 80s.

The Movements

At the beginning of the 80s political vitality in the US is around other issues. For unions and black organisations are neither militant nor effective. Actions by union members are likely to take the form of insurgencies while black communities surge with leaderless anger. Current political life is occurring around feminist, environmental and neighbourhood issues.

All three movements are raising basic transformational questions. The feminist movement faces employment discrimination and, in the US, is broadening analysis and policy by constructing an argument about 'comparable work', which goes beyond 'equal pay for equal work' or 'equal access to jobs', to differences in pay in different jobs which require similar levels of skill. The crowding of women into 'female jobs' keeps wages in such jobs below 'male jobs' which do not require any higher levels of skill.

The radical feminist movement points to fundamental tensions in the nature of production and reproduction. Are routinisation and hierarchy the only or even the most efficient ways of organising work? How does patriarchal family structure harm all members of the family unit? Some important changes have occurred in consciousness of both men and women, despite backlash and the anti-abortion movement. The most profound issues of structural and psychological change are raised by some sections of the movement. The feminist movement will face important difficulties in the 80s, and will become sharply focussed on employment issues. Some issues will gain wide support because all stand to gain, as in the effort to 'take back the night', which endeavours to protect women (and men) against assault in city streets in the evening. On the other hand, the declining economy will support arguments that women should be at home taking care of families. As the birth rate continues low and perhaps even dropping in poor or uncertain economic conditions, with the new outlooks of many women, and as the percentage of women in the paid labour force increases, the argument is not likely to be persuasive. But reduced employment opportunities may make concentration on the family a forced alternative for many women.[12]

High levels of unemployment and increasing competition for the limited number of good jobs are likely to result in weakened affirmative action to open up jobs to women. Competition with blacks over jobs may increase, as the divide between good and poor jobs becomes more extensive and deep. The re-structuring of industry is likely to reduce the number of jobs available to entry-level workers, to wider inequalities among jobs, and to make internal promotion more difficult. A segmented labour market in a period of high unemployment creates grave tensions. The beginning gains in reducing employment discrimination against women may erode in the 80s unless political pressures by organised groups of women grow strongly.

The environmental movement has engaged many people. Though frequently denigrated as a middle-class movement about consumption not production issues, it does directly involve production issues in the case of occupational safety and health. The environmental movement is also very broad, having concern for air and water pollution, nuclear energy dangers, the disposal of poisonous wastes. It confronts potential threats to most people even if they are reluctant to envisage them. The environmental movement raises fundamental questions about the right of present and future generations to a decent, unrisky environment and about the balance between material gains in goods and a safer environment.

A variety of other formations exists. But I will move on to urban social movements, local or neighbourhood organisations. Peter Dreier[13] has argued that relatively more people are involved in such activities than were participating in political and quasi-political organisations in former years in the United States. Apathy, his argument runs, does not characterise the American situation despite the decline in participation in electoral politics. In other countries, urban social movements are important though beginning to wane in the turn into the 80s.

The strength of these movements is their local basis; that may also be their weakness. They mobilise people around immediate, close, visible, personal issues. Frequently, they are 'against' movements, trying to prevent something from happening rather than advocating a positive set of actions. They are usually short-lived. As they win their point, make a gain or lose on an issue, they dissolve, become shells, or have an organisational form without active supporters. They are small in size, tend to be unconnected to other organisations, lack a national agenda and eschew national action. They are of, for, and by the neighbourhood.

In the US some neighbourhood-oriented organisations like Massachusetts Fair Share and Ohio Public Interest Campaign seem to be overcoming many of these difficulties. They are staying afloat for a longer period, no minor accomplishment; they deal with more than one issue, e.g., plant closings as well as fuel price adjustments or traffic lights; they are becoming politically effective, and are developing a broader political and economic agenda. They may become potent political forces although they currently avoid partisan electoral politics. That is likely to shift as members run for elective office, which is beginning to happen, and as their issues become ballot and legislative questions.

Many of the effective organisations concentrate on white working-class and lower middle-class neighbourhoods and avoid divisive social issues of race, public assistance or abortion. Some organising is occurring in black and poorer communities. The economic and political strains of the 80s will likely facilitate such organising.

A major problem of the 80s is to draw the neighbourhood groupings toward a national economic and political agenda without weakening their strength in the neighbourhoods. That is no easy matter and the movement can become encapsulated in its neighbourhoods or lose its base by wandering in the corridors of power. ·

A great hope of the neighbourhood movement is that it demonstrates the possibilities of local citizens taking charge, of new forms of democratic participation. Decentralisation and 'empowerment' are the themes. One difficulty is that decentralisation and neighbourhood forms may not be internally democratic and may be manipulated by organisers, despite the latter's good intentions, since they have a different orientation from the neighbourhood members. Some of the more successful organisations have a very conventional organisational structure. A second problem is that local empowerment or control can result in local exclusion, keeping out undesired ethnics, resisting efforts at desegregation and the like. These doubts should not obscure the potentials of the neighbourhood movement in affecting political and economic life and demonstrating new organisational forms.

They are likely to have continual success in the basic organising of neighbourhoods because of crass business policies that exploit consumers by raising oligopolistic prices and that disrupt communities by closing down plants without consultation with the workers or the community and because of governmental policies of reducing public spending and services. Successes in such struggles may lead neighbourhood-oriented organisations to become emboldened and to broaden their outlook and construct a national political and economic agenda. The linking of neighbourhood-based organisations to each other, now beginning to occur, and to national organisations and issues, especially around economic policies dealing with inflation and employment, will be the key organising question for the left.

The three movements briefly discussed above, especially the first two, are frequently described as single-issue movements. They are regarded as narrowly focussed because they are largely unconnected to national political parties, mainly deal with specific issues in specific localities, and do not exclusively revolve around workplace issues. But the single-issue term is not accurate when, for example, the feminist movement affects over 50 per cent of the population and ranges over a wide set of problems.

Two contrasting views of the movements exist. The positive view is that they do achieve important gains or reduce losses for important sections; consciousness is raised; people who have been inactive become active and develop organising skills; they serve as socialist demonstration projects, indicating what a better world could be like; over time the specific or local actions will connect up with broader, national economic and political issues as it becomes clear that problems cannot be resolved at the local level. The opposing view is that these activities compete with each other, divide ethnic and racial communities, dissipate energies, become becalmed at the local level and have little spread effects. That is, they do not reshape other political formations and movements.

An important tendency within each of the movements is the recognition of the need to broaden out, to face national economic issues. (The US environmentalist movement contains an organisation called Environmentalists for Full Employment which directly addresses broad economic issues, seeking to join environmental concerns with economic concerns and not to treat them as in competition.) Many feminist leaders are concerned with broad economic policy which affects employment possibilities. These tendencies are not dominant but they are likely to become stronger as economic conditions decline.

Two institutionalised forces have been underplayed in the foregoing discussion: unions and political parties. Their behaviour will have important effects on the three movements and more broadly. Unions in the US are undergoing important changes as non-manufacturing unions grow, and minority and women members become more numerous. In a difficult economic environment, they are likely to face militant corporate opposition as the larger firms try to break down the tolerated area of agreement which prevailed through the late 50s and 60s and to win back some of the gains that unions have won. As pointed out earlier, internal conflict is likely to expand within unions as corporations toughen their resistance to raising wages or improving or even maintaining working conditions. Some unions, perhaps a majority, are likely to concentrate on fighting internal dissent and placating employers but there are already signs that at least a few unions will be broadening their agendas[14] and seeking allies among the movements. Joint action on specific issues rather than continuing and broad coalitions is the likely form of mutual aid because the agendas of the unions and movements do not fully converge and suspicions of each other are still strong.

The possibility of large-scale change through political parties is discouraging. First, can a left or even a liberal-oriented faction win the continuing support of the Democratic Party? (In somewhat different terms, the same question applies to the Labour Party.) Second, can its programme be the basis of winning elections? And, third, if elected, will the party be able to carry through its left-leaning programme without substantial dilution? To carry through a left-liberal programme requires broad and strong popular sentiment and support and low business resistance (because companies see some gains coming from the left policies as in the Keynes-Beveridge proposals). In the 80s these conditions are unlikely unless the economy plunges to such lows that the current conventionalities of economic policy and political life are smashed.

Two non-institutional forces may be important in the 80s. One, already mentioned, is militancy and violence on racial lines that would be politically disturbing, particularly for the US, as 'the leader of the Free World'. The other is new insurgencies around unemployment, social programmes (e.g., new welfare rights movements), or foreign and military actions (e.g., failed Middle East military intervention). One does not have to agree with all of the arguments of Frances Fox Piven and Richard Cloward in *Poor People's Movements* to recognise the impact that non-institutionalised action can have. It can create shocks to political life—especially for a hegemonic power that needs internal cohesion for foreign adventures. While the timing and specific character of this insurgent shock cannot be predicted, it is likely to happen during the troubled 80s. It should be recognised, as mentioned above, that governments are much better prepared strategically and logistically to handle such shocks than they were a decade ago. But even the potentiality of such actions unhinges much of organised political life.

Finally, the Left as organised political force may influence the intensity and character of political life in the 80s. The following, concluding discussion takes up some issues facing the Left.

The Left

At the beginning of the decade, two surprising developments are evident. Distressing economic conditions which usually are regarded as building left support are not having that consequence. Left groups appear to many to be sectarian, ineffective or irrelevant to the economic and social difficulties of the day. (Note: 'irrelevant' was a powerful radical epithet in the 60s; now, it is used against radicals.) The Left does not seem to have a confidence-building approach. At the same time, the public seems critical of established political parties, political leaders and of business, government and unions. Dissatisfaction is high and widespread but the Left is unsuccessful in responding to it. Therefore, this discussion does not refer only to the small radical caucuses and parties in the US but also to the much greater number of persons of Old or New Left persuasions who maintain radical outlooks but who feel politically homeless.

The other unexpected development is that intellectual life on the Left is lively, interesting and informative in contrast to left political life. Left analyses and studies today are much more penetrating and less dogmatic than the literature of the 30s, certainly in the US, and probably in Britain and France. In recent years, left scholarship and analyses in many fields have made great gains and are influencing orthodox scholarly work. This is particularly true in historical analysis. I do not want to lure myself into portraying this period as a golden age of left writing but even a cursory glance at 1930s work suggests great gains, even if off-the-Marxian-Bible deductionism and textualism still abound.

But the growingly rich left corpus[15] is largely unconnected to the interesting actions of the day. That is not true of some socialist feminist writing and other exceptions exist like the work of the Institute for Workers' Control. But by-and-large political practice, e.g., the spread in the US of neighbourhood groups, is unconnected to radical theorising. Urban social movements are being studied, I should add, by many sociologists and planners who have been stimulated by Manuel Castells. The connections of such studies to action is very thin in the US and UK.

Linking theory and action is an old call. Two things that are frequently ignored will be particularly important in the 80s. One is that often (most of the time?) action precedes and influences theory; the theoretically-inclined then respond to clarify recent and current actions and to debate alternatives and consequences. Practice is never a simple derivative of theory. Frequently, theory is the late response to 'spontaneous action' though it may be important in later developments.

The other neglected point is that when the break between theory and practice is discussed, intellectuals and academics are usually castigated for their unwillingness, incompetence, arrogance, or class biases in not overcoming the break. These are important, frequently on-the-target points, but much of the difficulty arises because action movements feel too busy to try to connect with intellectuals or do not know how, or want to use them only in propagandistic or sectarian ways, or do not pay attention to where the action or organisation is going ('the action-action' mentality), so there is little need for trying to understand what is or might be happening. The theory-practice-praxis break occurs then at two points not only one. While I do not believe in the magical effect of the connection, it is an important link which has not been made effectively as the 80s begin.

The theory-and-practice split does have an immediate significance. An important strand of left theory in recent years has stressed the role of the state in aiding monopoly capital and the importance of the issue of the legitimation of the state. These orientations lead to strong criticism of government and approval of the weakening of support for the state as an institution. On the other hand, the re-capitalisation strategy results in contracting public social expenditures. Left groups then are fighting for at least maintaining governmental services. But the theoretical perspective is of sharp attacks on these services and on liberal or social democratic governments in general. It is not a paradox to be critical of inadequate or coercive or coopting public services and to feel nonetheless that they are needed and should be defended. But the theoretical analysis and political rhetoric have not faced the practical situation of defending public services against massive reductions, while denouncing the capitalist state.

The defence against social service cuts—at least in the US—has not been sophisticated or politically wise. The support for Proposition 13 measures which reduce taxation and public social expenditures shows the widespread dislike of how the welfare state functions, its economic burden, and its reputation. Liberals and radicals share much of the critique. The welfare state has to be defended while criticised. Social programmes have to be changed while protected. The public employees' unions have been slow, at least in the US, in recognising the new political terrain and the need for improvement in public services, not just the continuation of past practices. Nor have the Left and liberals proposed wider changes.

That last sentence suggests two important issues. One is that it asserts that liberals, right-wing social democrats and radicals may have a similar concern for public services. That outlook leads to questions of coalitional activities, joint actions, overcoming the divides between liberals and radicals in a perilous situation, especially for poor people. (Earlier, a parallel point was made about the clash in interests of multinational firms and smaller companies. Can the latter be connected to a socially-useful agenda?) The hoary, unresolved, perhaps unresolvable troubling point of the role of reform is again to the fore. In the 60s in the US, 'reform' was an epithet for many on the Left. In the 80s, it might be a vain hope. All eras have to confront the issue of reform in specific, concrete, historical terms. That will be a prime issue in the 80s, though I have the impression that many radical groups are sliding into reform and coalition with less radical groups, even if their (implicit) theories do not explain their behaviour.

The other issue is that liberals and radicals are on the intellectual defensive. As I said above, they do not have a politically attractive, economically viable set of alternatives about the welfare state nor economic policy. Nationalising a firm or sector does not address inflation or assure employment. Nor do price-wage controls settle issues of which kind of growth. The absence of an attractive alternative is an immediate defect.

For radicals (and for liberals and social democrats too) a longer-run question is the vision of the better society for which they strive. Bureaucratic, authoritarian socialism is repellent even if not grounds for a life-threatening Cold War. Creeping socialism through nationalisation offers few transformational possibilities. The mobilised communitarian models of China, Cuba, and Tanzania, once deeply attractive to many, have been tarnished. Where is the 'good socialism?'

The picture is not completely bleak, for decentralised visions of a 'socialism' seem to be emerging. Frequently, they are naive about the need for centralised economic and political activity. For which industries and regions should be aided to grow? Or, how to limit inequalities if there is no attempt to smooth out regional imbalances? Decentralists ignore Bertram Gross's rule that every act of decentralisation requires an act of centralisation and vice versa. The decentralist perspective implies greater democracy but small places can be coercive and authoritarian too, sometimes even more personally intimidating than large, impersonal pressures.[16]

Despite the limitations of the decentralists, they attempt a transformational perspective, a vision of a society attractive of itself, not only a patch-up of what is visibly wrong with the workings of a capitalist economy. Some vision of this kind is needed even if the 80s will be largely dealing with immediate, disturbing questions of protecting vulnerable populations, preventing devastating wars and ecological catastrophes.

The 80s will likely see a variety of interesting experiments (e.g., workers' control situations which attempt to change the labour process as well as protect jobs). They do not add up to a socialist vision but they could be the proving ground for a non-bureaucratic, democratic, economically effective and just society. One of the great tasks—which radicals have avoided until recently—is the effort to learn how to build or convert larger-scale organisations to a human and humane scale. The study and transformation of bureaucracy as a prime socialist project for smallness cannot be the answer to everything.

This essay will be notable as one of the few political economy articles written in and about the 80s which does not display the word 'crisis'. Of course, whether a crisis does emerge partly depends on the definition of that term. But I eschew the definitional quarrel. What seems more important is that despite their economic difficulties British and American capitalisms will not experience great political strain unless there is strong opposition to economic policies. Whether that will occur is the great although not the only issue of the 80s.

The Left has to learn how to deal with the developing policies and forces of re-capitalisation in ways that contribute to the mobilisation of opposition. Unrest may emerge regardless of what the Left does and the most appropriate left efforts may not shape unrest. But it is clear what the tasks of the Left are—to provide a way of understanding the unfolding issues, helping to organise actions, sketching a vision of a better society. Paul Sweezy and Perry Anderson separately have pointed out that social systems do not suddenly collapse; they are supplanted over centuries. In that perspective, the 80s are a very short period. But they are still likely to be a crucial one for consciousness may be deeply changed and lower standards of living accepted as necessary and fair; private enterprise may be given fuller sway and levers of control over it dismantled; and left proposals may be further marginalised as ineffective and impractical. These would not be minor shifts. While there is much useful action occurring, the Left is ill-prepared for this new and uncertain economic and political phase. But events and political organising may make a radical movement in the 80s.

NOTES

1. In thinking about structural developments in the 80s, it might be useful to think about what could have been predicted in 1970 about the course of the 80s. To what extent were accidents (of at least the exact timing) such as the formation of OPEC crucial in what took place? Was the impact of Watergate something that could not be anticipated? Was inflation inevitable in the 70s or could it have been avoided if the Vietnam war had not continued or if Nixon had not tried to make himself electable by heating up the economy in 1972? Was the failure of the Heath and the Wilson-Callaghan governments to improve the economy inevitable? Could the failure have been less pronounced? (Roy Bennett and I did talk about the possibility of an OPEC-type action in an essay criticising Harry Magdoff's *The Age of Imperialism* but we did not believe that it would occur only three years later and in an already inflationary situation. Timing does make a difference.) ('Does the US Economy Require Imperialism?' *Social Policy*, September-October and November-December 1970.)

2. Editors' Review, 'U.S. Foreign Policy in the 1980s' does a good job of dispelling the belief that international relations form a zero-sum game where a decline in US power necessarily means a gain in USSR power. *Monthly Review*, 31, 11, April 1980, pp. 1-12.

3. See R.W. Wilson, 'The end of the American Era', *New Society*, 24 April 1980. The similarity of Johnson's title to Williams' shows how long the decline has been under way (or at least envisaged).

4. American economic and political weakening is parallelled by its intellectual and academic decline. In the Fifties, social science was regarded as largely what occurred in the USA. That was always a gross misunderstanding; today it is completely out-of-date. In the 70s, American social science (and literature) no longer dominated, e.g., the emergence of French structuralism, and in the 80s the US will be further eclipsed. To a large extent, intellectual and academic fashions follow the flag.

5. Richard Barnett and Ronald Mueller, *Gobal Reach: The Power of the Multinational Corporations*, New York: Simon and Schuester, 1974.

6. The degree of success of the European Community in reducing systematically steel production, capacity and, therefore employment among its members will be a good indication of the ability of the capitalist countries to concert their activities and deal with their long-term problems.

7. In focussing on Cold War issues and symptoms, the internal problems of the

Soviet Union and Eastern Europe are largely undiscussed and Cuba and China ignored. The heterogenity among socialist nations is considerable and deserves attention.

Eastern Europe and the Soviet Union face grave economic difficulties. They are caught in the contradiction between the need or desire for controls to combat inflation, to direct investment, and to limit inequalities and the need for the relaxation of central planning in order to increase efficiency and consumer sensitivity. Allocational priorities and efficiency are often in conflict.

8. I know that this statement is alien to much left thinking. Instead of an extended discussion, I can refer readers to my and Roy Bennett's disagreements with Harry Magdoff's analysis in *The Age of Imperialism*. While the data in the articles are not up-to-date, they do point to a different mode of analysis in differentiating among the participants in trade and capital flow. See 'Does the US Economy Require Imperialism', *Social Policy*, September-October and November-December 1970; also, *A Neo-Imperialism Critique: Does the Rich Nation Need the Poor?*, *Policy Papers*, New York University Centre for International Studies, 1971.

9. S.M. Miller, 'The Re-Capitalisation of Capitalism', *Social Policy*, November-December 1978. An earlier version appeared in *The Journal of Urban and Regional Research*, 1978.

10. The importance of small- and medium-sized firms is discussed in S.M. Miller, 'Notes on Neo-Capitalism', *Theory and Society*, 2, 1, 1975.

11. See the debate about this contention in the May-June and September-October 1980 issues of *Social Policy*.

12. The decline in birth rates may result in labour shortages by the end of the decade. If demographers were not predicting such an occurrence, I would have more confidence in its happening. Despite demographers' poor prediction record, demographic factors are important and neglected in left analysis. Certainly a very important one is the growth in the number of one-parent families.

13. 'Socialist Incubators', *Social Policy*, 10, 5, May-June 1980.

14. Despite left denigration of unions in the recent past, the AFL-CIO has been in the forefront of many economic and social issues and George Meany, its late president, early and vociferously attacked the economic policies of the Carter Administration as harming workers and the poor. The Progressive Alliance, a union-led alliance of trade unionists, environmentalists and minority groups is a second example of union leadership in the current US political scene.

15. I deliberately say 'Left' rather than 'Marxist' or 'Marxism' to underline that an analysis need not be conceived or be defined as in a Marxist tradition to be important and useful to radical political movements. That set of blinders is sectarianism incarnate.

16. The problems of small, communally-oriented formations are honestly analysed in John Case and Rosemary Taylor, eds., *Coops, Communes and Collectives*, New York, Pantheon, 1979.

THE LABOUR MOVEMENT AND THE LEFT
IN THE UNITED STATES*

Stanley Aronowitz

During the 1960s and early 1970s, majority sentiment on the American left held that the American trade union movement had become a relatively conservative interest group. It fought within the Democratic Party, and in direct bargaining with corporations and government, for an increasingly narrow vision of its interests. For example, when confronted with the demands of blacks for full equality within the unions as much as within society as a whole, labour leaders responded with a dual position. The unions remained committed in general to civil rights at the legislative level, but were primarily protective of their members' immediate interests in higher pay and job security. When these interests were in conflict with the demand for full equality, some unions abandoned all but a *legislative* commitment to civil rights.

On the question of the Vietnam war, most unions were either bellicose supporters of the Johnson policies, or remained silent, due either to the ambivalence of some leaders about the war or to unresolved debates among members. The left was aware that a section of the trade union leadership distinguished itself from the generally conservative policies of a section of industrial unions around the ILGWU, the building trades, and most of the old-line union leaders (all of whom grouped around George Meany). This more liberal wing of the labour leadership was led by the United Auto Workers (UAW) and included most of the old CIO unions except the Steelworkers, as well as some former AFL unions (notably, the Amalgamated Meatcutters, some sections of the Machinists, and the State, County, and Municipal Employees). These unions were motivated by at least two different impulses: their ideological antipathy to the persistence of cold-war alliances into the 1960s when reflex red-baiting seemed beyond reason, even in the midst of the Vietnam war; and the influx of large numbers of youth, racial and ethnic minorities, and women into the ranks of the industrial unions. These influences combined with power struggles against the Meany administration to produce a (loyal) opposition at the leadership level of the labour movement. Yet in almost no case outside the public-sector unions, where organising the unorganised took on

---

*This article first appeared in the March-April 1979 issue of *Socialist Review* and is reprinted by kind permission of the Editors.

the dimensions of a crusade, was the leadership of the 'progressive' unions committed to qualitatively different policies from those of the dominant wing of the AFL-CIO on issues at the level of the shop or office floor. The opposition was largely confined to different positions on national political questions and international cooperation against multinationals. For the most part, there was no effort to secure membership participation in any mass activities against the war, although, in the early 1960s, the progressives mobilised for civil rights.

The predominant left view was that following World War II, after a brief period of militancy engendered by wartime wage- and price-freeze policies, the unions had settled down to riding the new wave of American world economic and political hegemony. The trade unions had been able to win substantial concessions in union contracts until the late 1960s despite four post-war recessions. Union leaders had joined in the cold-war chorus that resulted in the expulsion of Communists, the easing out of militants, and the erosion of internal union democracy. Unions had become bureaucratic and their social vision was blurred, if not obliterated[1]; they were mired in business practices, and even the elements of social-democratic ideology that infused the CIO during the 1930s were gone.

It was acknowledged that organising and strike activity had not disappeared in 1946-70. Wildcats (unauthorised strikes that were directed as much against the unions as against the company) and authorised long-term strikes such as the 116-day steel walkout in 1959 or several lengthy rubber and auto strikes continued. And there were rank-and-file movements formed, for the most part, in protest against the abrogation of democratic practices or the loss of militancy among union leaders. But for most of the American left, these signs of militancy were far outweighed by the evidence that the unions increasingly played the role of labour lieutenants of capital, in Daniel DeLeon's famous phrase.

With the growth of Marxism among new leftists in the late 1960s the tendency to write off the working class became untenable. To be sure, there were signs that the situation had altered somewhat in a few sectors: the most notable change was the rise in union membership among public employees in the 1960s, spearheaded by teachers' union organising and the phenomenal growth of administrative employees' unions, particularly AFSCME and the Government Employees.* Postal workers were also growing restless during the early 1970s inflationary spiral. The massive entrance of blacks and women into public employment also helped to produce the largest wave of union organising since the 1930s in the public sector.

As dramatic as the 1970 national postal strike proved to be, and the

---

*This growth was as large as that of the recruitment of the CIO in the late 1930s.

almost annual strikes by teachers in many major cities, it cannot be claimed that the inspiration for a resurgence of left-wing interest in the working class was based on an understanding of the new features of class struggles or the changing composition of the working class. At a time when millions of women were entering both the labour force and the labour movement, the left discovered the working class through its reading of Marxist theory. For most, the working class was defined as those who produced surplus value, or even as only those engaged in the process of the production of material goods. And, in the classical formulation, a special interest focussed on those who produced the means of production—the miners, steel-workers, transport workers, and, because of their centrality to all these industries, the consumer-goods-producing auto workers. The argument for 'concentration' on these sectors has been that the 'basic' industrial workers hold the key to the economic mechanism. Their unions, the UAW, USW, Teamsters and the UMW, are the most militant, are largest in the American labour movement, can stop production in many other sectors, are the most advanced detachment of the whole class, etc.

Whether these arguments correspond to the reality of contemporary developments within the class, the economy, or the unions has been largely irrelevant to the left debates. The majority of the left parties (the CP, Maoist or neo-Maoist groups, and the Trotskyists) have adopted theoretical and practical perspectives on a rigidly doctrinal basis. The white-collar and public-employee sectors of the working class are either labelled 'secondary' in importance or are dismissed as petit bourgeois who are little more than 'allies' of the working class. (Some attention is conceded to consumer goods industries where black, Chicano and Puerto Rican workers predominate, because these are among the most 'advanced' workers despite the marginal character of the industries within which they work.)

Moreover, citing Lenin, the trade unions are regarded as 'schools for communism' despite their 'reactionary leadership' or their 'reactionary character'. For most of the socialist left, working-class organising has effectively meant work in trade unions.[2]

Neighbourhoods, community colleges, informal work groups, women's and poor people's organisations are not viewed as arenas of working-class activity, even when they are acknowledged to have some importance. Thus much of the left has reproduced, on the basis of no concrete analyses, perspectives based on the experience of European and United States communist and socialist movements of the last century, until World War II, perspectives that do not take account of the actuality of the last thirty years in the United States (as well as Europe). The analyses of the new left that did offer insight into the new configurations of work, politics, and culture within the working class have remained marginal to virtually all of the practical activity of the left in relation to the labour movement in the last decade.*

In what follows, my intention is to discuss the specific problems faced by the working class in this historical period, its changes, possibilities, and limitations. I will first look at the labour movement in its overall social context as a constellation of institutions that have arisen in response to these problems. On that basis, I will examine the main features of the strategic perspectives of the major existing left organisations, before presenting my own views on the questions involved.

Two points are particularly important throughout this article. First, it is argued that there exists a many-sided crisis of the labour movement in the framework of a tendency for the political and economic power of the working class to decline. Second, while much of what follows centres on the trade unions, they are treated as a specific form of workers' organisation, which even if the main form, does not exhaust the range of organisational settings that are of vital importance for any left strategies.

PART I

THE WORKING CLASS AND ADVANCED CAPITALISM

The American working class and its unions struck a definite bargain with the corporations and the government after World War II. While not surrendering the right to strike, or to oppose management policies on the shop floor or at the level of public policy, the labour movement became part of an alliance that aimed to maintain the United States' economic and political hegemony in the capitalist world while opposing the class struggle on the political level at home. This bargain did not extend with uniform success to the economic level or to the workplace, despite the efforts of most of the labour leadership to promote class collaboration within the collective bargaining process. Although rank-and-file unionism declined appreciably after the war[3] as most unions became more centralised, more businesslike and bureaucratic, in thousands of factories and offices, an eroded rank-and-file steward system of militant local union leadership battled the attempt of capital to dequalify 'free' labour from the workplace by means of automation, changes in work organisation, and mechanisation.

In many instances, notably the steel, auto, and mining industries, new management strategies met with stiff resistance. Workers defended their work rules made on the shop floor with line supervisors, and only yielded to new processes under severe pressure from their union leadership and the 'starve them out' policies of a resolute management willing to take long strikes in order to gain full control of the labour process. To this day, the

---

*There are, of course, some exceptions, but virtually none concern the traditional left parties.

efficiency experts and the engineers have not succeeded fully in taking power away from the workers in many industries. The class struggle has determined the shape and the pace of technological changes as well as the forms of work organisation.[4]

Yet anticommunism and union bureaucracy have largely been successful in integrating the working class into advanced capitalism. Of course, the powerful world position gained by American capital enabled the emergence of another crucial force: the ideology and practice of consumerism. New patterns of industrial decentralisation produced the exodus of workers from the cities and resulted in their relative isolation in suburbs and smaller cities. The political, social, and class solidarity produced by the concentration of capital in a few large units that had contributed decisively to the industrial union successes of the 1930s and early forties in cities like Detroit, Pittsburgh, New York, and San Francisco was now challenged by the advent of mass one-family private housing, cars, and, above all, the fragmentation of working-class life away from neighbourhoods into suburban tract housing and isolated forms of social life.

If the segmentation of plants within the same or related industries was the necessary condition for the break-up of class consciousness, the ideology of consumerism was its sufficient condition. The *displacement* of the conflict between labour and capital to consumption had the effect of depoliticisation within the working class in the postwar period.[5] Workers became privatised, concerned chiefly with the house, car, and other payments, and thus came to regard high wages as the central trade-union demand. In the process, many hard-won gains at the shop floor were systematically, if slowly, surrendered. Many workers came to regard their unions as insurance societies (Marx) at best, and often viewed them with hostility, even if they remained loyal to the trade union principle itself.

By the late 1960s the last of the generation of union leaders who had been formed by the period of mass organising and relative radicalisation were gone from the scene: John L. Lewis retired and yielded his mantle to a corrupt business unionist, Tony Boyle, whose demise was to be closely associated with the resurgence of the movement for democratic unionism a decade later; Walter Reuther was killed in a plane crash as the 1960s decade came to a close, a tragedy symbolic of the end of an era. Reuther and Lewis were honest, but also had been engineers of the collaboration between the unions, the corporations, and the state. Lewis gave up the workers' and unions' control over working life, permitting the industry to mechanise rapidly in the 1950s in return for health and retirement benefits. Reuther and his steel union counterpart, David McDonald, never tired of insisting that the fate of the workers had to be tied to their willingness to yield to productivity in order to safeguard their living standards and job security. The class struggle was seen as anachronistic, although Reuther often backtracked from this line during bargaining.

By the early 1970s, it became apparent to many observers that the honeymoon between labour and capital was also coming to an end. America's world economic position was severely challenged by Germany, France, and above all Japan. In addition, nationalist claims to oil resources in the Middle East placed in question the dominant position of American corporations in that area. At the same time, European capital was matching and exceeding United States production in 'durable' goods sectors such as autos, steel and electrical instruments.

The development of conglomerates and multinational corporations changed the shape if not the substance of class struggles. It was perfectly consistent for a multinational corporation to be based in the United States but in control of a major electronics manufacturer in Japan, and, at the same time, be adversely affected by the rising proportion of imports threatening its domestic operations. Companies like General Electric and General Motors maintained large operations in both home and foreign countries, often choosing to divert capital abroad in order to safeguard their corporate position. But the gradual de-industrialisation of the United States and other advanced capitalist countries in the wake of competition from both the Third World and Japan began to corrode the balance-of-payments position of the United States, and became a serious factor in the inflationary spiral beginning in the 1970s putting enormous pressure on the working class and the trade unions.

Structural Changes in the Working Class

These general tendencies have occurred in the context of a major recomposition of the working class; the two primary features of this process have been the relative decline of the industrial working class and the vast expansion of the service and administrative sectors.* At this point, only the most narrow conceptions could deny that the size and character of the industrial labour force is rapidly changing. With few exceptions, old skills have been made obsolete and the industrial labour force has been materially reduced by the movement of plants overseas and to the southern and south-western parts of this country, in combination with the rapid mechanisation of key industries.

For example, in 1947 there were more than six hundred thousand workers in the basic steel industry. Today fewer than four hundred thousand produce twice the amount of steel their counterparts made thirty years ago. Not only are older plants shutting down (Youngstown Sheet and Tube, Bethlehem's Lackawanna plant), but the existing mills are being modernised. Not all mills have introduced new processes, but

---

*The absolute number of workers in manufacturing has not declined, but the labour force has expanded from about 60 million in 1947 to more than 90 million in 1977.

those that wish to compete with the Japanese, the French, and the Germans are forced to move in the direction of modernisation.

Similar developments in the chemical, electronics, and information industries and in auto parts manufacturing forecast sharp reductions in size of the operating work force, while many of the functions usually performed under the old technology by semi-skilled and skilled workers have been transferred to maintenance and 'inspection' processes. The inspector becomes the representative of the engineering and scientific function, which has now become the major productive force in continuous operations industries.

These developments do not signify the disappearance of the industrial worker, but do signal a change both in qualifications and in function. The worker performs either a traditional 'technical' role in the production process or is responsible for keeping the automatic machines running. The old skills are reduced, new skills are introduced. The steel mill of the future will have a majority of workers with some kind of technical training, either in community colleges or four-year postsecondary technical and liberal arts schools. And there will be fewer workers, even if they occupy the central position in the labour process. The number of persons in the industrial labour force will continue to decline because of the more rapid introduction of *processes* that eliminate whole stages of production, in contrast to mechanisation, which may only reduce the number of workers required in each stage.[6]

The trade unions view their situation with alarm, but have agreed, in the main, to heavy investment programmes. Many militant unionists and democratically-run internationals with honourable traditions have been obliged to go along with management programmes because of the shut-down or plant removal threat, which is no longer merely a bargaining tactic by the corporations, but a serious challenge to the assumptions of 'class-struggle' unionism. Class-struggle unionism requires not only an expanding economy both in production and employment, but also a stable configuration of industrial possibilities. These are precisely the conditions that are being removed by international competition and productivity changes. Multinational corporations control American production just as they control the major productive forces in every leading capitalist country of western Europe and North America, if not Japan. The widening of their net also signifies the widening of their operations and the intensification of the *international* division of labour. With the growth of the secondary (industrial) sector in the Third World and those countries like Spain that may be said to lie in the semi-periphery, both basic and consumer-goods industries in this country are threatened, even in good or boom times.*

---

*In a recent visit to Kaiser Steel I was struck by the limits imposed on trade unionism by the investment programme of that corporation to bring production up to the level of sophistication of Japanese competition. The union has not insisted

In many cases, workers have been forced to cooperate in management's productivity efforts, as in the machine-tool industry, where bidding on both private and public contracts is now world-wide. These developments indicate clearly that the national union, one whose vision is confined to the borders of its own country, social conditions, and political life, is simply archaic in an increasing number of cases. Although there are a few cases where unions in the United States have joined in some consultation with counterparts, notably the Metal Workers and Chemical Workers federations, the progress is slow and the membership has been dimly apprised of these developments.

The Public and Service Sectors

The productivity rise in manufacturing that has accompanied reorganisation of the work processes and mechanisation means that fewer workers can expect to become employed in the production of goods, where unions are relatively strong, working conditions relatively enforced by collective action, and the level of wages higher than in other sectors. Since 1947, the increase in the size of the public sector together with the growth of service industries has matched the growth of the labour force.* There are no significant manufacturing sectors except chemicals that account for the creation of new post-war jobs. Now almost one of six workers is employed in the public sector, and another fifth in retail, wholesale, and financial services. Added to the five million workers in administration, almost 50 per cent of all employees are in public and private administration and services.

Two main conclusions follow from this growth: first, the size of the labour force employed in activities of coordination approximates those

---

on enforcement of that provision of the contract that insists on observing 'past practices', a euphemism for union control over the introduction of new labour processes. With half of the plant shut down due to archaic processes, the only hope for the corporation is to 'modernise'. The hope of the members to keep their jobs is to cooperate at least to the extent of permitting attrition rather than layoffs to become the key mechanism for reducing the work force, and to save the jobs of the remaining workers by relaxing past-practices clauses. Of course, seniority and other protections still exist in the plant and the union has fought for more stringent safety measures. Yet it cannot be denied that in the interest of saving jobs by preventing plant shut-downs and removals, some sections of the union have cooperated with management to raise productivity by relaxing certain work rules. In one instance, 'workers' participation' has been the vehicle for raising production. In the tube mill, a plant hard hit by competition, the workers saved the mill by agreeing to abolish their informal work quotas; the mill is producing more, and layoffs have been reduced to just a few workers in the past several years.

*At the end of World War II there were about 4 million public employees in the United States, not specifically related to defence industries and the armed forces. By 1975, the number had increased to 16½ million. Service employment grew similarly.

who are being coordinated. This function, centralised in the state, large financial institutions, and corporate headquarters, includes a considerable number of the women who have entered the labour force in the past thirty years. These 'unproductive'* workers administer production, distribution, marketing, and consumption activities to a degree unknown forty years ago. Thus the role of these groups is not *merely* a drag on capital accumulation: they are absolutely necessary for the accumulation process itself; a need is also a constraint. The attack on the public sector and administration by the large corporations (organised to some degree by the right) is an attempt to reduce the costs of coordination and also, by cutting back social services and therefore some taxes (property as well as income) to lower the cost of the reproduction of labour power. This is a solution to the crisis of accumulation that produces the economic basis for right-wing politics and ideology.

The second consequence of the growth in the unproductive sectors is the decline of trade unionism as a political as well as economic influence in the country as a whole. Most of the new, employment growth sectors are

TABLE I

TRADE UNION MEMBERSHIP IN THE UNITED STATES

1930-1974

	Union membership (in millions)	Percentage of the labour force	Percentage of the non-agricultural labour force
1930	3.4	6.8	11.6
1935	3.5	6.7	13.2
1940	8.7	15.5	26.9
1945	14.3	21.9	35.5
1950	14.3	22.3	31.5
1935	16.8	24.7	33.2
1960	17.0	23.6	31.4
1965	17.3	22.4	28.4
1970	19.4	22.6	27.5
1974	20.2	21.7	25.8

In 1974, 12 per cent of women in the paid labour force were in unions; 30 per cent of men in the paid labour force were in unions. By sector, 42 per cent of union members were in manufacturing, 44 per cent in private non-manufacturing, and 14 per cent in government.

SOURCES: *Directory of National Union and Employee Association*, 1975 (Bureau of Labor Statistics, 1977); *Handbook of Labor Statistics*, 1975, Reference Edition (U.S. Department of Labor, Bureau of Labor Statistics).

---

*'Unproductive' in the Marxian sense, that is, workers who do not directly produce surplus value.

non-union, with the notable exception of public employment.* In fact the decline of union representation in the work force may be in large part ascribed to the non-union status of this sector, since manufacturing, transportation, and public employment have either maintained union strength since the end of World War II or increased union membership (see Table I above).

The Labour Movement during and after Vietnam

These changes in the structure of the working class and the international balance of forces among capitalist countries began to have serious effects on the labour movement in the mid-to-late 1960s. For some sections of the working class, it became clear that the post-war formulas would no longer assure even the maintenance of their living standards.

The wave of union militancy that broke out in the heavy industrial sectors in the late sixties was determined, in part, by the international problems confronting American capital, and partly by the contradiction between the new generation of workers not accustomed to work degradation and the increasingly repressive trade union leadership. Workers fought on three levels: in the late sixties there were many efforts to slow down or prevent plant removals in the machine, food, and auto industries, with varying success.† Second, workers organised rank-and-file movements for union democracy with the aim of electing officers who would be responsive to the membership and more militant. Third, workers rejected union-negotiated agreements in growing numbers until 1974, and used the strike weapon in preference to more conciliatory methods of dealing with grievances and contract disputes.+

But these moves have not resulted in the development of a comprehensive labour programme to deal with the chronic issues of structural un-employment (where layoffs are not due to the slow economy alone, but also to specific investment decisions that produce technological un-employment and runaway shops), health care, and labour reform. The majority of labour unions remain tied to the liberal, anticommunist wing

---

*One outstanding exception to this pattern is the retail food field, where the Retail Clerks union has organised a majority of chainstore employees together with the Meatcutters, who represent most butchers in retail chain stores.

†One example: in the 1967 struggle to keep the Schaefer brewery in Brooklyn, workers chained themselves to machines to dramatise their refusal to accept the closing of this large plant. On the other hand, there were a number of uncontested closings of oil refineries in the same period.

+Some 'rank and file' movements in the 1960s were really palace revolts, such as within the Teachers, Oil and Chemical Workers, Government Workers, and State, County, and Municipal Employees. Although the new leaders were recruited from large local unions, most of them had already been full-time officials. It is estimated that about one-third of all proposals were turned down by members from 1967 to 1974 (see the various issues of *Monthly Labor Review*).

of the Democratic Party, and have refused to ally themselves with even the reform elements who captured the party in 1972 (which remain a strong but declining force). In the wake of a more or less concerted corporate-led assault on labour's legal rights as well as contract protections, the unions have found their alliance ineffective to win even minimum demands; Democratic leaders in Congress and the Democratic administration are now wedded to 'anti-inflation' policies such as wage and social-welfare restraint, and cutbacks. The dominant mood of the large corporations, to 'take back' many contract protections won by workers and to force concessions by the federal government in tax and import levies is reflected in the refusal of the 'moderate' wing of the party to wage a struggle for labour reform legislation that would ease somewhat the way for union organising, for a national health insurance programme needed by workers, poor people and retirees to offset the skyrocketing health costs, as well as other measures traditionally associated with liberal-state expenditures.

Part of the problem stems from the disintegration of the *active* base of the unions, which, as late as the 1950s, could still be mobilised for legislative action. This base, developed during the upsurge of the 1930s, left the plants and the offices in the late 1950s and 1960s or was forced out because of the conservative turn in union politics. Apart from the growth of retail and public-sector unionism, which has only partially restored the membership base of union activism, only the Teamsters, Steelworkers and Mine Workers have shown much evidence of an active rank and file, and then only in some districts where an opposition to the leadership has emerged. In many cases, this opposition has confined itself to demands for democratic unionism, concentrating on a programme of rank-and-file approval for union contract settlements, regular conventions, and militancy at the bargaining table. With a few exceptions, notably District 31 of the Steelworkers, the new impulse for democratic unionism remains *economistic*, that is, confined to issues bearing on wages, benefits and working conditions.

The Decay of the Unions
The disintegration of the active base of the unions resulted from multiple sources rather than from a single cause. For most left-wing commentators on the post-war labour movement, the decline of the unions as a significant social force in American life has been ascribed nearly completely to the severity of the political repression of the first post-war decade. This central ascription is combined with a 'misleadership' thesis according to which the 'social-democratic' (Reuther) or conservative (Meany) leaderships were responsible for both expelling the left-wing rank-and-file-oriented leadership of the movement and 'the bureaucratic evolution' from democratic, social unionism to business unionism.[7]

According to this view, the split in the left/centre coalition that had built the CIO and many AFL unions was fundamentally a cold-war phenomenon. A variant of this position is offered from the Trotskyist perspective: the CP's collaboration with the wartime policies of the Roosevelt administration after the invasion of the Soviet Union in 1941 was the decisive cause of the decline of the labour movement. The Stalinist left's interpretation of the strategic requirement to form a united front against fascism produced, in this view, the gradual move of the unions away from class-struggle politics both in the shops and at the ballot box.[8]

In fact, the success of the collaboration between the unions and the employers and the unions' support of the cold war cannot be accounted for by a theory that looks *exclusively* to policies of this or that wing of the labour movement, or even to the repressive policies of the state. The partial eclipse of labour's rank and file was linked to changes in the character of social life after the war: the unique position of American capital in the world that permitted nearly thirty years of expansion; the break-up of traditional centres of working-class power by industrial decentralisation; the rise of consumerism as a social force; and, linked to these, the long-time tradition of American ideology that privileges the practical over the theoretical, the short-run over the long-run, the expedient over the principled. Union members were increasingly discouraged from participating in the everyday activities of their organisations. Discouraged, for example, by the increasingly large number of union agreements that reduced the power of the stewards and established company- or union-paid full-time grievers in the plants;[9] discouraged by the routinisation of union affairs and their reduction to matters of contracts and bargaining; discouraged by the loss of the social ideology of the democratic unions that had emerged in the 1930s, an ideology that was incipiently democratic and class-independent.

Within the context of the bureaucratisation of unions, the concept of the union as an insurance society grew dominant among the vast majority of members. Where rank-and-file committees once formed the core of union organising efforts, the task was now relegated to full-time officials. Where workers fought directly to protect their measure of shop-floor control over the labour process, contract unionism urged, cajoled, and sometimes forced them to change their orientation to wage demands, and to permit corporations to take command of the plant by means of new methods of work organisation and technological innovation.

The 116-day steel strike of 1959 and the 1955 auto wildcats only served to illustrate the degree to which some workers remained dedicated to their power at the workplace. But auto and steel were not typical of the working class as a whole. By the mid-1950s oil refineries and chemical plants were firmly in the hands of management and a plethora of new industries and processes were introduced that circumvented the class traditions. Electronics and computers began to be the motive force, not only of administration, but also of production.* The great, militant traditions of the brewery workers were destroyed by plant removals and electronically-based processing; the food-processing industry became a model of the 'continuous flow' operation and literally buried another long-time socialist-minded sector of the working class. The Packinghouse Workers and the Bakery Workers unions, whose traditions had been models of class-conscious struggle, were beaten not primarily by red-baiting or bureaucracy, but by the 'march' of labour-saving technology.

The West Coast Longshoremen's union suffered from a gradually aging and collaborationist leadership, which has been weakened by its relative isolation from the mainstream of the labour movement. Yet, next to the mechanisation and modernisation agreement of 1960-62, the issue of the subjective character of the leadership or left policy pales. There were no alternatives proposed to an agreement that purportedly secured the well-being of most of the workers in exchange for permitting the Pacific Maritime Association to load cargo by containers rather than human muscle. In the wake of the international introduction of this method, the long-time left-wing president of the union, Harry Bridges, saw no way of holding back assent. It appeared that despite the legendary solidarity of the longshore workers, the rank and file was not prepared to hold out against a degrading technology that undermined the foundation of their social power.† How was this possible, when on many occasions the leadership had been unable to enforce its policies among the membership?

These multiple determinations produced a new ideological and political orientation among the membership of even the most progressive of the unions. The working class lost the confidence in itself that had been acquired in the 1930s and early 1940s, particularly in its ability to take the initiative. Organised defensively into trade unions whose normal method of operation was to pick up the pieces created by the logic of capital, it became more open to regressive ideologies of racism and sexism on the one hand and to consumerism and privatisation on the other. The

---

*This process is still under way and meeting with considerable resistance in the machine-tool industry, in contrast to steel, where automation has moved much more rapidly. numerical controls are still incompletely introduced in the machine-tool industry, in part because of skilled workers' resistance.

†The mechanisation and modernisation agreement provided guarantees of full-time work for remaining union members, a liberal pension programme, and safe working conditions. In recent years, those guarantees have been seriously undermined by the employers, especially in the San Francisco Bay area. Among the most important of union conditions that have suffered erosion is the tradition of almost no permanently hired workers. The union's power was reinforced by the hiring hall, a device that gave workers primary identification with the union. Recently, stevedore companies have been employing permanent people, an issue the last contract negotiations did little to resolve.

basis for the development of these ideologies was the position of American capital in the world as much as the bureaucratic development of the unions. Yet the autonomous role of the ideological shifts among the working class in causing its decline as an active class cannot be ignored. Explanations for the disintegration of the active base of the unions that rely on misleadership and political or corporate repression assume that the workers are always ready to fight, are class-conscious, and are democratic, but are only deterred from the outside. My contention is exactly the opposite. On the one hand, the American working class is heir to a variety of influences that stem from the development of American capitalism and its specific ideologies, the most important of which is that the class was constructed out of immigrant and black slave sources in the nineteenth century. The fragmentation of the American working class remains a crucial element in its historical development. On the other hand, the changes in social life after the war meant that the working class was re-divided internally by a new way of life that subordinated production to consumption at the ideological level. As work and living places were widely separated and the cultures created in the bars and social, fraternal, and political clubs were disrupted, white male working-class culture disappeared from many places. For women, the situation was even more difficult. Once a majority of working-class women shared a neighbourhood life that was closely linked to certain industries, particularly garments, textiles, and food processing. Now these industries disappeared from most neighbourhoods and moved to company towns in the South and Southwest where communities still exist to some degree, but without the links to militant working-class traditions or even Democratic liberal political traditions. Working-class women's culture has shifted decisively to the workplace, although women still form the base of church organisations and parent groups.

Industrial workers' wages and benefits have barely succeeded in keeping up with inflation in the monopoly, unionised sectors such as auto, steel, and electrical. In the unionised competitive manufacturing sectors such as clothing, shoes, and textiles, where the extent of union organisation has slipped badly over the past decade and international competition has had a material impact on employment and prices, union wage settlements have failed to keep up with inflation. In non-union sectors (now 80 per cent of the wage and salary labour force), only the threat of unionisation has succeeded in enabling workers to make wage gains. (This is particularly true of the textile industry, largely a non-union Southern employer.) For workers on fixed salaries or where the political climate prevents unions from winning wage increases, such as in the public sector, particularly at the local level, the decline in real wages has seriously affected living standards. In sum, the working class is undergoing a severe loss of economic, social, and political power. The corporate offensive that followed the boom years of the Vietnam war is succeeding, due in no small measure to the ascendancy of right-wing ideological and political initiatives, as well as the growing gaps between union leaders, the rank and file, and the leadership of the Democratic Party.

The Labour Movement and the Democrats

In contrast to the New Deal and Fair Deal periods (1933-1968), when a majority of union members voted Democratic and an even larger majority of unions were oriented to the Democratic Party and exerted a considerable influence over its policies, if not always on its candidates, the Nixon presidency was accompanied by deep and perhaps permanent splits in the party. Splits have always existed, but were reserved for conventions and congressional battles. The traditional Democratic division had been between its conservative southern wing and its northern 'corporate-liberal' majority, which was dominated by a sector of the capitalist class but included a coalition of labour, black, and middle-strata forces. Organised labour always played the role of junior partner, but retained its independent legislative position. It has been the coalition's driving force on almost every piece of social legislation, including civil rights, social-welfare programmes, and labour rights.

The Democratic primaries and convention battles of 1968 witnessed virtual labour unanimity behind the candidacy of Hubert Humphrey despite his identification with the war policies of the Johnson administration. But by 1972, the McGovern candidacy produced the first major split in labour's ranks since John L. Lewis refused to back FDR in 1940. Most of the progressive union leaders supported the South Dakota senator, both because of his anti-war stand and because he had become the candidate of the Democratic Party. The bulk of union leaders refused to back McGovern, but could not overtly support Richard Nixon either. Labour's official abstention may not have changed the votes of most rank-and-file union members (who stayed with McGovern), but it withdrew moral and financial support from the Democratic challenger, and was part of the reason for the enormity of his defeat. (McGovern's percentage of the popular vote was only 3 per cent less than that of Humphrey in 1968. The main source of Nixon's wide margin was the absence of George Wallace or another major third-party candidate.)

Labour's 'neutrality' was part of a widespread election defection of the so-called Jackson wing of the party and much of the Humphrey wing as well. Following the 1972 elections, George Meany and a majority of his executive council began to support Senator Henry Jackson's bid for the 1976 nomination. When that campaign failed to get off the ground in the wake of the Carter blitz, the unions united solidly behind Carter, but the fissure in the party and the union ranks widened despite the 1976 Democratic victory. McGovernites and progressive unions stayed close to the traditional liberal policies of the party and were joined shortly after the election by Meany, who began to perceive the Carter administration as a captive of big business. But the party had split in a new way: the liberal ranks went in two directions. One drew closer to the administration's strong anti-inflation programme and energy programme, both of which implied substantial cuts or stagnation in social programmes.* The other, headed now by Senator Edward Kennedy of Massachusetts, insists on the old programme, even if it cannot mount an effective attack against Carter's policies.

Today union influence in the Democratic Party is quite muted owing to the convergence of Democratic and Republican economic policies that call for both wage and social austerity. The question raised by the new developments among Democrats is whether the Democratic Party can any longer be the arena through which the traditional liberal coalition may operate.

The Corporate Offensive

To some degree, the corporate offensive and the right-wing resurgence overlap, but are not identical. The large corporations have mounted a major assault on Congress and have thwarted nearly all liberal social legislation. At the bargaining table, company policies have resisted major improvements in pension and health plans and have insisted on long strikes in many cases rather than acquiesce to union wage demands. In some instances, there have been 'take backs', such as in the steel industry where the Experimental National Agreement requires the workers to forsake the strike weapon for six years, to relax enforcement of limits on work rules and past-practices changes, and to tie their wages to increased productivity on a more global scale than ever. In the public sector *de facto* wage-freeze policies are in force in many localities, with the reluctant agreement of the unions. While some uniformed service employees (police, fire, and sanitation) have successfully broken away from wage restraints, and at least 15 per cent of the country's teachers went on strike to win their demands for higher wages, thousands of administrative employees were laid off or had their wages frozen, gutting their pension and health programmes to save jobs in many instances.

The attack against the public sector is determined by a number of factors: first, small and medium-sized employers in the private sector have insisted on tax breaks as a price to stay in town or in the United States while many others have escaped to regions at home and abroad offering lower wages and other concessions. Second, the revenue-sharing programme

---

*Glenn Watt, president of the Communications Workers, joined Carter's anti-inflation crusade, prefiguring his probable emergence as a leader of labour's pro-Carter forces in the 1980 primaries.

introduced during the Nixon years requires local communities to match federal funds on a dollar-for-dollar basis, with few exceptions. With shrinking revenue bases, federal spending for subsidies to local areas in the field of social welfare has declined in real terms, even if dollar amounts remain the same. Third, many working people and middle-strata employees have been attracted to the tax revolt led by the rentier class of savings and loan associations, real estate boards, and landowners who have supported, financially and politically, the programme of the right wing to cut or eliminate property taxes. (Proposition 13 attacked this regressive form of taxation, but in such a way as to benefit property owners.)

The decline of real wages and the urgent need experienced by many workers to find some relief has been crucial. This is not to minimise the extent to which racist ideology has influenced the success of right-wing efforts, or the role that sexist and sexually-regressive ideologies play in the ability of rightist appeals to find a mass base. I would only argue that the economic malaise constitutes the *detonator* for bringing these fears and prejudices to the surface. Since the left and the liberal wing of the Democratic Party and the trade unions have conducted only ritual education on the ideological level and have paid little attention to problems of social and private consumption, the economic crisis was displaced to the social level where a vacuum existed; and the response has been a mass turn to the right.

One of the distinctive features of the present period is the split between the organised workers and the middle strata, whose alliance formed the basis of traditional liberal Democratic politics and public support for labour's rights. Labour has not relinquished its own liberal position, even if there have been some rank-and-file breakaways to the right. It is the middle strata that have become politically unstable in proportion as labour has failed to make its own power effective politically and ideologically. Right now, labour has found itself isolated, both to its left and to its right, and there are few signs of efforts to rebuild or create alliances.* In the main,

---

*Some exceptions can be noted. The best examples of a labour-middle strata alliance have been the boycott campaigns of the United Farmworkers and the Amalgamated Clothing and Textile Workers in recent years and the limited success of the environmental-utility coalitions in attracting some labour support, particularly among progressive unions outside the construction industry. In the first instances, unions found that their weakness at the picket line or their weak legal position demanded another approach to winning union recognition, one that required 'public' backing. The heartfelt support rendered by young people and professionals to farm workers and textile workers attests to the large reservoirs of sentiment for workers' struggles that exist among some sectors of the middle strata. In the latter case, the issue groups, composed largely of members of the middle strata, approached unions for support, sometimes urged by socialist members of the coalitions. In many localities these two types of coalition efforts have helped bring liberals, socialists, and trade unionists closer together and paved the way for joint work on other issues. But these examples are still sporadic, and do not signal a more broadly based rapprochement between labour and its erstwhile allies.

unions still operate at the top with the leaders of the Democratic Party rather than at its mass base. Labour has no independent political role, and seems incapable of conceptualising, much less implementing, an independent line around its own demands.

PART II

LABOUR AND THE LEFT

At present, the largest left groups in the trade unions are the Communist Party, Democratic Socialist Organising Committee, the Socialist Workers Party (SWP), the International Socialists (IS), and the two 'new left' Marxist-Leninist groupings, the Revolutionary Communist Party (RCP) and the Communist Party (M-L) (formerly the October League). A group with some local influence is the Communist Labour Party. The New American Movement's influence is confined to public-sector unions, particularly in health and education.

The following short sketches of the origin and development of these groups will necessarily be incomplete. To those readers familiar with these groups, my apologies for too simple characterisations. In discussing these groups and their roles in the labour movement, two points should be kept in mind. First, the influence of even the largest among them is very small within the labour movement as a whole, and is generally concentrated within a few sectors and geographical areas. Second, there are many individuals active in various parts of the labour movement who share the general perspective of one or another of these groups, but are not organisationally affiliated.

The Left Groups

The Communist Party is still the largest organisation with a stated socialist perspective. Founded in 1919 out of the left wing of the Socialist Party, it has always had some fairly substantial working-class roots, particularly among immigrant minorities, blacks and Chicanos, and American-born white workers in some basic industries such as steel, electrical, and mining.[10] It reached its membership peak in 1937-47 at the time when the Party's participation in labour and popular struggles was extensive. Its size has been drastically reduced since then by ideological anticommunism among the workers, state repression, and its own policy of unyielding support for the Soviet Union and the Eastern bloc. Nevertheless, its working-class membership is relatively high, at least in comparison with other groups. It still retains influence in widely scattered sectors of industry. Its policies have ranged from warm support of progressive union leaders to oppositional union politics.

The criterion of class struggle or democratic unionism does not seem to play a dominant role in its labour policy; more important is its conception of overall issues. For example, the Party is now militantly anti-Carter and has taken a left turn because of Carter's apparent anti-Sovietism. On other occasions it has restrained its dedication to class-struggle unionism when it believes that overreaching issues preclude such leftism. The CP, of all left groups, has the most flexible policies, depending upon conditions of time and place, within a framework of general defence of the Soviet Union, and uniting with progressive forces in the Democratic Party and the labour movement. The Party has spoken much of its independent role, but became reluctant to use it after the 1940s, partly because of the fear of repression, and partly because of the limits imposed by its small size.

The SWP was formed in 1938 out of defeated or expelled members of the CP, and retains many of the Leninist principles of party organisation and political orientation. Its composition historically resembled that of the CP, and it played a similar role in the organisation of the industrial unions in the 1930s, but on a smaller scale. Its membership is now far more composed by younger people from the middle strata formed in the new left, because it was decimated in the 1950s both by government attacks and by numerous internal splits. Once a respectable force in the labour movement's left wing, with a fairly consistent commitment to rank-and-file democracy and labour militancy, the SWP is now rebuilding its base in the unions by means of 'colonising', i.e., sending people into 'key' industries. This represents a real switch from the 1960s concentration on students and other members of the middle strata.

The IS made its 'turn to the working class' earlier than the SWP. The historical antecedents of the group date from an SWP split in 1940 which gave birth to the Workers' Party. The Independent Socialist League, the WP's successor, played an active role in the post-World War II struggle to rid the unions of Communist influence, and has had its own splits: to the left, a recent series of 'pure' Trotskyist tendencies have accused the organisation of a flagging commitment to class struggle; and to the right, in the 1950s, many, including its founder, decided that Marxist-Leninist socialist politics had to give way to democratic socialism and efforts to influence the left wing of the Democratic Party and the trade unions. (Michael Harrington joined this split and has since helped to form the Democratic Socialist Organizing Committee.) The present-day IS is a small organisation with one redeeming activity: its single-handed initiative in building a mass organisation of rank-and-file teamsters, and its active support of the rank-and-file movements in communications, auto, and other industries where it has had some members.

The RCP and Communist Party (M-L) are both, in various ways, products of the love affair of sections of the new left with the Chinese Revolution in the late 1960s. They both have entered the labour field with implacable anti-leadership perspectives. Far more energetic than some of the other organisations, they suffer from no historical legacy or perspectives and have succeeded only in a few places in doing sustained trade union work.

The Communist Labour Party grew out of black and Chicano struggles in Detroit and other places, where some of its leading figures came directly out of the shops and had engaged in mass rank-and-file national presence.

The Rank-and-File Perspective and its Limits

Today, there are two lines pursued by left-wing organisations and militants. The first, dominant among Maoist and Trotskyist groups and some sections of the independent left, has been to enter the unions (primarily in the basic industrial sectors) with the strategic goal of transforming them into democratic, rank-and-file-controlled institutions capable of leading a 'class struggle' approach to collective bargaining. This objective is often made ancillary to the long-range goal of making unions 'schools for communism', or transforming the trade unions into revolutionary or at least socialist-minded organisations. In practice, this position has led those of the left who adopt it to work towards the organisation of rank-and-file caucuses that contend for leadership against the entrenched bureaucracy. In some cases, these caucuses are little more than 'fronts' for the particular left vanguard that creates them, since the real objective is not to change the unions, but to recruit among the 'advanced workers' in the plant or office for the socialist group. In others, work by leftists in the rank-and-file movement is genuinely oriented towards electoral struggle within the union. Many groups work together within a caucus provided its aims are restricted to union democracy and militant unionism (not always the same thing).

The 'sectarian' side of this position consists in using the caucus form for narrowly organisational ends. Even though some workers are temporarily attracted to the group, believing its criticism of the union leadership and democratic aspirations are genuine, many quickly fall away when they learn that the left group is interested mainly in organisational aggrandisement. One can often detect the signs of this approach in the propaganda of the caucus, when it is strident and doctrinaire and lacks an effort to understand the history of the plant, the historical role of the union and left groups (if any) within it, and the specific grievances of the workers. The tendency of the left sectarians is to make wanton attacks on the manifestations of collaboration and bureaucracy without shedding light on it theoretically or politically.

Even when left intervention is motivated by a serious commitment to provide the means by which democracy may be restored to the unions, much rank-and-file activity suffers from other problems, principally the lack of understanding of workers' consciousness and of the role of unions both at the shop level and in society as a whole. A major tendency in left-wing union policy is to make the assumption that the workers, or at least a large portion of them, are 'instinctively' revolutionary, or at least radical, and that they are aching to be liberated from their bad leaders. On the basis of this assessment, strategy and tactics in trade union and factory work aim *exclusively* toward the formation of oppositional rank-and-file caucuses whose object is to win union leadership.

Rank-and-File Movements

Forming rank-and-file movements *is* one proper focus for left strategy in the workplace. But whether these movements enter the unions in order to overturn the leaders depends on the specific situation. A workers' organisation is not simply a union caucus. At certain times, an independent workers' organisation such as TDU or Miners for Democracy may enter the fight for union leadership on a programme of class-struggle unionism and union democracy. But its reason for being cannot be confined to these objectives. Workers' organisations have other functions: to educate on problems of shop-floor control; to fight the tendency of technology to pull workers apart by isolating them spatially, by creating hierarchies in job classifications, and by reducing, if not destroying, skills; to provide social and cultural life for their members; to undertake political education on general issues of local and national concern as well as on those that immediately affect people as workers; and to remain an independent force in the workplace that is friendly to the union. Such organisations may elect members to union leadership but do not confuse themselves with the union apparatus. *

To many accustomed to considering the role of the left in the working class to be primarily, if not exclusively, that of building rank-and-file movements that can transform the unions into democratic organisations that express workers' class as well as sectoral demands, this position may appear confusing. First, let me say that I believe that building rank-and-file opposition to an existing leadership is not a question of principle. The formation of such a movement presupposes at least two conditions: a militant union history that is perceived by the membership as highly desirable, combined with a widely-held belief that the existing leadership has violated these traditions; and a core of militants with sufficient sophistication to withstand the co-optation and the repressive moves of that leadership. (Co-optation is likely because, in a union with democratic traditions, the leaders are usually fairly able, having come up from the rough-and-tumble of the mass meeting, the shop floor, and the picket line.)

---

*During the first half of this century, this form of organisation was important among ethnic minorities. The Nationality Federations associated with the left wing of the Socialist Party and later the Communist Party were workers' clubs that supported militant unionism without being a part of the union itself. The nationality organisations often constituted the core of CIO organising committees in steel, electrical, and auto campaigns in the 1930s, especially in cities like Chicago, Pittsburgh, and Buffalo.

Unless the union has retained many of the forms of democratic process, even if bureaucratic procedures derived from contract unionism have subverted their content, neither the legal nor the political basis is likely to exist for anything more than the fight to create these forms. Thus, the steelworkers' and the teamsters' movements for democratic unionism may be considered a necessary step, since in neither case does the rank and file possess the legal power to decide on the disposition of the agreement between union and management. The fight for democratic unionism *concentrates* the ideological and the political splits between the membership and the leaders, but it is a *displaced* demand from class issues. It becomes necessary because these unions are not avenues for broad cultural and political development of the membership. At the same time, because the members of these unions have not acquired the skills of political combat and ideological disputation, the rank-and-file movement finds itself with no leadership depth. After the few key people at the top, and some in the locals, it cannot supply its own cadre needs. This requirement for leadership within the movement raises the question of whether the rank-and-file opposition can hope to succeed without a broad programme of political education and cultural development. That is, the extension of the opposition to the cultural and political realms is not external to its democratic demands, but most likely a condition of their victory.

In many unions bureaucracy has so eroded the forms of membership participation that trying to form a rank-and-file movement is really more light-headed than developing a programme and institutions that train workers to be in a position to run their unions. Thus, the 'simple' demand for rank-and-file-run shop committees, or for some kind of educational programme for stewards, may be a necessary precondition for even raising the question of oppositional politics.

A different type of situation is presented by unions in which traditions of democratic participation are more or less intact. The auto workers' union has deteriorated in the past twenty years in this respect, but it is far better than the Teamsters, for example. Here, the question of 'advanced' organisational and ideological forms may be raised both within the rank-and-file movement and in the union as a whole. In auto, electrical, and West Coast longshore unions, broad issues of policy (the relation of the union to the split in the Democratic Party, the relation of the union to the multinational corporations that run the industry, etc.) can be raised. Since forms exist to open these debates, whether the left can connect immediate issues (of shop-floor control, health and safety, etc.) to broader questions may depend on its ability to overcome its own economism.

The unevenness of the development of the working class and its unions demands a multi-layered approach to the intervention of socialists within the factories and offices. In one place the task is to help form a trade-union-conscious membership and a group of militants able to take care of the business of the union rather than relying on full-time leadership. In another place, the condition for building a viable union is connected to electing a new leadership. In a third place, the problem is that the rank and file has lost interest in its union, even though the tradition exists and the forms for democratic control are available. So to raise the slogan of the rank-and-file caucus around the demand for democratic unionism is not appropriate in every instance. In some cases, for example, building a strong stewards' council within the existing framework is far more important and practical than the abstract demand to throw the rascals out.

What I am opposing is the prevalent tendency of radicals to ignore the key problem: in most cases, there is no rank-and-file base in the unions possessing the ideological outlook and the political skills to contest for political power either in the workplace or in the unions. The development of that group of activists takes place as a result both of the experience of militant opposition to the company and the union leaders (if they are collaborating with the company to defuse the rank-and-file thrust) *and* of the cultural development of the membership so that it has a grasp of how to fight around its own problems and take control of its own organisations. Sometimes that grasp is best gained within the existing union framework. At other times, workers' organisations oriented toward the union but independent of it are a better vehicle for such development.

Many left groups consider that *their* organisations are the appropriate forms through which political, educational, and cultural development of 'advanced' workers best occur. (Advanced workers, in the jargon, are defined as those who have class rather than trade-union consciousness, and are interested in becoming socialists or at least learning more about the socialist movement and its programme.) But in the recent period few left organisations have performed the function of cultural development among workers. They have, in the main, constituted themselves as organisers of rank-and-file movements, contenting themselves with day-to-day involvement in union struggles on the shop floor or in locals.

Maoist and Trotskyist groups share a total antipathy to elements within the union officialdom who call themselves socialist or progressives. While they correctly insist that the existence of a rank-and-file caucus or independent workers' group is necessary within unions that have espoused 'social' rather than business unionism (even where, as in the case of the UMW, the democratic forces have succeeded in capturing leadership), their policies regarding coalition work remain inflexibly sectarian. In effect, they have adopted the old slogan of 'united front from below' without regard to specific circumstances. The idea of working with sections of the leadership around legislative issues or trade union demands, finds most in the 'new communist movement' and some in the Trotskyist tradition spouting anticollaborationist slogans against those on the left who believe that coalition work at the top can, under some circumstances, be a valid move.

As a result, the 'left' tendency of socialists working in the unions has become narrowly economist. That is, the left maintains a sharp separation between trade-union and political and cultural questions, except when it gathers around itself a few workers who are interested in broader questions. In practice, the left tendency stays aloof from both electoral politics (except the SWP which supports its own candidates), and political questions that do not directly impinge on trade union concerns. It is the union leadership that asks the rank and file for support for such measures as national health insurance, labour-law reform, and full-employment legislation. For some left tendencies, action around these issues is considered 'social democratic' or 'reformist' and unworthy of socialist intervention. Thus, the far left is (unwittingly to be sure) part of the process of depoliticisation among the working class. Lacking an approach to the neighbourhood or community as well as the workplace it was rendered silent on some critical issues of working-class struggle over the past several years: inflation, especially in food and housing; taxes; and the environmental issues of pollution, occupational and community health and safety, etc.

The Problems of Coalition Work

The other main tendency, represented by the Communist Party, DSOC, and many independent leftists, (including some individuals in NAM), holds the position that socialists must work at all levels of the labour movement, including cooperation and coalition work with pro-gressive top leaders (Fraser, Winpisinger, UE, ILWU). While placing some emphasis on supporting rank-and-file movements for democratic unionism, these groups have often taken the corporate offensive to signal a need to bury their differences with the labour leaders, blunt their criticisms, and place coalition work *above* building rank-and-file organisations.

The CP vacillates between these two orientations (rank-and-file vs coalition work). In its 'left' periods it is perfectly capable of shrieking as loud as the Maoists about 'collaboration' by the top leaders, and forming and joining coalitions from below. But the dominant tendency of the CP, since the cold war became an anti-communist purge, has been to seek support for progressive issues at the top, to play a progressive role in the political coalitions of labour and liberals that surround the Democratic Party, and to act as staff employees within the labour bureaucracy or to assume elected union posts as *militant trade unionists rather than socialists*. The CP is perhaps the classic case of the separation of economics from politics; thousands of party members have functioned and still operate as good trade unionists, following the official policies of their unions, and trying to push them to the left on a few issues such as the Vietnam war or struggles against joblessness. Since it has been the largest of socialist groups, the CP must be held responsible both for whatever reputation the left has earned (or suffered) in the labour movement, and for the general left tendency to subordinate socialist politics and culture to trade-union reform concerns.

The Democratic Socialist Organizing Committee has perhaps of all socialist groups dedicated itself most consistently to the policy of unity of the most progressive forces in the labour movement with the liberal, minority, and women's coalitions in the Democratic Party. Its membership is sprinkled liberally with middle and top officials of the progressive unions. Though it supported Sadlowski's challenge to the Abel-McBride leadership of the Steelworkers, it functions primarily as an influential leadership caucus within the left wing of the Democratic Party. It cannot be said that DSOC is particularly narrow; on the contrary, its concern with electoral politics and legislative action seems to dominate its activity to the detriment of any serious programme on issues bearing on the internal life of the labour movement.

The fundamental problem of DSOC's emphasis is not its specific policies regarding the Democratic Party nor its attitude towards the progressive unions. The basic issue is that DSOC has decided that these are not the times for a mass politics based on the assumption of the possibility of political radicalisation among the workers and portions of the middle strata. On this premise it has opted for coalitions from above and a rather cautious programme of political education around the issues that historically propelled the left-liberal wing of the Democratic Party.

DSOC's 'united front from above' strategy can be defended on the basis of the political realignment position according to which even the most modest liberal positions become radical these days, because the contradictions of American capitalism have forced the moderate as well as conservative Democrats closer to the Republican antipathy toward social reform. DSOC has *entered* the Democratic Party as the only practical way to conduct politics in a period when the working class and the trade unions show no propensity towards political action outside the two-party system. This posture has made DSOC something less than a radical organisation. Instead it functions as an organiser for the left wing of the Democrats, who seem to lack the energy to mobilise around their own concerns. What is implicit in DSOC's approach is the view that the workers and their unions are really not socialist-minded, or even hospitable to radical ideas. The premise is that the liberal alternatives have not been exhausted. Although the CP functions, in practice, on the same assumption, it has not been willing to own up to it.

It is not the substance of the CP's or DSOC's position that is necessarily objectionable, so much as the way in which the position is carried out. Anyone can find in the resolutions of both organisations support for the position of work at *all* levels. In practice, these groups tend to work primarily at the top because of their estimate of the current situation as well as their composition (both have relatively large numbers of officials among their members and their periphery). These organisations allow a socialist sympathiser in the labour movement to be a member of a socialist organisation without performing responsible political work. Their members in the trade unions are often exempted from recruiting tasks, selling literature, and conducting socialist education, and from advocating the policies of the organisation where those policies depart from the line of the progressive wing of the labour leadership.

Of course, this laissez-faire attitude is more prevalent in DSOC (or NAM) than in the CP. The CP encourages 'secret memberships', undoubtedly a carryover from the repressive period of the post-war era and from the experience of the international Communist movement where secrecy was the sine qua non of personal survival in many countries. Perhaps the CP has had reason for its circumspection under some circumstances, but I believe its hesitancy to conduct overt socialist education and propaganda among workers is a product of its belief that socialist ideas have no currency in the working class and that efforts to speak of socialism would result in certain isolation from the workers. (This aspect of CP practice is gaining ground among far left groups as well.)

In sum, most left groups have based their labour activity on one of the variants or styles of economist activity: on the one side, a rigid line on overturning entrenched union leaders and replacing them with democratic rank-and-file caucus leaders; the political and ideological role of these caucuses remains ambiguous. On the other side, there is in most instances a subordination to progressive leaders, an emphasis on making alliances that in practice unnecessarily limit what is politically possible.

To be sure, some left activity in both modes has produced valuable work. The role of parts of the left in helping to democratise the UMW, advancing the rank-and-file opposition in the Steelworkers union, and organising and building public employees' unions has been important. Teamsters for a Democratic Union (TDU) is perhaps a model for building a national workers' organisation that sees itself as independent of the bureaucracy (though it has not evolved a programme that addresses workers' needs beyond the union). A number of left groups have made significant contributions, and continue to infuse their work with dedication and seriousness.

Yet almost all left groups have built whatever strategic and programmatic base they have among the working class within the confines of *contract unionism*. In effect the left is a tendency among the trade unions and has failed to grapple with problems of the class they may go beyond the capacities of the unions. Further, even in relation to union work, the policies of the left are not built around *class demands,* are not directed to development of class as well as trade-union consciousness. Finally, the left is not playing a *political* role in the unions or among the workers. Instead, its practice is *trade-union* politics, informed by the ideology of democracy and militancy and little else. There is little socialist politics within the working class, either at the level of concrete struggles or at the level of education.

PART III

PROBLEMS OF A LEFT LABOUR POLICY AND STRATEGY

What follows is written from the perspective of someone active in one socialist group, NAM, and is necessarily an argument about how that organisation ought to view the present situation and its own activity. Yet it is also written with a clear understanding that NAM is not by itself capable of undertaking all the tasks suggested, and that a broadly cooperative left effort would be necessary to have a major impact, however dim the prospects of such cooperation often appear.

If the previous analysis of the economic and political position of the workers, their unions, and the middle strata is correct, we cannot avoid recognising that the labour movement is itself under attack. Because of the deterioration of democratic forms within the unions and the falling away of their active base, the unions have become less able to defend the elementary interests of their members on the shop floor, in legislative arenas, and in the community. Unions are no longer adequate defensive organisations of the workers, much less offering a road toward offensive activity. This does *not* imply that unions can be replaced either by dual revolutionary organisations or by the left itself. But it implies that the left must take an active role in union revitalisation.

The left should direct its labour activity to breaking the ghetto-isation between workers' struggles in the economic sphere and politics. The job is to create or join in those forms that engender the politicisation of workers, the development of workers, the development of their power in the electoral, community, social, and cultural arena, so that offensive action and, above all, socialist and class-conscious elements may arise within the class.

Revitalising the Unions

Unless unions are revitalised to become defensive organisations capable of meeting the challenge of capital's attack on workers' living standards, there is a chance that the 1980s may reproduce the conditions of the 1920s. I do not mean to draw a mechanical parallel between the two periods. Unions will probably not lose membership, because members have come to regard them as *necessary* evils. But they have lost their character as *social movements* capable of mobilising their members for political as well as contract struggles. The union halls are empty, except for a few officers and their followers. They fill only during negotiations, when strikes appear likely or contract approvals must be secured.

In the coming period, the unions cannot be adequate defensive instruments unless they are popular organisations with an active rank and file, especially when the corporate offensive demands that workers defend, with their jobs if necessary, hard-won gains. In turn, there are not automatic formulae for making sure that the rank and file emerges; if not, their gains will be eroded by inflation, lost and costly strikes, and relative passivity when capital moves to greener pastures. The unions can only become vital if they regain their social vision, if they are dedicated to building a unified membership that understands the large corporations and the national administration as class enemies, and is capable of extending the struggle politically as well as on the shop floor—in short a *movement* as opposed to a series of organisations.

It is not determined *in advance* that this task can be accomplished, even if the left were much more powerful and influential than it is. Nor is the union leadership capable of reorganising the unions into a movement, even the progressive leaders. For unions are in a bad way. The deterioration has gone so far that the old progressive union ideology is partially discredited among the rank and file, because new ideologies have emerged to describe and explain the weakened position of the workers. There has occurred an ideological shift among large sections of the working class. The anti-business ideology that motivated the upsurge of the 1930s and 1940s has been replaced by an anti-black and anti-government ideology that argues for the old values of individualism rather than collective action. To lose sight of this fundamental change is to keep our heads in the sand. The progressive leaders have no marching hymns capable of attracting a following. They are fairly isolated and have relied for nearly twenty years on well-oiled machines or full-time officials that are often sustained largely by the indifference of large sections of their ranks to whatever they do. While workers want union protection, it is not clear that they want a labour movement in the old established sections of the unions. The new groups of Southern workers embattled by voracious company attacks, farm workers, and many public workers have a different conception of their unions—for them the union is still a movement, in many instances. But the older segments of the labour movement require revitalisation because of the fissure between the members and the traditional ideology of unionism.

In connection with the task of union revitalisation, the struggle to democratise the labour movement should go hand in hand with the fight to democratise the workplace. Most fights for union democracy are at best implicitly directed towards building workers' power at the workplace. In the example of the miners, the reforms introduced by Miners for Democracy into the union structure were substantial. Workers have the right to vote on the contract, to hold regular conventions, and to elect all of their officials directly. But the union leaders who emerged from the reform struggle became reluctant to fight for such workplace issues as the right to refuse to work under unsafe conditions, the right to strike over grievances, etc. The fight for democracy involves change—both within the union and on the job. Offensive efforts for demands such as narrowing the pay differential between lower and higher job classifications, rigorous enforcement of job health and safety rules, and an active steward system able to deal with grievances on the shop or office floor are all part of a left programme.*

Union revitalisation involves organising the unorganised, especially among clerical workers and in the growing industrial South and Southwest. Rank-and-file organising committees could be joined to caucus movements or urged upon an officialdom completely absorbed in its own maintenance and committed to professional paid organisers for expanding their membership. Under some circumstances, leftists may become paid organisers, but should see their task (as distinct from those organisers who work as bureaucratically as the officials) in terms of building the *active* rank and file, even where not connected to caucus movements. In the 1930s many unions and left activists were trained in organising campaigns rather than caucuses. They learned how to give a speech, write a leaflet, meet with a committee and train it, and how to fight against employer resistance in unionisation campaigns. Among the sources of the decline of the labour rank and file has been the reluctance of the leadership, even in progressive unions, to draw their members into any kind of activity, even when this activity benefits the union, such as in the case of organising. When a union is prepared to undertake a campaign, the left should not stand off on the grounds that we do not approve of the leadership. If our analysis of the growing role of the right, the offensive of the corporations, and the weakness of the unions in the working class is correct, then any efforts to bring new workers into the unions must receive strong left support.

In the current situation, with the efforts of the Business Round Table (now the leading corporate political action group) and members of the Carter administration to make the labour movement an official arm of the corporate-government alliance, any forces within the labour unions willing to preserve the independence of the unions by shaping a legislative and bargaining programme that challenges corporate priorities must be

---

*Even where there are elected stewards, few unions have retained vigorous educational programmes to train them in grievance handling, much less providing opportunities for stewards to understand labour's legislative and political programme. One reason for this decline of union education is that the stewards system has been replaced by business agents and other full-timers.

supported. At the same time, we can learn from the mistakes of the past; we should *never* abandon our policy of helping to build rank-and-file forms; to abandon it creates the conditions for the hegemony of bureaucratic styles of union leadership, the class collaboration of leaders, and the depoliticisation of the membership. Where the rank-and-file movement has successfully elected a democratic leadership to union offices, it should be helped to retain its autonomy, its ability to propose its own policy and to have an internal political, cultural, and educational life. Its attitude toward the *union as an institution* cannot be one of complete confidence because contract unionism—with its no-strike provisions, its full-time enforcement of restrictions on worker actions, its complex grievance procedure, and its economism—will still tend to erode the spirit and the independence of the rank and file.

Unions and Politics

We should work to broaden the scope of the rank-and-file movement beyond its traditional programme of democratic unionism. Socialists should help rank-and-file movements to get involved in community struggles and, in certain circumstances, electoral action. At the same time, the rank-and-file movement could be a force for making the union a political voice of its members' needs. Legislative battles for a national health programme paid by the government, for lower prices, against wage-freeze policies of government, and around international issues such as nuclear survival and against war could be encouraged by socialists. Our expectations of the rank-and-file caucus movement exceed those of many workers who wish merely to replace the existing leadership with a new, honest and democratic administration of the union. Electing leaders is insufficient for solving the problems inherent in bureaucratic unionism that has become enmeshed in administering contracts on a businesslike basis, no matter how honestly. Of course, we should enter whatever movements workers have created to make their unions more responsive to their needs, but our approach should always be to raise the level of programme and action of these movements without unprincipled attacks on the existing caucus programme.

Many leftists active in the labour movement are reluctant to make such efforts to broaden the scope of whatever democratic movements exist, in part because of fear of appearing to wish to impose a narrowly sectarian political agenda on what are most often fragile organisations. It is important to recognise that alongside the routine economism of most of the efforts of left parties to intervene in the labour movement, there has been a related tradition of demanding adherence to one or another political position for organisational purposes, even when the issue is not directly relevant to the problems facing the union or caucus. These demands have often caused destructive splits within the left organisations themselves, when members within the labour movement simply refused to go along with organisational directives.

Given this history, it is necessary to be extremely sensitive in raising broader political issues. At the same time, the analysis of the state of the labour movement presented here indicates that this broadening is crucial for the accomplishment of even the most minimal objectives in a period in which the labour movement is internally weak and isolated from many of its traditional allies.

Consequently, a series of questions that are usually held to be of importance not for left activity within the labour movement but for general strategic orientation are immediately relevant for whatever programme is conducted within the contemporary labour movement.

The question of the relation of mass work to recruiting individuals to socialist organisations, one which has never been solved by any American left movement, suggests some of the issues at stake. The history of the CP and the SWP is replete with examples of deep involvement in popular struggles. The role of these organisations in building the CIO in the 1930s, and helping to organise civil rights, women's, and youth movements down to our day was both important and often heroic. Yet neither was able, in the main, to function consistently as an openly socialist organisation within mass movements. Their critical role in building the labour movement subordinated the function of the development of socialist education and culture.

I believe that most of today's left shares in the reticence of our forebears to make our socialist politics integral to our mass work. Among the reasons for such reluctance to deal boldly with the ideological and political consequences of opposition to capitalist policies is that we are not sure that those we work with are sympathetic to socialism. We have revolutionary aspirations, but these do not seem to correspond to the situation. To be blunt, workers are not socialist-minded, nor sympathetic to socialist organisations.

Among the causes of this anti-socialism is that the Soviet Union has been held up by many leftists (and anticommunists) as the model of socialism against which we must measure our own conditions. The legacy of attacks against Communists combined with blind and often mindless pro-Sovietism (or anti-Sovietism in the case of social-democrats and Trotskyists) has turned many workers off. The subordination of the left to either the politics or the vision of the Soviet Union, China, Cuba or any other country calling itself socialist has had disastrous consequences for building a socialist movement in the United States. While we cannot adopt the political lines of these countries, we must have a balanced critique of their history and their role in world affairs. Working people cannot respect, much less join, a socialist organisation whose members have not grappled with the realities of socialism as it actually exists, with the working class in those countries, the problems of democracy in the actual socialist world, and our relation to those realities. Thus we must commit ourselves to dealing with these issues as a crucial part of spreading socialist ideas and encouraging organisational affiliation.

One thing is certain: despite the decline of virulent anticommunism in the United States since the 1960s, no socialist movement can grow unless it deals with socialism as it really exists. This is particularly true within the working class with its high proportion of people from eastern and southern European backgrounds, where communist and socialist ideas and politics have dominated since the end of World War II.

Any possibility of a substantial expansion of the role of socialists in the labour movement requires, among other things, a fairly sophisticated and balanced analysis of actually existing socialism. In the present juncture, when many of the crucial questions within the labour movement concern efforts to establish, redefine, and expand democracy, it is not possible to function effectively as socialists without deciding some elementary questions regarding the problems of socialist transformation if we are to have more than a marginal effect even in the immediate situation, when an actual socialist transformation is far away.

There is a growing body of discussion in other advanced capitalist countries on these questions. The ideas grouped around the label 'Eurocommunism', while not a recipe, may offer some assistance, given a careful examination of American history.[11] Because of the achievement of universal suffrage in our country after 1920, the legalisation of trade unions in 1935, and the enactment of civil rights in the 1950s and 1960s (for the second time), there is no longer any question of whether socialists should declare their full support of all democratic rights and forms. We must declare that *both* parliamentary and industrial democracy are crucial in a new society, that free trade unions independent of the state are to be strengthened and that the right to strike is inviolable. Further, we do not endorse a one-party socialist state, but anticipate the participation of many socialist parties (and of parties that do not accept socialist ideas) in the democratic process.

If we are committed to democracy as an end, not just as a slogan or a 'transitional' position, can we speak of the dictatorship of any class and expect American workers to respond affirmatively to programmes in which socialists play a significant public role? I believe that it would ignore both the specificity of the struggle for democracy as an end in itself in Western capitalist countries, and the contradictory experiences of actually existing socialism, to think so.

The Labour Movement and the State
Beyond affirming—and practising—a basic commitment to democracy, contemporary socialist involvement in the labour movement requires a

theory of the state that does not rest content with the formulation that the state is the instrument through which a ruling class assures the continuation of its rule by force. The development of the modern state in nearly all countries has enlarged its functions considerably; a substantial portion of the working class is now employed directly by the state, and many industrial jobs in the private sector depend on their creation and maintenance on the 'contract' state.

From the point of the view of the industrial worker in the pre-New Deal era, the state was clearly an instrument for the preservation of class rule, by coercion at all times, and by force if necessary. The image of the state was the swinging billy club and the repressive courts that regularly granted employers injunctions against mass picketing, threw radicals in prison, and declared unions a conspiracy to restrain trade. From the perspective of union and radical militants struggling for their elementary rights, the state appeared as just another arm of the capitalist effort to prevent workers from organising on their own behalf, and to preserve private property at all costs.

Unfortunately this conception of the state, born of the practical experience of thousands of militants in the pre-war era, has changed little for most of the socialist left in the past forty years. It was always only a partial truth that the state expressed the ruling class's drive for profits and domination. For the state preserves more than property; it preserves a *system of social relations* that has to do with the reproduction of labour power as wage labour, *the reproduction of the ideologies of domination* as well as its material side.[12] It consists in a wide variety of institutions such as schools, the media, health institutions. The state is also the coordinator of the economy, and a major source of investment. In short, its enlargement since the New Deal has touched the lives of all people well beyond its repressive apparatus. As a matrix of *ideological* apparatuses and a source of capital accumulation, it has become part of society in a way that obliterates the traditional base-superstructure distinction.

The enlargement of the state's intervention into the economy and daily life means that our posture towards it must decisively change. Public employment accounts for more than one of every six jobs. Public investment accounts for more than half of all investment, first of all in the war sector, but second in health, education, and transportation. The expansion of the state bureaucracy has taken place in a new way, compared to the nineteenth century when only important elements of the middle class entered public employment as a vocation, and workers became employees of the state mostly via the armed forces and police. Moreover, the expansion of health, education, and social welfare has brought millions of people into the state both as political actors and workers. The state becomes, in this period of capitalism, a new and important arena for contestation. It does not only *mirror* the contradictions of capital, it *constitutes* a new set of contradictions.

First among these is the contradiction between the state's accumulation functions and its ideological functions. We can see this operate with the cutbacks in public services that result from the primacy of accumulation in the context of world economic competition and conflicts. The development of struggles within the public sector to preserve existing 'social programmes' challenges the priorities of capital that privilege investment in arms, energy, and a general cutback in state expenditures not directly useful to accumulation. This has become perhaps the key political issue of our period. [13]

Second, there is a contradiction between the tax burden on working people and the need to generate as much capital as possible for durable-goods investment to meet international competition. The large public sector helps cause inflation at a time when American production of material goods is limited by sharp competition from abroad and a stagnant market at home. Yet the private sector cannot absorb the employees released by cutbacks from public-sector work. One of the consequences of this contradiction is that large numbers of workers become persuaded by the ideology of 'big government' as enemy because they perceive that high taxes are produced by a large public sector. In any inflationary economy racism and anti-bureaucratic ideologies constitute adequate explanations for the decline of real wages. At the same time, 'buy American' campaigns and import curbs are viewed as serious answers to foreign competition that results in job migrations.

The question of how to fight in the public sector has become increasingly complex in the past five years. Socialists have a chance to work among public employees faced with job losses due to cutbacks. Alliances with client groups, tenants, and others adversely affected by cutbacks may be forged where socialists are involved in public-sector unions and community organisations. But the problem of developing a *class* alliance has become infinitely more difficult since many workers in the private sector have shown interest in fighting for tax cuts under conservative banners such as were provided by Proposition 13-type initiatives in the 1978 elections.

These are difficult issues to resolve with a simple slogan or two. The division of labour and fragmentation of the working class into sectoral ghettoes makes a united programme impossible to envision except on the basis of some rather fundamental redistribution of the tax burden from individuals to corporations, the elimination of taxes on small property, and a determined effort to prevent runaway shops from cities like Cleveland, Los Angeles, and New York.

It is evident that the left must intervene in struggles to maintain public-sector jobs and services. But it cannot rest content with a merely defensive posture, as insistence that jobs simply be preserved, as most public-sector unions have done. The fact is, union demands for the status quo are not popular, even among union members. The uniformed services (police and fire and sanitation) have managed barely to hold their own through strikes and job actions, in part because administrative employees and many service workers have not resisted the cutbacks with the same determination. In the long run, defensive strikes among public-sector workers have their limits unless they become general strikes at a city-wide scale. Unions must take the political offensive if their defensive programme to preserve jobs is to succeed. This entails an examination of the federal and local policies of the business groups that have been demanding cutbacks, and a political struggle to fashion a pro-labour programme on taxes, economic development, and other issues bearing on the urban crisis. Socialists have a role here, but only if they understand how crucial the attack on public-sector unions and the cities really is. Forming unions has been a major focus of many left groups in the past decade. But too many socialists, many of whom have been elected to office in public unions, have settled down to bargaining postures, leaving behind not only their socialism, but also their vision. As militant trade unionists they have mobilised some struggles against cutbacks, but have not succeeded, except in a very few instances, in building community/political coalitions around health and education.

The relative failure of socialists to struggle within the public sector beyond purely trade union demands for jobs and salary increases may be partly attributable to their misunderstanding of the specific configuration of the capitalist crisis in the present period. Armed often only with the myopic vision of the primacy of the industrial proletariat under all circumstances, many sections of the left have abandoned or otherwise downgraded the significance of struggles in the public sector. The public sector is where the crisis of capital accumulation in Western capitalist countries has become concentrated, rather than in basic capital and consumer-goods sectors.* The crisis is manifested in several different ways: first, large cities are saddled with a 'fiscal' crisis which is merely a displacement of the movement of industries to the periphery, the concomitant exodus of large sections of the middle strata and the skilled workers, and the severe reduction in federal aid. Second, the 'unproductive' character of the underclasses that remain in the core cities removes the impetus for providing social services on an expanded scale. Large sections of these underclasses appear more or less permanently displaced from the industrial and private service labour force and can only find work in the public sector, if at all. This situation places considerable pressure on city finances, especially as revenue sharing requires local government to match federal funds in order to receive them. Thus the cutbacks in social welfare, education, and even police and fire departments.

*There is a crisis of overproduction in most Western-capitalist countries, but it is made more complex by the unevenness of its effects in different sectors.

The business right-wing offensive is largely successful in the wake of the decline of liberalism. In the first place, many organised workers in basic industries and services are no longer residents of large cities and cannot be counted on to support the programmes that have sustained the underclasses, even at low living standards. Second, the public-sector unions have rarely attempted to forge alliances with left-liberal forces who remain in the cities among the middle strata, and the underclasses who find themselves isolated from other classes. The role of the left within the unions should be to advocate the formation of alliances with other forces around the defence of services and jobs, and to develop alternative policies to those of the banks and the right wing. Although this is not the place to suggest specific programmes that might constitute an effective counterweight to budget cutting, the first step is to recognise that such programmes must emerge if jobs, salary levels, and services are to be preserved.

The involvement of socialists in struggles within the state, including the army and the police force, as well as the administrative apparatus as a whole, was important during the Vietnam war and the 'war on poverty'. Now, most socialists in the public sector have helped form unions; while the creation of trade unions is necessary, it is not sufficient to define our relation to the state.

Socialists can help to develop, as a task that concerns the entire labour movement, both a theory and a strategy for conducting democratic struggles within the state at the level of its administrative functions as well as its legislative role. In this regard, a coherent approach to electoral work is urgently needed.

Many socialists continue to disdain the electoral process on grounds that are not novel. Elections are a sham, it is argued, and more and more people are recognising this by abstaining. There are times when socialists might boycott elections—when they really are nothing but a sham conducted by an authoritarian regime, or when, in certain revolutionary situations, they express only the tactical efforts of a parliament that is nothing but an organisation of the ruling groups in the face of popular organs of political and economic power.

Yet neither situation now exists, and the attitude of abstention is inappropriate. It amounts, in effect, to a replication of the economism that has plagued the left's efforts in the labour movement. We are in a period of widespread depoliticisation among broad sections of the population, born largely of a sense of isolation and powerlessness. The right has seized the time to use the electoral process to roll back social-welfare gains won by the working class in the past forty years and to attack the social and cultural gains made by women, by youth, and by gay men and lesbians in the 1960s.

Moreover, the Congress has, after more than a decade, become a major arena for the defence of the right to strike, for workers to defend their living standards, and for the ability of unions to organise. Blacks and other minorities are locked in combat to force Congress to pass a full-employment bill, and we are all suffering the lack of national health insurance.

For the left to abdicate the electoral arena is tantamount to betrayal of the interests of minorities and women as well as the working class as a whole, since it is in this sphere that the anti-popular forces have mounted their most effective offensives. Socialists must be among those who encourage the trade unions to wage an aggressive struggle in their members' interest in the electoral arena, especially on crucial issues that affect labour's rights and the living standards of working people. At the same time we should advocate a labour politics that is independent of the Democratic Party, is not narrow and parochial, and involves work with environmental, women's, and gay rights groups on the broad issues of democratic liberties and social advances.

Labour and the Democrats
What is an independent labour politics in relation to the Democratic Party? Historically, much of the left has defined this as the formation of a labour party of the British type as a necessary, transitional step towards revolutionary struggle. The argument for a labour party consists in the contention that all electoral politics in a non-revolutionary period is necessarily social-democratic and that leftists need such an arena for the promulgation of revolutionary ideas among larger constituencies than are available to the revolutionary left in its own name. Second, working people need a party through which they may participate in their own name in the struggle for reform. A labour party, in the traditional socialist view, educates workers towards their class, rather than sectoral interests, and provides a forum for combat with the forces with whom alliances can be temporarily made.

In the United States, such thinking has had little practical relevance since the Roosevelt administration because the Democratic Party, operating within the context of long-term economic expansion and abetted by the disdain for ideological politics among wide sections of the population, has performed many of the functions of the British Labour Party. (This is not to claim that the two parties are entirely similar—but their relationships to the working class have shared many features.) Under these circumstances, the slogan advanced by sections of the left for a labour party was merely agitational and had no practical result. The sharp turn rightward by the Carter administration and the festering split in the Democratic Party impels a re-examination of labour's perspectives on political action. As noted earlier, the realignment perspective of DSOC is predicated on an assessment of the realities of labour's unwillingness to consider seriously forming its own party at this juncture, despite the considerable evidence that the Democrats have become distinctly inhospitable to labour's demands over the past decade. Whether progressive unions and rank-and-file forces make the fight to reform the Democrats via demanding that substantial programmatic commitments be taken seriously, or choose to break away, will not be determined by the desires of the socialist left. In this context, the issue of independent progressive political action must still be raised, without reducing that issue to the question of the organisational relationship to one or another section of the Democratic Party.

The first element of an independent politics is for labour to develop its own programme that goes beyond its narrow self-interest. The Democratic Agenda, inspired by DSOC, corresponds at least in its broad outlines to this concept. In essence, it means that the labour-progressive forces would have coherent programmatic alternatives to the two party platforms. For example, a different posture on arms spending would imply a different position on many international issues. Another example: demands for the nationalisation of rail transportation, municipalisation of power, a programme of serious energy alternatives, etc. This perspective would go beyond the traditional demands for expanded health care and education, but would include them, and would entail a new tax programme. Over a period of years the Democratic Party will either reintegrate the unions by making substantial new concessions, or will move further right, opening the way for new electoral possibilities, not the least of which would be an independent labour/progressive party.

We must place the relationship between electoral and extra-electoral action in a broader perspective. Struggles in shops, offices, and neighbourhoods for greater popular control over the conditions of work and community life are primarily undertaken outside the electoral arena; yet most of these efforts, even narrowly defined, have an electoral component, which at some points may be primary. If we understand that a labour strategy is only partially a trade union strategy, but entails an approach to the multiple problems of the working class, its social and cultural life as well as its working life, in the community as well as in the shop or office, then we must think through a wide variety of problems: taxes as well as the runaway shop, the quality of schools, day-care facilities and recreational centres in the city or town, marriage and family life when both partners work.

Not a single left organisation currently possesses the range and size to deal with the totality of everyday life, without a division of labour that often results in one-sided political development. The 'working-class' organisers become pure and simple trade unionists who are willing to fight the boss, but cannot get a handle on capitalism, and who tend to view issues around sexuality, family life, and personal relations as foreign territory, while other activists struggle around reproductive (or tenants') rights, but plead ignorance on 'workers' ' issues.

PART IV

PROSPECTS

The strategic considerations contained in this article have centred on the argument that the fundamental break that needs to be made involves consciously going beyond contract unionism in the left's conception and practice of 'labour's strategy'. These considerations are grounded in two basic arguments. The first is that economistic labour practice has reached the limits of its effectiveness, not only in socialist terms, but in terms of the ability of the unions to conduct wage and benefit struggles—the heart of contract unionism. Political intervention by labour is necessary to maintain existing living standards, to achieve what bargaining used to be more or less sufficient to win.

Second, I have argued for union revitalisation as a key task of the left, even if one must remain pessimistic that even the most progressive unions—who recognise these problems—can act to change their situation. The left here is defined as both socialist organisations and those who consider themselves radicals or socialists, but work either as individuals or in small, local groups. The possibilities are probably limited for the established left to agree on a broad strategy of revitalisation on the basis of a programme of independent labour political action, establishing and assisting rank-and-file movements that can address both the problems inherent in the undemocratic and class-collaborationist drift of large numbers of unions and the political and cultural development of the rank and file.

The reasons for this pessimism involve both the extent of antagonisms between existing socialist organisations, and the unhappy fact that many left groups are stuck in a series of propositions about American reality that are at best half true and at worst entirely out of phase with what is happening. The history of these propositions is linked to the notion of a 'key sector' and ranges from a mechanical adherence to the view that the industrial working class is the only properly revolutionary force in our country to a view that only blacks and other third-world peoples are revolutionary while almost everyone else is infected by the virus of 'white skin privilege' (a tepid reformulation of Lenin's labour aristocracy thesis).

In the present period, an 'industrial' concentration policy would amount to a reflexive return to (the errors of) the past, applying abstract criteria to the development of labour strategy. The question of both the middle strata and organisation among public-sector and administrative employees cannot be relegated to second place; the growing significance of services and administration in the politics and economy of the United

States shapes crucial aspects of the immediate political situation.*

With the exception of the International Socialists, who have taken a lead in the formation of several rank-and-file caucuses, most left groups work at the local level, contenting themselves with vying for union office, recruiting some workers to their organisations, and becoming good trade union militants. But there are few instances of growth in genuine socialist influence among workers or systematic political and cultural education by these groups. Even the Teamsters for a Democratic Union suffers from contractitis, a dearth of leadership, and no perspective on a broad range of political questions. Not all of these weaknesses are attributable to the IS leaders, since the workers themselves have emerged from several generations of reliance on contracts, strikes, and bargaining to safeguard and advance their interests. The IS has been a valiant catalyst, but is clearly caught up in the mechanics of organising the caucus, its strategy limited to winning local offices, projecting an opposition to the incumbent president, and building for the long run, around job dissatisfaction.

And the IS is head and shoulders in advance of all the rest in understanding the need for national coordination of rank-and-file opposition. Elsewhere, in Detroit, Chicago, New York, and West Coast cities, local affiliates of established left organisations are getting involved in union work to a degree unprecedented in the past twenty years. Yet it cannot be claimed that the influence of the broad left wing is growing within labour's ranks. The gradual decline of the West Coast longshore union, the relative stagnation of the United Electrical Workers, and the virtual disappearance of the Mine Mill union into the Steelworkers has deprived the left of important institutional bases. If some progressive weight remains in the Meatcutters and Machinists, it is not a rank-and-file phenomenon, but a function of the survival of the old left leadership of the Fur and Leather Workers and the Packinghouse workers in one case and the survival of dim socialist traditions in the case of the Machinists.

Perhaps the most interesting new development has been the rise of the rank-and-file movement in the Steelworkers, led by persons who had some ties to the Chicago left-liberal traditions. As I have noted, there are signs that this movement goes beyond the limits of contract unionism and may become a stable force for a broader left-progressive coalition in that region.

---

*In stressing the growing politicisation of trade union struggles, it is possible to point to almost any aspect of labour activity. In struggles around the introduction of new technologies and occupational health and safety programmes, the site of conflict has shifted somewhat from the shop floor (where the battle cannot be won, but must be waged) to political and international trade union cooperation. In a sense, the question is not whether this politicisation will occur, but over whether it will be possible for the left to assist in the development of a political orientation different from that implicit in the willingness of substantial sections of the labour movement to accept a new kind of subordination to government and corporate plans, in the hope that such cooperation might prevent the worse.

But the extent of political development among the rank and file remains circumscribed by fear of red-baiting, a lack of middle and low-level leadership within the Fight Back organisation, and the ambiguous traditions of the union itself.

It is in the public and clerical sectors that much of the new left's influence has been felt, in the teachers' unions, AFSCME, SEIU (Service Employees International Union), and the Office and Professional Employees, a medium-sized union of private-sector clerical and technical employees. Many socialists have been elected to local union offices in these sectors. NAM, for example, has a rather large number of members who are on union staffs or are elected officials in these unions, in addition to a greater number who belong to the AFT or other public-sector unions. But most NAM people and other leftists are not elected as socialists; they become respected fighters for the everyday interests of the members and are logically put forward for union office or staff jobs.

Becoming a *socialist* union member is a long process in the light of the past thirty years. Nobody in her or his right mind would enter a workplace announcing radical—much less revolutionary—sympathies, not only because dismissal might immediately follow, but because it might arouse either suspicion or antipathy among co-workers. But unless one has an approach to becoming an open socialist, the tendency to become a progressive (literally, a liberal) union activist is hard to resist. In a time when workers are not seeking socialist solutions to their problems, the task of finding a way to make these solutions available and palpable is not easy.

Dissatisfaction is now widespread throughout labour's ranks, but in only a few places is it organised. One of the reasons is that there is no organised left presence in the unions that has a broad vision of what the tasks are in this period. Leftists do not develop such long-term theoretical and strategic perspectives because they don't think such work is important, compared to the practical day-to-day tasks of organising among workers. Even if we wanted to define these tasks in the light of the economic, ideological, and political tendencies of our period, the left would still have to face its own theoretical and historical impoverishment. Until there is a commitment to strategic thinking and theoretical assessment these problems will not go away because the 'situation' will not by itself produce radicalisation.

The pragmatic orientation of the left, its reluctance to engage in political debates except about questions of 'the party', has been debilitating. We are stuck with the classic texts and have a clear aversion to facing reality. Some of us are stuck on the shop floor around issues of workers' power over production and seem oblivious to the syndicalist implications of such a position. Others are stuck at the intermediate level of the union office—processing grievances, organising the unorganised, and engaging in the necessary political machinations within a local union. Some leftists are the best grievers in the labour movement because they have political experience. But they never look below or above the ranks of middle-level trade union leadership. Others are swimming in union staff jobs trying to influence progressive leaders to do more and better things, but have not figured out how to connect with the rank and file or with their socialist conscience. Finally there are a few socialists at the top, most of whom function as left liberals. These leaders are not to blame for the 'opportunism'; since socialist consciousness is, by definition, not an individual matter, but depends on the demands of the class as well as the quality of socialist leadership within the class, we can only try to encourage these forces on the basis of what we do below.

The most realistic assessment of the current situation centres on the ideological shift within the working class, a shift qualitatively different from any in the recent past. Here the triumphalism of the left becomes a serious barrier to grappling with difficult problems. In my opinion, we can no longer assume a propensity among sizeable sections of white workers towards progressive social attitudes and conceptions of the social world on the broadest level. The success of consumerism and racism as ideologies consists in their ability to provide *imaginary* explanations and suggest general courses of action for the decline of real living standards, the growing turbulence in the economic and social situation, and the sense of transition to an uncertain new situation.

The left has no explanation for these phenomena that can capture the imagination. Since the left aims its efforts against the corporate capitalist class, and not within the working and underclasses, and the concrete conditions do not favour class unity but instead lead toward further fragmentation, left ideology is headed for even greater marginality unless it admits that the *class* is turning right-ward, rather than ascribing right-wing influences to purely external or conspiratorial factors. It is not because workers are *happy* that the right grows in influence. It is precisely the opposite: workers grasp at right-wing programmes because they offer a way out of the dilemmas of inflation and insecurity. They blame the victim, the underclasses, the gays and lesbians and other groups who have challenged familiar ethical systems.

Yet most of the left persists, in practice, in downgrading personal life within working-class struggle. No serious left influence in the working class is possible without addressing the issues on which the right has attacked. What do we think of the ethical systems (hard work, family life, hetro-sexuality) and what alternative can the left offer to the tax revolt, which is grounded in the right-wing critique of centralisation and bureaucracy?

An authoritarian left is helpless to address these questions except with the most stereotyped arguments against libertarian right-wing programmes, such as: 'socialism will bring solutions through collective ownership', 'the state is necessary in the transition period and bureaucracy will go away as private property is abolished', 'democracy is reserved for the progressive forces and consists more in true economic security than in free speech', 'repression and central planning and power are necessary to save the revolution from its enemies'.

Thus a break with the authoritarian and bureaucratic elements of traditional life ideologies (both Leninist and social-democratic) is a political imperative. It is necessary not simply to 'have' but to develop practically a critique of bureaucracy and centralisation, and to counterpose a political vision that (1) agrees with parts of the libertarian right-wing critique of bureaucracy, while parting with it on the question of free enterprise; (2) acknowledges that the family is crucial for many people who have lost community ties, without trying to conceal the ways that the conventional family is no longer viable; (3) defends freedom of sexual preference while understanding why people experience sexual misery and find themselves attracted to repressive attitudes toward gay and lesbian preferences; and (4) agrees that taxes are too high and government is wasteful while criticising the attitudes toward social services and their recipients often implicit in such statements.

Most of the established left seems unable to do more in the present period than organise resistance to the efforts of the corporations and national government to make the workers pay for the crisis. The resurgence of socialist influence within the working class cannot be projected onto a new depression, mass strikes, or other apocalyptic events. Traditional liberalism is unlikely to rebuild an active mass base of the type that developed during the depression and immediate post-war periods.

That is to say, a hard, realistic view of the current situation is required. The prospect of a significant long-term decline in living standards for perhaps a majority of workers is apt to move them to the right, sometimes radically, given the present alignment of political and social forces. And the ideological points of combat will not be concentrated, necessarily, within the economic sphere, even though an increase is likely in defensive strikes and rank-and-file opposition to established leaders. To those who object that my insistence that questions of personal life, concepts of decentralised popular socialism, and education for political as well as economic action at the base fails to provide specific strategies for the left, I would argue that the theoretical and strategic debate is now as important as tactical plans, and that the latter can only make sense in the context of general strategic agreement in relation to groups and organisations that have some chance of implementing them.

NOTES

1. Sidney Lens, *The Crisis of American Labor*, (New York: A.S. Barnes, 1961); Stanley Aronowitz, *False Promises*, (New York: McGraw-Hill, 1973).
2. See Lenin's *Left-Wing Communism: An Infantile Disorder*.
3. Lens, *Crisis*.
4. For theoretical discussions of this point see Mario Tronti, 'Workers and Capital', *Telos* 18; also Stanley Aronowitz, 'Marx, Braverman, and the Logic of Capital', *Insurgent Sociologist*, Winter 1978-79,
5. See Henri Lefebvre, *Everyday Life in the Modern World*, (New York: Harper Torchbooks, 1971).
6. Thomas Hogue, *The American Steel Industry*, vol. 4.
7. This is the standard position of the 'new communist movement' adopted from Communist Party leader William Z. Foster's post-war writings. See especially his *Negro People in American History*, (New York: International Publishers, 1970), and *History of the Communist Party of the United States*, (New York: Greenwood Press, 1968); and *History of the Three Internationals*, (New York: Greenwood Press, 1968).
8. For a typical formulation, see Art Preis, *Labor's Giant Step*, (New York: Pioneer Publishers, 1971).
9. Aronowitz, *False Promises*, ch. 4.
10. There are two comprehensive histories of the Party: Foster's *History of the Communist Party in the United States*, and Irving Howe and Lewis Coser, *The American Communist Party*, (New York: De Capo, 1974). These books may be regarded as two sides of the same coin. One is relentlessly apologetic, while the other is thoroughly vituperative.
11. See Santiago Carrillo, *Eurocommunism and the State*, (London: Lawrence and Wishart, 1977), and Fernando Claudin, *Eurocommunism and Socialism*, (London: New Left Books, 1977).
12. See Claus Offe, 'Theses on the State', *New German Critique* 4.
13. James O'Connor and Jürgen Habermas have, in different ways, pointed to this 'legitimation' crisis. See O'Connor, *Fiscal Crisis of the State*, (London: St. James Press, 1973), and Habermas, *Legitimation Crisis*, (London: Heinemann, 1976).

THE FRENCH COMMUNIST PARTY
AND FEMINISM

Jane Jenson

Introduction

In France, as in the rest of the advanced capitalist world, the women's movement has come to stay. The movement's demands for changes in the status of women and the new content which it has brought to politics can not be ignored. The political context which the French women's movement faced in the past decade was a Left revitalised around an alliance of parties, *Union de la Gauche*. This has meant, in contrast to Britain or North America, that a lively and socialist Left already existed with which the movement had to deal. And the parties of the Left, with their own analyses of advanced, monopoly capitalism could not ignore the women. A confrontation was inevitable; a resolution of benefit to both was more problematic.

The mobilisation of women was only one of the many new social movements which characterised politics in the late 1960s and 1970s. Ecologists, students, consumers, anti-war activists, homosexuals, women, came together, in more or less formal organisations, to press their demands for social and political change. These 'single-issue movements' posed profound questions about traditional left practices of mobilisation and activism. In earlier years the parties of the Left were frequently the carriers of some of the concerns which later motivated the social movements. In recent times, however, the movements have developed their own organisations which are, or attempt to be, autonomous of the parties. This autonomy plus the social base of many of the most important movements—in the 'new middle class'—has raised important strategic questions for the left parties. The classic left problem of making alliances with non-working-class strata is posed in new terms. Will the existence of such movements reinforce the political parties in their projects, or will they draw activists and supporters away from the more general work of political change toward an issue-focussed and more short-time intervention in political action? How the French Communists tried to cope with these new problems, as manifested in their changing relationships with the French women's movement, is the subject of this article.

Coping with social movements has always been complicated for the PCF. Theoretically, the Party has been able to choose from among three

121

possible approaches. The PCF could accept the legitimacy of a social movement and allow it to flourish outside the control of the Party; the Party could attempt to direct the movement itself (by creating front organisations and/or using mass organisations as transmission belts for Party policy and mobilisation needs); or the PCF could wage war on the movement, as unprogressive. While these are three logical possibilities, the latter two are by far the most common in PCF history.

The PCF, in its earlier history, dealt with social movements according to the strict criteria of the Party's *ouvrieriste* theoretical perspective. Such movements had to be fitted into the class reductionism of this *ouvrierisme*— if the movement's goals could be reduced to 'the interests of the working class', or its allies as defined by the Party, especially with reference to wages, working conditions, and living standards, then that movement was eligible for PCF attention and support. If the movement's goals did not conform to these strict criteria, it might be banned to the pale of 'petit-bourgeois' distraction from the real goals of class struggle. Using these criteria, the PCF focussed much of its work on mass organisations like *La Confédération Genérale du Travail* (CGT), *Le Mouvement de la Paix*, and *Le Mouvement de Défense des Exploitants Familiaux*, for example. The traditional pattern of work with social movements was to develop an organisation closely connected to the PCF—composed only of Communists or of Communists and non-Communists (with control over strategic decisions assured by the Communist leadership).

The Eurocommunist changes of the last two decades seemed to call this traditional pattern into question. The PCF developed a new economic theory and class map, along with the strategy of *Union de la Gauche* and notions of a 'revolutionary-reformist' transition to socialism. The Party's goal in all this was to create an alliance between a plurality of progressive political formations, animated by the PCF, which would open the way to a peaceful and democratic transition to French socialism. Such changes in theory and strategy also implied new approaches to autonomous social movements. In the words of the XXII Congress of the PCF, *le socialisme, c'est la démocratie jusqu'au bout* (socialism is democracy to the fullest). This slogan implied that, as the monopoly capitalist state became less able to guarantee democratic forms and relationships, struggles for democracy would also be struggles against the state, against capital, and for socialism. It also implied that the Party would seek to find new ways of working with the democratic struggles of groups which arose outside the Party's own orbit, if those groups were involved in expanding the limits of democracy.

By the 1970s then, which were the years in which the women's movement in France was increasing its influence, the PCF was simultaneously changing its perspective on social movements. Clearly the women's movement was a struggle for greater democracy—in the workplace, in society, in the family—and as such should have been a prime candidate for PCF support and encouragement. However, the real history of Party reaction to the movement was much more complicated than one might have expected from simple knowledge of the Party's doctrinal changes. The reasons for this complexity are found in the contradictory ways that the PCF 'Eurocommunised'. Its 'Eurocommunisation' was incomplete because the Party had advanced more in some spheres of Party practice than in others.[1] The incomplete nature of the PCF 'Eurocommunisation' and the contradictory processes which underlay this incompleteness were perhaps nowhere better illustrated than in the Party's efforts to cope with the women's movement.

The Pre-Eurocommunist Analysis of the Situation of Women

Prior to 'Eurocommunisation', the PCF had a well worked out analysis of women in capitalist society and it was from this beginning that a new analysis and alliance strategy came. The earlier approach to *la condition féminine* and blueprint for liberation was derived from the Marxist classics and the example of the socialism of the Soviet Union. The participation of women in the wage labour force was the most important step to change. Only such participation would begin creating the personal independence and political consciousness which would engage women in the struggle for socialism. Only socialism could bring their full liberation from the exploitation of capital and of men. Following Marx, Engels and Lenin, as well as Bebel and Fournier, the PCF's analysis of the situation of women in capitalism included recognition that formal equality of rights did not automatically entail real equality. Women were doubly exploited because they played a dual role—in production and reproduction—in capitalism. However, capitalism refused to recognise the social character of maternity. The analysis continued to note that the division of labour within the family resulted in women being saddled with the suffocating daily round of domestic labour. Moreover, women had become a source of cheap labour—part of the reserve army of labour—for industrial capitalism. Thus capital had every reason to attempt through various institutional, legal and ideological mechanisms to reproduce the subordinate status of women.[2] The PCF's model for the reforms necessary to begin changing women's situation was always the Soviet Union. Communists' efforts in favour of women in capitalist society would win women to the long-term struggle for socialist transformation by drawing them to the PCF, as *militantes* and as voters.

In the 1950s, while the theoretical analysis of the condition of women was the one outlined here, most mobilisation of women, *qua* women, was done through the *Union des Femmes Françaises* (UFF), a mass organisation of primarily non-salaried women. The UFF campaign foci were usually bread and peace and appeals were directed to women as mothers, as housewives, and as peace-lovers by nature. However, in a 1961 re-evaluation of the work of the UFF and the success of campaigns directed towards women, a change occurred.[3] This change in focus (or a recognition of an earlier gap in mobilisation) corresponded to an understanding of the restructuring and modernisation of the French economy which the post-war years had brought. PCF campaigns throughout the sixties always emphasised that women were super-exploited and that they must demand to be treated as the equals of male workers, not accepting capital's claim to pay them less because they 'needed' less.

Therefore, the PCF appealed to women as working mothers, forced by capital to perform a *double journée du travail* under conditions of great hardship, and subject to an ideological campaign which claimed that the real function of women was as mothers at home, so that, if they did work, it was only to earn a supplementary income or to fill a few hours of free time. Against this view of women's work, the PCF counterposed another. The picture of the ideal woman painted by the PCF was that of an independent woman, involved in her work and the struggle for socialism, who returned to her family with the interests and enthusiasms inherent in such involvement. At a time when the dominant ideology celebrated *la femme au foyer*, even while the reality was higher levels of salaried employment for women, this position of the PCF was dramatically different and not unprogressive.[4]

We can see that the PCF position on women, from the years of Thorez up until the late sixties, shared most of the characteristics of other PCF campaigns. The appeal to women was fundamentally economistic, focussing on women as workers, albeit workers with special needs because they bore children, and as consumers, responsible for running a household on an ever-tightening budget.

Before 1968 the PCF had a near monopoly on 'progressive' positions on women. There were few competitors in the field. From its position of strength the PCF could afford to judge autonomous feminist efforts harshly. Communist understanding of the 'women's movement' was drawn from experiences with feminists in the earlier part of the century, who were vilified as a bourgeois distraction from the 'real' issues of class struggle.[5]

Such thinking was bound to lead to difficulties once the modern women's movement arose *and* once the process of 'Eurocommunisation' was carried forward in the PCF. The Party and the movement would probably never have encountered each other in any fundamental way if the movement for women's liberation had developed before 1968. Before then the PCF's Stalinism held solid and its sense of self-righteous vanguardism was unchanged. Thus the Party and any women's movement would probably have sailed right past each other, with much sound and fury and very little mutually advantageous illumination. However, after 1968 and especially in the 1970s, the PCF encounter with women was much more nuanced and much more complicated because the PCF itself had begun to change.

The Women's Movement

The modern French women's movement followed the events of May-June 1968, as did so much in French politics today.[6] It is worth noting that the women's movement arose, in large part, out of the very process which the PCF had been advocating—the massive entry of women into the salaried workforce. While the PCF's analysis of the status of women called for activity outside the home as a preparation for the transition to true liberation, it was the increasing participation of women in salaried work which led to the confrontation with the inadequacies of the traditional analysis. As women entered the world of the salariat, they encountered inequalities *beyond* those of lower wages, unequal access to training, and problems of maternity. In other words, the status of women could not be derived *only* from the desire of capital to have a pool of cheaper, less organised, and more exploitable labour. The experience of women in the modern capitalist system (as industrial workers but especially as service sector, professional, and intellectual workers) raised questions of domination and subordination between men and women in work, in the family, in the couple, and in sexuality—issues which the traditional Marxist analysis of the PCF could not answer and which the PCF could not incorporate into its economic mobilisational approaches.

At the same time, the women's movement which became the carrier of these issues posed a serious problem for the PCF. As the Party developed its Eurocommunist perspectives it specified that democratic mass struggles would be the core of any French transition to socialism. The women's movement looked very much like the kind of democratic struggle which the PCF had in mind. It became impossible, therefore, to disqualify the women's movement as 'mere reformism' or a petit-bourgeois attempt to undermine the class struggle. The *couches intermédiaires* which were the primary home of the women's movement were also the social groups targetted by the PCF for the expansion of Communist strength upon which the success of *Union de la Gauche* would depend.[7] Granting to these strata a real interest in socialist transformation, even if that interest were derived from somewhat different concerns than those of the working class, also implied granting a certain legitimacy to the demands of the women of these strata for liberation and for changes in male-dominated, male-constructed French society and the PCF. Thus, the old tactic of dismissing the initiatives of non-working-class women was no longer possible.

The women's movement challenged the PCF to consider inequalities due to the historical workings of patriarchy in addition to the inequalities of class. This partriarchy was observable not only in the classification of 'women's work' as less important and therefore less remunerative than that of men (a tendency which the PCF had already uncovered and taken on) but also more generally in authority patterns, in relations within the family and the couple, and in sexuality. This emphasis challenged the usual distinction between the private arena and public concern's and raised to the status of the 'political' matters which had previously been 'personal', as much for the PCF as for the rest of French society. The theory of partriarchy, by including all men as its carriers, refused to grant an exemption to the working class, even its Communist vanguard, from participation in the reproduction of patriarchy. Finally, seeing *all* women as the victims of patriarchy, the theory blurred boundaries between classes, identifying instead the specificity of women's situation, which needed its own movement and organisations.

The attention paid by the women's movement to sexuality, to relations between people and within the couple, to new forms of authority, did not immediately resonate within a Party which for many years had 'understood' the concerns of women (housing, children, better jobs, working and living conditions for themselves and their husbands) and which envisioned a world in which women would be like men, except for the fact that they would also have children. Moreover, while the earlier economistic analysis of women's place in capitalism required no political formation other than the Communist Party to advance the cause of women, partial 'Eurocommunisation' implied that there was room for a progressive social movement, mobilising women, as women, for their own struggles because the Party could not necessarily encompass all struggle.

In this way, the development of the women's movement, coincidental with Eurocommunism, set up a tension within the PCF. It provided a test of the practical commitment of the Party to its own theoretical change. The tension produced both drama and intense struggle within the PCF. The rest of this paper is a discussion of change and struggle within the PCF around women's issues, focussing on two levels of Party practice— theory and strategy and rank and file life.

The 'Eurocommunisation' of the PCF's Analysis of Women's Situation
These implications of Eurocommunism for the PCF's relationship to the women's movement are derived from an interpretation of the logic of Communist theoretical changes of the late sixties and early seventies. New Communist understanding of the importance of the women's movement did not actually emerge until rather late in the process of 'Eurocommunisation', however. If the report of the XXII Congress of the PCF in 1976 can be read as representing a summary statement of the Eurocommunist position within the PCF, attention paid to women was minimal at that time. Women, as carriers of specific needs and requiring

special efforts to assure their liberation, even into the stage of building socialism, were not mentioned.[8] The only place that women received special reference was with regard to their promotion within the PCF itself. This reluctance to focus on women, as late as 1976, indicates the slowness with which the PCF translated its Eurocommunist innovations into some spheres of Party practice. The XXII Congress showed that the Party was moving ahead in theory and in developing an alliance strategy appropriate to that theory *vis à vis* political parties. Yet, at the same time, the full implications of such theoretical changes for dealing with new social movements were not yet appreciated.

The absence of attention to women at the time of the XXII Congress meant that the way was left open to continue old-style approaches. In the flurry of explanatory publications directed at special interest groups, around the time of the Congress, one was written for women. Madeleine Vincent, the member of the *Bureau politique* responsible for women, published *Femmes: quelle libération?*.[9] This book followed the traditional pattern of emphasising the material gains to accrue to women and their families if a government of the United Left were to come to power. The primary goal was one of promoting equality, which would follow from better training, wages, and working conditions—essentially from struggles for the implementation of the Common Programme and for *Union de la Gauche*.

Only in the year preceeding the 1977-78 electoral campaign did the reasoning of the PCF about women and the women's movement begin to undergo substantial change.[10] Georges Marchais, for example, in December 1977 spoke to Communist women in Paris and talked of the *mentalités retardataires* (backward attitudes) which existed in the whole of French society, including within the PCF. These attitudes, the Secretary-General claimed, paid too little attention to women's liberation problematic. Thus, changing the status of women was acknowledged to be a more complex matter than the economistic analysis of earlier years would have allowed. At the same time, however, while Marchais provided neither a real analysis of the sources of these attitudes nor concrete suggestions of what to do about them, he expressed a voluntaristic confidence that they would disappear, once exposed for what they were. He engaged in self-congratulation that the PCF had already begun to take steps to ensure that the special needs of women militants were considered.

However, in this same statement there were also signs that more fundamental re-thinking had occurred within the PCF and that the voluntarism of Marchais was inconsistent even with some aspects of his own views. In particular, he announced that struggle for women's liberation would be necessary well into the construction of socialism. In other words, there was no longer an assumption that sex-based inequalities would automatically disappear with the elimination of classes. The women would have to ensure their own equality. This newly-discovered need for a specific women's struggle in building socialism was linked to an analysis of the prehistoric sources of sexual inequality founded on a sexual division of labour. If the inferiority of women and their work pre-dated private property, then sexual subordination, although clearly extended and codified in class society, preceeded class society. In addition, while acknowledging the necessity of profound change in the relations between classes in order to do any thing fundamental about the situation of women, Marchais stressed the value of women's own political activity and visibility at the present time. The women's movement was a movement which could help to build Left unity and social change.[11]

These remarks by the Secretary-General of the PCF reflected a major theoretical change for the French Communists. The specific parameters of the change were best set out in *La Condition Féminine,* a book produced by the Party's *Centre d'Etudes et de Recherches Marxistes* (CERM) and made up of a series of essays by PCF researchers.[12] One important article, by Maurice Godelier, provided an anthropological examination of sex-based subordination in pre-class societies, rejecting Engels' designation of women as the first class.[13] The political implication of this analysis is that if sexual domination did not arise with classes, it will not automatically disappear as classes disappear. Struggle around specific sexual inequalities will have to continue well into the transition to socialism. Indeed, Godelier's conclusions may have been the source of Georges Marchais' remarks cited above. Such an argument also demanded a re-consideration of the treatment of women in socialist countries.

Other articles in the collection also criticise the situation of women in the socialist countries and argue the need for a separate women's movement throughout the pluralistic process of building socialism. For example, one chapter locates the subordination of women within the needs of capitalism for free domestic labour for reproduction of the labour force.[14] Since women's domestic labour (or more generally, someone's domestic labour, whether women's or couples') is not optional to capitalism, struggles to break down the domestic economy are struggles against capital. Many of the authors stress that it is a separation between public and private economies which provides the foundation for the subordination of women, even in socialist countries. Thus, programmes to re-assign the costs of domestic labour and to break down the ideological forms which reproduce this gift of free labour will both help the liberation of women and advance the cause of socialism.

In the CERM book there are also a number of studies which examine the mechanisms by which the ideology which assigns women a minor status is reproduced—for example, women's magazines, television and school books.[15] Finally, two important articles examine the successes and failures of the PCF in its promotion of women within the Party and its relationship to the women's movement.[16] Careful documentation of the progress of women within the Party points to areas where the promotion of women has been slow. The same author warns that the mere presence of women in governing positions of the PCF will not solve all problems. In another piece the PCF's new attention to democracy (especially *autogestion*) is used as the justification for struggles against attitudes which subordinate all women.

The CERM volume was eagerly received by the many militants who had been searching for new positions which they could defend inside the Party connecting Eurocommunism and women's issues. The book legitimated support for an autonomous mass movement, criticism of the Soviet model of the 'liberation' of women, criticism of the past and present treatment of women within the PCF itself, and it provided new ammunition for Communists in their political work with women. Analyses like those of the CERM authors, especially as they were reflected in the pronouncements of PCF leaders, encouraged rank-and-file Communist women to incorporate appropriate parts of the women's movement's understandings of patriarchy into their own theory. They also enhanced pressures to make women more active and vocal within the PCF. However, the changes which the Eurocommunism of the PCF brought to its relationship with the women's movement and to its analysis of the female condition were fragile. As the Party changed again, so might these positions.

The core of the PCF's Eurocommunist strategy was an alliance with other Left parties in *Union de la Gauche*. However, as the campaign for the 1978 legislative elections approached, the PCF faced a deteriorating balance of forces *vis à vis* its major ally, the PS. For this, and other reasons, relationships between the two parties strained to the point of division. The disunity which resulted probably cost the Left the election. At the core of the Communists' own pre-electoral anxiety was its failure to convert Left unity into increased PCF support from the French electorate. Its hopes for increased strength in the middle strata were particularly frustrated. At the same time, Socialist electoral strength, in general and in the middle strata, increased dramatically. The PCF's response to this weakness was to substitute an electoral strategy designed to re-inforce its appeal among the part of the electorate it could most count on—the working class. Thus, the PCF's campaign was progressively more marked by *ouvrierisme*, well-symbolised by the campaign slogan, 'Make the Rich Pay'. Such themes were carried into the immediate post-electoral period. The PS was held totally responsible for the electoral defeat because of its alleged 'right turn'. This shift by the PS back to social democracy, as the Communists put it, made the Socialists an unreliable and unattractive ally.

The ultimate result of the PCF's reflections on the electoral experience was a strategic change—to *union à la base*. The purpose of 'unity from below' was to demonstrate to French workers that the PCF, and only the PCF, was on their side. Only the Communists could lead their struggles and protect them from the effects of economic crisis. If it worked, unity from below could block the Socialists from further inroads into the Communists' working-class base and expose the Socialists as potential 'managers of capitalist crisis'.

The 'unity' line began to unfold very soon after the election and dominated PCF politics for the following year. It was in many ways a return to older forms of PCF practice. *Union à la base* had been PCF strategy in the isolated Cold War years, and the 1980s version seemed to share some characteristics of the earlier form. It emphasised the implantation of the PCF in the working class plus economism in mobilisational approaches to workers. Most importantly, it marked a retreat from a number of Eurocommunist perspectives. It was a line which de-emphasised PCF overtures to the *couches intermédiaires*, and at the same time it retreated from the more ecumenical approach to new social movements of the mid-seventies. Moreover, the return of workerism brought with it attempts to revive older, more centralised and less open forms of internal Party life.

Progress on women's issues was, as has been suggested, closely tied to the general process of 'Eurocommunisation' in the PCF. Any retreat from Eurocommunism would call such progress into question. It was precisely retreat from Eurocommunism which characterised the PCF after September 1977 and especially after the electoral defeat of March 1978. It was not surprising, therefore, that post-electoral strategic change also brought a substantial retreat on women's issues. Older themes were re-emphasised. Women were appealed to primarily as workers, as poor people, and much less often as victims of sex-based subordination. The shift to workerist perspectives on social movements also led the leadership, as part of its campaign to blame electoral defeat on the Socialists and on opportunism, to condemn the women's movement as merely 'feminist' and as dominated by either the Socialists or the Trotskyists.[17]

In general, the abrupt change in Party strategy was difficult for many Communists to accept. Beginning in 1978, the Party was wracked by unprecedented internal conflict. The leadership's retrenchment policies led much of this conflict to focus on issues of democracy. The PCF's position on women's issues were, to some Communists, a vital aspect of democraticisation. As a result, some women's groups joined in the chorus of dissent which rocked the PCF in the spring of 1978.[18]

Rank-and-File Communists and Party Crisis
To this point this paper has described the changes that 'Euro-

communisation' implied for the relationship between the PCF and the women's movement as well as for the Communists' own understanding of the status of women in capitalist society. However, the analysis has focussed only on the upper levels of the Party and on theoretical and strategic spheres of Party practice. It is useful at this point to shift to the rank and file and to the spheres of Communist mobilisational practices and internal Party life. Doing this will provide new insight into the ways that 'Eurocommunisation' affected one group of ordinary Communists and how they reacted to the Party's retreat away from it. The group in question was a section-level *commission féminine* (women's commission) which was created to put into practice some of the promise of the XXII Congress. In the months of Party crisis the women's commission quickly became an arena within which the conflict between strategic currents which characterised the PCF in the post-electoral period was acted out in one section of the Party. Its experience documents the fragility as well as the importance of the 'Eurocommunisation' which had occurred. It illustrates the effects on the rank and file of the leadership's move away from the decade-long strategic perspective in several areas, including effects in the areas of internal Party democracy and mobilisational strategies.

This description will draw on the findings of a participant-observation study of a cell and section in the PCF between March 1978 and the XXIII Congress of the PCF in May 1979. The section in question, Paris South, was one of the most committed to Eurocommunism in France. Communists within it were therefore very much caught up in the effort to understand and deal with the changes in the PCF line that followed the defeat of March. An important part of the section's story was the process of learning experienced by its women's commission whose existence was a source of pride for many in the section. In the months after March, the commission was deeply implicated in the effects of closing down the Eurocommunist strategic option and the search for some meaning for *union à la base* that might satisfy their desire for continued openness and Eurocommunism.

Paris South's commitment to Eurocommunism derived not only from an understanding of the general conditions of European society which made a strategy of a peaceful, national road to socialism desirable, but also from its own sociology. The Paris South area (as all of Paris, in fact) was not primarily working class in social composition and the membership of the section reflected this. Most of the section's Communists were white collar—office workers, a goodly number of lower or middle managers, with a few professionals and intellectuals. Paris South had a long and noble history of Party work, from the Popular Front and the Resistance, and this history was a source of considerable pride. In the 1960s, as Gaullist-inspired urban renewal re-made the social map of Paris, the section developed an active practice of out-reach toward the changing population. It had also developed a position of autonomy in the Party. The section leadership, from at least 1968 on, had followed a strategy of protecting the section from undue interference from above such that independent initiatives might be taken, both within the PCF and in mobilisation work in the neighbourhood. The section (a large one of about 300 Communists in 1977-78) had developed a certain reputation within the Paris federation for creative and enthusiastic Eurocommunism, for taking the notions of democracy and pluralism very seriously.

The section saw its *commission féminine* as a very important part of this political position. The commission began as a small group of militants who met to discuss and initiate Party work in areas of concern to women. The group grew from a few young, 'new-middle-class' Communist women to include about fifty people who came with greater or less regularity to the monthly meetings. It included Communists from both the local and workplace cells of Paris South. Its social composition was similar to that of the section. Most of the women were white-collar workers, professionals or intellectuals. One aspect of the commission which was of particular note was its willingness to include both Communist women from other sections and non-Communists in its early meetings.

The *commission féminine* was created after the XXII Congress and took its mandate from the Congress' broad exhortation that Communists be 'creative'.[19] The commission was struggling to be 'creative' in two areas—internal Party life and the mobilisational practices of the PCF, especially as they were directed to women. Although it accepted the traditional PCF organisational form of the women's commission (which exists at most levels of the Party to carry out work among women) the Paris South group was designed to introduce into the section some of the concerns of women who were close to the women's movement. It had two different kinds of goals, therefore. The first was to provide an alternative place where Communist women could come together and reflect on their situation as women and as Communists. The commission was to provide all the familiar support functions of a women's group. The second goal was to develop within the commission new political understandings of what the PCF could and should do in its work with women.

Rapid growth of the PCF in the early seventies, promoted by the Eurocommunist ambition to create a mass Party, had had an interesting effect on the Party's internal life. The 'Eurocommunisation' of French Communists' theory and strategy had been almost directly grafted onto a Party organisation designed for a very different kind of transformational scenario (a Bolshevik-style scenario). A mass membership developed without a re-examination of the part played by that membership in Party life. There had been no real re-evaluation of what it meant 'to be a Communist'. However, a mass Party was a new Party, in effect. The post-Common Programme militants had been promised 'democracy' in the transition to socialism not only in society but also within the PCF. Yet, the failure to explore the full implications of Eurocommunism for internal Party democracy set up the possibility of crisis. While such problems touched most militants, they had special effects on women, especially as they tried to introduce their concerns into the PCF.

With the huge expansion of the PCF's membership in the 1970s, more women became Communists. Their numbers increased both absolutely and in relative percentages. The leadership, in line with its traditional strategy of imposing quotas to produce certain demographic 'profiles' at all levels of the Party, installed more and more women in official organisational slots. As a result, women began to appear almost everywhere in positions of responsibility. These women were more than 'token'; they did become important within the PCF.[20] (In Paris South, for example, the section's First Secretary was a woman, while large numbers of women served on the Section Committee and in its *bureau*.) But the progress of women within the Party brought with it new complexity.

The Party's female comrades confronted a double barrier. First, the PCF's traditional *pur et dur* style of activism devalued any personal content or consideration in favour of complete and asexual devotion to leading the class struggle, as defined by the Party leadership. Superimposed on this was the society-wide reaction to women. Over the years the PCF had developed certain expectations of its *militantes*. They were to be as active and committed as men, devoted to 'passing' the Party line to the world by approved top-down mobilisational methods. However, because they were women (the family and maternity was always a big value for the PCF), once they had young children, they were expected to retire from the front ranks of activity and occupy themselves with their families—they were 'honourably' excused. In the past, women with young children had therefore been systematically relieved of their responsibilities or not promoted. In the France of the Napoleonic marriage laws, and thus for the Communists of France, children were the responsibility of the mother. A *triple journée*—of work, family and Party—was considered beyond the capacity of even Communists. In the past, then, only certain kinds of women—young, without children, or past the age of young families—were eligible to become *militantes*. However, once women began to refuse this exclusion and to insist that the Party develop a different conception of female activism—more reasonable, less demanding of time and energy, more considerate of children—the PCF's old habits would have to change.

The new demands and interests of women would also challenge the definition of 'politics' and political discourse in the PCF. The old-style PCF had a very clear vision about what constituted political activity and how such activity was to be carried out. Politics was about capital and labour, wages and prices, conditions of work and living, crèches and schools. One major type of activity within the Party, in cells and elsewhere, was speeches to elaborate on such politics and make a connection between the dynamics of capitalism and state policies and the PCF's programmes. Speeches were formal, often quite long, prepared in advance (almost always for higher instances of the Party; less often in the cell) and had to be clear. Their purpose was to help fellow militants acquire examples and arguments for future use. In the PCF good militants were those who spoke well and clearly about the Party line especially as it touched their own local (but very rarely personal) situation.

Obviously not everyone was a good militant in this way. Of all Party members, workers and women were most likely to have problems with this form of political discourse, both for the same reason. French society is very verbal. Linguistic elegance is highly prized, but it is also unequally distributed. Workers acquired less than their full share because of poor schooling, among other things. Workers, even if they suffered relatively within their own party, had two advantages over women, however. First they could recognise themselves and their needs in the pro-working-class politics of the PCF. Second, the PCF, as a party, bent over backwards to make sure that workers were heard. Particular efforts were made—quotas, special encouragement to speak, acceptance of and real attention to what workers said. Not so for women. There was little in the internal norms of the Party, or its traditions, that encouraged women to speak. If they did it was fine; if they did not, that was fine too. Unlike workers, then, women did not benefit from any special arrangements which might have overcome their difficulties in speaking in public.

There was an additional, and more complex problem, however, which was that when women did speak, they were often not 'heard'. This failure to communicate successfully had two main causes. The first was that their contributions might be presented in a different way than was the norm. Thus, the motivation of an intervention by a 'personal' rather than a 'political' experience, in a briefer form, or even in a different tone of voice might result in not being 'heard'. The second failure to communicate arose from the fact that women did not always recognise themselves or their most pressing concerns in what the Party said about women—issues were often narrowly confined to material and family benefits and the struggle of women to interject new concerns into Party discourse often fell on very deaf ears. These then were the two problems of women within the PCF—to make themselves 'heard' within the Party and to be 'heard' about new and less traditional matters.

The women's commission of Paris South worked hard to introduce women's voices into the PCF in their area and they had some successes of which they were proud. Several *militantes* who, despite having been elected to the Section Committee had never spoken out in meetings of that committee, found their tongues after attending the women's commission where the reasons for such silences were discussed and where they gave each other support and encouragement. Similarly, the woman who was the First Secretary of the section found that she could count on the women's commission as one of the major sources of support for the feedback about her work. She relied upon the friendship of the group as sustenance in her difficult job. Moreover, after a year of experience with the women's commission, a strong feeling of solidarity was created among the group. When they met again outside the commission, in cell or section-level meetings, such solidarity helped the very timid to participate. In addition, the sense of solidarity encouraged women in their cells to raise matters which had previously not been considered within the purview of Communist politics. Several cells in Paris South at this time held both informal and formal meetings devoted to consideration of rape, of sexuality, of relations within the couple. The existence of the women's commission and the solidarity of its membership also encouraged women to confront their male comrades about their sexist expectations and the more blatant expressions of sexism.

Nevertheless, these kinds of activities, while considered important, were not the primary goal of the group. It wanted to work with women in ways which were different from what the Party had done in the past. It was in this attempt that they had the most trouble and the post-electoral events weighed most heavily. The women's commission of Paris South had been caught up in the constant electioneering that had characterised all Party activity in the years leading up to March 1978. The group complained that their efforts to be 'creative' were being stifled by the upper levels of the Party which were interested in them only as propaganda machines for electoral campaigns sent down from above. As the 1978 electoral campaign unfolded in its obvious inappropriateness for the Paris South area (where *couches intermédiaires* were more numerous than blue collar workers) and as the content of the campaign directed toward women became more and more economistic, the women's commission's sense of being stifled grew.

Before the election the Paris South women's commission had proposed that the Arrondissement organise a day-long session for women in the area to raise and discuss some of the issues they considered missing from traditional Party programmes. In particular they wanted to talk about sexuality. The Arrondissement refused and instead organised a very traditional electoral meeting to discuss the election promises and programmes of the PCF. When a few feminists tried to raise some of their concerns in questions from the floor, they were effectively put down in a series of speeches, especially one from the official of the Arrondissement responsible for work with women. For the members of the Paris South women's commission, this kind of response was another demonstration of the way that the Party was in retreat from its post-XXII Congress position.

It also increased their wariness of any initiatives coming from upper levels of the PCF, the Arrondissement in particular. After the election they were even more discouraged. In June 1978 a very important day-long study session on women was held (at Argenteuil, June 10 and 11) in which the new *union à la base* strategic perspective, as it related to women and the women's movement, was set out. The most notable events of this session were an attack on the women's movement as an unreliable and therefore unavailable ally, a return to an emphasis on working women and their material situation, and, in the course of the meeting, a criticism of the activities of the Paris Federation of the PCF in its Eurocommunist-inspired work with women.[21] This meeting made it very clear that something of great importance was gone from the old strategy but it was not clear to the women's commission what had been put in its place. However, the anger generated by the campaign and post-electoral analysis of the PCF, could simmer throughout the summer of 1978.

In the fall, the first intimations of what was to be a year-long struggle over strategy, broke out in Paris South and the first focus of difficulty that arose was in the internal life of the Party. What came to be at issue was the extent to which Eurocommunism had brought a more open Party, with room for autonomy of decision-making at the lower levels. The troubles began when the section, inspired by the women's commission, attempted to do what it had done in 1977 (before the rupture with the Socialists) at the *Fête de l'Humanité*. The commission had devised a Eurocommunist programme for the section's booth at the *Fête,* organising a bookstall to sell literature about women—both Party publications and other progressive works. In the context of the *Fête*, probably one of the major social events of the French Left, the women of Paris South helped to contact both Communist and non-Communist women and men for discussion and to display what they, as a group, were doing. The booth had been a success in 1977 and the plan was to continue it in 1978.

However, things were very different in the summer of 1978. Two weeks before the *Fête* the Arrondissement sent out a directive that the Paris South bookstall was not to sell non-Party magazines. This suggestion was very badly received by the leadership of the section and in a stormy August session, the *bureau* of the section voted to defy the Arrondissement's instructions on the grounds of democracy and independence. The section's earlier decision to sell the magazines was reaffirmed and battle was engaged. Drama was high at the *Fête* itself, as the Communists of Paris South waited to see how the Party leadership and other Communists would respond. Initially, the leadership of the higher levels resorted to social pressure alone. The woman who was the Communist deputy in the legislative constituency next to Paris South (and therefore, in many ways, 'their' deputy) refused to enter the bookstall in her rounds of the Arrondissement's booths. The leaders of the Arrondissement followed the same tactic. In contrast, many Communists from other sections all over France visited the booth and expressed their amazement that the Paris South women's commission could convince the section to focus its booth on women and in this way. Thus, with such responses, the section leaders felt vindicated and the sense of confidence of the women of Paris South (and their male comrades) increased. They put the troubles with the Arrondissement down to its own silliness or backward ideas. That the 'backwardness' might be more widespread was not yet clear.

The events of the *Fête* provided much of the focus of discussion throughout the section in subsequent weeks. The section's defiance of the Arrondissement had been daring and the section had to be ready for the after-effects of such actions. However, the event of the booth soon came to be overshadowed by something else which had happened at the *Fête*. Some of the women in the section, including the First Secretary, had given an interview to a leading women's movement magazine, in which they discussed their lives and their experiences within the Party. Most of the comments, although very thoughtful, were critical of the Party and the magazine emphasised the criticisms in its article. Needless to say, at a time when the appearance of Communists in non-Party media was problematic (after the many articles by dissident Communists in French newspapers the previous spring), this interview was explosive in its effect.

For the First Secretary of the section the situation which followed was extremely difficult. She was summoned to the Arrondissement to 'explain' her decision to grant the interview. She defended herself on two fundamental grounds. The first was that she had said nothing which was not true and nothing which was dangerous to the Party. Her argument was that the truth must be exposed rather than hidden away under the facade of unanimity which had always characterised the PCF's democratic centralism. For her, her Eurocommunism implied more open discussion of all questions. Her second defence was that, in the earlier times of expansive Eurocommunism she had spoken to the Arrondissement leadership about an interview requested by a Catholic magazine. The answer given by the leadership at the time was that Communists 'should go about everywhere' to publicise the Party. In fact, she had been told that her checking such a request was really unnecessary and she should use her own judgement. Second time around, however, things had changed. What had previously been possible was now impossible.

The situation of another woman of Paris South was more dramatic. Her part of the interview (which was very prominently played up in the article) emphasised that the PCF reproduced the patriarchy of French (and all) capitalist society. Her position was summarised by the banner used to publicise the magazine in the news stands of Paris—'if I can be a Communist and a woman, that is paradise'. This phrase represents her developing conviction that the Communist position on women and women's movement position on women were, if not contradictory, at least not being reconciled. She spoke in the interview about the prospect of having to choose between the two positions and was eloquent about the pain involved in such a choice. She was, and had been for almost a decade, a good and loyal Communist. She believed that the Party was leading the historic struggle for change and she feared 'being left out of history' if she failed to participate in the Party's struggles. However, by November, she had left the PCF.

To her cell she explained that she was making a *personal* choice, but a choice nonetheless. Her choice was not to be interpreted as the necessary one for all Communist women, even those deeply committed to the women's movement. But it was a personal decision also because she could no longer, *as a person,* live within a Party which reproduced the patriarchy of capitalist society and within which she felt like an appendage. Her explanation of her leaving the PCF contained two important themes, then. The first was a criticism of the Party's stance on women's issues and its failure to get to the roots of patriarchy. The second theme was a more general assessment of the authority structure within the PCF. Her argument was founded on a political criticism of the way the PCF used its ordinary members—both female and male. In her opinion all Communists were reduced to the status of minors in a Party which was authoritarian in its structures and its operation. She felt that the independence of Communists, the possibility of exercising their own creative powers, was severely curtailed by the internal working of the Party. The reaction of the upper-levels of the Party to the initiatives of the section at the *Fête,* the criticisms of her interview in the magazine of the women's movement, and the critiques of the activities of the women's commission itself had forced her to a choice. She had concluded that it was no longer possible for someone like her to do what she judged most likely to advance the cause of the Communist Party. Now one had to be cautious, to calculate the balance of forces within the Party and to play a careful political game within the PCF, in ways which meant that the original purpose of the action was sometimes lost. For this *camarade* The Eurocommunist past, and its promise, had gone. The new situation demanded fundamental compromises which she was unwilling to accept. Whereas it had been, for a time, possible both to support the women's movement and to be a Communist, this possibility was fragile. The PCF's opening to the woman's movement was dependent upon its Eurocommunism and this was in retreat after March 1978. With the retreat, some individuals were forced to choose between the Party and the movement, and institutions like the women's commission of Paris South had to re-think their possibilities.

The cell's, and then the section's, consideration of this dramatic resignation of a *camarade* went a long way towards clarifying the situation within the PCF at the time. The women's commission and its

activities were caught in the general evolution of the Party's strategy and
the conflicts which surrounded it. As the PCF as a whole moved away
from *Union de la Gauche* towards *union à la base* and as a more 'workerist'
strategy replaced the Eurocommunist perspectives of the previous decade,
all spheres of PCF activity were affected. In other words, it was not only
the internal life of the Party—democracy and the creativity of militants—
that caused problems but also questions of mobilisation practices of the
PCF. In the case of Paris South, these questions came to focus on the
work of the women's commission as it attempted to continue its search for
new forms of contact with women and the women's movement. However,
in this sphere of Party practice, and in contrast to its work within the
PCF, the women's commission was quite at a loss. The members knew
what they did not want—traditional electioneering, top-down campaigns
directed toward women, exclusively economistic discussions of women's
situation—but they had not yet developed, in their own work, any suitable
substitutes. Their search, moreover, came to an abrupt end as the PCF as a
whole moved towards its post-electoral version of *union à la base*.

The Paris South women's commission was at a disadvantage because it
had not been able to delineate clearly its own mobilisational activities
prior to the shift in strategy. Most of its efforts had gone into providing
support for women Communists within the PCF or into electioneering.
Thus, when confronted with the leadership's instructions to proceed to
union à la base in the context of a return to *ouvrierisme*, it was at a loss
about what to do. Other parts of the PCF faced the same problem, in
particular cells which had no clear idea of what to do in the absence of
any elections and without the possibility of joint actions with the
Socialists and other Left political formations. The retreat into isolation
that *union à la base* seemed to represent was impossible to countenance
for an institution like the women's commission whose activity was
premissed upon a more open strategy.

Therefore, in the autumn of 1978 the women's commission of Paris
South found itself vulnerable to the efforts of the leadership of the PCF
to 'take in hand' the Party and close down the discontent which had been
rampant since March 1978. This taking in hand involved the leadership
organising the rank and file's work around a series of specific campaigns,
the purpose of which were to keep the ordinary militants constantly
occupied with tasks approved by the leadership of the Party. One of these
campaigns focussed on the Party's work with women and all levels of the
PCF were expected to undertake new action to expose to French women
the policies and programmes that the Communists advocated for them.
This was to be done in the new context of *union à la base* and was
supposed to demonstrate the effect of *union* on women.

Two initiatives in this campaign affected the women's commission of
Paris South—one local and one national. The local campaign was directed

by the leadership of the Arrondissement and was designed to publicise Communist policies *vis à vis* women. The technique chosen to contact women was a 'questionnaire' to be filled out by Communist and non-Communist women asking for their views on a series of matters like 'equality', discrimination, relations within the family and the couple, child-care, etc. This 'questionnaire' technique was familiar to the women's commission of Paris South because in reality it was little more than a political tract with a few 'questions' attached. The format was the following: it began with a bold title statement that women 'want to live better'; continued with a listing of Communist policies, both past and present, to show that the PCF knew what to do for women; and concluded with the 'questions', which were of the most banal sort (for example, Do you feel that you are treated unfairly? Do you want more for your family?).

In the meeting called to consider this initiative the women of the Paris South women's commission reacted with verbal violence. The questionnaire was analysed as nothing more than another effort by the Party to contact women from the outside, to impose an agenda of change on them, and, in that agenda, to emphasise the most workerist of positions. The major criticism was, however, directed at the style of the approach—it came from the outside without an effort to engage the women themselves in thinking about change and it neglected to solicit their feelings about the change that *they* wanted. What was being rejected, then, was a reversion to the PCF's traditional mobilisational practices. As was clearly stated at the meeting, the grounds for the rejection of the questionnaire initiative was the need to develop Eurocommunist practices which would make women (and all people) responsible for the changes in their lives and not leave the definition and implementation of change to politicians and parties.

In framing their objections to the questionnaire, the Communists of the *commission féminine* insisted upon the need to develop new methods to approach women, new ways of engaging them in conversation and analysis of their lives, and the responsibility of the women's commission to discover such methods in its own work. They looked upon the questionnaire as both a diversion from this more important task and as a way of undoing any work which they might already have accomplished in their contacts with women. Since they were determined not to play the Arrondissement's game, they therefore refused to have anything to do with the questionnaire. As the section had done earlier on the issue of the booth at the *Fête de l'Humanité,* the women's commission of Paris South decided to ignore an instruction from above and not to carry out the tasks assigned to it.

At issue next was a 'national campaign for women', essentially a call for several demonstrations organised around the slogan 'live better, equal and free'. One demonstration was to take place in Paris and to focus on questions of women's employment, working conditions, and opportunities.

The call for a massive demonstration was supposed to point to the Communists' continuing concern about women's problems and to stress that Communists could advance the cause of women without resorting to an alliance with the women's movement. The demonstration clearly indicated, then, the return to an economistic perspective of emphasising only issues of employment, taxes, prices, and living and working conditions. The official tract distributed by the PCF said little about backward attitudes which might retard the liberation of women nor did it encourage any thought of the legitimacy of the women's movement as an ally in the construction of socialism. The Paris South women's commission recognised the *manif* (demo) for what it was and refused to attend, they refused to make a banner (or some other identification of the section's presence) and they preferred to indicate their objections by abstention. This absence was noted! Later, the behaviour of the women's commission—its failure to participate in the questionnaire distribution and its absence from the demonstration—provided ammunition for those who wanted to see the elimination of what was considered to be the undue influence of 'feminists' within the section.

The women's commission of Paris South was vulnerable to the critiques of the Arrondissement and other members of the section who disagreed with its stance on women's issues in part because it had not succeeded in finding its own programme and tactics for working with women. Having been completely absorbed in the electioneering of the campaign period and the discovery of the commonality of its members' experiences as women, it had not yet undertaken any real work of its own. In the fall of 1978 the commission's members had two plans about how to proceed. The first was that the commission would continue to raise and discuss general questions which Communist women had not yet adequately addressed. The first of these questions was that of children. A meeting was devoted to general discussion of the women's feelings and reactions to children— their own children and their lives as children. The meeting was interesting and thought-provoking, but it did not lead to any immediate conclusions or programmatic proposals. It was, rather, a time of collective reflection. However, by the fall of 1978, the ability of the women's commission to sit back and reflect together had been curtailed by events in the section and the Party-at-large. In the context of controversy which surrounded the commission, it had to do something which would get it back into the good graces of the rest of the Party. Therefore, the discussion of children which a year before would probably have been termed a great success in itself, was in the new situation seen as little more than 'wheel-spinning' even by the strongest supporters of the commission.

The second plan for action seemed somewhat more promising. The women's commission dusted off its idea of a day-long meeting of the section to discuss the situation of women in general and to talk about the

Party's reaction to the *militantes* and its work among women. However, for all the generally acknowledged successes of the women's commission in helping women within the PCF, its members did not know how to approach their *camarades* (for the purpose of the meeting was to engage men as well as women in commitment to the commission's work) on these issues. Discussion of the proposed study day was begun by the women who had the most experience in the Party (35 years) who argued that it was essential to link explicitly the situation of women and the class struggle. Only if this articulation were made could the men be engaged in discussion because class struggle was what they understood. Beginning there it would be possible to raise other matters—of ideology, of patriarchy, of non-economistic questions.

However, the planning of this study meeting soon dissolved in a swamp of desultory conversation because, for the first time, the divisions which had appeared throughout the PCF, between Eurocommunists and those advocating a return to the *ouvrieriste* strategy, began to penetrate the *commission féminine* itself. The presence of a woman, not ordinarily an attender, who advocated more 'workerist' positions, caused the fragile unity of the women's commission to collapse into inaction. The meeting of the commission turned into a head-on conflict between 'feminists' and 'workerists', each of whom had very clear ideas of how to cope with women's needs in Paris South. The member of the group who was most committed to the analyses of the women's movement (and who eventually left the PCF, as described above) began by proposing that the planned meeting, instead of following the traditional Party format of beginning with a report by someone, should call on the men to testify about how they lived with the pain which they caused themselves by participating in the subordination of women. Most everyone at the meeting realised that such an initiative would fall flat. Indeed, it boggled the imagination to think of how the *camarades* of Paris South might react to such an open-ended proposal! While meetings in Paris South were less structured and more democratic in their proceedings, such testimonials were far beyond the realm of the conceivable. Beyond this, however, the proposal drew the fire of the 'workerist' woman who had come to the meeting especially to monitor the discussion of this matter. She announced passionately that the 'women in her cell' were not concerned about the pain of their subordination but rather how they were going to put food on the table.

This 'workerist' critique had its intended effect. It did in fact touch a weak spot in the work of the women's commission. Its members were aware that they had not succeeded in making contact with working-class women in the section and in finding out their interests and needs. In fact, they had tried in the past to approach these women and met with embarassing failures. Therefore, while not granting the validity of the argument that women were *only* interested in 'getting food on the table', the women of the commission realised that their work was vulnerable to criticism. Added to this vulnerability was the fact that, with the leadership's several campaigns to 'take the Party in hand' in full swing, there were no dates available for the meeting to be held. In the atmosphere of tension and disagreement which surrounded the women's commission, the lack of a date was seized upon by those present as somehow indicating that there was no longer any commitment within Paris South section to the work of the commission.

The result of the combination of time pressures, attack from the 'workerists', and the failure of the women closest to the women's movement to translate their concerns into a useable formula was that the day-long study session was never held. The idea was shelved and the women's commission never did develop a forum for presentation of its work to the rest of the section. Ultimately this proved to be the downfall of the group. More broadly, the commission was a victim of the general taking in hand of the Party in the fall of 1978. Because the commission refused to accept the leadership's direction, it was vulnerable to criticism. Because it did little effective work of its own (because of its lack of experience with being 'creative') it had nothing successful to counterpose to such criticism. Gradually the women's commission closed down. In a context in which the Party's line moved rapidly towards *ouvrierisme* the women's commission was unable to find a viable place for itself. It limped through the winter of 1979 in a crippled state and virtually disappeared in the months of preparation of the XXIII Congress.

Conclusion

The last part of the year following the electoral defeat of March 1978 was taken up with the preparation of the XXIII Congress scheduled for May 1979. The attention paid to women in the Congress document was much greater than in the past. Women's concerns for equality, for dignity, were placed on the agenda of struggles to be supported by the PCF as part of the Party's *union à la base* activities. However, at the same time as stressing the importance of struggles by women, the document reasserted traditional PCF attitudes towards women. Women were described as especially susceptible to the appeals of the bourgeoisie, appeals playing on the supposed fears of women of real social change. Thus despite its efforts to single out the significance of women's issues, the PCF was placing women in a 'minor' status again, implying that they, more than other social categories, did not know their minds and could not recognise the need for struggle to achieve real change. Such an emphasis of course, would make it difficult to promote joint actions with the women's movement in the context of *union à la base*. In fact, in the months after the Congress, the PCF became even more isolationist in its relationship with the women's movement, to the point where it refused full participation in national actions around the extension of French abortion legislation *(loi Veil)* in the fall of 1979.

What we see from this examination of the activity of the PCF, both at the highest level of the Party and in the rank and file, is the impossibility of considering the reaction of the PCF in one sphere in isolation from others. The PCF does not have a 'position on women' separate from its general strategic and theoretical stance. To the extent that these stances evolve, change, or develop, the relationships with mass movements and positions on their issues will change. The PCF was forced to do something 'about' women because of the changed social climate of the post-68 years. However, *what* it did (whether to be supportive or dismissive), *how* it was done (in alliance or isolation), and its successes and failures were determined not by the specific problems of women, but by PCF general strategy. With Eurocommunism, the PCF opened to 'new' women's issues and to the women's movement for a time. In the retreat to *ouvrierisme* after 1977, the Party began to back-track on women's issues too, as the old responses of dismissal, fear, and challenge re-emerged.

More generally, the processes which we have examined in this paper underline two central dilemmas which not only the PCF but all formations of the Left must confront. The first is a crisis of *militantisme*. It is no longer possible to count on completely devoted and single-minded militants, ready to serve the cause, in ways defined by the leadership, at any cost. In mass parties especially, many militants have developed new expectations about their role in the Party. They expect to be able to participate in strategic decision-making and to design their own contributions to political action. Party democracy means, for these militants, that their own creative abilities are honoured and their political judgements respected. The Left can either encourage such democratic creativity or it can confine the rank and file to the instrumental role of merely implementing the directives of the top leadership. For the PCF in 1977-78, the return to *ouvrierisme* brought a re-imposition of traditional controls over the actions of the rank and file of the Party, after the experience of earlier years when some practice had been more open and democratic. There were women in the PCF who expected their Party to support their struggles, to be more democratic, to listen to their voices. When these expectations were frustrated, the women provided a focus for discontent and challenge to those who would return to workerism. The story of Paris South demonstrates that these women were discouraged—either leaving the Party or moving on to other concerns. However, the legacy of the women's commission—as an effort towards the implementation of a Eurocommunist strategy—remains. Whether the effect will continue depends on how the general strategic conflict within the PCF evolves.

The second dilemma confronting the Left is a crisis of mobilisation.

In advanced capitalist societies a revolutionary strategy which relies exclusively on the working class has become less and less plausible. Some kind of alliance strategy is essential. A series of changes in post-war capitalism—universal education, consumerism, omnipresent electronic media, for example—have homogenised society to some extent, such that the boundaries between the industrial working class and other social categories are more blurred. Moreover, as the traditional industrial working class has either stagnated or decreased in size, changes in the occupational structure of the modern industrial system have created new work and workers with variable connections to that working class. A revolutionary party must design an alliance strategy, with the working class at its centre, which can engage these new social forces in a movement for radical change. Such forces may have an interest in profound social change. But this interest will be theirs, and not the working class's, at least to begin with. The strategic task of a revolutionary party must, therefore, involve the articulation of these different perspectives on change into a greater whole. This will not be easy. Not only do such new social groups develop their own notions of what kind of change they want, but also the kinds of organisational forms with which they feel most comfortable. Modern 'single-issue movements' (women, ecologists, students, consumers) seem to be characteristic forms of protest of such groups. The Left cannot afford to ignore or dismiss such movements. It must develop, with parts of these movements, a connection which is consistent with the Party's political goals and strategy for transition to socialism. The PCF currently faces this crisis of mobilisation, a crisis whose evolution and resolution depend upon the strategic choices that Party makes. The PCF is engaged in the process of choosing—choosing whether to push forward with a strategy which accommodates, based on understanding, the modern social movements of advanced capitalism (which are likely to be located outside the control of the party of the working class) or whether to dig into *ouvrierisme* and wait for the 'final crisis' of capitalism.

NOTES

1. For a discussion of the development of Eurocommunism in the PCF and a description of the uneven process of change in several spheres of Party practice, see J. Jenson and G. Ross, 'The Uncharted Waters of De-Stalinisation', *Politics and Society*, Vol. 9, no. 3, 1980.

2. The single best collection of the pre-Eurocommunist PCF thinking about women is *Les Communistes et la condition de la femme* (Paris: Editions sociales, 1970). This is a revised edition of *La Femme et le communisme* (Paris: Editions sociales, 1950). Another useful summary, especially because it lists the demands of women for reforms, is 'Le Role des femmes dans la nation', the report of the study session of February 1968 at Ivry, supplement to *Cahiers du Communisme*, Vol. 44, March 1968. The 1970 pamphlet publication, *Le Femme aujourd'hui demain*, the report of the study session of May 23-24, 1970, at Vitry, gives the

PCF's position as the Party entered the pre-Common Programme stage of Eurocommunism.

3. A rationale for the shift of attention toward working women, including an evaluation of the success of the UFF, is reported in Jeannette Thorez-Vermeersch, 'Pour la défense des droits sociaux de la femme et de l'enfant', report of a study session, October 24-25, 1964. The UFF did not disappear after this shift in attention, however. It remained the primary mass organisation for contacting women, except for the CGT unions. See, for example, Madeleine Vincent, 'Aller aux masses', *Cahiers du Communisme*, Vol. 45, December 1969, pp. 51ff.

4. One of the most problematic stances of the PCF *vis à vis* women in this period was taken on birth control. For more than a decade the Party campaigned against birth control, which was presented as a malthusian plot developed by the bourgeoisie against the working class. Internal opposition to this stand broke out in 1956, at the same time as the XX Congress of the CPUSSR and Hungary and was a major factor in deepening and sustaining the internal Party crisis of that time. Even in the mid-sixties antagonism to *planning familial* continued. By the 1970s, contraception was accepted as legitimate but the PCF always hastened to warn that no *individual* solutions could substitute for profound social change which would give all women the right and ability to bear children willingly. See, Jeannette Vermeersch, 'Faut-il choisir entre la paix du monde, l'interdiction de la bombe atomique ou le contrôle de la natalité?: Contre le néo-malthusianisme réactionnaire' in *Les Femmes dans la nation* (Paris: PCF, 1962); Jean Baby, *Critique de base: Le Parti communiste français entre le passé et l'avenir* (Paris: Maspero, 1960), pp. 75-86; *Femmes de XXe siècle*, La Semaine de la pensée marxiste (Paris: PUF, 1965); and 'Les Communistes et la famille' in *La Femme aujourd'hui demain, op. cit.*

5. The PCF was always very critical of the 'feminists' who were characterised as petit bourgeois, concerned only with legalistic improvements, or actually involved in diverting women from the real questions of class struggle. As late as 1970 the PCF reproduced Lenin's exchange with Clara Zetkin on the 'proper' type of work among women for revolutionaries. This violent critique of discussions of love and sexuality as an aspect of Party work, formed part of the PCF inheritance on the 'women's question'. There was usually an expressed fear that 'feminists' would mislead women, especially working-class women, into a mistaken judgement of the enemy and away from an understanding of the need for fundamental social change. Women were seen as particularly susceptible to promises by the bourgeoisie that change could come without overturning the established order of things. See, *Les Communistes et la condition de la femme, op. cit.*, pp. 107ff; 77-80; 120.

6. For a description of the women's movement in France see, Joelle R. Juillard, 'Women in France' in L.B. Iglitzin and R. Ross, *Women in the World* (Santa Barbara: Clio, 1976). For an analysis of the connection between this social movement and the political parties see, 'Interview with Christine Buci-Glucksman', *Femmes en mouvement* no. 12-13, December 1978-January 1979.

7. On the question of the strategy of the PCF in expanding into these *couches intermédiaires* see Jenson and Ross, *op. cit.*

8. PCF, *Le Socialisme pour la France* (Paris: Editions sociales, 1976).

9. Madeleine Vincent, *Femmes: quelle libération?* (Paris: Editions sociales, 1976).

10. After the XXII Congress of the PCF in 1976 there was a certain disparity between the tone adopted by Georges Marchais, Secretary-General of the PCF, and Madeleine Vincent, the member of the *Bureau politique* responsible for work with women. Such differences emphasise the only partial acceptance of Eurocommunism within the PCF. Marchais stressed the fundamental change

involved in women assuming greater roles in society, which he called an historic movement. He spoke of women's desire for dignity, for meeting their own aspirations to escape from the status of a minor in society. He emphasised that the PCF should do more, including bringing more women into the Party. Vincent, in contrast, was careful to draw attention to the fact that 'feminists' attacked men as the enemy and that they were easily victims of the majority's campaigns to trick women into thinking that real change could follow from the bourgeois parties' policies. She stressed that women were not all the same and that putting all women's concerns together 'under the same "female condition" so as to erase the realities of class would falsify the problem and mask the real solutions.' See 'Pour la femme: une vie heureuse, libre et responsable dans l'égalité'. Report on the Central Committee of the PCF, November 9-10, 1976.

11. *Femmes: pour changer votre vie,* the speech of Georges Marchais, Secretary-General of the PCF, Paris, December 3, 1977. (Paris: PCF, 1978.)

12. Centre d'Etudes et Recherches Marxistes, *La Condition féminine* (Paris: Editions sociales, 1978). While the book was published in 1978, after the electoral defeat, some of the themes and work had been in circulation for a number of years, some since *La Semaine de la pensée marxiste,* in 1975, which had taken as its theme, 'Femmes, aujourd'hui, demain'.

13. Maurice Godelier, 'Les Rapports hommes-femmes: le problème de la domination masculine', in *La Condition féminine, op. cit.*

14. Jean-Louis Moynot, 'La Force de travail féminine dans la production et la société', *La Condition féminine, op. cit.*

15. See, for example, M. Guilbert, 'Les Femmes actives en France, Bilan 1978'; A-M Lugan-Dardigna and L. Blanquart, 'La Reproduction des modèles dans la presse féminine. A qui profite le rêve des femmes?'; M-J Chombart de Lauwe. 'La Transmission sociale des catégorisations relatives au sexe', *La Condition féminine, op. cit.*

16. Yvonne Quilès, 'L'Idéologie sexiste, ça existe, je l'ai rencontrée' and Yann Viens, 'Femmes, politique et Parti communiste français', in *La Condition féminine, op. cit.*

17. 'Avancer vers la libération de la femme', the report of the study session, Argenteuil, June 10-11, 1978. Further developments in this direction of workerism are given in Gisèle Moreau, 'Pour accèder a l'égalité', *Cahiers du Communisme,* October 1978.

18. See *Le Monde,* June 11-12, 1978.

19. *Le Socialisme pour la France, op. cit.*

20. The CERM book, *La Condition féminine* indicated that the PCF federations had not all equally taken the advice of the leadership to promote women. See Viens, *op. cit.*

21. For important new information about the problems created by Eurocommunist women's expectations at another level of the Party—the Paris Federation—and the crack-down on women at this meeting, see Henri Fiszbin, *Les Bouches s'ouvrent* (Paris: Grasset, 1980).

HUGH GAITSKELL (1906-1963): AN ASSESSMENT

John Saville

The British Labour Party, since its early days, has always been a party of social reform whose ideas and policies have been largely articulated within a socialist rhetoric. There are certain crucial differences, at least in theory, between a party of social reform and a reformist socialist party. The former, whatever its social basis, may be defined as a party within a political democracy whose aims and purposes are the introduction of social reform into the existing structure of capitalist society; and whose objectives in no way challenge the fundamental property relationships of that society. A reformist socialist party, by contrast, is one whose long-term perspectives are the transformation of capitalism into one or other versions of a socialist society, to be accomplished through the steady modification of existing institutions, and by parliamentary means. The rhetoric and terminology of reformist parties are socialist; their practice is invariably moderate, involving piecemeal social change. These reformist socialist parties always have a Right, Centre and Left within their organisations, and it is, of course, the Left which will especially emphasise the long-term objectives of a socialist transformation. On these definitions the British Labour Party, once it adopted the Constitution of 1918, has been a reformist socialist party whose practice in and out of office has been discrete social reform.

Those who established the Labour Representation Committee in 1900—which became the Labour Party in 1906—inherited a body of ideas which were the Fabian version of liberal collectivism. The crucial assumptions may be summarised as the use of state power to remedy social injustice and, as far as practicable, social inequality; a neutral theory of the State which involved a passionate belief in the primacy of Parliament, and in the possibilities of absolute control by a working-class party once an electoral majority was assured; a firm conviction that there were 'rules of the game' to which all responsible political parties would adhere. For those who were the architects of the Labour Party in the early twentieth century, whatever their particular commitment to any particular version of socialist doctrine, a parliamentary majority equalled state power; and the history of the widening political democracy in Britain before 1900 was for them ample justification for their argument.

The basic assumption about political behaviour has always been the firm

148

conviction that political parties will play the parliamentary game according
to its traditional rules; and this is interpreted to mean that Conservatives
will accept the will of the majority at a general election, and will not seek
to subvert that will. But the thesis went further in the belief that there were
no forces in society that would be able to withstand effective political
control emanating from a majority government at Westminster. C.R. Attlee,
leader of the Labour Party between 1935 and 1955, made explicit these
ideas in a book written in 1937: his most radical political years, it may
be noted:

> The Labour Party opposes Government policy, and seeks to convert the country to
> its point of view, but it does not carry on a campaign of resistance, passive or
> active, to hinder the ordinary functions of government being carried on. It accepts
> the will of the majority, which has decided that the country shall be governed by a
> Capitalist government, and it expects its opponents to do the same when it is
> returned to power.[1]

There are certain corollaries of this general thesis that need emphasis.
The argument embodies the assurance that since real power resides in those
who control Parliament, the owners of economic wealth and strength can
either be legislated out of existence, or effectively curbed and regulated. It
follows, if these things are true, that there is no basis for the concept of
class struggle as in any way central to the dynamics of capitalist society.
'Interests' there are, of course; and many such interests will be so selfishly
motivated that only the most stringent management and administration
will curtail their anti-social effects. But this is far from any comprehension
of the meaning of class struggle; and it has always, therefore, been possible
for the Labour Party, and more particularly, the Labour Party leadership
to think and talk and act in terms of *national* interest rather than in terms
of working-class or socialist interest. And this approach—the concept of
national interest—has found expression in many different ways, from the
explicit statements of Ramsay Macdonald on the eve of the first minority
Labour Government in 1924 to Attlee's return from Potsdam in 1945, when
he recalled 'that our American friends were surprised to find that there was
no change in our official advisers, and that I had taken over with me [as my
Private Secretary] Leslie Rowan, who had served Churchill in the same
capacity'.[2]

There are two other consequences of the 'national interest' approach
that need emphasis. One, the supposed neutrality of the civil service, has
already been suggested. The other, the identification of Labour leadership
with the Conservatives over matters of foreign policy, is of great
importance and significance, and establishes the limitations of the social
parameters within which a Labour administration allows itself to operate.
The conflict over appeasement towards the Fascist powers in the 1930s
temporarily obscured what had already been an agreement over funda-

mentals before 1933; and it was during and after the Second World War that the acceptance of consensus in foreign affairs began to be taken for granted. After 1945, for a number of additional reasons this meant a position of subservience to the demands of American foreign policy, and although the reformist left wing of the Labour Party has usually had a different approach and stance, it has rarely been influential as a pressure group, and never effective against the basic conformity of the Labour leadership with Conservative assumptions and policies. There have been certain exceptions—the important matter of Indian independence is one—but in no area of parliamentary politics is the impact of socialist rhetoric so feeble as it is in foreign affairs; and in no period has this been so striking as the last 20 years.

The most important achievement of British labour in the twentieth century, now rapidly being undermined by the Thatcher Government, was the progressive incorporation of welfare policies into social life. The political strength, density and cohesiveness of the propertied classes in Britain have always been so powerful that advances in social welfare have come about only after intense political struggles; and the bitterness of the conflict has led many outside the Labour Party, as well as those within its ranks, to exaggerate what in practice has been obtained. Social welfare is quite commonly identified with socialism, and this supposed correspondence has been much fostered by successive Labour leaderships. What is remarkable here is the poverty of social-democratic theory in this, as in other contexts, and equally remarkable has been the failure of the Left, within and without the Labour Party, to offer a popular alternative: popular in the sense of its penetration into popular consciousness.

The leadership of the British Labour Party has undergone interesting, indeed significant changes in its social composition over the past eighty years. The Party emerged in the early years of the twentieth century out of the political alliance of the trade unions with numerically small groups of socialists; and it was the socialists who largely engineered the break with liberalism and the Liberal Party. Their support in the country at large was working-class and most of the leaders were of working-class origin, as were the majority of the Parliamentary Labour Party down to the Second World War. Within the Parliamentary Labour Party there has taken place, however, a gradual shift towards an increasingly influential middle-class stratum, professionally or university educated; and the change has been especially marked since 1945. It is not argued here that social origins are more than one factor in a constellation of complex forces determining political attitudes, or the balance of political forces within a Party of the Left. But life styles, and their changes over time, are not unimportant, and in the case of the subject of this present essay—Hugh Gaitskell—we have one of the more extreme examples of a Labour politician whose origins were far removed from the working people his Party was in existence to represent, and whose own upper-middle-class life style was in no way altered throughout his adult years.

The recent biography of Hugh Gaitskell by Philip Williams provides the opportunity for a re-appraisal. The work has been executed on a massive scale: 787 pages of text with another 212 pages of notes and index; and whatever the merits or otherwise of the volume, it offers an immense quarry for future research workers into the history of the Labour Party in the middle decades of the twentieth century.[3]

Gaitskell had almost no experience of the life of the Labour Party at its local levels, or of the wider movement in general. In this he was similar to Wilson, and unlike all the Labour Party leaders who preceded him: Keir Hardie, Ramsay Macdonald, Lansbury and Attlee. His father was an Indian civil servant, working mostly in Burma, and the family had a long tradition of service in the army. Gaitskell was educated at an upper-class prep school in Oxford, and then went to Winchester, a haven for the sons of the professional upper middle class which was supposed to be somewhat more intellectual than the general run of public schools. Winchester's impact on Gaitskell, according to his own account, was emotionally and intellectually stultifying. A good deal later in life Gaitskell wrote to his daughter Julia about the transition from the smothered atmosphere of Winchester to the heavenly freedom of Oxford: 'The great thing for me was the flowering of intellect and personality—much repressed at Winchester. Feeling oneself developing was exciting—and also getting rid of a lot of adolescent shames.'[4]

It is necessary to listen to the tone of Gaitskell's phrasing as well as to his actual words. He remained to a notable degree within an undergraduate vocabulary and intonation for the rest of his life. 'Heavenly freedom' was his phrase in 1959, four years before his death; and like so many among the British upper classes, he was marked by his school and university experiences to a quite extraordinary extent. Gaitskell's school career had been fairly undistinguished—the phrasing is that used by the public schools about their pupils—and in the closed circle of ex-public school boys in Britain, school careers have never been unimportant. Here is Philip Williams, discussing the relations between R.H.S. Crossman and Gaitskell in adult life, in terms that in most countries would be regarded as no more than adolescent chat, but which in his biography are presented as matters of fact; and which presumably are meant to be taken seriously: 'Crossman too was a Wykehamist: indeed their relationship was always warped, as Crossman (typically) recognised, by his own far more glittering record at the school.'[5]

Gaitskell's career at Oxford was interesting, not because his contemporaries thought him outstanding in any way, which they did not— he was academically quite good and got a First—but from the style of his life there. 'Oxford in the middle twenties' he wrote in 1959:

was gay, frivolous, stimulating and tremendously alive—it was a brief blessed
interval when the lives of the young were neither over-shadowed by the
consequences of the last war nor dominated by the fear of a future one. Most of
us sighed with relief and settled down to the business of enjoying ourselves.[6]

There is a revealing passage in Williams, again told straight, which is
instructive not only about Gaitskell but about university life at Oxford
in these years. In his first term Gaitskell went for elementary economics
tutorials to Lionel Robbins, then a very young tutor. Williams got the
story from Robbins. 'He would sit on Robbins' sofa reddening with
suppressed mirth at the mild impertinences of his Australian fellow pupil
until his decorous Wykehamist reticence broke down in peals of helpless
laughter.'[7] In other words, in his nineteenth year, still a giggling school-
boy. He was never, in his Oxford years, seriously interested in ideas; he had
no time for undergraduate or, except occasionally, for national politics;
he made what was regarded in the intellectual backwater that Oxford was
in the inter-war years—at least in the social sciences—the 'adventurous
choice' of Modern Greats (i.e. PPE: Philosophy, Politics and Economics);
he moved occasionally 'on the fringes of a homosexual set whose tastes
were then quite prevalent among the aesthetics'[8] and altogether he 'spent
much more time with girls than most undergraduates did', but many years
later he 'sharply denied having been a ladykiller'.[9] It is not clear whether
'ladykiller' is Gaitskell's word or a description by Williams. The former is
more likely, for Gaitskell never appears to have moved beyond a callow
appreciation of himself, and he seems to have had an unfortunate habit for
summing himself up in clichés. A few years before his death, when he was
in his early fifties, he wrote to a correspondent: 'To thine own self be true
was the great creed of my developing phase at Oxford. And I still believe
it is the most important thing of all.'[10] 'To thine own self be true': as
canting a phrase as the 'integrity' which Williams scatters through
many pages.
    It is difficult to discover what intellectual influences played upon
Gaitskell in his Oxford years. Housman was a favourite poet; Proust,
and the inevitable Lawrence, were among his admired authors; when he
was secretary of his College play-reading society 'he broke with custom
by bringing in modern authors like Ibsen and Strindberg'—a nice touch
of Oxford parochialism, Ibsen having been first played in London in the
late 1880s, and Shaw having written *The Quintessence of Ibsenism* in
1891. In his second year at Oxford Gaitskell began to read some socialist
theory which, except for half of volume one of *Capital*—which half is not
noted—was in the British Fabian tradition: Dalton, Tawney, the Webbs and
J.A. Hobson. Presumably a reading of this kind of literature was encouraged
by the choice of his degree, and he must have begun to think about social
questions; for the turning point in Gaitskell's career came at the time of the

1926 General Strike, when he took a decision that went against the stream:
he supported the strike.

This decision, of course, is of the greatest interest to the historian, for it
led to changes which affected the whole future life of Gaitskell. How did it
come about that the repressed adolescent from Winchester took this quite
momentous step out of his own class background? We are told that
already during his first summer vacation he was showing signs of
challenging certain traditional values, and there are other, quite minor,
pieces of evidence which point in the same direction; but the question is
not really confronted by his biographer. One must not, however, make too
much of a mystery of the affair. It only needed a modicum of decency to
overcome the accretions of class prejudice and refuse support to the
hard-faced mine-owners and their ministerial supporters; and at the same
time, it is necessary to note the limitations of Gaitskell's own support for
the strike. He thought the miners were being badly treated by the
Government, and he continued to collect money during the lock-out which
followed the ending of the General Strike. But intellectually, as against his
political commitment, the Strike does not seem to have made much
difference to him. He admitted—very much later in 1958—that 'I did not
honestly think a great deal about it. I knew that once the chips were down
my part was on the side of the strike. I considered that the Government
had behaved badly to the miners and that was that'.[11] The most important
personal, and political, consequence of his support was that it led to the
beginning of a close association with G.D.H. Cole. It was the latter's
influence that decided Gaitskell to take the British labour movement as a
special subject in his third year. Cole taught it, and this was Gaitskell's
first serious contact with some parts of the past history of the labour
movement. One of his undergraduate essays—on Chartism—was later
published as a WEA booklet. It is written very much in the Cole tradition
of these particular years; less radical, for example, than the Hammonds.

Oxford in the middle twenties; and G.D.H. Cole. One of the remarkable
features of British university life in the 1920s was the general absence of
anti-war sentiment and feeling, and a prevalence of liberal-conservative
politics among the very small minority who were politically-minded. There
was certainly a widespread, for the most part inarticulated, pacifist and
anti-war mood in the country as a whole—Wertheimer commented on it in
his 1929 volume on the Labour Party[12] but it was not until the late
twenties and early thirties that occurred the great outpouring of books,
plays and poems with their themes of bitterness, disenchantment and
betrayal.[13] During Gaitskell's years at Oxford anti-war themes were largely
absent; certainly Gaitskell himself left no record of being in any way
touched by them, and their absence is a not unimportant face in his
intellectual history. As to Cole, the interesting thing about him at the time
he became friendly with Gaitskell is that he was in the most reformist

phase of his whole political life. Guild socialism had come to an end, and the trauma of 1931 was still in the future. This was the period when Cole was working on the volume which was published in 1929—*The Next Ten Years in British Social and Economic Policy*—the most parliamentarian and Fabian of all his political policy statements throughout his career.

In the summer of 1926, then, Gaitskell made what was to become a lifetime commitment to the Labour Party, although no one could have predicted that at the time. There is no evidence that during his Oxford years he was involved in any personal or political experience that could be in any way described as radicalising; and it is interesting that the generation of Oxford socialists who were his contemporaries and who became well-known politicians or theoretical writers, all exhibited the same politically moderate stance as himself. Most of them, like Gaitskell, were certainly influenced by Cole; and these personalities include Colin Clark, E.A. Radice, John Parker, Douglas Jay and Evan Durbin, the last named being probably less persuaded by Cole than any of the others mentioned.

By the time Gaitskell left Oxford he had moved from a non-political liberal conservatism to a moderate labourist approach to political problems. But he was emphatically not a very political person in the way that Crossman was, and this was to remain true for many years afterwards. As a result of Cole's influence, Gaitskell spent a year as a WEA tutor in Nottinghamshire; and this is made much of in all accounts of his life. This was the time when he was supposed to have come closest to working people; when he taught 'unemployed miners at Nottingham, whose sufferings he never forgot'. This is Williams, writing on p. 767; but Nottingham, as he also told his readers on p. 22, 'was prosperous in 1927-8, and the coalfield was one of the least badly hit'. The miners' union was among the most politically moderate in the whole country, and in the aftermath of the General Strike it was the centre of the most serious breakaway union from the MFGB, that of George Spencer. Gaitskell in his own lifetime, and Williams in his biography, squeezed as much political capital as possible from this year among the workers, but the reality was somewhat different from the myth that has been allowed to form. Naturally Gaitskell learned something from the social contact with working people he now made for the first time in his life. But how much he learned, and the ways he learned it, and what he thought about his new experiences, need to be carefully examined. He was, it is clear, highly uneducated for the job of tutor to which he had been appointed. The first lecture he gave to a miners' class was on Saving and Economic Progress: 'the full classical doctrine in which thrift. . . is crucial'. Gaitskell was telling this story in 1952, and confessed he was surprised at what he called his 'audacity'. We get a remarkable insight into what Gaitskell really thought about this Nottingham year in a letter he wrote on the 9th December 1927—after he had been in Nottingham for just about two months. Williams quotes the three extracts given below in three different places, and most readers would not know, without a careful search of the footnotes, some 750 pages on, that it is one letter which is being referred to. Which order the extracts come in the actual letter cannot be judged; but they are quoted here in the order in which they appear in the biography. The first is a pleasant example of the, mostly, unconscious paternalism and snobbery of an upper-class Englishman towards the lower orders. The miners, Gaitskell wrote:

> the nicest sort of people—indeed I like very much all the working people I have met. . . more honest and natural than the Middle Class who are always trying to be something they aren't and who are never quite sure whether they are saying the right thing.

The second extract is an illustration of his intellectual naivety, and of the narrowness and parochial quality of his Oxford education:

> I am very interested in the question of 'class'. I would like to write something on it some time. It's quite extraordinary how important the thing is as a whole and historically though it does not exactly make my work difficult (sic). But of course meeting so many people who have lived and do live so utterly differently from oneself is peculiar.

And finally, the crunch: what he really felt about Nottingham and why he could not get away quickly enough. This third extract comes in the same letter, let it be said again, written about two months after he had arrived in the town:

> I see tremendous danger of stagnating here. I went to London a few days ago. The difference is quite remarkable—there is so much more vigour and better taste and better intelligence and more personality in the atmosphere.[14]

So by early May—not much more than six months after he had arrived in Nottingham, he had accepted another job. Not for him a commitment of any substance for his lovely miners—the 'nicest sort of people'. His less 'honest' and less 'natural' Middle Class friends and acquaintances were pressing him hard to find something more congenial to his own class and education; and when Noel Hall, of University College, London, offered him an assistant lectureship in economics, he took it, on the advice, among others, of Lionel Robbins. But Nottinghamshire, and the suffering miners, remained a most useful reference point. For the future Labour politician it was the answer to the question: 'And what did you do in the war, Daddy?'!

Gaitskell remained at University College for eleven years. As an economist he was of no more than average ability: W.A. Robson describing him as 'a nice, ordinary competent economist, we all meet dozens of them'[15] Gaitskell was not, from Williams's account, seriously concerned with the fundamental disagreements that existed among economic theorists during this decade, between the neo-classicists and the Keynesians; and in this un-concern he was following the leading personalities in the economics depart-ment of LSE. When Gaitskell first went to University College he attended the LSE lectures of Lionel Robbins, partly to learn something about lecturing techniques, partly to remedy his own intellectual deficiencies in the subject. Robbins was an extremely competent performer at the lectern, and he belonged to the extreme liberal tradition within orthodox economics. His practical politics, expressed mainly in the pages of the *Lloyds Bank Review,* were in the tradition now accepted by the Thatcher Government, and even Robbins in his autobiography had to refer in mildly disparaging terms to his own practical offerings at this time.[16] LSE economics was the bulwark of conservatism in the thirties against the heretical views coming from Cambridge. What economic teaching at LSE added up to was an intellectual mish-mash, contributed to by Arnold Plant, T.E. Gregory, Benham and, of course, 'the most distinguished muddle-head in Europe', as Keynes once described Friedrich von Hayek. Only a few of the younger tutors, in particular Kaldor and Lerner, seemed to be fully aware of what was happening at Cambridge before the *General Theory* was published in 1936. Now Williams does not help to situate Gaitskell at all clearly in these doctrinal conflicts, but the impression is that Gaitskell, who was neither very competent in theory, nor very interested, showed no signs of leaning towards Cambridge, and he remained uncritical towards LSE orthodoxy. The matter is by no means unimportant, since it confirms once again his easy acceptance of the ideas and values of his own conservative upbringing except where his direct, and narrow, political concerns were involved. There does not appear to have been any tension arising out of Gaitskell's acceptance of bourgeois values in general, and his social-reforming propensities; and one must assume that this was the consequence of the character and the nature of Gaitskell's reformist socialism, which in no way involved the vision of a radically different kind of society. He certainly pursued with vigour the exploration of reforming policies for future Labour governments. He became assistant secretary of the New Fabian Research Bureau, established by Cole in March 1931, and he was also chairman of the economics section. With Dalton and Jay he became a member of the XYZ, a select dining club where City sympathisers met for economic and financial discussions with certain of Labour's top leaders. Like many of his Labour friends, Evan Durbin in particular, Gaitskell was greatly impressed with the experience of Sweden. He was theoretically in favour of an extension of public ownership, equivocal on the subject of workers' control (which in fact dropped out of the discussion) and like all his Labour colleagues, was increasingly impressed with the supposed growing influence of the Bank of England and the Treasury over the City. The deduction was obvious: nationalise the Bank of England and the basic financial levers of control would be in a Labour government's hands. By the end of 1936 Gaitskell and Durbin had agreed that provided the Bank was nationalised, the socialisation of the joint stock banks was no longer a necessary condition for a short term programme.

What has often been missed in the discussion of the thirties was the effective consolidation and success of the right-wing theorists within the Labour Party. During the previous decade it had been the ILP intellectuals who provided blue-prints such as the Living Wage policies—never used, of course—but after 1931 it was the right wing which produced the ideas that proved lasting. It was not Cole, now returned to a more radical phase, nor Laski, nor the theoreticians of the Socialist League who were to underpin the post-1945 Labour Governments with their socialist theorising, but Dalton and the New Fabian nursery who elaborated the practical policies carried through in the aftermath of the war. It was certainly not obvious before 1939 that Gaitskell would be the most successful politician of the future, but it was the group of which he was a part who articulated the assumptions upon which the Attlee governments were to legislate. The group included George Catlin and Douglas Jay, Evan Durbin and Michael Postan. Both the latter were bitterly anti-communist and anti-Marxist; both were markedly revisionist (of traditionalist socialist theory) and Postan was closely involved in the discussion of the key text which Durbin published in 1938: *The Politics of Democratic Socialism*. So was Gaitskell, and after the initial wave of social radicalism in the two years or so immediately following the end of the Second World War, it was the ideas of the Dalton group that formed the staple theory of the Parliamentary leadership throughout the 1950s. Gaitskell later summarised the main objectives of the group as they evolved in the second half of the thirties:

> They believed in making the economy more efficient; they believed in the possibility of full employment; they believed in social reforms which would gradually undermine the class structure, so that in due course a happier and more socially just society emerged. These were the ideals they held in front of them, and it was in order to advance these that they had gone into politics.[17]

This was written in 1951, and there is a precision in the statements almost certainly the result of hindsight—the reference to full employment, for example—but in fundamentals this is an adequate summary. What is interesting about Gaitskell in this decade before the wars, however, is not that his economic policies were moderate and cautious—he *was* concerned about the possible flight of capital in the event of a Labour victory, but he did not think the problem at all insoluble—but that his political attitudes do not seem to have been even mildly radicalised. It has been a common historical phenomenon of the past forty years that many socialists who went through the thirties became at the time much tougher, more radical, in their political ideas and practice while their fundamental philosophy remained unchanged; so that when full employment and welfare policies became normal, it was not difficult to slough off the more militant political postures of the earlier period. Not so with Gaitskell, for whom the thirties was not a radicalising experience at any level. For a couple of years after 1931 he used fairly strong language on the platform, as did almost everyone who had not gone Macdonald's way; but with Gaitskell this phase did not last long. His Vienna experience was, in this context, quite crucial for an understanding of his personality. He went to Vienna in the autumn of 1933, attached to the university for the whole of the coming academic year. The Nazis had taken power in Germany in the spring of 1933; and Gaitskell was present in Vienna in February 1934 when Dollfuss ordered the attack on the socialist workers' tenements. Gaitskell acted in an exemplary way in succouring his socialist comrades, but the political effect upon him was to strengthen his support for parliamentary democracy, and to harden him against the political radicalism that was so commonly expressed within the Labour Party at this time. And it was in these years that he declared his total rejection of Marxism; hardly a point worth noting since his interest in the subject had never been more than marginal.

Before he went to Vienna he had become Labour candidate for Chatham. He was adopted in 1932, was a good candidate and effective campaigner, and polled reasonably well in the general election of 1935. He decided not to stand again for Chatham, and in 1937 rather reluctantly accepted an offer from South Leeds. His reluctance was because 'he had intended to concentrate on academic work and drop politics for the time being'[18]—an instructive comment for the year before Munich, and for a future leader of the Labour Party. But he was still not a political sort of person. This biography by Williams is massive, and nothing Gaitskell was concerned with, or interested in, is likely to have been missed. So when the very detailed index has no reference to any of the Hunger Marches (not even to Ellen Wilkinson's Jarrow march) or to the Left Book Club, or to George Orwell, or to John Boyd Orr or Dr. McGonigle, it must be assumed that these were not matters or events or personalities that greatly concerned him. There is one reference, and one reference only, to the Spanish Civil War where in a private letter Gaitskell expressed his anger against the Chamberlain Government; and unlike his close friend Evan Durbin he was unequivocally against Munich.

He remained, then, down to the outbreak of war, what he had been since his Oxford days: a collectivist liberal who like so many of his generation saw the Labour Party as the only political force capable of effecting radical social reform. Beatrice Webb, whose political evaluations and prophecies were by no means consistent or correct, seems to have got some things at least right about Gaitskell, following a visit from him to the Webbs in February 1936:

> [He] is said to be one of the rising young men in the socialist movement. Like Durbin he is fat and self-complacent; clever, no doubt, but not attractive; like Durbin, he is contemptuous of Cripps and a follower of Morrison and Dalton, and, I think, he is anti-communist... Gaitskell altogether demurs to our view that the younger generation are going definitely communist... The Trade Union Movement is today, he thought, stale-mated as a progressive force in Great Britain as it is in the USA... With a mass of unemployed, strikes are of no avail. Political action of a reformist character—including municipal administration, was the one and only way according to Gaitskell: he was in fact an orthodox Fabian of the old pre-war school. What is wrong about this group of clever and well meaning intellectuals... is the comfort and freedom of their own lives; they have everything to gain and nothing to lose by the peaceful continuance of capitalist civilisation.[19]

Gaitskell became a civil servant as soon as war began in September 1939; and after serving as a fairly low grade officer, he became *chef de cabinet* to Hugh Dalton when the latter was appointed Minister of Economic Welfare in the Churchill administration of May 1940. When Dalton was transferred to the Board of Trade in February 1942 Gaitskell went with him, and was first concerned with fuel policies and then with a wide range of problems connected with the home front. He proved an excellent administrator, and in these years learned a great deal about the relationships between the Civil Service, their Ministers and Parliament. In the general election of 1945, which brought a massive Labour victory, Gaitskell was easily elected for South Leeds, spent a year on the back benches and then in May 1946, became Parliamentary Secretary to Emmanuel Shinwell, the Minister of Fuel and Power. When Attlee reshuffled his government in October 1947 Shinwell was moved to the War Office, and Gaitskell took his place. Alf Robens became his parliamentary secretary. In the last year of the 1945 government, because of the increasing illness of Stafford Cripps, Gaitskell began to take on special responsibilities at the Treasury, a tribute to his growing reputation as an efficient administrator and Minister. After the general election of 1950, which left Labour with an overall majority of five, Gaitskell was made Minister of State at the Treasury, directly understudying Cripps, and in October 1950 he succeeded the latter as Chancellor of the Exchequer. He was only 44, and from a number of points of view it was an unusual appointment. For one thing, up to that time, senior members of Labour administrations normally had some standing with the rank and file of the Party; and Gaitskell had none. And there were serious rifts within the Cabinet—the position of Bevan being the most difficult—which might have been at least partly healed if a different appointment had been made. For Gaitskell was now confirmed and accepted as on the right wing of the Party, and in his own career it was the first major step towards the Party leadership. How far his academic and bureaucratic experiences over the previous two decades had hardened him into a revisionist of the existing reformist socialist approach is made clear by his biographer, summarising a comment made by Gaitskell at this time:

> On first learning that he was to take Cripps' place, Gaitskell had told William Armstrong [Cripps' private secretary, and now his own: later head of the Civil Service] that over the next ten years the principal task of a Socialist Chancellor would be the re-distribution of wealth, which unlike the greater equalisation of incomes was not generally accepted; once that was accomplished, the philosophical differences between the parties would gradually diminish and their rivalry would turn increasingly—as in the United States he said—into a competition in governmental competence.[20]

It may be noted at this point that Gaitskell's attitudes towards American political parties remained the same for the rest of his life. In visits in 1956 and 1960 he underlined the close parallels he found between the Democrats and the British Labour Party; and he found John Kennedy's administration especially sympathetic.

There is a further comment to be made about the Armstrong quotation. Greater equalisation of incomes, Gaitskell had said, was generally accepted—unlike the need to re-distribute capital wealth more equitably. Here he was at one with his colleagues and friends on the Right of the Party—now including Crosland—who in these years of the Labour Governments were seriously arguing that social changes of great magnitude had occurred, and that Britain was no longer a capitalist society in the hitherto accepted sense. This was the theme which dominated the symposium, *New Fabian Essays,* published in 1952. C.A.R. Crosland put the argument most emphatically in his contribution to the *Essays,* and not all his fellow contributors accepted completely his thesis; but all were agreed that changes of a quite fundamental kind had occurred. Crosland himself, while to an extent modifying his earlier thesis, was still writing in 1956 (in *The Future of Socialism*) that 'capitalism has been reformed almost out of recognition. Despite occasional minor recessions and balance of payments crises, full employment and at least a tolerable degree of stability are likely to be maintained'.[21] It was this belief that the unemployment and unused resources of the inter-war years were now no longer possible, together with an unqualified faith in the power of governments to legislate social reform of an egalitarian kind, that were the main intellectual foundations of the post-war Labour revisionists. They believed that the world boom they were living through was the result of improved economic techniques at the disposal of governments; that it was within the competence of governments, through financial policies, to control output, investment and the levels of employment in ways which would eliminate the sharp fluctuations of pre-1939 capitalism. It was, further, the continual refrain of Liberal and Conservative as well as many Labour commentators, that against this background of full employment in Britain there had taken place a marked diminution of economic inequality; income and wealth, and especially the former, were being more equally distributed; widening educational opportunities were increasing social mobility; the 1930s levels of poverty had gone for ever; and that there was developing a re-casting of the social structure, in Western Europe in general, whereby the working class and the middle classes were converging, in income levels and in life styles, and not least in social expectations.[22]

It is necessary to underline how widespread these ideas and beliefs were among Labour intellectuals of Gaitskell's own generation: those who supported him in his successful bid for the leadership of the Labour Party, and who sustained him thereafter. It is also necessary to note how close the connection was between the arguments of Crosland in the fifties and the earlier work by Evan Durbin, *The Politics of Democratic Socialism*, first published in the late 1930s and republished, with a preface by Gaitskell, in 1954. Durbin, until his death by drowning in 1948, had been Gaitskell's closest friend; and Gaitskell's preface to the 1954 reprint emphasised his intellectual debt to Durbin. The revisionism of the 1950s was for him, therefore, not a new mode of thinking about society; the experience of the war years and the period of Labour rule after 1945 did no more than confirm the political and social trends which he and his friends were already accepting before 1939. The new factor in the post-war years was full employment. Keynesianism offered a theoretical basis for what, in fundamentals, was already appreciated as the basis for their social reformism.

Gaitskell's promotion to the Chancellorship of the Exchequer was in October 1950. A few months earlier, in August, in response to strong American pressure following the outbreak of the Korean war, the Labour Government had agreed to increase substantially its armament programme: to £3,600 million over three years. On the 29 January 1951 Attlee told the House of Commons that the Cabinet had agreed on a further expansion to £4,700 million. The sum stated was a trebling of resources for armaments over a year earlier, and it represented an increase from 8 per cent of GNP to 14 per cent: the highest proportion in NATO, and exceeded only by the United States. There was, it should be added, no possibility that national resources could be made available on the scale proposed; indeed the Tories, when they returned to office, reduced the targets set by Labour. But the Attlee government had totally accepted the American version of world politics, and their agreement to increase their spending on armaments— which could only mean an end to an already greatly reduced commitment to social improvement—was wholly within the anti-communist spirit of the world reactionary crusade that America was leading. Inside the British Cabinet Gaitskell was a firm and undeviating supporter of the proposals for increased defence spending, and it was his Budget of April 1951, which imposed certain health charges in the interests of finding extra finance for armaments, that led to the resignation of Bevan and his colleagues. Throughout the last period of a faltering Labour administration—with most of its senior members ill or desperately tired—Gaitskell emerged, in Roy Jenkins' words, 'as the one strong man of the Labour Government's last year'.[23] And when the Tories won the election in October 1951, the most significant thing about Gaitskell was that he continued to push himself into a national role. It could easily, of course, have been otherwise. Gaitskell still had no base in the movement; the trade unions hardly knew him; and he was yet to make any mark in the annual party conferences or within the PLP. But Gaitskell had developed a shrewd sense of power, and he was extremely ambitious: characteristics which his biographer is oddly reluctant to accord him. But in the world of politics no one gets to the position of national leader by default. It has to be worked for.

The years which followed the defeat of Labour at the general election of November 1951 saw bitter internecine struggles inside the Labour Party. Attlee was 69 in 1952, and it was expected that his successor would soon be chosen. There were two obvious contenders: Herbert Morrison and Nye Bevan. Morrison had many enemies; the Left detested him; he suffered from Attlee's personal dislike; he had few friends among the trade union leaders; and his performance on foreign affairs had been disastrous. Nye Bevan, from a very different standpoint, also suffered from many of the same disadvantages, notably from the ferocious hostility of certain leading trade unionists, and the opposition of a majority of the Parliamentary Labour Party. But he had one outstanding area of support: the constituency parties. At the first Party conference after the Labour government's resignation—Morecambe 1952—Bevan headed the poll in the election for the constituency members, and Bevanites took six of the seven seats.

Gaitskell, by the time of the Morecambe conference, was just beginning to enter the arena in the contest for the leadership. He had continued to speak in favour of the rearmament programme after Labour left office—an unpopular stance with the rank and file of the Party—and already by the spring of 1952 some journalists were beginning to speak of him as the obvious rival to Bevan. What made Gaitskell's position clear beyond doubt as the future leader of the political Right of the Party happened in the immediate aftermath of the Morecambe conference. During the conference Arthur Deakin, bringing fraternal greetings from the TUC, had commented sharply on the 'struggle for the leadership'. His remarks included advice to the Bevanites to 'get rid of their whips, dismiss their business managers, and conform to the party constitution. Let them cease the vicious attacks they have launched upon those with whom they disagree, abandon their vituperation, and the carping criticism which appears in *Tribune*'. Much of the rest of his speech was lost in what Michael Foot described as 'Vesuvian' interruptions.[24] Four days later Gaitskell expanded on Deakin with a McCarthyite speech which immediately made him the obvious front runner for all right-wing trade unionists. Gaitskell himself had stood for the executive committee in the constituency section, and had polled 330,000 votes against 620,000 for Crossman, who was the lowest successful candidate. Gaitskell spoke to a small audience at Stalybridge, and what he said, whatever excuses his friends later made for him, he believed. While he claimed that the Party leadership had won all the major policy decisions, he alleged that many resolutions came from the *Daily Worker*. Here are his words:

> I was told by some well-informed correspondents that about one sixth of the Constituency Party delegates appeared to be Communists or Communist-inspired. This figure may well be too high. But if it should be one-tenth, or even one-twentieth, it is a most shocking state of affairs to which the National Executive should give immediate attention.

In another part of the speech he attacked the Bevanite press, and insisted that 'the solid sound sensible majority of the Movement' must reply. It would not endanger the unity of the Party:

> For there will be no unity on the terms dictated by *Tribune*. Indeed its. . . vitriolic abuse of the Party Leaders is an invitation to disloyalty and disunity. It is time to end the attempt to mob rule by a group of frustrated journalists and restore the authority and leadership of the solid sound sensible majority of the Movement.

It was a speech characterised in other places at this period as witch-hunting and inevitably it reverberated throughout the Labour Movement; it made any general rapprochement between Left and and Right out of the question; and it was the beginning of the alliance between Gaitskell and the right-wing unions—who commanded the majority bloc vote in Labour Party conferences—that was to bring him to the leadership of the Party.

The Stalybridge speech was calculated. As early as the previous July Dalton had noted in his diary that he found Gaitskell 'very tense and unsmiling. . . in danger of having an obsession about the B[evanite]'s' About the time of the speech itself Gaitskell wrote to a correspondent: 'it is clear to me now that we must fight. The worm must turn'. Four days later he wrote to another correspondent that if Attlee continued to remain silent, the morale on their side would collapse.[25] And after the

Stalybridge speech Gaitskell continued to enhance his role as the new, tough leader of the political Right that the unions had been looking for. They gave him the Treasurership of the Party, and he took a prominent part in the campaign to support German rearmament. In the attempt to expel Nye Bevan from the Parliamentary Labour Party Gaitskell once again exhibited his intransigence. After the failure of the last bitter episode in the affair he wrote in his Diary:

> [M]ost of my friends think I was very foolish to allow myself to be carried on by the 'right wing', with the inevitable result that the Bevanites 'framed' me as the 'Chief Prosecutor'... I always find it difficult to behave in these matters in the subtle way which my own friends seem to expect. I don't see how one can have strong loyalties with people like George Brown and Alf Robens, not to speak of the T.U. leaders, and continually refuse to do any of the dirty work for them and with them... my own position is no doubt weaker... but I cannot regard that as the only thing that matters. One would get no fun out of politics if one spent all one's life thinking in terms of the single object of one's own political success.[26]

Within less than nine months Gaitskell had been elected leader of the Parliamentary Labour Party; his 'fun' paid dividends.

With Gaitskell's accession to the leadership of the Labour Party the revisionist current entered into the mainstream of Labour Party policy-making. In the years from 1956 the re-statement of Labour policy in revisionist terms went ahead steadily, obscured for many by the conflicts over foreign policy and the nuclear debate; and although Gaitskell formally lost the constitutional battle over Clause 4—the wholly logical development of his own and the Party's revisionism in the 1950s—it made no difference to the reality embodied in Labour's programme. In the years immediately preceding his death in 1963, Labour Party policy was reduced to reformist objectives which now no longer even involved the rhetoric of the trans-formation of society into a socialist commonwealth. This was Gaitskell's main contribution to the history of the Labour Party in the twentieth century; and the limited perspectives for change which he offered to the Party over which he presided have lasted from his day until the present. Wilson, when he succeeded to the leadership after Gaitskell's death, followed carefully the Party policies Gaitskell had established; only his accent and intonation were different. And in Wilson's language it all sounded very different. As Crossman wrote in his Diary on 5 March 1963— less than two months after Gaitskell had died—the programme Wilson was articulating 'sounded astonishingly left wing... no one had any idea until that weekend that the Labour Party had quite radical policies on every subject under the sun.'[27]

While its socialist rhetoric in domestic matters has markedly weakened during the past twenty years, the Labour Party's conservatism is nevertheless most clearly pronounced in the area of foreign affairs. Here, since 1945, there has never been any pretence. Labour ministers in the war-time coalition had accepted Churchillian conservatism in world affairs; in office themselves after 1945 and led by Ernie Bevin, Labour's foreign policies were never seriously questioned by the Conservative Party: a statement which even includes the acceptance of Indian independence. Acquiescence in reactionary policies abroad cannot be combined with radical policies at home—radical, that is, in socialist terms; and to use this touchstone to evaluate Gaitskell's politics reveals his traditionalism in the context of any serious structural change in the organisation of society. During the Second World War his biographer offers no suggestion that Gaitskell ever had doubts about Coalition foreign policies, of which Greece was one of many which seriously troubled British socialists. In the Attlee Government after 1945 Gaitskell was a close and earnest supporter of Ernie Bevin; an early convert to the Cold War; and among the Cabinet's most resolute supporters of the vastly increased rearmament programme, for which as Chancellor in 1950-51, he had to find the money. Inevitably, he supported America over Korea, and equally inevitably, he supported and vigorously advocated German rearmament. In October 1954 *Tribune* quoted him as saying: 'I doubt if foreign policy will play a big part in the next election—not because it is not important, but because Mr. Eden has, in fact, mostly carried on our policy as developed by Ernest Bevin, in some cases against the views of rank and file Tories';[28] and at the time of the 1955 election Gaitskell wrote to Dalton that he was 'quite sure that. . . the less we bring foreign policy in the better'.[29] Throughout his years as a leading Labour politician Gaitskell was an enthusiastic, committed and undeviating supporter of the American alliance. After the 1952 Morecambe conference, at which the Labour right wing were so decisively rejected by the constituency parties, he told a journalist: 'There is only one thing we have to do in the next few years, and that is to keep the Labour Party behind the Anglo-American alliance'.[30] And the climax of his support for the alliance in general, and for the conservative establishment at home, came in the bitter debates at the end of the decade over the nuclear bomb; which he won.

Gaitskell came to the leadership of the Labour Party partly, at least, because of the electoral history of the previous three decades. The Party leaders between 1945 and 1951 were already prominent figures before the war began. But in 1931 the Parliamentary Labour Party had been reduced to around 50, and the 1935 general election only gave them another 100. When Attlee came to choose his government in 1945, there was at least one missing generation in the middle ranks of experienced politicians. Gaitskell became Minister of Fuel and Power at the age of 41; Harold Wilson went to the Board of Trade when he was under 30. With a larger field to choose from, it is unlikely Attlee would have nominated Gaitskell as Chancellor of the Exchequer when he did.

Gaitskell proved to be a not very effective politician, and on a number of tactical issues within the Party he made serious mistakes. He was, indeed, an appalling tactician. What sustained him, in his struggle for the leadership, and subsequently, was the block vote of the right-wing trade unions. It is true that by the time of his death his authority within the Labour Party was greater than it had ever been, and was, in fact, unchallengeable. But Bevan by this time was already dead, having several years earlier made his political accommodation with Gaitskell and the right wing of the Party; the Left without Bevan, and defeated over the nuclear issue in 1961, were in disarray, their situation apparently made more confusing by the anti-EEC stand that Gaitskell was beginning to advocate—a position, it should be added, that had nothing to do with socialism.

Gaitskell, by upbringing, education and professional training, was well conditioned for the role of a very moderate political leader in the particular and peculiar moment of time represented by the 1950s. 'He was' his biographer summed him up,

> the standard-bearer of Attlee's post-war consensus, labelled and misinterpreted as Butskellism: the mixed economy, the Keynesian strategy, full employment, strong but not overweening trade unions, the welfare state, the Atlantic alliance, decolonisation, and a tacit understanding that governments, whether moderate Conservative or democratic Socialist, would not strain the tolerance of the other side too violently. That legacy makes him a natural hero for social democrats.[31]

No doubt: except that some things are missing from this nostalgic account of life as it was in the decade or so before 1963—such matters as British Guyana, Cyprus and Aden, for example; or the extraordinary profiteering bonanza that the 'new-style' capitalism enjoyed in Britain in the 1950s; or MacCarthyism, an international as well as an American phenomenon; or the rapid slide towards full-scale intervention in Vietnam in the years immediately preceding Gaitskell's death; or Nasser's nationalisation of the Suez Canal, one of the very obvious signs of the stirrings in the colonial and neo-colonial world. The 'post-war consensus' in Britain was a short-lived, parochial and myopic response to a rapidly changing world that within a decade of Gaitskell's death would be in long-term crisis: its tensions and contradictions obvious to all, including even social-democrats. Moreover, on his own home ground Gaitskell misread the course of social change. In the year before Gaitskell died, Richard Titmuss published his *Income Distribution and Social Change,* in which the widely accepted beliefs of the supposed income-levelling trends in British society were sharply denied; and since 1962 the literature on social inequality and the 're-discovery' of poverty has been extensive, and its documentation has destroyed the easy generalisations of the Labour revisionists of the 1950s. But when all has been said about Gaitskell's lack of skill as a political leader or his failure to understand the contradictions developing in the world or the naivety with which he approached the economic complexities of his own society, it is the English middle-classness of his political attitudes and reactions that remains with the reader of the Williams biography. Here, as a last example, is part of a letter Gaitskell wrote to a friend at the height of the crisis in France in May 1958, two days before de Gaulle became prime minister:

> Oh God isn't the news awful? de Gaulle doing his best to lose us the Cold War and Cousins doing his best to lose us the Election. I feel very sad about France—worst of all is the hypocrisy—Army officers seizing power and trying to pretend it's all quite legal—People assuming that this old egotist of 67 can solve their Algerian problems. . . when it's all really just this bad temper induced by humiliation and inability to accept the facts of life.
>
> I'm afraid that what looks like being a military dictatorship in all but words will have a terrible effect on NATO and the West. The Communists will gain as the 'resisters'—neutralism will spread—and left-wing parties everywhere will be driven further left—or at least become pacifist. It's bad enough having to back reactionary feudal regimes in the Middle East and I've never been very keen on Portugal as a nice representative Democratic State—but to have France like this![32]

The writer of these words was the leader of the British Labour Party who, had he lived, would have been a Labour Prime Minister. Instead, the Labour movement got Wilson who sounded, but was not, different.

The Gaitskell biography by Philip Williams is a long drawn-out argument for the defence. Williams liked Gaitskell, and greatly respected him, and while there is a large amount of information provided for the reader, it leans very obviously to Gaitskell's side. This enormous volume is useful because it offers the possibility of a discriminating analysis different from that put forward by Williams. The biography, it must also be said, is hopelessly ill-proportioned; it would have been a good deal more useful if cut to a third of its present size, and it needed to be more sensibly balanced between its different parts. The war years and the Attlee governments do not require for example over 150 pages to explain the main trends of Gaitskell's career over this period. There are, too, some methodological questions to be scrutinised: the large scale use, for example, of oral testimony. Obviously, a biography of this kind must rely quite heavily upon the opinions of contemporaries, but the evidence offered needs always to be very carefully evaluated. There are some respondents used by Williams in whom one can have no confidence; there is at least one who is widely known as a very intelligent story-teller of half-truths and falsehoods, when it suits the purpose. Oral historians cannot afford to be promiscuous in these matters. It may be doubted, to quote a trivial example, whether Gaitskell's impact on people really was 'absolutely magical' to quote one gushing respondent from the war years;[33] and on a more serious level, is it possible that Eric Roll thought Gaitskell 'tremendously impressive' when they met at a weekend conference in the 1930s? Twenty years later Roll might well have made this judgement, but in the earlier decade Roll was well-known as a Marxist economist whose name was often coupled with that of Maurice Dobb, and it is improbable that he would have given any marks at the time to one of Dalton's revisionists.

In the same month that Williams' biography was published in the autumn of 1979 Dora Gaitskell gave a remarkable interview to Polly Toynbee which was published in the *Guardian* on 15 October 1979. We must make the assumption that Polly Toynbee got most things right, and that her straight quotations from Dora Gaitskell are accurate. The marriage, it was made abundantly clear, was a happy one; but the interview confirmed that in his personal attitudes as well as his political life Gaitskell remained to a marked degree the product of his conservative upbringing. He treated his wife kindly, affectionately, but not generously. She knew nothing of his considerable investments—the result of a large legacy left him when he was a young man—and during his lifetime Dora Gaitskell never had much money of her own. More telling was his general attitude towards her as a person in her own right. Here are her words as quoted in the *Guardian* interview:

> I think that he never really gave me as much confidence in myself as he could have done. He never really encouraged me at all. I was only for domestic life, and I feel now I could have done more with my life.

The central problem of this biography, however, remains its assessment of Gaitskell as a political figure. Williams sums him up as the outstanding leader lost to Britain in the last twenty years of decline, a theme taken further by a number of reviewers of the volume. But there is nothing in Gaitskell's career to suggest that he seriously comprehended the world in terms that were qualitatively different from those understood by his Labour Party successors, or that he could have provided solutions to the world crisis of capitalism that has been steadily growing during the past decade. Wilson and Callaghan followed the lines of country that Gaitskell had already mapped. The fundamental consensus with the Tories that Gaitskell bequeathed to those who followed him became deeply embedded in Labour Party thinking and practice; and the logic of that kind of accommodation, when set against the background of worsening crisis, led inexorably to the revisionism of the radical Right which the Thatcher Government represents. On the world scale, Gaitskell's defeat of the anti-nuclear movement in Britain, and his fundamentalist support for the

American alliance, have contributed to the increasing militarisation of the world today and have made immeasurably more difficult a movement for disarmament and a lowering of tension. Gaitskell's legacy to the British Labour Movement, continued by Wilson and Callaghan, has had disastrous results, the consequences of which are only today beginning to be seriously debated in the aftermath of the electoral defeat of 1979. There is a very long way to go.

NOTES

1. Attlee, C.R., *The Labour Party in Perspective* (1937), p. 219.
2. Miliband, R., *The State in Capitalist Society*, (1969), p. 111.
3. Williams, Philip M., *Hugh Gaitskell, A Political Biography*, (Cape, 1979). Where only page references are quoted, it is this volume to which they refer.
4. Williams, p. 15.
5. p. 14.
6. p. 13.
7. p. 16.
8. p. 14.
9. p. 14.
10. p. 13.
11. p. 19.
12. Wertheimer, E., *Portrait of the Labour Party*, (1929), esp. Ch. 4.
13. For a brief discussion, see John Saville, 'May Day 1937' in Asa Briggs and John Saville (eds.) *Essays in Labour History*, (1977), esp. p. 248 ff.
14. pp. 22-29.
15. p. 81.
16. Lord Robbins, *Autobiography of an Economist*, (1971), Chs. VI and VII.
17. p. 72.
18. p. 75.
19. pp. 61-2.
20. p. 240.
21. Crosland, C.A.R., *The Future of Socialism*, (1956), Ch. 2.
22. See John Saville, 'Labour and Income Redistribution' in *Socialist Register* (1965) pp. 147-162; J. Westergaard and H. Resler, *Class in a Capitalist Society*, (1975) esp. Part I.
23. Jenkins, Roy, 'Leader of the Opposition' in *Hugh Gaitskell, 1906-63*, (ed. W.T. Rodgers, 1964), p. 118.
24. Foot, M., *Aneurin Bevan, Vol. 2, 1945-1960*, (1973), p. 381.
25. p. 304.
26. p. 345.
27. p. 785.
28. Quoted in R. Miliband, *Parliamentary Socialism*, (1961), p. 333, note 1.
29. p. 352.
30. p. 308.
31. p. 779.
32. p. 518.
33. p. 30. The quotation from Eric Roll, which follows in the text, is on the same page.

ZIMBABWE: THE NEXT ROUND*

John S. Saul

Marxists and other progressives have quite correctly celebrated the success of the Zimbabwe African National Union (ZANU) in the Zimbabwe elections of 27-29 February of this year as a triumph of heroic proportions. Whatever the difficulties which may now confront the Zimbabwean revolutionary process the fact remains that in those three days over 80 per cent of the adult African population in Zimbabwe (those who voted for ZANU and the other wing of the Patriotic Front, the Zimbabwe African People's Union—ZAPU), stood up, quite literally, to be counted in the final act of wresting their freedom from settler political domination. And they did this in spite of attempts to blunt any such statement, attempts made by British officialdom (through the terms imposed during the Lancaster House agreement and through the activities of Lord Soames and his team on the ground), by the structures, very much intact, of the Rhodesian settler state itself, and by Bishop Muzorewa and his cronies (including his huge private army, albeit one well subsumed within the white military hierarchy, of 'auxiliaries' and such backers as South Africa and a wide array of international economic concerns). Moreover, contrary to the claims of some unsympathetic journalists, the vote was for far more than merely ending the war. Most Zimbabweans sensed that the Patriotic Front, and particularly ZANU, also bore the promise of a new social order, one defined, however vaguely, in ways which would serve the interests of the broad mass of the impoverished black population and, in particular, the interests of the country's rural dwellers.

The immediate aftermath of the election came as something of a surprise, however. Here was the Prime Minister-designate Robert Mugabe, the Marxist wildman of settler and South African propaganda whose party's militant Maoist formulations had scorched the pages of its journals, *Revolutionary Zimbabwe* and *Zimbabwe News*, for a number of years, announcing calmly that

*This essay was originally presented to the 'Conference on Zimbabwe' held at the University of Leeds, June 20-21, 1980. Although all customary disclaimers to collective responsibility apply, the author wishes to thank a number of friends in Toronto (especially Steve Gelb and Susan Hurlich), in Leeds (especially Lionel Cliffe), and in Binghamton and Los Angeles, for encouragement and assistance, and for the opportunity to discuss the issues involved.

as far as we are concerned, we have stated quite clearly that we are not going to interfere with private property, whether this be farms, or the mining sector, or the industrial sector... We recognise that the economic structure of the country is based on capitalism and that whatever ideas we have must build on that. Modifications can only take place in a gradual way.

True, he looked eventually to 'meaningful change in our lives' and spoke, in following days, of the need to deal vigorously with the land question. But even the relatively modest statement of intent to 'evolve a socialist pattern' for the Zimbabwe economy which appeared in ZANU's electoral manifesto was noticeably downplayed. Now such 'socialism' as came front and centre referred primarily to the desire to meet the welfare require-ments of the mass of the population in terms of health and education. Far more dramatic than any socialist themes in his initial statements, in fact, was Mugabe's embracing of General Walls, Commander-in-Chief of the Rhodesian Armed Forces and the man who had directed the carnage inflicted upon Zimbabwe (and upon neighbouring Mozambique and Zambia) during the war. The latter was being asked to preside over the integration of the three forces (Rhodesia's, ZANU's and ZAPU's) into a single national army, working, it was announced, 'in conjunction with the ZANLA and ZIPRA commanders' and with 'the assistance of British military instructors'. Beyond that, 'co-existence' with South Africa was stated to be a central feature of the new government's policy!

Had the electoral denouement to the eight-year war (and much longer political struggle) merely brought forward a neo-colonial anti-climax? Initial reaction was only somewhat mixed as white settlers, South Africa and western media-mongers alike rushed to embrace this show of 'pragmatism'. 'To believe it is a Marxist government seems to be totally fallacious', stated Sir Ian Gilmour, Britain's Deputy Foreign Secretary, almost at once in Parliament when taxed by the right wing of his own party for allowing Mugabe to slip into power. 'How Mugabe changed his spots', read the headline in London's prestigious *Observer*.

Though *Business Week* still worried 'whether Prime Minister Robert Mugabe will—nor indeed can—stick to the moderate line he has taken' (5 May 1980), Bridget Bloom of London's *Financial Times* had soon seen enough encouraging signs to conclude that 'for those people in Britain who thought that ZANU meant communism, Mr. Mugabe's victory ought to be especially poignant'. 'Perhaps', she added, 'it may become an object lesson for those who are so apprehensive about change in Namibia and South Africa!' Similarly *African Confidential,* a London-based and some-times well-informed scandal sheet, emphasised that 'Mugabe's victory was based primarily on military stamina and traditional nationalism, not on Marxism' and looked to a 'technocratic core' in the new Cabinet to help Mugabe with 'the key theme of (his) next few months': 'the cooling of his own militants'. Even the *Financial Mail*, South Africa's most intelligent and hard-headed business journal, which had warned darkly of a Marxist takeover of Rhodesia only weeks before (and hinted at a possible case for South African intervention to prevent such a result), began almost immediately after the election to speak of Mugabe as a possible 'force for stability' and within weeks stood in praise of 'the renewed and continuing evidence of moderate pragmatism from Mugabe himself'.

Clearly some of this enthusiasm was genuine, whether based on a careful (if controversial) reading of the auguries by certain analysts or merely on a massive sigh of relief (the reaction of many settlers). At the same time some of it no doubt reflected the belief that even if Mugabe's concessions were merely tactical they should be encouraged in the hope of eventually hardening them into a pattern of compromise with Zimbabwe's capitalist infrastructure from which it would be difficult for the new government to retreat. Perhaps no-one presented the basis for this alternative reading of the situation as subtly as David Willers (of the egregious South Africa Foundation) in a special column of the *Financial Mail* (4 April 1980) 'What can an Italian political prisoner, who died of maltreatment by Mussolini's secret police in a fascist prison in 1937, have in common with Robert Gabriel Mugabe, Prime Minister-elect of the new Zimbabwe?', Willers asked, and answered his own question: 'Perhaps plenty'.

For in Willers' view Mugabe is 'no wishy-washy African socialist'. Like Gramsci, who avoided premature confrontation and counselled 'tactically winning influence and control over the trade unions, cultural agencies, media, education, religion and the main production centres', Mugabe 'appears to be following the Gramsci line in every respect and (has) thus far averted a rebellion by the bourgeoisie'.

> Tactically, Mugabe has been without fault: a primary objective, namely to persuade the Rhodesian *bourgeois* whites that ZANU-PF is a national, credit-worthy party of reconciliation, free of obedience either to the Russians or the Chinese, has largely been achieved. The emphasis, aimed at wooing the middle classes, has been on moderation. Lulled into a sense of security by a projection of ZANU-PF as a party of economic sanity, the bourgeoisie have not complained.
>   . . . One hopes that Rowan Cronje will be proved wrong when he feared that whites would be kept on in Zimbabwe merely for economic expediency or as neutral factors of production. However, it is difficult to escape the conclusion that Robert Mugabe will soon be taking far-reaching and meaningful steps to turn his country into a socialist state on the Gramscian model. . .

Willers' conclusion: 'There will be plenty of scope for free enterprise, but the advantages will lie with those businessmen who have learnt their dialectics!'

What are those on the left to make of such diverse interpretations? In an interview with Karen Gellen (*The Guardian*, New York, 26 March, 1980),

Kumbirai Kangai, the new Minister of Labour, challenged the 'ultra-"left" criticism already coming from some elements of the U.S. left (which says) that ZANU. . . has "sold out" the Zimbabwean revolution'.

> The goals we were fighting for have not been abandoned. We think people should give us a chance and see what is going to happen in our country. . . We believe we are going through a national democratic revolution whereby the institutions, the society has to be democratised. This is a national democratic phase but it is also a transition to socialism. Our leader has made it clear that we envisage a socialist society in the final analysis. Of course things can't be done overnight—we have to reeducate some Zimbabweans as we go along. But the means of production will have to be controlled by the peasants and workers themselves, and we are moving toward that goal.

In and of itself such a statement does not prove Willers' point, though it certainly lends it weight. Nor is it an argument for suspending judgment altogether, an error the left has made all too often in the past with reference to various presumed 'transitions to socialism'. Still, it may serve to remind us of how early in the process of defining a new Zimbabwe the present moment is, and serve too as a warning that humility and caution are in order in commenting on such a situation. Where, then, to begin an analysis of the 'next round' in Zimbabwe?

I

Obviously in making sense of the current situation much will depend upon our reading of the character of ZANU, of the class forces which it represents and of the kind of politics and ideology which it has come to embody—of how well, in short, ZANU itself really has 'learnt its dialectics'. Such a reading is no very straightforward exercise, however; the evidence is slippery, as we shall see, and the scope for difference of opinion and of emphasis vast. For this reason there may be some point in bracketing temporarily the ZANU question in order to look at the actual terrain for manoeuvre which confronts a Mugabe conceived, for the moment, as Willers' consummate Gramscian tactician. It is, in any case, a way of posing the issue from which Marxists can hope to learn. Lenin's enforced reversion to the New Economic Policy, Mao's early post-1948 dalliance with China's 'national capitalists', suggest that, in the transition to socialism, the shortest distance between two points is not necessarily a straight line, that 'ultra-leftism' can sometimes be as dangerous as going too slow. What of the Zimbabwean case in this regard?

Certainly the inherited terrain is formidably congested and the need for tactical dexterity patent, even if (especially if?) a transition to socialism is on the agenda. A good starting point would be to remind ourselves that Zimbabwe possesses a notably dependent capitalist economy, yet one which is at the same time much more developed than is the norm in Africa. Well endowed with minerals (chrome, copper, nickel, asbestos), gold is at present the country's largest foreign exchange earner, while on the agricultural side, as much as one-half of Rhodesia's agricultural production is exported, contributing a third or more of foreign exchange earnings. Nonetheless, this is also an economy where a quite highly developed manufacturing sector accounts for about a quarter of gross domestic product; this sector expanded notably after the Second World War when Southern Rhodesia was hub for the Central African Federation, grounded itself (with considerable government encouragement) during the UDI and sanctions period, and is now of substantial importance.

Despite such diversification, however, concentration of ownership and a very high degree of external control has remained one of the economy's two most distinctive characteristics (the other being the fact that black Zimbabweans are estimated to control no more than 12 per cent of the productive capacity of the economy!) Thus domestic capital—in agriculture, light industry, commerce and services—merely fill the gaps in an economy, described by Stoneman, Bratton, Clarke and others,[1] in which 7.6 per cent of manufacturing firms produce 68 per cent of total output and where, of the country's fifteen leading profit-earning companies, twelve are foreign-owned (as are all four banks), in which mining production, having quadrupled in value between 1964 and 1976, is almost entirely dominated by foreign firms (88 per cent of jobs and 95 per cent of output), and in which, even in agriculture, perhaps as much as three-quarters of profits accrue to externally-owned plantations and estates. A number of very large companies control key sectors—Turner and Newall (asbestos), Union Carbide (chrome), Lonrho (mining and manufacturing), Delta (South African Breweries)—while the South African giant, Anglo-American, which is in mining (nickel, copper, coal), iron and steel, agriculture (Hippo Valley for sugar, Mazoe Estate for citrus), and milling and which has one or more directors on eighty-two different companies, has spread itself right across the economy. Indeed, the only real shift in this pattern during the UDI period was towards a much higher stake for South African capital in the mix, the latter now beginning to rival British capital for the lead in this respect (with American and other capital further back, though by no means absent from the game—especially in mining).

Of course these firms all rely on migrant and low-wage labour and have almost all been involved in high levels of remittance of repatriated profits and dividends, two things the Mugabe government can be expected to bridle at. But even in noting these facts in a recent special supplement on Zimbabwe, London's *Financial Times* could still smugly affirm that 'foreign-owned companies provide many jobs which the new Government cannot afford to jeopardise when it already has widespread unemployment to cope with. They are a primary source of imported technology for the relatively sophisticated manufacturing sector. They can provide expertise in finding export markets. . . and they have ready access to sources of international capital.' On balance the FT apparently concludes that possession of such bargaining counters does make private capital relatively immune from radical governmental action. Note, too, the conclusion of Duncan Clarke, an economist very much more sympathetic to the cause of a transformed Zimbabwe than the *Financial Times*:

> It is hard to find a sub-Saharan African example comparable to the Zimbabwean case, in which the role of foreign investments has been so long established, as deeply integrated into the sectors producing the bulk of output, so strongly interconnected with local capital, and in consequence probably as difficult to foresee being quickly and successfully altered.

Under such circumstances, it is not difficult to understand and indeed sympathise with the statement in the ZANU electoral manifesto to the effect that 'one of the existing practical realities is the capitalist system which cannot be transformed overnight.' Yet what meaning is then to be given to the attendant formulation that 'private enterprise will have to continue *until circumstances are ripe for socialist change*' (emphasis added)?

In fact, it has been tempting for Mugabe, on at least one occasion, to present the substantial state sector which does exist—marketing boards, electricity, railways, airline, post and telecommunications, an Industrial Development Corporation, all these together accounting for one-third of the country's total economic activity—and the quite diverse assortment of available state controls—over prices, imports, foreign exchange, new projects, many of these worked out to enable the settler state to battle sanctions—as some initial approximation to socialism. He must know better but, as hinted, it may seem to him dangerous to claim much more at present. The economy, despite an initial post-UDI decade of dramatic expansion, has more recently (since the mid-70s) experienced a serious crisis, structural in essence given the marginalisation of so much of the population, but compounded by rising oil prices, the spill-over of South Africa's own crisis, and the high costs of the war. Now that the lid is off fuller African participation in the economy (and sanctions lifted), Mugabe seems content to let businessmen, and market forces, get things moving again, rather than risk the short-term uncertainty, disruption (including possible food shortages) and *increased* unemployment that could follow from a deeper-cutting approach to the private sector and any resultant flight of capital and personnel. Certainly, right from the outset of their term, Mugabe and his ministers have striven mightily to scotch rumours that nationalisations in the industrial and mining sectors are on tap; moreover, it is obvious that the rather startling appointment of the Rhodesia Front's David Smith, once Ian Smith's Finance Minister, to the Commerce and Industry portfolio in the Mugabe cabinet was designed to deliver a similar message to the private sector.

Only limited clues are available as to which way the new government is prepared to go in the longer run. It goes without saying that many (most?) elements in ZANU ultimately would be much more comfortable with a production pattern which, even at the minimum, serviced the 'basic needs' of the population in ways that 'market forces' are never likely to do. And then there is the recently published UNCTAD report, 'Zimbabwe: Towards a New Order', whose preparation was supervised on behalf of the Patriotic Front by Bernard Chidzero, then a U.N. functionary, though now Zimbabwe's Minister of Economic Planning and Development. This report, in advocating the move from political to 'economic independence', does call for a markedly increased range of state action: nationalisation of banks, extended control over industry and mining (including the possibility of nationalisation of the latter sector), and significant regulation of private sector investment decisions. In addition, it lays considerable emphasis upon the establishment of workers' control in all economic sectors. Chidzero, now receiving the report in his new role as Minister, emphasised that no 'precipitate or unconsidered measures' would follow from it. Nonetheless, the fact that Information Minister Nathan Shamuyarira affirmed 'the general thrust of the report (to be) in step with government thinking on major issues' does seem a promising augury.

Yet the *Financial Mail* (23 May, 1980) and other business papers received even this report calmly enough, the FM arguing that 'because (it) was largely prepared when the country was in the throes of a bitter war, some aspects reflect a harder line than is now likely to be adopted'. Moreover, 'it is a fact that as the ministers become more familiar with their tasks, their views on future policy are likely to change somewhat. It is one thing to adopt a firm socialist line outside government but quite another to hold firmly to that line when in office'. The FM did expect that 'economic uncertainty' and some delay in investment decisions would continue 'until the new economic policy is formulated and publicised' in detail. However it is obvious that the voices of capital, whether correct or not in their interpretation, continue to be remarkably confident that they hold a winning hand. And, after all, the FM had been able to bray only the week before at Mugabe's hasty retreat from the rather modest statement that investment, while welcome, 'must be Zimbabwe-oriented—in other words majority shareholding must remain inside the country (!) and profits reinvested'. For 'within forty-eight hours', Mugabe was assuring the AGM of the chamber of mines 'that the operative word in his (Bulawayo) trade fair speech had been "persuasion", not "compulsion".' Stating that 'it is not my government's intention to legislate against the repatriation of profits but rather to invite investors to join in the spirit of our Zimbabwe-anisation programme', he also denied reports that the government planned to take a stake in the mining industry or even to push a programme of workers' committees. Obviously this is not very revolutionary stuff, any of it, and merely demonstrates the tight leash Mugabe feels himself to be on just at the moment.

The second conditioning factor in Zimbabwe's political economy is the land question, source of much of the heat behind the country's revolutionary thrust over the years and now a policy area of considerable challenge for the new government. The basic statistics are graphic enough. Historically, the country's land has been divided by statute into 45 million acres for Africans and 45 million for Europeans, a figure which takes on even more meaning when one realises that in 1976 there were approximately 680,000 African and only 6,682 European farmers! Add to this the fact that the so-called 'Tribal Trust Lands' occupy much the worst land, land which (as seen) is criminally overpopulated and overgrazed (in some areas 40 per cent of those between 16 and 30 are landless), and land which, in consequence, has deteriorated ecologically at a disastrous rate. Add, too, the impact of the war—the widespread and disruptive establishment of strategic hamlets, the flight of people from the war zones to the cities and across the borders (an estimate of at least one million displaced persons out of a population of seven or eight million would not overstate the case), the planned destruction of African agricultural capacity in order to deny the guerillas food (the notorious 'Operation Turkey')—and one has not only a compelling argument for structural change but also a short-term crisis of serious proportions.

Solving the short-term resettlement crisis (with its attendant problems of starvation and disease) will take considerable energies and resources. But it is clear that the redressing of the black-white imbalance in the rural sector represents a promise of such importance to the African population that the government cannot delay in fulfilling it. Yet here too there are constraints. For one thing European agriculture (which, incidentally, employs 38 per cent of the black labour force) has been responsible for 92 per cent of marketed output, and is therefore crucial not only to export earnings but, perhaps even more importantly, to the country's ability to feed itself. The government has made an unequivocal decision not to jeopardise this productive capacity for the foreseeable future, a decision which has been an important premise for the overall package of compromise and outreach towards the white community which has marked the Mugabe government's approach since it has taken office. It is also a fundamental factor in determining the shape of such land reform initiatives as are likely to be forthcoming.

For there has seemed to be a way to have land reform without, in the short-run, rattling the existing commercial sector. The efficiency of European agricultural enterprises is notoriously uneven, running from the 60 per cent of farms which pay no income tax at all (and whose failure has been subsidised by a wide range of government assistance programmes) to the 271 European farms which in 1976 contributed 52 per cent of taxable income (these including such giants as the million acre-plus estates owned by Leibig and Lonrho). And, as Roger Riddell, an admirably trenchant observer of Zimbabwe's rural scene, has pointed out,[2] inefficiency is often combined with almost criminal malutilisation of land; vast amounts of commercial farm land are unused (and some even abandoned), and the figure for land available in these terms might even reach as high as 60 per cent or more when underused land is also included. It is on some of this land that the government has now set its sights for the first stages of large-scale African movement into the former 'European' area; indeed Dennis Norman, president of the white Commercial Farmers' Union, had already begun to calculate this possibility even before the ZANU victory, and this must account in part for his presence—a presence which is in any case reassuring to his fellow white farmers—as Minister of Agriculture in Mugabe's cabinet.*

Not that this approach is itself entirely straightforward. One of the greatest compromises made by ZANU and ZAPU at British dictate during the Lancaster House Conference was to accept the entrenchment (effectively for ten years) in the Constitution's Declaration of Rights of a stringent section on 'Freedom from Deprivation of Property'. Summarising the implications of this recently in the *Financial Times,* Michael Holman writes that

> compulsory acquisition can only take place when it is for the 'public benefit' or 'in the case of underutilised land, settlement of land for agricultural purposes'. Acquisition can only be lawful provided there is 'prompt payment of adequate compensation', remitted abroad 'within a reasonable time'. The provisions are justifiable and thus the High Court—at present without a single black judge— could have a vital role. Much is left to the judges since there is no definition of underutilised land, adequate compensation or prompt payment.

The result seems likely to be a very high price for land indeed (including court costs) and great foreign exchange problems, so much so that as sympathetic an observer as Riddell (quoted by Holman) can conclude: 'Even if the new Government of Zimbabwe were committed to implementing a comprehensive land resettlement programme. . . under the constitution it would be well nigh impossible to carry out'.

In short, the British, with this section in the Constitution, have tried to corner the new Zimbabwean government (and control the pattern of expropriation) even more effectively than they cornered the new Kenyan

---

*Of course, there has also been created a Ministry of Lands, Resettlement and Rural Development under a ZANU minister, and it has been stated that this will be the coordinating ministry for rural development purposes. The precise division of labour which is worked out between these two ministries will obviously be of considerable importance.

government almost two decades ago. Ironically, the UNCTAD report (cited above) warns quite specifically against a replay of the costly Kenyan model—the use of externally-borrowed funds to compensate white farmers—yet the government has felt compelled to reaffirm its commitment to the Lancaster House agreement and to the avoidance of expropriation. It will, therefore, be particularly instructive to see how it plans to fight its way out of this corner as it begins to spell out its land reform. For fight it must if its revolution is to have any substance at all. Equally instructive will be the pattern of productive relations which is encouraged during the actual process of rural transformation: ZANU's election manifesto, very different from any Kenyan intentions, promised the promotion of 'collective villages' and 'collective agriculture'. But this is an issue to which we will have occasion to return.

The strategic positioning and exaggerated dominance of the white community—settler and multinational—in Zimbabwe's industrial and agricultural sectors is paralleled in all spheres, of course, though most dramatically within the state apparatus and, especially, within the military. White power is much more immediately vulnerable in the civil service (where the number of Africans in established posts have only recently passed the 10 per cent mark, with these, in turn, mainly concentrated in technical grades—teachers, doctors, nurses) then elsewhere, and there can be little doubt that accelerated Africanisation will be well up on Mugabe's agenda. Nonetheless, the new government apparently feels that caution is necessary even here in order to ensure a continuity of expertise and experience and, more generally, to underwrite the viability of the whole 'stability' package. Yet 'expertise and experience' are not politically neutral, as a number of first-hand observers have found in reporting the apparent incomprehension of incumbent officials when fielding questions about the implications for their ministries of various newly-styled progressive government policies. Examples in education and health—where African needs have conventionally had a very low priority—have been cited but clearly in all sectors ZANU's long march through such institutions is bound to prove a treacherous one. Even more serious is the related danger that change which is 'slow but sure' may run the risk of reducing itself to *mere Africanisation* of the established state apparatus, rather than premissing any more fundamental remodelling of it.

Needless to say, the handling of the military apparatus presents an even more daunting challenge to the new government. While the unambiguous nature of ZANU's electoral triumph helped pre-empt any extreme white backlash, Mugabe's decision to incorporate the formidable General Walls in his team—as coordinator of the process of military integration—may have been the necessary icing on the cake in this regard. Hailed by many observers as a brilliant tactical move in defusing general settler anxieties, this step was probably equally important for its facilitating the demobilisation of various extremely dangerous special-forces units within the Rhodesian army (the Selous and Grey Scouts, and the Rhodesian Light Infantry, among others), these being composed of the worst detritus from failed empires around the world, as well as the most ruthless of local elements, both black and white. The need to be seen to be dealing even-handedly and fairly with the numerous and well-organised (if much more conventionally trained) forces from ZAPU, the other liberation movement, also has encouraged adoption of as apparently neutral a process of blending the three armies as is now underway.

The main long-term danger in this process also will be evident. For the strength of ZANLA (the ZANU military wing) lay in its development of a classic guerilla army, a process still unfinished at the time of the Lancaster House Conference but characterised, nonetheless, by a practice on the ground and vis-à-vis the peasantry which had begun to give ZANLA a distinctive political cast. It also has been argued that ZANLA, in consequence of this practice inside the country, had become the source of much of the pressure towards radicalisation of the parent movement, ZANU, over the years. Does the possibility arise that in order to placate a settler army a people's army will have had to be demobilised? And what kind of standing army will emerge from the ministrations of a General Walls and of 'British military instructors'? Time alone will tell.

British military instructors. These are, in any case, merely a small fraction of the external actors who will now be active in the attempt to lock the new government's various compromises firmly into place. In the first instance there is South Africa itself, its private sector increasingly prominent in the Zimbabwean economy, its state a backer of Muzorewa and military partner in the settler cause, especially towards the end of the war. The ties to South Africa which remain are extremely tight, reinforced by large debts (unlikely to be repudiated) accumulated during the war and by that country's considerable competitive advantage in transporting land-locked Zimbabwe's goods to and from the sea. Eventually current efforts to develop regional multi-state alliances outside the South African sphere of influence, and the reconstruction of alternative transport linkages (via Mozambique, for example), may help Zimbabwe to draw more firmly north but South Africa has great clout at present. And not just clout in the metaphorical sense. Prime Minister Botha's first response to Mugabe's victory was a very heavy-handed warning to the new Zimbabwe, and South Africa is both strong and ruthless enough to do considerable damage both above and below ground. Mugabe has associated himself strongly with OAU positions on the necessity for change in South Africa but for the moment will necessarily proceed with caution on this front.

Other imperial actors will be more subtle. We will return to this point, but here it bears noting that such actors have been crafting the 'false decolonisation' of Zimbabwe for some time—at least since Henry

Kissinger's dramatic reversal of field in 1976 when he and Anthony Crosland first plotted a pre-emption of the further militarisation and radicalisation of the struggle in Zimbabwe. It is worth recalling Crosland's remark, made at a NATO Foreign Ministers' meeting at the time of the Geneva Conference, that

> if the British government gave up hope (of negotiated settlement), there would be no doubt over who would eventually win on the battlefield. But if the issue were settled on the battlefield it would seriously lessen the chance of bringing about a moderate African regime in Rhodesia and would open the way for more radical solutions. . .

One can then trace the various permutations and combinations of that strategy—a strategy only temporarily complicated by Smith's playing of his own (quite unconvincing) neo-colonial card, the Internal Settlement—which eventually brought the liberation movements to the bargaining table at Lancaster House.

Of course, the military advance of the liberation movements was also setting the pace here, and it has not always been clear just who was manoeuvring whom. However, on the imperial side it can at least be said that the plotting has been broad-guaged. Thus, attendant upon the David Owen-Andrew Young 'Anglo-American Plan' (a reincarnation of the Crosland-Kissinger initiative) was an elaborate aid package, the Zimbabwe Development Fund, designed not merely to smooth, but to shape, the transition to black majority rule. Indeed, as stated, the question of how best to shape the transition has been a long-term preoccupation both of U.S. imperial planners in particular (witness the 1977 reports by the Southern African Task Force of the African Bureau of USAID and, also for AID, by the African-American Scholars Council)[3] and of multi-national capital in general (witness the development of possible reformist scenarios by the corporate-funded Whitsun Foundation within Rhodesia itself). In light of this, it will appear as no accident that it was the United States who came forward at a particularly delicate moment in the Lancaster House parleys with a promise of economic aid for judicious land reform when the terms regarding that item on the agenda became contested.

Strikingly, the U.S. seems to have moved with speed, since the February elections, to reinterpret the terms of its commitment on that item, and even to have reduced the level of its promised aid in spectacular fashion (to a mere $27 million—to be shared with Zambia and Mozambique—in 1980-81, compared with the $1 billion-plus package considered at the time of the Anglo-American Plan). Indeed, a relative shortfall in aid seems to be the picture right across the board, even though significant amounts will come (and even though these amounts will still be designed to service the various neo-colonial purposes, mentioned above, which lie behind them).* The Zimbabwe government seems confident it can handle any such inputs on its own terms, and, in fact, looks directly to the United Kingdom as its principle source of help. Thus Simon Mzenda, Deputy Prime Minister and Foreign Minister, stated in this connection that 'the one country we can be closest to is the country which colonised us', while among Mugabe's first diplomatic initiatives was a journey to meet Mrs Thatcher in order to discuss the possibility of her increasing assistance. Nonetheless, the shortfall is there and it would seem to reflect the growing confidence in western ruling circles—parallelling that in the business press, as cited above—that the terms of the Lancaster House agreement and the stranglehold of private capital are themselves pretty substantial guarantees of continuity. They might even reason that a stickiness with aid could actually be a positive thing, encouraging the government in Salisbury, in the words of the indefatigable *Financial Mail,* to deepen its acknowledgement 'that private sector capital is going to have to play a vital role if black economic and social aspirations are to be met in the Eighties and Nineties'.

Perhaps this smugness is reinforced by the thought that Zimbabwe really has nowhere else to turn as long as it continues to play a quasi-conventional development game. For better or worse strong links to the Soviet Union do not exist, and will not easily develop, even though ZAPU, the Soviet Union's much preferred liberation movement during the armed struggle, is now a junior partner in the ZANU government. Such links as ZANU itself had during the struggle were, initially, with China, with such countries as Rumania and Yugoslavia, and with a number of African states; the Soviet arms which they did obtain came via third parties, Mozambique and Ethiopia for example. Yet none on this list is a strong counter-pole of attraction away from the tactic of bidding for a share of apparent western abundance. All of which is not to prejudge the question of where the Zimbabwean government will eventually locate itself on the world stage. But so far, in line with its caution on other fronts, it is playing a hand which could scarcely be styled anti-imperialist.

In summarising this section, then, it can be confirmed that the constraints are real enough. It is not beyond reason for the new government to see a pressing imperative in keeping the whites in place, international capitalism on side, and South Africa at bay in order to avoid short-term economic disruption—or worse. In Mozambique the precipitous departure of the colonialists (though even there there was no precipitous break with Mozambique's own South African connection) did in fact bring the economy near to collapse, especially since this departure was attended by considerable, and quite ruthless, sabotage. This had the

---

*An added irony will arise if a great deal of this 'aid' (including loans and the like) goes toward compensating settler farmers (see above) and paying the pensions of former Rhodesian civil servants, as the new government has committed itself to do.

advantage of creating in certain sectors something of a *tabula rasa* upon which to build new institutions (the state farms and the industrial production councils, for example) and quickly to acquire new skills; considerable creativity was displayed by FRELIMO in power in these various areas of challenge. But the process was also costly—not least in the agricultural sphere—and it seems that Samora Machel, himself now forced by the fragility of his economy to make real compromises regarding the pace of socialist advance, may have been one of those who counselled Mugabe to move gingerly.

Yet the latter approach carries dangers which, if less dramatic than short-term economic crisis, are perhaps even more serious in the longer run. For there is the very real possibility of becoming *trapped* on the terrain of short-run calculation, 'circumstances' never quite so 'ripe for socialist change' (to return to the words of the ZANU manifesto quoted above) as to make realisation of such change a straightforward exercise. Then, with powerful forces acting quite self-consciously to reinforce pragmatism and caution, long-term goals of transformation may, without ever having been quite 'ripe', merely wither on the vine! For a transition to socialism is never risk-free; the deftest (and most successful) of revolutionaries have been those who have pushed carefully but creatively at the margin of risk, expanding that margin and increasingly controlling it. This may be happening in Zimbabwe; once again there is no intention of pre-judging the situation there. But these formulations, taken together with what we have seen so far, may at least serve to underscore how much more fraught with complexity is this round of the Zimbabwean revolution than the armed struggle which preceded it.

Nor are the new government's calculations with reference to this complexity being made in a vacuum. Bourgeois commentators summarise the other side of the Zimbabwean coin by talking of a possible 'crisis of expectations'; Mugabe's party, the *Financial Mail* notes, 'has promised free schooling, free health services, a social security system for all the people, more and better paid jobs. . . more land for blacks'. And Mugabe himself has spoken quite explicitly of the difficulties he has in striking a balance 'between maintaining white confidence and also satisfying the expectations which our people have'. Even phrased in such conventional terms this is not a contradiction which is easily resolved. Already, for example, there are signs that deepening the tax bite sufficiently to cover such programmes will not be taken lightly by capital, and that some modification of goals in this sphere may therefore be necessary.

Yet even if some greater risk is likely to be run in order to meet some of these goals than might be the case in other policy areas, there is an additional danger in being forced to deal with the situation in these kinds of terms. For viewed from another perspective such expectations are real *class demands,* coming from those exploited classes in Zimbabwean society who not only wish to redress their historic situation of deprivation but who also have every reason in so doing to see the white settlers and the multinationals as their class enemies. Moreover, it is precisely in the class-conflictual nature of mass demands that there lies the possibility of workers and peasants coming to see in socialism a broader solution to their deprivation, and of their coming to support a genuinely hegemonic project aimed at the fundamental transformation of the productive relations of Zimbabwean society.

In contrast, it is when such a transformatory project is not in train that class demands can dissipate into mere 'expectations' (the understandable, but economistic, drive for *more* education, *more* health, *more* pay, *more* land) and the movement's response transmuted into mere welfarism. In the latter event, such demands are then too easily construed as 'problems' to be dealt with administratively—the social-democratic trap—rather than becoming the substance of prioritisation and self-conscious planning by the dominated classes themselves. Class alliances fragment, and politicians, far from being catalysts of socialist consciousness, begin to outbid each other to deliver sectoral and regional favours. Or, alternatively, they become the instruments for suppressing such 'unreasonable' demands altogether!

Phrased in this way the contradiction which now confronts Mugabe is seen to be even more fundamental than his own formulation, quoted above, allows. For the problem comes into clearer focus when the danger inherent in leaning too far towards 'maintaining white confidence' is seen to lie not so much in a failure to 'satisfy popular expectations' as in *a demobilisation of the class struggle*. Short-term tactics may dictate that the class enemy be embraced as friend and helpmate, that social ownership or even any very firm governmental control over the private sector be defined as inappropriate at this time, and so on. The difficulty arises when knowledge that this is mere tactic must—again, for apparently very good reasons—remain the profane, tactically-suppressed, knowledge of the vanguard: how do you bring the popular classes into this kind of game without giving the game away? yet if they are not in on the game how do you keep the class struggle alive?

In short, any very Gramscian notion of developing a new hegemonic project could be the loser here, with Mugabe then finding himself less a Gramsci than a Thomas Munzer—as described by Engels in words which do provide one plausible reading of the current Zimbabwean situation:

> The worst thing that can befall the leader of an extreme party is to be compelled to take over a government at a time when society is not yet ripe for the domination of the class he represents and for the measures which that domination implies... What he can do contradicts all his previous actions and principles, and the immediate interests of his party, and what he ought to do cannot be done... In the interests of the movement he is compelled to advance the interests of an alien class, and to feed his own class with talk and promises, and with the

asseveration that the interests of that alien class are their own interests.[4]

Engels concludes that 'he who is put into this awkward position is irrevocably lost'. Yet even if this is in fact plausible, there are also signs that more is in motion, in class terms, within the Zimbabwean revolution than this formulation might imply. These are signs which Kangai's claim that present 'democratisation' points the way towards a transition to socialism is perhaps designed to epitomise. To this, and related considerations, we can now turn.

II

We can begin, then, to remove the brackets we have placed around such tactical questions by attempting to assess the moment in the Zimbabwean class struggle which now presents itself. Let us first return, for a moment, to Willers' 'bourgeoisie', those whites—only a couple of hundred thousand in a population of six million—who nonetheless continue to dominate the infrastructure of Zimbabwean society virtually across the board. As any number of commentators have pointed out this is far from a uniform group, being divided, however roughly, between settlers—farmers, skilled workers, small businessmen and civil servants—and those local actors who are attendant upon, or employed by, the large multinational enterprises mentioned above.

For obvious reasons it is the former group which has felt itself to be most directly threatened—in their land, in their jobs, in their life-style—by African advance, and has been both most enamoured of the UDI experiment and most supportive of the extreme limitations upon reform inherent in the Internal Settlement and the Muzorewa government. In contrast, it appears that multinational capital could have lived, on the terrain of neo-colonialism, with a much more adventurous version of black advance from a quite early period and can still plan to do so comfortably. Not, of course, that the interests of these two elements of the white community are even then to be distinguished too sharply. Inevitably there has been considerable overlap of self-identification and interest within the white community* and, in any case, multinational capital must certainly be fearful of too precipitous a rate of change, even if such change were merely to be in the direction of the judicious Africanisation of established structures which it is prepared to encourage. For it must see itself as being at least as reliant, in the short-run, on the 'expertise and experience' of the settler element as Mugabe apparently sees himself to be. Any indecently accelerated departure of the white community such as might threaten stability and

---

*Indeed it would not be surprising if a number of those now in the civil service were to move directly into the private sector. (Of course, in contrast, there will be whites, including some returnees from abroad, who will choose to play a progressive role.

business as usual would not be welcome. Nonetheless, the multinational fraction of the 'bourgeoisie' does have considerably more room for manoeuvre in the long-run than its 'settler' counterpart, and can be expected to continue to use it in an attempt to pre-empt any renewed radicalisation of Zimbabwean nationalism.

Gramsci is again relevant here, though in ways which go far beyond Willers' interesting but still rather jejune use of his theories. For the game of the most intelligent of this white bourgeoisie must now be—in Fanon's words—'to capture the vanguard, to turn the movement to the right, and to disarm the people'. Part of the tactic here consists, as we have seen, of threat, tacit or otherwise (capital flight, flight of personnel, industrial and agricultural collapse), and part will consist of the most obvious of carrots (promotions, agencies, directorships, even bribery, on the Kenyan model). But part of it, too, will be to draw 'the vanguard' ever more firmly onto the cultural terrain of international capitalism and to make the values and *modus operandi* of this global system the 'common-sense' of the new African petit-bourgeoisie-in-the-making. This will mean, in the Zimbabwe case, encouraging the making of a virtue of the necessity of 'pragmatism' and 'compromise'. It will be a part of the class struggle which will be fought not in the bush but on such prosaic 'battlefields' as the sundowner circuit, the ministerial office and the business meeting over lunch at Meikle's Hotel or the Salisbury Club. And it will be fought by the more sophisticated of white civil servants, military officers, and local managers of multinational firms as they regroup on the ground, and by the purveyors of aid, capital and technology who are even now descending upon Salisbury airport. It would be a mistake to underestimate the importance of this aspect of struggle.

There are limits upon such bourgeois action, of course; white supremacy is not merely a calculating machine and sheer racism will sometimes intervene. Doris Lessing, most acute of observers of white Southern African society, caught the nuance well. Martha Quest, her heroine, is bantering with Mr. Maynard, a cynical but sophisticated member of the colony's establishment (the time is the late 30s). 'Why not abolish passes altogether?' she asks.[5]

> 'Why not? I suggest you put pressure on your Parliamentary representative to that effect.'
> Martha laughed again (and Mr. Maynard continues).
> 'I am firmly of the opinion that the sooner a middle class with privileges is created among the Africans the better it will be for everyone. Unfortunately, the majority of the whites are so bogged down in intelligent considerations such as that they wouldn't have their sisters marrying black men, that they are too stupefied to see the advantages of such a course.'

Lessing then writes that 'Martha was several years from understanding this remark', but at this late date no-one else need be so naive. For even if racism does impede the process, it seems safe to say that real settler die-hards (always assuming a white counter-coup is avoided) will be among the first to go. At this point in Zimbabwe's history Maynardism must be, will be, ever more urgently the white-cum-bourgeois strategy. For Mr. Maynard, self-evidently, had learnt his dialectics!

Are there African recruits for such a strategy? Continue to bracket the question of the nature of Patriotic Front leadership and look instead at the overall class structure of the African community. Viewed in these terms and in continental perspective it would be surprising if there were not such recruits and more in Zimbabwe than in many other ex-colonies. Despite massive educational deprivation at the base, and real shortfalls in black skills relevant to such a relatively sophisticated economy, Zimbabwe does have a larger pool of trained Africans than other newly-independent African countries. Thus, some estimates set the figure of blacks with higher education as high as 20,000 including up to 8,000 people who have completed or are still undergoing training abroad. Complementing those already *in situ*, many of the latter will be returning to claim their place in the sun, often from western-sponsored programmes which have been more or less self-consciously designed to groom them for such a moment. In addition, as Colin Stoneman has recently documented in detail, there are in most sectors, public and private, skilled and semi-skilled Africans whose advancement up the job ladder has been artificially constrained by racist definitions of competence.[6]

As Stoneman puts the point, such facts 'present both an opportunity and a danger', the danger lying 'in the possibility that some fundamental characteristics of the white economy, in particular the extreme inequality in wealth, income, land distribution and decision-making, will survive, with the skilled and educated blacks slipping into white shoes', and thereby creating themselves as a 'black middle class. . . with interests directly at variance with the majority of the population (and in support of) growing integration with and subordination to the world capitalist economy in exchange for external support'. This is a familiar enough syndrome else-where in Africa to be a particularly salient possibility under Zimbabwean conditions. It is also worth reminding ourselves that there has been just enough scope for African agricultural activity—in the Native Purchase Areas (specifically set aside for African 'Master Farmers') and in parts of the Tribal Trust Lands where a certain measure of class differentiation has taken place—and entrepreneurial activity to sow the seeds for development of a private sector petit-bourgeoisie. True, settler economic control was sufficiently all-encompassing that these seeds are not quite parallel to the quite vigorous African private sector which had begun to bloom (in agriculture, trade and services) in Kenya even before inde-pendence. Still, there are elements here to complement and interpenetrate with any 'new' or 'bureaucratic' petit-bourgeoisie which may now begin to form around the state and corporate hierarchies, and perhaps in future there will also be private sector opportunities for the latter to exploit for themselves. In short, black advancement will now be the name of the game and in that context it will not be the availability of recruits for 'mere Africanisation' which is in question. Rather, the crucial factor will be the political and ideological context in which such potential recruits now find themselves and in which they must define their practice.

We return by this route to the question of how a Gramscian Mugabe could hope to structure a counter-hegemony resistant to the cooperative wiles of Maynardism. It seems clear that members of the Zimbabwean petit-bourgeoisie-in-the-making can be recruited for more radical undertakings, as well as more conservative ones, but this possibility does not remain open indefinitely. In fact, it is in this connection that we can specify quite concretely another of the dangers of Mugabe's 'pragmatism', as analysed at the conclusion of the previous section. The point should by now be obvious: any tactical reluctance to generate revolutionary political institutions *and* a genuinely revolutionary culture could allow to breed, in the interstices of short-run compromise, precisely those people who will want to make that 'virtue of necessity' mentioned above. Marcelino dos Santos, a senior FRELIMO leader, once said that the most important way to guarantee against any such degeneration in Mozambique was 'to popularise' the revolutionary aims and to create such a situation that if for one reason or another at some future time some people start trying to change these aims, they will meet with resistance from the masses.'[7] What, in Zimbabwe, of Kangai's rather similar proposed innoculation against degeneration of the revolution there: 'democratisation'.

Fortunately, Kangai is not dragging this concept in arbitrarily from left-field. It has a basis in Zimbabwean history, and that basis is the armed struggle itself. For Zimbabwe has had, to this point, no straightforward transition to neo-colonialism, the strategists of international capitalism having been forced—in significant measure by unilateral settler action—to leave the process of cooptation until rather late in the day. Is it necessary to remind ourselves that Zimbabweans have acted in heroic fashion not merely to vote for their freedom, overwhelmingly, in the very last round of the independence struggle, but actually to wrench it from the settlers by force of arms: no successful guerilla war and Ian Smith would still be ensconced in power in Salisbury. Moreover, we have already suggested that that phase of the struggle had many of the attributes of a people's war. What are the prospects for a *people's politics* to safeguard the integrity of the new phase of the Zimbabwe revolution?

An initial key to this should lie in the role of the peasantry since it was among the peasantry that the Patriotic Front found its popular base for advancing the armed struggle as effectively as it did. It is at this point in our analysis that we begin to enter the zone of controversy surrounding evaluation of the component elements of the Patriotic Front, ZANU and ZAPU, alluded to at the outset of this paper. But in the case of ZANU, in particular, much of this controversy is over how far the movement had gone in grounding its military struggle in a parallel process of political mobilisation, not whether that process had begun at all. Perhaps ZANU did have a penchant for overstating the extent to which it could lay claim to fully-liberated areas (and in truth establishing such areas would at the best of times have been far more difficult in Zimbabwe than in relatively backward Mozambique, given the dense infrastructure of settler control and the scattered character of the land allotted Africans). Yet impressive developments were in train as Lionel Cliffe, an unofficial observer at the Zimbabwe elections, has had occasion to note: 'Prone to assess the liberation movements by the exile leadership, many of us who sympathised with the liberation cause underestimated what had been achieved in the link between guerillas and people over a very wide spread of these fragmented pockets of the TTLs.'[8] Cliffe and other observers brought back accounts of the *pungwes,* or all-night meetings, ZANU cadres had consistently held with local populations during the armed struggle, and of the dense network of *mujibas,* or young apprentice militants, which had complemented the guerillas in building a new political infrastructure among the people, a political infrastructure which, in turn, took the form of impressively functioning 'people's councils' in many areas. It was precisely such political realities, important, obviously, to the military success the liberation movements had, which also laid essential groundwork for the self-conscious militancy expressed by the African population in the February election.

But what of the main bearers of this process, ZANLA, the ZANU army. Some of its members apparently stayed out of the assembly camps (set up to field the guerilla armies during the electoral process) and did play a mobilising role in the election itself. But René Lefort, writing in *Le Monde Diplomatique* (May 1980), has suggested that some ZANLA people have seen in the compromises at Lancaster House and in the guerilla army's own incorporation into the new overarching standing army, an undercutting of the political process, established in the semi-liberated zones and sketched above, which had focussed popular energies and given them revolutionary thrust. Indeed Lefort goes so far as to argue that, as a result, 'the party runs the risk of being reduced to a leadership which is saddled with a very weak apparatus, one hastily constructed for the purpose of fighting the election and controlled by local "notables".' A serious risk if true—the spectre of the absorption of apparent 'parties of mobilisation' into class-differentiated social structures which has occurred elsewhere in Africa looms large here—though it is probably an over-statement of the case. Still, in querying the straightforward continuity of development out of the armed struggle, Lefort's observation does under-score the main question of the moment: what political institutions can be generated (or, at least, freshly reminted for the new purposes at hand) on the ground in order to consolidate the popular base for further change?

To be sure, old structures are already in disarray because of the war, the people's councils already exemplify something of a new alternative, and in addition, further breaks with the past are implicit in the necessity for refugee resettlement and in the movement of people within the pro-gramme of land reform. Assuming the sheer immensity of these latter undertakings does not bury political creativity in a technocratic maze, and assuming that ZANU's break with the political imperatives of the armed struggle is not as sharp as Lefort might fear, there remains considerable opportunity here to have 'a rural political and administrative apparatus of potentially revolutionary design'.[9] Perhaps for ZANU the key is to be found in its proposed programme of collectivisation. The movement's electoral manifesto is quite explicit about this: 'peasant agriculture, at present predominantly private, will be the basis of collectivisation', although, to be sure, 'such collective agriculture will be by persuasion rather than compulsion'. For 'it is essential that peasant land holdings are combined to constitute viable collective units on the basis of which State assistance, technical and financial, can be granted'.

When established such units could also provide the socio-political basis for the peasantry's organisation as an even more fully self-conscious class, though it must be admitted that one would feel more comfortable with such an extension of the argument if these possible positive implications for Zimbabwe's class struggle were actually to be found in the Manifesto itself rather than having to be sniffed out of it by sympathetic observers. For we know that such 'collective units' have often degenerated, else-where in Africa, into mere instruments of state control of peasant agriculture and peasant surpluses. What, in this case, will be the methods of political work which exemplify 'persuasion', what the countervailing mechanisms of popular participation and control, what the balance between leadership and mass action, remains to be seen. Let us assume, for the moment, that the instinct for 'democratisation' carried over from the armed struggle is still alive and well in Zimbabwe. Even then, to repeat, it is the way in which this instinct is given *current* expression in the rural areas as institutionalised and focussed peasant power that will be the litmus test of the direction the Zimbabwe revolution is taking. Unfortunately, the mere raising of such a question is as much as developments to date (and available information) permit us to do.

What of the Zimbabwean working class, an obvious candidate for guarantor of a socialist transition?[10] Of course the category 'working class' is a slippery one under Zimbabwean conditions; as in most Southern Africa settings much of the work-force is in migratory movement between urban and rural settings and therefore not easily categorised. Moreover, this work-force (of roughly one million persons) is quite diversified; figures for 1975 show 38 per cent in agriculture (in this sphere, in particular, some are migrants from beyond the border); 6 per cent in mining; 14 per cent in industry; 7 per cent in construction; 21 per cent in services. The bases for extreme working-class discontent are also patent; in one recent year the average white monthly wage was $423, the average black wage $39. Indeed, between 1965 and 1975 the wage gap between black and white had actually doubled, and one estimate from several years ago suggested that less than 15 per cent of the blacks in non-agricultural employment earned above the Poverty Datum Line. Small wonder that with the electoral demise of white power the top blew off the Zimbabwean industrial relations system, and the new government was met immediately with successive waves of strikes, involving thousands of workers, in the private sector.

Presumably ZANU would not want to query the logic of such demands, since in many cases they are directed merely to drawing workers up past the Poverty Datum Line, or to guaranteeing workers sufficient income to facilitate the movement of their families out of the inhuman syndrome of migrant labour and into more permanent urban habitation. Given the vast discrepancies in income and life changes in Zimbabwe one must be cautious about using labels like 'economism' or 'labour aristocracy' to characterise the thrust of such labour action even when it does come, as is sometimes the case, from those sections of the work-force which are (relatively) least deprived and best organised. Two difficulties arise, however. First, it must be emphasised that the terrain for working-class organisation is already partially occupied. Despite settler-government restrictions (and security activities) there are a number of African trade unions, many with some history of struggle (albeit struggle defined, by and large, in quite apolitical terms and directed towards fairly narrowly-defined objectives). Less satisfactorily, some such unions have a history of extensive penetration by the most dubious of western influences (the ICFTU and the AFL-CIO, for example) and these are influences which are at present again zeroing in on the African working class in preparation for the next round in Zimbabwe.[11] Clearly the problem of adapting such union structures to any new nationally-defined purposes raises a whole set of questions of its own, though Mugabe has already commented on the virtues of constructing a single new national union structure. Second, there are potential contradictions of a different order that a party like ZANU must confront in dealing with the working class, contradictions exemplified in the possibility that any dramatic wage increases might have to be purchased at the expense of the peasantry or at the expense of those who are without work (unemployment being already a serious problem in Zimbabwe). As seen, only the development of a self-conscious alliance of workers and peasants—with appropriate political institutions—capable of arbitrating competing demands by the popular classes and resolving such contradictions relatively non-antagonistically can then provide the key to future advance.

Such realities can help us avoid romantic oversimplifications regarding the role of the working class in the Zimbabwean revolution; they may suggest, too, some of the advantages which arise when the assertions of the working class are located under the umbrella of a broader hegemonic movement. But this merely serves to bring us back to the general formulation sketched at the end of Section I, a formulation which we can now hope to specify further. For the chief contradiction which ZANU must now confront antecedes any fine shading regarding the terms of a proposed worker-peasant alliance. As implied earlier, it will be difficult for a movement to mediate between classes and to propose terms for a class alliance when the very class character of the revolution is itself being downplayed. And it will be difficult for ZANU to present itself as a vanguard for working-class action in the context of its commitment to the health of the private sector. Under these circumstances an assertion by the party and its state that, to take one possible example, it is acting to balance off worker interests against legitimate claims to the surplus on the part of the peasantry and the unemployed might well be interpreted by the workers as a mere safeguarding of the profits of the bourgeoisie! So salient is this contradiction that the *Financial Mail* has even assumed that the government will be reluctant to press its (inevitable) reform of the old Rhodesian Industrial Conciliation Act too far: 'The old adage of poacher turned gamekeeper is... likely to apply. Legislation which seemed discriminatory and restrictive while one was in opposition may appear less so from the other side of the desk, and unions in Zimbabwe may be disappointed by the extent of the amendments, once they reach Parliament.'

ZANU's response to such difficulties is still being worked out, but they do present the movement with a real challenge in the labour sphere. For ZANU, despite the fact that it does have a notional trade union structure of its own (the Zimbabwe Trade Union Congress), has been largely a rural-based movement. True, it amassed a considerable number of votes in the urban and white farming areas but it will have to move creatively to give that immediate working-class support long-term focus and a revolutionary role to play. And that is the rub, for, as Mugabe noted disarmingly in an interview given just after the election, on this novel terrain it is necessary that ZANU 'first study the workers, how organised they are'![12] It is not too surprising, then, that the reaction of Kangai, Mugabe's Labour Minister, to the aforementioned wave of strikes reflected some of the uncertainties here. On the one hand, and despite statements of sympathy for the workers' demands, he was reduced to recommending the draconic

Industrial Conciliation Act as the established procedure which must be used.* On the other hand, in the conversation with Karen Gellen cited above, he went rather further:

> We think this development (the strikes) will help us to talk to multinational companies about the fact that there must be changes. . . (T)his uprising that is on will help us in forcing and persuading some people in Zimbabwe to accept that change is forthcoming. We think the workers should continue to work, but their demands will push those who have been controlling the economy to see that there must be fundamental changes immediately, because that is what the struggle has been all about in Zimbabwe.

It is not clear what form, if any, Kangai might hope this kind of expression of working-class energy to take in institutional terms, but it is the case that he is here striking a general note which other evidence suggests to be actively premissing at least some party activity on the ground. Thus a recent article in the *Johannesburg Star* (10 May, 1980), with a Salisbury dateline, notes that party cadres have linked up with workers, especially in the white agricultural sector where ZANU 'cells' are reported as being formed in the compounds to press grievances against the farmers. The *Star's* interpretation is that

> there are people in ZANU (PF) far more radical than Mr. Mugabe. To a certain degree he rides a tiger and cannot be seen to be too conciliatory towards whites without harming his own image both inside and outside the party. And here lies another problem. It does not necessarily matter how pragmatic Mr. Mugabe is at governmental level because individual businessmen, civil servants, and farmers will still have to deal with party officials on a day-to-day basis, officials who may adopt a harder line towards whites than that advocated by the Prime Minister. . 'It is not Mr. Mugabe we talk to, nor his ministers but his party workers in the field and believe me these people can make life very difficult for us', said one dairy farmer. Commerce and industry has not yet been affected by this unauthorised 'interference' by party officials but some businessmen believe it will come.

Whether the *Star* is correct or not about Mr Mugabe, there is promise here, promise of a party which, on some fronts, is indeed beginning to embed itself within the dominated classes in facilitating the pressing of their class demands. The impact upon the party itself of such on-going practice could also be considerable.

Of course any promise here is still promise, performed on a tight-rope, given the government's overall tactical posture towards commerce and industry. There is, however, one other mechanism the new government

---

*Indeed some of the statements made by Kangai in this respect (but also by Mugabe himself) make particularly chilling reading, as witness the material included in the article 'We are all speaking—the Strike Wave' in *Zimbabwe Information Group* (London), 14, Summer 1980.

has begun to push which some see as having long-term promise of eventually resolving contradictions in this sphere in favour of the dominated classes: the workers' committee. True, the government's signals here are still a little mixed. We cited earlier one apparent retreat from this concept, though Mugabe has mentioned it positively on a number of other occasions (once adding—as if again to underscore the contradictions involved—that 'you've got to (establish committees) with the cooperation of the entre-preneur in every case!)' More vocal is Dr. Chidzero who has highlighted the committee concept in many of his public utterances. And it is also a prominent item in the aforementioned UNCTAD report, an item singled out for special mention by Nathan Shamuyarira in his press conference welcoming the document when he emphasised that party thinking squared fully with the proposed 'democratisation' of socio-economic institutions through the 'participation of workers and peasants in decision-making processes of the institutions in which they work'. What this will mean in practice remains to be seen, especially in light of the initial strongly negative reaction from the business community to such proposals. Like collective villages, workers' committees are a two-edged sword, and can become either a means for advancing the class struggle—building strength for the eventual confrontation or of domesticating and containing it—in the 'public interest' and/or in the interest of capitalist allies. Nonetheless, in David Willers' opinion there is no doubt that the committees represent the Gramscian tactic *par excellence:*

> There are already indications that Mugabe will eventually achieve the progressive transformation of the capitalist Zimbabwean economy into a socialist one through means other than the blunt instrument of nationalisation. One such is greater participation in management decisions.

The meaning of this could be clearer, but one can only hope that Willers' fears are justified.

In summation, we find that it is more than mere rhetorical flourish to affirm the strong class base for a continued deepening of the Zimbabwean revolution; as noted earlier, workers and peasants have deep-seated grievances in an inherited situation of gross exploitation, deprivation and alien control. However, as also noted, it is precisely because these grievances do not automatically find expression as a fully-fledged socialist project that questions of broader forms of organisation and ideology are so important. In Africa, the lead in focussing class struggle, building class alliances and generalising the impact of such endeavours has tended to come from nationalist movements and, at the helm of such movements, petit-bourgeois intellectuals. More often than not the trajectory of such organisations and such leaders has meant, in the end, a pre-emption of the further radicalisation of the struggle and an eventual demobilisation of the dominated classes. Yet sometimes, particularly under the conditions of protracted armed struggle and often twinned with ideologically-premissed struggles within the petit-bourgeoisie itself, they have facilitated the advance of these classes towards power. It is with reference to these two trajectories that Marcellino dos Santos, in the interview quoted above, elaborated the distinction between 'primitive' or 'bourgeois' nationalism on the one hand and 'revolutionary nationalism' on the other, with the latter, defined as realising 'the interests of the people as a whole' rather than 'the interests of a small group', permitting a 'true revolutionary leadership' (supported by 'resistance from the masses' against any backsliding) to open up 'real possibilities for an advance from liberation to revolution'.

There are those who are profoundly sceptical regarding such a scenario, hastening past the nationalist-cum-petit-bourgeois terrain (and often past the vast mass of the peasantry while they are at it) towards the goal of a 'working-class party'. The latter is not, however, the option which ZANU offers in present-day Zimbabwe. At its best (and in the present author's opinion this would be very good indeed) it offers some kind of expression of revolutionary nationalism, one (by definition) already transfigured by the entry of the popular classes into its politics and one which can facilitate the further expression of the revolutionary energies of those classes. The experience of the guerilla war demonstrates that this process was already underway during that period; some of the post-electoral evidence presented in the immediately preceding pages suggests that it is still alive and may be beginning to premise precisely that 'democratisation' which will be crucial to keeping alive the long-term question of structural transformation even in the teeth of short-term compromise. But considerable controversy swirls around the question of how strongly to affirm this point, of just what kind of promise of continued forward movement ZANU has to offer.

The difficulties which both wings of the Patriotic Front, ZANU and ZAPU, have had historically in moving past 'primitive' nationalism towards revolutionary nationalism are well known. An article which I wrote a number of years ago on precisely this topic occasioned considerable controversy because it emphasised the ways in which 'petit-bourgeois politicking'—the jockeying for position within and between movements which was clearly sub-ideological and premissed on factionalism and personality and, to some extent, even the instrumentalisation of ethnic counters—had forestalled a deepening of the Zimbabwean revolutionary project.[13] Yet these problems did not disappear, and have continued to be commented upon by other observers since. Thus in 1978 even such sympathetic observers as the editors of the *Review of African Political Economy* could wonder aloud whether the fierce internecine strife then on-going within ZANU represented 'petit-bourgeois factionalism' on the one hand or 'a gradual purge of the more militant' on the other.

Moreover, an editorial drafted for the *Review* in early 1980 (after Lancaster House but before the election) carried this argument even further, suggesting that many liberation movement leaders still saw armed action primarily 'as a means of pressurising the British to intervene and negotiate a settlement' (hence Lancaster House). This in turn may have influenced 'the *kind* of struggle that was being waged: over-reliance on outside bases rather than guerillas operating within the country amongst the people, on military as opposed to political forms of struggle' and so on.

> All these tendencies were most marked within ZAPU in recent years but were present in some of the thinking of ZANU leaders too. Such tendencies, within movements each of which were broad fronts, probably came to be more dominant even within ZANU in the last three years as a result of changes in the leadership cadres that have brought in more of the old-guard nationalists who had been in prison or in more distant and comfortable exile as academics and the like and who had no first-hand experience of the guerilla struggle at the expense of seasoned but younger militants. The continuing conflict for power and the processes of learning through involvement will go on but are likely to be inhibited in the transition.

In consequence of this analysis Cliffe feels driven to the conclusion that 'even if the Zimbabwe movements as entities have not required the highest level of ideological clarity, there are still many outstanding cadres that have emerged during the last years of struggle, whose difficult position at the present time will need our understanding and whose continued efforts to see that the Zimbabwe revolution still lives will require our continued solidarity.'

Chilling stuff, though there may be grounds for thinking that the situation is a little less straightforwardly polarised than Cliffe suggests. The war did deepen after 1976 and this did have a continuing impact on the movement. In particular, an even stronger base of peasant support and militancy began to crystallise, a reality Cliffe himself was quick to acknowledge in light of his observation, as cited above, of the electoral process. This is a point to which we will return, but here we may also raise the question as to whether Cliffe's 'old guard—younger militant' dichotomy quite captures the terms of the on-going struggle which he correctly sees to be likely within ZANU's ranks. Certainly wasting internecine strife of no very edifying variety continued among ZANU politicos through the late seventies. Certainly, there remained a disjunction between the political advances forged through guerilla struggle within the country and any parallel transformation within the movement's overarching political structure (the latter being the chief reason for unease at the apparent swallowing-up of ZANLA into the new army and at the absence of guerilla personnel in key decision-making circles in the new government—a situation so very different from developments in

Mozambique for example).

And certainly there are those in the political leadership for whom the steamy Maoist terminology of the armed struggle (and of the hey-day of Chinese support) remained mere rhetoric—and now, of course, never to be heard on their lips—with any militancy they permitted themselves being more comfortably phrased in conventionally 'black nationalist' or virulently party-partisan terms; these and others are indeed possible recruits for Maynardism *within ZANU itself*. Yet it has also been suggested that there are those among the so-called 'old guard' (and its allies) comprising the political leadership whose nationalism runs deeper, whose commitment to the military struggle was not fragile, whose identification with popular aspirations is not merely rhetorical, and whose possible recruitment to a more revolutionary project cannot be ruled out.[14] Under these circumstances it is tempting to argue that the war itself has kept ZANU on the boil and in a sufficient state of flux, that Cliffe's 'outstanding cadres' are still to be recruited at a number of different levels within the movement.

'Still to be recruited'—this is the key in any case. For the class struggle in Zimbabwe is scarcely to be considered over just because the guerilla war did not resolve as many of the contradictions in the nationalist camp as might have been hoped. Even if this process (political transformation premised on the logic of protracted struggle) had gone further—as perhaps it did in Mozambique—it would in any case merely have provided a running-start on the next round of struggle, the complex struggle over the terms of socialist reconstruction once in power. Moreover, this latter round has its own difficulties, whatever a movement's historical point of entry into it (as, again, Mozambique is discovering). It also has its distinctive opportunities. The peasant factor, mentioned above, becomes relevant here and the land question provides one such opportunity. ZANU epitomises peasant hopes and aspirations and that pressure will continue to stir within the movement. So, too, will the pressure from the working class which we have discussed. To the extent that these pressures make themselves felt Mozambique's (much criticised) encouragement of ZANU to run the risks of Lancaster House in order to reground the struggle on this novel and difficult—but perhaps ultimately more promising—terrain will not seem so amiss!

There is class pressure, then, in Zimbabwe to shake down the leadership, potentially revolutionary pressure to elicit militancy at the top. And there are those spread across the movement who, on this new terrain, can be expected to respond, and in turn to lead—thereby possibly rejoining the revolutionary dialectic at a level in advance even of that exemplified during the armed struggle itself. Only those who accepted uncritically all the things ZANU said about itself during the latter phase will be surprised to hear that it is no uniformly militant vanguard arbitrating the class struggle from an attained position of exemplary clarity and coherence.

But only those who ignored the drama of the armed struggle will be surprised to hear that the on-going class struggle is likely to take place, in important and potentially positive ways, within the movement itself.

To attempt to specify the players in this game with any further precision would smack too much of Kremlinology. Right-wing commentators make much of the possible differences between cabinet and central committee, between 'technocratic core' and 'hard-line militants', and the like—and they even name names. We will not so indulge ourselves here except to note that, however sensationalised and conventional their terminology and their speculations, they are probably not mistaken to be so preoccupied. As we have seen, there must be further struggle, class struggle, in Zimbabwe and within ZANU—at all levels including amongst the 'petit-bourgeois leadership' and over most of the concrete issues we have been discussing in this essay—as well as swirling around it. We will merely note that, and one more thing: how often speculation about Mugabe himself looms large in calculations about the future (*viz.*, 'How Mugabe changed his spots'). In contrast to the un-equivocally militant image forged for him by the media in recent years, events since Lancaster House have found him cast more in the role of Sphinx, as he guards his options and seems deliberately to muddy the ideological waters, as when he stressed that 'the principles of common togetherness' which motivate him are 'really holy principles which find a basis not only in Marxism-Leninism but also in Christianity and other humanitarian doctrines'!

What then? Willers' consummate Granscian tactician? or the business papers' consummate pragmatist? or merely another fuzzy-minded 'Nyerere-style leader'—albeit 'in a Kenya-style economy', as one mordant wit put it recently? One hopes not the latter, though it is sometimes difficult to escape a rather clammy sense of *déjà vu* as 'waiting for Mugabe' threatens to become the 1980s equivalent of the rather feckless 'waiting for Nyerere' in which many radicals, indigenous as well as expatriate, indulged themselves in Tanzania during the late 60s and early 70s. Somehow, reading his speeches and articles over the years, one senses that there may be more to Mugabe than this, that, however tight the corner he is in, Willers may just be right about him. And that, in any case, more is afoot in Zimbabwe, more steam in the kettle, more class actors who won't wait for anybody—because of the war, because of the developed and highly exploitative economy—than ever there was in Tanzania. In any case, neither comparisons with Tanzania (or, for that matter, with Mozambique) nor appeals to the past are likely to help us much. The class struggle in Zimbabwe is indeed joined on new terrain and at a new level. It is what happens in the next round that counts.

At the risk of anti-climax we must add one final complexity to our analysis of Zimbabwe which even now remains bracketed off. For the class struggle which we see must cut across ZANU itself is at present taking place on a much more open political terrain than parallel processes in Mozambique and Angola where one-party systems have emerged from the liberation struggle. As already noted, this has implications for class-corporate organisations like trade unions and in this connection presumably will be hailed by some both on the right and on the left as a great advantage. On the right it will be hailed, for example, by those connected to such western trade union organisations as are prepared to work over-time to help pre-empt a politicised workers' movement, on the left by those who see in the existence of autonomous workers' (and peasants') organisations—however bankrupt these may be in the short-run—the basis for a class politics of resistance to future exploitation by state and capital. Such critics, the latter in particular, will see dangers where Mugabe sees challenge, the challenge of creating a single trade union centre, for example, or of making the party-cum-government sponsored collective villages the principle vector of peasant political activity. Of course, it is the broadest kinds of questions about the institutions most relevant to a transition to socialism which are being raised here, not merely the question of the likely capacity of ZANU *per se* to facilitate such a transition, and these are questions which will remain with us.

More immediately relevant, however, is the fact that this 'open terrain' contains other political organisations, and, in particular, ZAPU (or, as it is now somewhat confusingly called, the Patriotic Front (PF), having taken exclusive possession of that name when ZANU—as ZANU (PF)—chose to enter the election independently of the Patriotic Front alliance). We have already alluded to the fact that ZAPU's military strategy was from an early date of much more conventional cast than ZANU's, and that ZIPRA, if a more disciplined military force, did not acquire as many of the attributes of a people's army as ZANLA. Yet it would be a serious mistake to make too stark a distinction between the two movements on the basis of that difference. Joshua Nkomo, powerful, even authoritarian, and not notably progressive, may have kept a tighter lid on ZAPU after his resumption of active leadership than Mugabe ever did in ZANU, but there can be no gainsaying the fact that the Zimbabwean class struggle cuts across ZAPU, even across its petit-bourgeois leadership, in ways that parallel the ZANU situation. For, unquestionably there are exemplary militants who will engage creatively with the complexities of this next round and there are those who will adapt comfortably to the softer options.

Mugabe's approach has been to welcome ZAPU into a share of power, Nkomo himself, after having declined the offer of the largely ceremonial role of President, taking the Justice portfolio (albeit a portfolio stripped of some of its most important police powers by the time he received it). To be sure, the pickings have been slim—three relatively unimportant ministries in addition to Nkomo's—and some grumbling has been heard from ZAPU about this. But the move towards a greater degree of unity, if difficult to accomplish (the antagonism between the movements is adhered to particularly venomously by some if for no other apparently very good reason than the self-reinforcing reality of a long history of rivalry), is particularly important. Not least because it can help pre-empt the temptation open to opportunistic politicians of seeking to cut across class definitions of politics with regional and ethnic definitions.

It is true that, contrary to the predictions of many bourgeois commentators, the ethnic variable was not a dominant factor in the Zimbabwean election. Indeed ZANU managed completely to wipe out electorally those politicians who sought to build constituencies on the basis of sub-tribal, intra-Shona groupings. Nonetheless, even if the elections were not about ethnicity, they were played out on a counterpane of ethnic identification. The people voted first and foremost for genuine liberation—in effect, for the Patriotic Front—but they did vote for that wing of the Patriotic Front whose image had become linked to their own *ethnie*. Various efforts by the movements themselves to escape such exclusivism notwithstanding, the elections found ZAPU with virtually a clean sweep of the vote from that 20 per cent of the population which is Ndebele-speaking, and ZANU the overwhelming choice of the majority Shona-speaking peoples.

Clearly the Ndebele peasants and workers must be involved in any hegemonic socialist project which may be forthcoming in Zimbabwe (just as, paradoxically, it is only such a project that will serve to make their participation in the Zimbabwe revolution *as Ndebele* even less salient in the future than it has been in the past). For this reason, ZAPU participation at Cabinet level in defining that project is an important step in forestalling a possible wasting fissure in the class alliance for change. How far can such a process go? Certainly unity has been an elusive, frustrating phantom in the past. Still, it is hard to see how progressive forces in either movement can hope to benefit from its absence,* for the chief imperative that both must feel is to raise the class struggle in Zimbabwe above the lowest common denominator of that 'petit-bourgeois politics' which feeds on catering to 'expectations' and facilitating fragmentation. Thus *the extent and the content* of the unity established between the two liberation movements may well be yet another index of how positively the revolution is progressing in Zimbabwe.

*   *   *

---

*This in spite of the fact that it is precisely among the more militant elements that there may be more grounds for ideological difference than between the two movements taken as a whole—ZANU militants being somewhat more inclined to favour Maoist definitions, ZAPU militants to favour Soviet-style definitions.

At the minimum, then, the Zimbabwe elections represent a high-water mark in the political history of that wave of African nationalism which has crested across the continent since the Second World War. For in those elections Zimbabwean Africans spoke out as vocally against white-minority rule (albeit in the final round a white-minority rule which was fronted, however transparently, by a thin veneer of black puppetry) as any colonised people ever has. One needs only to have read Doris Lessing's *Going Home,* with its grisly portrait of smug Rhodesian settlerdom, to realise how important it is to have at least consigned the settler's political order to the trash-can of history.

Revolutionary nationalism? Socialism? How much more can be expected? It will be evident by now that there are no easy answers to these questions. Perhaps the best we can hope for is that the preceding essay will have posed such questions clearly. However, one final point does bear emphasising. Let us repeat that the electoral success of ZANU and ZAPU has premissed on the military success of the Patriotic Front in stalemating, even defeating, the settler regime. With ZANU in power nothing in Southern Africa can ever be quite the same again, whatever machinations South Africa and the West, and recalcitrant members of Zimbabwe's own petit-bourgeoisie, may contrive. For the Zimbabwean example is already alive and well in South Africa 'where Robert Mugabe's election victory. . . is still a daily source of consciously inspirational news.' 'Mugabe pledges support for the freedom movement in South Africa' said a front-page story on Monday in the newspaper *Post* about what, to a non-South African, looked like a routine and formal promise by the Zimbabwean prime minister to help the Organisation of African Unity.[15]

Indeed, 'Zimbabwe's independence is mentioned repeatedly as a factor in the new wave of African unrest (in South Africa). "People look at Zimbabwe and see violence used creatively", says (Zwelakhe) Sisulu. "After the riots of 1976, there was a mood of despair in Soweto. That's been completely removed by Mugabe's victory", says Fanyana Mazibuko, secretary of the Soweto Teachers' Action Committee.'* Whatever the difficulties, we can expect more progress in Zimbabwe itself. But such reports document that Zimbabweans have also made a major contribution to the future of the region as a whole. A future which in any case is, self-evidently, their own, since the eventual toppling of powerful, parasitic South Africa will magnify the opportunity for all countries there, including Zimbabwe, to shape their destinies for themselves. *A luta continua;* one struggle, many fronts: for few areas of the world are these sayings as true as they are for Southern Africa.

---

*This last statement may, in turn, overstate the exclusive impact of specifically Zimbabwean developments since South Africa's growing internal contradictions and dramatic ANC actions (the sabotage at SASOL, for example) are of at least equal significance, but this is an important reality nonetheless.

NOTES

1. See Colin Stoneman, 'Foreign Capital and the Reconstruction of Zimbabwe', *Review of African Political Economy*, 11 (January-April 1978); Michael Bratton, 'Structural Transformation in Zimbabwe: Comparative Noted from the Neo-Colonisation of Kenya', *Journal of Modern African Studies*, 15, 4 (1977); and Duncan Clark, *Foreign Companies and International Investment in Zimbabwe* (Catholic Institute for International Relations (CIIR), London, 1980); see also Financial Times (London), Special Supplement: Zimbabwe (22 April, 1980).
2. Roger Riddell, *The Land Question* (CIIR, London, n.d.); much of the data used in this section regarding the land question is drawn from this excellent pamphlet.
3. Sean Gervasi and James Turner, 'The American Economic Future in Southern Africa: An Analysis of an AID Study on Zimbabwe and Namibia', *Journal of Southern African Affairs*, 3, 1 (1978).
4. Frederick Engels, *The Peasant War in Germany* (International Publishers, New York, 1966), pp. 135-6.
5. Doris Lessing, *A Proper Marriage* (Panther, London, 1966), pp. 220-1.
6. Colin Stoneman, *Skilled Labour and Future Needs* (CIIR, London, 1978).
7. Marcelino dos Santos, interviewed by Joe Slovo, in *The African Communist*, 55 (1973).
8. Lionel Cliffe, 'Zimbabwe Independent: View From the Grass Roots', *Canadian Dimension*, 14, 7 (June 1980); further detailed documentation of these and other points is to be found in the papers on the Zimbabwean elections presented to the Leeds Conference by Cliffe, Barry Munslow, Joshua Mpofu and Barne Mazanzu.
9. Michael Bratton, *Beyond Community Development* (CIIR, London, 1978).
10. Information on labour as well as on many other relevant aspects of Zimbabwe is presented usefully in *Zimbabwe: Notes and Reflections on the Zimbabwean Question*, prepared by the Centre for African Studies, University of Eduardo Mondlane, Maputo, in 1977.
11. See Clyde Sanger, 'Trade Unions in Zimbabwe: A Report to the Canadian Labour Congress' (27 April 1980), which is useful both for the information it contains and the assumptions it reveals.
12. 'Interview with Mugabe', in *TCLSAC Reports* (Toronto, April-May 1980).
13. 'Transforming the Struggle in Zimbabwe', first published in *Southern Africa* (February 1977) and reprinted as chapter 5 in John S. Saul, *The State and Revolution in Eastern Africa* (Monthly Review Press and Heinemann Educational Books, New York and London, 1979).
14. Terence Ranger in making some of these points in a recent unpublished paper attacking both Cliffe and myself ('Politicians and Soldiers: the re-emergence of the Zimbabwe African National Union') runs the risk of going to the other extreme in uncritically hailing the 'old guard' to a man, in effect disposing of the need for any on-going manifestations of class struggle within ZANU itself. One hopes this is not a foretaste of the kind of celebrationism all too familiar from the Tanzanian literature and reaching its apogee in rather similar terms, in Cranford Pratt's *The Critical Phase in Tanzania* (Cambridge University Press, 1976).
15. This and the following quotation are from Jonathan Steele, 'Why Soweto is holding its fire', *Manchester Guardian Weekly* (8 June, 1980); I am grateful to Jonathan Barker for drawing this article to my attention.

RETARDED CAPITALISM IN TANZANIA*

Susanne D. Mueller

Tanzania: Narodism and the Articulation of the Modes of Production

To accuse an African ruling class of retarding capitalism and its principal classes is virtually unheard of. However, this is what has happened in Tanzania, where state capital has consistently acted to forestall the development of a bourgeoisie and a proletariat by basing accumulation on the expansion of middle-peasant household production. The reactionary utopianism of Russia's Narodniks** has actually been institutionalised here and labelled socialism. Lenin's predictions have come true; labour and capital have been confined to their most primitive state, and middle peasants are increasingly squeezed as the State intensifies the production of cash crops which demand more inputs and must conform to rigid quality and quantity controls.[1] From the perspective of the market, middle peasants are expected to act like capitalists while constrained by both their smallness and their lack of capital, and like labour without any of the benefits of fully socialised labour. With the intensification of commodity production, middle peasants are simultaneously subject to all the horrors of producing for an increasingly demanding market and none of the benefits of capitalism over previous modes of production. By forestalling 'the direct separation of household producers from their means of production', the State has fettered 'the accumulation of indigenous capital within smallholding production'.[2] (Cowen, 1977: 4.) This fettering plus the continuous expansion of smallholdings forecloses the possibility of significantly developing the productive forces. The result is overwork and underconsumption, the continuation of hand production, and the re-assertion of backward, semifeudal relations of production as middle-peasant producers who are unable to reproduce themselves under these conditions become informal tenants for others and whole families

*I wish to thank the following for useful comments on an earlier version of this paper: Grant Amyot, Michael Cowen, Jane Guyer, Colin Leys, Ralph Miliband, Phil Raikes and Nicola Swainson.

**The term 'Narodnik' and 'Narodism' are here used metaphorically insofar as a) no exact parallel with the material conditions in Russia at the time Lenin was writing is suggested; b) the Narodniks were a movement and not a state; c) the ruling class in Tanzania became 'populist' after becoming dominant in the State and not before. The metaphor applies in the sense that many of the Narodniks' populist ideas have been institutionalised in Tanzania with the results predicted by Lenin.

(including children) become part of this overworked and underfed work force.

In theory, the very considerable injection of international capital in Tanzania since 1974 should counteract the regressive effects of Narodism. In contrast to state capital, international capital enters as the advanced capital of a different form and period, acting to rationalise commodity production and to raise the productivity of labour through improved inputs and higher producer prices.[3] However, international capital (like all other capitals, as Marx noted) initially takes labour as it finds it and only later transforms it. By entering on the back of a state capital that has organised labour within a Narodnik framework, international capital is itself limited by the contradictions of attempting to transform the value of labour power within this framework. Consequently, improved inputs are used which theoretically increase the value produced by labour, but extraction on the basis of absolute rather than relative surplus value still predominates, as the formal and real subordination of labour to capital is inhibited by the confines of middle-peasant household production. Improved seeds, insecticides, and fertilisers are either counterbalanced by the effect of the hand hoe or demand more labour than can be supplied by a household which is too poor to hire in. Smallholdings limit the degree of mechanisation, resulting in outcries for so-called 'appropriate technologies' to stabilise Narodism in the fact of its contradictions.

As Lenin and Kautsky predicted, the middle peasant's land becomes his fetter under such circumstances. The formality of the land may mask his 'precarious position' of 'half peasant/half worker' (Lenin, I, p. 223), his eventual proletarianisation, and his interim status of 'wage labour equivalent' (Banaji, 1977: 33-34). However, once the laws of motion of capital predominate and become generalised, the middle peasantry is compelled 'to expand commodity production to reproduce the means of subsistence', (Cowen, NCCHP: 19) and it is this compulsion which determines its status.

The question of why the middle peasant's land in Tanzania has become his fetter is not to be answered by referring to some mythically resilient pre-capitalist peasantry. The middle peasantry is not pre-capitalist. It has been subjected to the laws of motion of capitalism and gets none of its progressive benefits. Its fetter is not itself, but the State which has legally restricted its freedom of movement, confined it to villages, and re-introduced minimum acreage requirements from the thirties. (Raikes, 1975, 1978; Coulson, 1975, 1977). Capital at the level of exchange is not articulating with some mysterious pre-capitalist mode of production. The laws of motion of the capitalist mode of production predominate with labour chained by the State to the most backward organisation of production, the most primitive productive forces, and thereby forced into the most primitive relations of production. The authority comes from capital. The limitations derive from the State and not a resistant pre-capitalist formation. To understand why capitalism is still so poorly developed and the reasons for the limitations on formal and real subordination that effectively institutionalise Narodism and pauperise a trapped peasantry, one must look to the State and its ruling class as the resistant class rather than to some resistant pre-capitalist formation. Furthermore, it should be stressed that the class itself is not pre-capitalist, but capitalist and petit-bourgeois. As such, the State is not against capitalism *per se*, but simply big capitalism out of its control as opposed to small capitalism within its control.

Why Narodism Became the Tanzanian Way

In Kenya, a nascent big bourgeoisie controlled profits as early as the 1930s, while in Tanzania, teachers, traders, and clerks were the mainstay of the independence movement, with kulak farmers participating (Awiti, Bienen, Hyden, Maguire), but never predominating as a class 'to the extent where they could become an important political force at the national level' (Shivji, 1976: 50).[4] In contrast to Kenya, Tanzania was not a settler colony[5] and had a lower priority for Great Britain. This junior status was reflected by its comparatively underdeveloped infrastructure, industrial and manufacturing sectors at independence in 1961.[6] Europeans in Tanzania alienated less than 1 per cent of the land, few restrictions were placed on what Africans were allowed to grow, and the official policy was to promote cash-crop production by expanding the number of middle-peasant household producers (Brett: 217; Iliffe, 1971: 36-37). Proletarianisation was minimal by comparison with Kenya, where the imposition of settler estate agriculture often necessitated separating the producer from his means of production, resulting in landlessness.[7] Unlike Kenya, where a future big-bourgeoisie berated the colonial state for being 'communist' (Njonjo) and not differentiating between them and the rest by allowing the 'better farmers' to plant coffee and have individual title to the land,[8] Tanzania's kulaks did not face the same impediments and were perhaps less insistent about controlling the independence movement. Although Kenya's nascent big bourgeoisie found its sphere of operation circumscribed by the colonial state, capital invested relatively heavily in this settler colony, creating ample opportunities to accumulate through trade and distributorships as well as by producing agricultural commodities which were less attractive to settler capital. Because Tanzania was, from the earliest times, a dumping ground for Kenya's developing industrial and manufacturing sector, opportunities for accumulation were more limited in Tanzania and a non-productive petit bourgeoisie predominated, with only a small number of kulak farmers emerging in the fertile areas of Kilimanjaro, Ismani, and Lushoto, alongside the European estates. These 'yeoman' farmers, as they were called, were not favoured by the colonial State against the 'peasant

cultivator' until the mid-1950s when the State attempted to encourage
' "the transition from native customary tenure into freehold in appropriate
areas" ' (Iliffe, 1971: 38). By this time, the independence movement was in
full swing and this policy, which clearly acted to stabilise kulaks in a class,
was roundly attacked by Nyerere, who claimed:

> If we allowed land to be sold like a robe, within a short period there would only be
> a few Africans possessing land in Tanzania. . . We would be faced with a problem
> which has created antagonism among people and led to bloodshed in many
> countries of the world (Nyerere in Iliffe, 1971: 38).

Kenya's big bourgeoisie came to power to strip capital of its racial fetters
and proceeded to smash its petit-bourgeois opponents who saw the situation
somewhat differently. Tanzania's ruling 'bureaucratic bourgeoisie', as it was
later called (Shivji, 1976: 66-99),[9] lacked the material base to act like its
Kenya counterparts and was not prepared to continue to support land
policies that would develop capital (out of its control) and proletarianise a
middle peasantry. Hence, while Kenya devised policies to support the
further development of a big bourgeoisie,[10] its poorer sister chose
Narodism to institutionalise a petit bourgeoisie and small capitalism.

Narodism Phase I: Ujamaa
Tanzania's Narodism has developed in two phases (1967-1973 and
1973-present) with tendencies to reproduce two different forms and
periods of capital. During the first phase, Nyerere presented his version of
'socialism', attempted to institutionalise it in the now famous *ujamaa*
(familyhood) villages, and began his attack on big capital.

Socialism, Nyerere argued, was 'an attitude of mind', and the immediate
task after independence was for Tanzanians to 're-educate' themselves and
'regain (this) former attitude of mind' (Nyerere in Clark, 1978: 42).
Capitalism, exploitation, classes and class struggle were all presented as the
unique product of a foreign, Western colonialism, rather than as a distinct
period in the development of commodity production. Nyerere therefore
insisted that Tanzania's task was to become 'self-reliant' and to develop its
traditional economy, which was already socialistic (Nyerere, 1968: 337-
356; 1966: 195-203).

The argument was not new. Almost one hundred years earlier Lenin
spent volumes attacking Russia's Narodniks who believed that socialism
there could be based on the *mir* (village commune) and its naturally
communistic peasantry (Lenin, I-IV especially). Lenin saw the Narodniks
as utopian, petit-bourgeois reactionary nationalists whose support of
Russia's 'small producer' was 'opposed to the interests of labour in general'
and was not an attack on capitalism, but simply big foreign capital (Lenin,
I: 440-441). Lenin roundly chastised the Narodniks for inventing 'a fiction

of the pre-capitalist order' (Lenin, II: 517), for their false assumption that Russia was still 'pre-capitalist' (Lenin, I: 384-385), and for their insistence on incorrectly seeing the Russian small producer as an independent proto-socialist rather than as a petit bourgeois engaged in the hopeless task of trying to stabilise himself as a small producer in the face of a developing capitalist economy (Lenin, I: 341-381). To prefer capitalism in its 'least developed' form, where both labour and capital are backward, was in Lenin's opinion to prefer capitalism in its 'worst form' (Lenin, I: 436). In designating 'independent undertakings', which depended on all sorts of personal exploitation, *moral,* and 'wage labour', which stripped 'exploitation of all its obscurities and illusions' *immoral* (Lenin, I: 384-385), Lenin accused the Narodniks of opting for 'stagnation' over 'capitalist progress' (Lenin, II: 519), and of fettering labour to the land rather than pressing for its freedom as a socialised commodity off the land, where it would be capable of confronting capital in its most advanced form (Lenin, I: 414).

In spite of its historical antecedents, Nyerere's radical populism had an initially strong domestic appeal and even more so abroad. Intrinsic to its success was the argument that socialism could develop apart from classes and class struggle, that everything could be improved without drastic change, that the peasantry was the 'natural fighter for socialism' (Lenin, I: 275) and that so-called traditional life would be preserved rather than destroyed. Even now, critics attacking the results of Tanzania's policies tend to defend the theory and/or the class behind these policies as 'progressive' (Shivji, 1976: 98; Saul, 1974: 362; von Freyhold, 1977: 85; Raikes, 1975: 36; Raikes, 1978: 269) with alternative positions branded 'pseudo-Marxist determinism' (Saul, 1974: 364). The historical analogue appears once again with reminders of Lenin's attacks on Narodnik reformism, their belief that Russia was 'exceptional' (Lenin, II: 518) and their underlying assumption that they, as intellectuals, could choose Russia's future apart from 'the independent trends of the various social classes which were shaping history in accordance with their own interests' (Lenin, II: 523).

Irrespective of the support it garnered from intellectuals and its own bureaucratic bourgeoisie, the Narodnik content of Tanzania's policies in this first phase was obvious enough. After repeated failures to attract foreign aid, the 1967 Arusha Declaration announced that Tanzania would base its socialism on 'self-reliance' at both the national and individual level. Banks, large companies, and big private estates were nationalised, with less than half of the transport and manufacturing sector left in private hands (Clark, 1978: 68). Shortly afterwards, the political party TANU passed a set of 'Leadership Guidelines' which prohibited members of the government, party and parastatals from holding more than one job, having directorships or shares in private companies, or from renting private houses to others. The agrarian policy was spelled out in two position papers: 'Socialism and Rural Development', and 'Education for Self-Reliance'. In the former, the state encouraged peasants to join *ujamaa* villages and farm communally in exchange for promises of increased social services. In the latter, proposals were made to dismantle the colonial educational structure and include agricultural work as part of the primary school curriculum so that peasant children would be prepared for their future with a realistic, relevant education. Somewhat afterwards, in 1971, TANU's 'Mwongozo' Guidelines theoretically opened the way for workers' participation and control by forbidding 'arrogant, extravagant, contemptuous and oppressive leaders' (Clark, 1978: 48).

Different classes in different parts of the country handled these pro-mulgations differently;[11] however, it would be a mistake to treat them as mere theory. The attack was against big capital and the development of wage labour as a commodity. The effect was to level class formation and simultaneously to introduce the more perverse sorts of differentiation predicted by Lenin. With state employees prohibited from engaging in private enterprise, personal accumulation did not stop, but depended on surreptitious business activities that were often unproductive (Shivji, 1976: 80-84; Raikes, 1978: 301-307; Fortmann, 1978c: 20) and on increasing the size of the state bureaucracy and the salaries of its upper echelons. In spite of the 'Mwongozo' Guidelines, the State clamped down hard on workers after a series of strikes in 1972-1973 (Mihyo, 1975: 64-84; Shivji, 1976: 23-45) revealing the anti-labour petit-bourgeois content of its socialism. With capital itself formally stymied, the size of the official working class also decreased (Raikes, 1978), in part the result of a cutback in sisal production (Rweyemamu; Clark, 1978: 55), in part a predictable conse-quence of Narodism. Furthermore, 'Education for Self-Reliance' appeared to apply only to the poor as differentiation continued (Mbilinyi, 1974; 1976) and other classes went on for secondary and university studies.

In the agrarian sector, this first phase attempted to halt the development of a politically and economically competitive class of capitalist farmers and to exert greater control over the sphere of realisation by encouraging communal production in *ujamaa* villages. Producer prices for agricultural commodities barely changed over a seven-year period, one example of state appropriation by unequal exchange. Another was its tendency to mimic merchant capital as it simultaneously entered the sphere of production sporadically and unevenly without transforming the productive forces, without decreasing the value of labour power and by appropriating through the extraction of absolute surplus value (Boesen, b; Coulson, 1975; Raikes, 1975; Shivji). Hence the predictable attempts by the ruling class to idealise the land, the village, and the hoe.

Kulak farmers responded in kind. Living in the most productive parts of the country on the periphery, they reacted by selling across the border to neighbouring Kenya and Uganda, where producer prices were often higher and the shilling was harder, following the dissolution of the unified

East African currency in 1966. Kulaks also used their control of the co-operative societies, through which credit was distributed and crops were marketed, to accumulate at the expense of both smallholders and the State (Raikes, 1978: 301-307; Migot Agolla in Widstrand; Fortmann, 1978c: 20; Cliffe et. al., 1975; Matango) and even managed on occasion to attract state resources to establish *ujamaa* villages (von Freyhold, 1977: 88; Raikes, 1975: 45-46). While the relationship between the bureaucratic bourgeoisie and individual kulaks remained somewhat ambiguous, the official policy of expanding middle-peasant household production fettered their ability to accumulate as a class. The thrust of the State's policies attempted to stymie the development of a class of competitive appropria-tors. Although the State might favour individual kulaks from time to time, as a class they became the scapegoat for the State's failures and the bureaucratic bourgeoisie mounted attacks on those farmers who could potentially become a 'focus of opposition against measures which affected the peasantry as a whole' (von Freyhold, 1977: 88).

During this period, *ujamaa* villages were voluntary and kulak farmers rarely joined with the exception of those who used the opportunity to attract State funds. *Ujamaa* villages were directed towards poor peasants; however, the much promised social services rarely came, no more than 15 to 20 per cent of the population ever joined, efforts to promote communal production were generally unsuccessful, and active political participation was discouraged to the point where one group of villages known as the Ruvuma Development Association was deregistered and banned (McHenry; Coulson, 1975; Raikes, 1975; Fortmann, 1978c). Although recruitment into villages was supposed to be voluntary, force was often used to re-locate peasants to sites where there was no water, no seeds for planting, no food during the relocation period, and where the land itself was poor, medical facilities were unavailable, and the lengthy distance from the market made it impossible to sell what was produced. Furthermore, with wage labour officially prohibited or discouraged, more perverse social relations of production appeared (Musoke, Bakula, Daraja, Mashauri, Mboya in Proctor). Leaders often had more land than others, penalised those who refused to work on communal plots, and used the labour power within villages as their personal servants (Proctor; Fortmann, 1978c; 42-43).

In short, the prohibitions on wage labour simply resurrected the various types of corvée labour described so well by Lenin in his critiques of the Narodniks (Lenin, DCR: 189, 605; Lenin, I: 216-217). While estate labourers had been relatively better off, as they were protected by a minimum wage (Fortmann, 1978b: 3), one Area Commissioner prohibited members of an *ujamaa* village from working in a nearby tea factory (de Vries and Fortmann, 1974: 15), and in another case the hiring of migrant wage labour was stopped. In Ismani, after capitalist farmers had their land appropriated and turned into *ujamaa* villages, the state used and 'directed' the labour of secondary school children and members of the National Service (Raikes, 1977: 306, 322) in preference to wage labour. In a village in Tanga, members became the 'personal servants' of the manager and were punished with double work loads if they did not perform the communal work assigned to them (Fortmann, 1978c: 42-43). Not surprisingly, 'labour organisation' was often perceived as 'problematic' during this period. However, the resistance of the peasantry could not be termed pre-capitalist. Given the choice between '*ujamaa* and working as a paid labourer, they chose the cash' (de Vries and Fortmann, 1974: 15); however, often the choice was not theirs. Decisions stemmed from the bureaucratic bourgeoisie that an 'idle and loitering' poor peasantry 'should be participating full time in agricultural production' (Boesen, b: 6) for the State. Predictably enough, with labour exploited by the State both in the sphere of realisation and exchange, agricultural production declined. Furthermore, the failures of this period were not the unfortunate mistakes of a 'well-intentioned' (Raikes, 1978: 269) socialism, but the predictable consequences of Narodism, which is anti-labour and reactionary where it appears. As Lenin noted,

> compared with the labour of the dependent or bonded peasant, the labour of the hired worker is progressive in all branches of the national economy (Lenin, DCR: 605).

> Not a single worker would ever consent to exchange his status for that of a Russian 'independent' handicraftsman in 'real', 'peoples' industries (Lenin, I: 216-217),

or, one might add, with a member of an *ujamaa* village.

The result by 1974 was stagnation in agriculture (Tabari, 1975: 90). With so few peasants in *ujamaa* villages and cooperatives still holding their own, state capital still had little control either in the sphere of production or exchange. Outside a few estates, the productive forces were still underdeveloped to the point of being backward (Boesen, b: 10, 7), inputs were not widely used, and surplus was largely appropriated on the basis of absolute rather than relative surplus value. With agricultural commodities forming one half of Tanzania's GDP and almost all of her exports, the consequences of a stagnating agrarian sector could not be overlooked. Peasants had to be kept on the land and producing to support a burgeoning state and insure its reproduction. The anti-proletarian content of Narodism was likely to become starker. The State needed to harness the labour power of the peasantry without creating surplus populations that 'could not possibly be absorbed' (Marx, *Capital*, I: 734). Furthermore, State capital itself was too poorly developed to support a large proletariat and was unwilling to allow a competitive capitalist class to accumulate at its expense.

Narodism Phase II: Villagisation

Faced with these crises, Tanzania embarked on a second phase characterised by the forcible villagisation of the majority of the population and a massive re-entry of international (mainly World Bank) capital of a different form and period. Villagisation had its greatest impact on weak and scattered populations in the poorest parts of the country. Here labour was uprooted and regrouped into legally constituted villages. Villagisation is best understood as the initial crude reorganisation of labour; as the formal subordination of labour to state capital. As such, it has more in common with Marx's description of early capitalism prior to mechanisation[12] (Marx, *Capital*, I: chapters XI-XIV, especially p. 322) than it does with the expansion of simple commodity production within the confines of a so-called 'peasant economy'. What has been described as the 'Resilience of the Peasant Mode of Production' (Hyden, 1978) exists only in the realm of mythology.

While the ideology of *ujamaa* was projected as a kind of sentimental Narodism, villagisation was presented in terms of modernisation theory. Peasants were no longer seen as proto-socialist, but as thorns in the State's side, whose 'problems were based fundamentally on their traditional outlook and unwillingness to accept change'. Ideologues argued 'the State had. . . to take the role of the "father" ' and move its citizens to 'a better and more prosperous life' (Mwapachu, 1976: 3). In 1973, Nyerere announced that 'to live in villages is an order', and justified coercion by a further notation that 'It's partly compulsory. . . so is vaccination', (quoted in Nsari, 1975: 116). From the standpoint of the State, the main objective of villagisation was

> . . . to make possible a better use of the existent and often underemployed rural labour. By working together. . . peasants are expected to engage in specialisation of functions and divisions of labour as well as increase their work and discipline. It is hoped that this together with the emanating village organisation would eventually lead to an increase in agricultural production and labour productivity (Maeda, 1977: 6).

One could hardly have asked for a better rendition of chapters XI-XIV of Marx's *Capital*, vol. I.

The State instituted its policy of forcible villagisation between 1973 and 1976. Communal production was largely abandoned and 13 million people were herded into nucleated villages with individual block farms, representing 85 per cent of the population and some 8,000 villages (Coulson, 1977). Regardless of intention, the initial impact of villagisation was not to produce primitive rural factories of organised labour. It was instead radically to disrupt rural life and to create a food crisis.[13] Government agents who ranged from the militia to TANU youth league officials to agricultural extension officers stripped peasants of their land, food, and possessions, burning their houses and crops along the way. Scattered populations were moved, in many cases from fertile to barren land, out of permanent dwellings, away from water, and to areas devoid of social services. Populations which had once been scattered were now concentrated. Ecologically sound land practices were dismantled. Land that was formerly cleared and kept under control through scattered dwelling patterns returned to bush. Villages were overpopulated and over-concentrated. Land began to erode under the pressure of too many animals and people, with sanitary conditions deteriorating rapidly. Whereas a farmer's field had once been close by his dwelling, the concentration of populations into nucleated villages now sometimes meant a five- to seven-mile walk prior to cultivating. Much of that land either returned to bush or, when it was farmed, was too far away to be protected from devastation by wild animals, bad weather, pilfering, etc. Consequently, a kind of illegal feudal subtenancy occurred with farmers who had land closer to the village subletting to those who had land further away, thereby creating 'a previously non-existent landlord class' (Fortmann, 1978c: 56). Villages were arbitrarily located near roads even when it was the least fertile land in the area. In practice, this meant that in some areas peasants were forcibly evicted from fertile hilltops to barren plains or vice versa depending on where the road was. The result in one instance was a 50 per cent decline in agricultural production (Operation Songeza, p. 6). Tanzania, which had been a net exporter of food between 1968 and 1971, was forced to import over 500,000 tons of maize between 1973 and 1975 to avert starvation (Lofchie, 1978: 453-455).

At the same time that villagisation was occurring, the State restructured its authority to deal with these new units of production. Freedom of movement was curtailed and minimum acreage requirements from the colonial period were introduced. Prior to the massive move, Government was de-centralised to the Regions in 1972 with a heavy concentration of administrative and legal authority directed to villages and village production. A hierarchy of command was established from the Prime Minister's Office (PMO's) to the village, and agricultural extension officers (bwana shambas) were only to report to the Ministry of Agriculture on technical matters, with the administrative authority (i.e. promotions, hiring, firing, orders) transferred to the PMO. In 1975, 'Villages and Ujamaa Villages (Resignation, Designation and Administration) Act' was passed to define what constituted a village and how its political and administrative affairs should be regulated. Village Chairmen and Secretaries became paid employees of the political party and assumed a greater responsibility for agricultural production at the village level. In 1976, cooperative societies were disbanded with agricultural credit (i.e. applying for, receiving, unlending, and recouping credit for improved inputs) and crop-buying arrangements filtered through the village as the legally liable unit, thereby eliminating the role previously enjoyed by kulak farmers. Parastatal crop-buying and marketing authorities were simultaneously established for almost every crop, again curtailing the kulak sphere of influence in an attempt to increase state accumulation. A year later, the political party TANU joined with Zanzibar's ASP to become CCM (Chama Cha Mapinduzi—the Party of the Revolution). With its new radical nomenclature, the party role nevertheless increasingly came to resemble that of the State's policeman in the countryside, as it assured a greater responsibility for agricultural production and the distribution of credit to the village level. However, the State decided not to leave village production to popularly elected officials and in December 1977 created the post of Village Manager (VM) and Village Management Technician (VMT) who were to be paid and accountable to the central government and responsible for the 'socio-economic take-off of the village as a production unit' (Maeda, p. 11). The position has been accurately described as 'the final stage of government penetration of the countryside' (Fortmann, 1978b: 19). However, with villages regarded by state officials as a kind of Siberia, few have reported for duty.

One must naturally distinguish between the State's vision and attempts at subordination and the reality which followed. Although in certain respects, villagisation as a classic form represented the 'enlargement of scale' (Mandel, 1977: 1023) which Marx felt was critical to greater formal and hence real subordination, the degree of formal subordination itself varied, creating various types of villages. Furthermore, even within classic nucleated villages, household production remains the dominant form, with the State doing little beyond supplying inputs to transform the value of labour power. The result in both cases is that there is a limit to the degree of subordination which can occur, thereby accentuating extraction by absolute surplus value, giving rise to the Narodism of an earlier period, and leading to certain contradictions for both state and international capital.

In the wealthy, densely populated, richer parts of the country, villages are often nothing more than legal composites of individual landholdings which are still scattered, sometimes unconsolidated, and cannot be visibly identified as villages. Following the assassination of a state official who tried to villagise the wealthy maize growers of Ismani, the State made no further attempt to move capitalist farmers and reorganise their production. Instead, the State's legal redefinition of these unconsolidated holdings as villages was directed towards subordinating the sphere of exchange by making it impossible for individual farmers to receive agricultural inputs outside of their village governments and making these governments the legally liable organs if they failed to recoup credit. Nevertheless, the State's policy of expanding household production and officially frowning on the hiring of wage labour both increases the difficulty of accumulating and concentrating rural capital and the likelihood that poorer middle peasants (themselves the product of the contradictions of Narodism) will be hired formally.

A second type of village is like the first, atypical, but in a different sense. Its population produces little for exchange value and really approximates a rural proletariat rather than the more common middle peasant wage labour equivalent—subordinated to capital, fighting to reproduce itself, and yet unable to sell its labour for the wage versus the equivalent. Such villages have little independent economic viability and are most accurately described as 'bedroom communities' to the large State or expatriate estates which they border. A number of such villages are new creations of the massive villagisation campaign. Typically, they have been sited on marginal land with poor productive potential; they are not considered creditworthy and produce little or nothing for exchange value. It would be difficult to say whether such villages are the result of bad planning or a strategic way of providing cheap labour for nearby estates. In the past, a number of attempts were made to recruit labour for state farms. When that failed, vagrants in town who could not show they had work were forcibly moved and trucked out to government estates. As most of the vagrants ran away, a more successful policy has been to relocate the peasantry to uninhabitable land, control movement between villages, and create a captive labour force.

A third type of village is also marginal, but unlike the second, there is no way the population can engage in wage labour. Here, the middle peasantry is experiencing the classic symptoms of Narodism and stands with 'one foot already in the swamp of pauperism' (Marx, *Capital*, I: 642). The population is too far away from the estates to sell its labour, too likely to be evicted from the towns if it tried, and too uneducated to succeed if it were not thrown out. The biggest problem of peasants in such villages is to ensure their own continuous reproduction—that is, to produce enough to eat. Normally, they grow two seasons of maize before they sell any because they fear starvation. As they generally have been relocated to uninhabitable land, their surplus is marginal, and they are no longer considered suitable credit risks. To the extent that freedom of movement has been curtailed by villagisation (and it is unclear how successful the State has been in its attempts to restrict migration), the land is likely to become increasingly marginal, leading to a situation in which poor middle peasants are less and less likely to be able to reproduce themselves. At present, these villages produce very little and sometimes nothing for exchange value. Hence, the essential condition which prompted capital to provide famine relief during the colonial period (Bryceson)—to ensure the continuous production for exchange value—does not arise. Nevertheless, to avert starvation, the importation of food and the exhaustion of foreign exchange reserves,[14] it is still important to the State that such peasants are able to reproduce themselves. State and particularly international capital have encouraged the growth of food crops through a variety of mechanisms including more favourable producer prices and by supplying inputs of credit for the production of food crops through programmes such as the National Maize Programme, which was jointly sponsored by the World Bank and AID. However, since the crisis of 1974, credit for the production of food crops is mainly given where cash crops are produced so that necessary labour time relative to surplus labour time will be reduced, thereby increasing the productivity of labour power from the standpoint of state capital. As these villages neither produce cash crops nor generally for exchange, they are by definition not creditworthy. Although credit was given to some of these villages experimentally following the food crisis of 1974, the result was either that credit was not repaid, or that the land was so marginal that the inputs had either no impact or a negative one (Fortmann, 1975).[15] It seems then that the continuous reproduction of this peasantry is not important for exchange value, but simply to avert starvation and/or the development of surplus populations. To ensure both, the State, in conjunction with the ILO and the UNDP is proposing to begin a 'Special Labour Intensive Public Works Programme in the Arusha, Dodoma, Rukwa, and Ruvuma Regions', which are some of the poorer parts of the country. The point of this project is to 'engage deployable surplus labour to build irrigation and water supply facilities, schools, health centres, housing, feeder roads and to carry out land reclamation' (UNDP, pp. 27-28). Labour power will either be paid below its value or compensated by 'food for work'. One is reminded of the German colonial periods when

> famine was made into a useful occasion for the administration to gain labour for its many 'projects of civilization'. The policy of 'quid pro quo' was proudly proclaimed. 'The governor does not intend to distribute the food free of charge, but rather to sell it cheaply or to exchange it against work performance. He hopes to generate some good results from this approach and to considerably increase the contribution of the local people to useful endeavours like road construction' (Kjekshus, 1977: 140-141, partially quoted in Bryceson, 1978: 17).

Whatever the initial reasons for moving scattered peasants off one piece of marginal land and concentrating them on another, it is clear that although these peasants produce nothing significant for exchange value, it is far easier for the State to subordinate and deploy rural labour from villages than from scattered settlements. From the standpoint of state capital, villages have many of the same attractions that factories did in comparison to scattered handicraft 'industries'. One is accessible, whereas the other is less so; one has functionaries (members of the village government, village managers, etc.) whose chief responsibility is to 'direct, superintend, and. . . adjust' (Marx, *Capital*, I: 330) the work process, whereas the other does not. Again, the fact that labour is not fully proletarianised, that it is in some sense still tied to the land but unable to reproduce itself off it, that it is paid below its value and subsidises this low payment by what it produces on the land is not the sign of a pre-capitalist peasantry. This middle peasantry is experiencing the classic symptoms of Narodism. It is being squeezed, trapped, and exploited by a poorly developed state capital attempting to transform itself without creating capitalists, workers, or surplus populations.

A fourth type of village has greater productive potential than those just described, primarily because of its location on arable land. Such villages have a special status for state and international capital. They are the focus of rural credit and 'integrated rural development' schemes and of programmes to expand the production of certain cash crops. However, even here peasants have received few increases in social services and little that would transform the quality of the productive forces. While the State views the village as a unit of production with stated targets, it has done little but to regroup labour. The middle-peasant household continues to remain the sub-unit of production, sometimes scattered, sometimes on individual block farms within nucleated villages. The hoe is still the main instrument of production, most villages are poorly connected by roads, many have no water, and the quality of extension services is often poor (Coulson, 1977). A climate of chronic uncertainty faces potentially productive peasants in potentially productive villages. A peasant may produce for exchange value only to find that the market does not provide for the purchase of use values, raising the obvious question of why produce if there is nothing to buy. Crop prices are variable, marketing is unreliable, and transport and storage are generally unavailable. Crops sometimes rot waiting for the State to market perishable produce, or prices suddenly change to the disadvantage of the peasant producer, putting him into debt or forcing him to underconsume. Liberal market incentives are too unpredictable to give rise to the degree of specialisation in production that one might expect. Instead, as a hedge against the State's poor prices and marketing, potentially high producers tend to diversify rather than specialise in one commodity and sometimes move more heavily into food production. Although special seeds, fertilisers, insecticides, and other improved inputs are supplied to such villages, the realisation of value still tends towards the extraction of absolute rather than relative surplus value, because the productive forces are so backward and their transformation is limited by the existing organisation of production. With minimum acreage requirements of the colonial period having been resurrected and the coercive apparatus of the State well developed down to the village, there is little direct confrontation of State authority. Instead, peasants engage in activities which are interpreted by the State as devious, stupid, uneducated or irrational, which give rise in turn to a further concentration of state authority at the village level. These activities are, in fact, the symptoms of Narodism—the contradictions of attempting to force out an increase in surplus value within the confines of middle-peasant household production.

Narodism and International Capital

This fourth type of village is the focal point for international capital, which now supplies Tanzania with 60 to 80 per cent of its annual development budget. It is directed primarily towards the promotion of certain cash crops or institutions and programmes which indirectly support that production. Continuity in production as well as quality and quantity controls are important aspects of supplying international markets with particular commodities. Both increasingly depend on the expansion and rationalisation of commodity relations in general. Hence, international capital is promoting projects to improve storage facilities for both food and cash crops, devise training programmes for village officials and agricultural extension officers, start small businesses within villages, improve the distribution of fertilisers and other inputs, and develop technical packages which are specifically designed to suit certain agro-economic zones.

To insure sufficient quantity and quality controls, it is necessary to force out an increase in the productivity of labour by using improved inputs. Tendencies towards a further extraction of relative surplus value depend on increasing the size of holdings, the hiring of wage labour, and the introduction of machinery, all of which are inhibited by middle-peasant household production. As the use of inputs increases and demands more labour than can be supplied by small households, a counter-tendency towards the extraction of absolute surplus value appears, in spite of the fact that international capital does enter as an advanced form of industrial capital with *tendencies* to produce higher yields of a specified quality. To insure a continuous supply of a commodity, there must in the first instance be a guarantee that peasant producers are able to reproduce themselves. In the second instance, commodity relations must be sufficiently generalised either to result in the ideal situation where producers purchase rather than produce the means of subsistence or where conditions encourage peasants to increase what they produce for exchange value and decrease production to reproduce the means of subsistence. To decrease necessary relative to surplus labour time necessitates supplying improved inputs for both food and cash crops, thereby increasing yields per hectare, decreasing the amount of land and labour time which must be used for production to reproduce the means of subsistence, and increasing production for exchange value, whether of food or cash crops. However, within the confines of middle-peasant household production, the tendency to force out an increase in the value of labour (i.e. the extraction of relative surplus value) is counteracted by the constraints of household production, resulting in a tendency towards the intensification of labour, overwork, and underconsumption, and the extraction of absolute surplus value. This is further heightened as producers are paid too poorly (below the socially necessary cost of labour) for what they produce for exchange. If they are paid too poorly for what they produce for exchange value, they will either go into debt as they attempt to pay for inputs received on credit, be unable to reproduce themselves, switch from one commodity to another in search of better prices, or attempt to retreat into production for consumption. In all cases, the *continuous* production of commodities for exchange value is threatened. Hence, in Kenya, according to Cowen, international capital fought against earlier forms of capital (in particular, estate capital) in their attempts to 'maintain producer prices' and sought to raise those prices to the international prices. Cowen demonstrates how estate capital as an earlier form extracted value on the basis of absolute surplus labour (by lengthening the working day, decreasing consumption, and/or paying value) and in doing so invited the pauperisation of the producer in contrast to international capital (Cowen, 1977).[17]

In Tanzania, the bureaucratic bourgeoisie has used the State as a vehicle of accumulation for itself as a class, with inflated salaries and numerous perks substituting for their inability to accumulate in the sphere of production. Furthermore, as real producer prices decrease relative to inflation, the salaries and costs of administering crop-buying parastatals have increased over time. The result has been that international capital has transformed the value of labour power with improved inputs at the same time that state capital has put a lid on producer prices, with the margin between producer and international prices increasing. Coupled with the obvious limitations of increasing the extraction of surplus value on small household units, international capital has mainly generated increased value for exchange through the expansion of the number of households engaged in the production of a particular commodity, rather than in any genuine transformation in the value of labour power.[18] While international capital has attempted to pressure for higher producer prices in some cash-crop commodities, it has simultaneously helped to support programmes that effectively increase the pressure on the small producer.[19] It has also effectively propped up the State and its ruling class during periods of economic crisis by supplying large amounts of capital and in some cases cancelling bilateral loans which have come due. Coupled with the obvious limitations of increasing the ratio of necessary relative to surplus labour time on small household units, international capital has compensated for the contradictions by generating increased value for exchange through the expansion of households engaged in the production of a particular commodity rather than in any genuine transformation of the value of labour power. However, the strategy itself may now have reached its logical limit. With overall agricultural production in stark decline, the IMF has recently insisted that Tanzania devalue its currency and introduce other stringent economic measures as a condition for future loans. (*New African*, 1980: 33-35). International capital, then, is like all other capitals faced with the law of values as its adversary and with the inherent contradictions of the Narodism it has subsidised. Nevertheless, to the extent (and it is in some respects quite considerable) that international capital can transform the value of labour power within the confines of household production, it postpones other confrontations—in particular, the confrontation with either indigenous capital or labour.

Faced with strong big bourgeoisies in various parts of Africa and elsewhere in the third world, international capital is finding its sphere of operations increasingly circumscribed (Swainson, 1977: 39-55). Hence, to the extent that production can be organised simultaneously to extract greater surplus value and forestall the development of a big bourgeoisie, it does not *immediately* go against the interests of international capital. The expansion of household production does this 'by tempering rather than accelerating the concentration of land within the hands of the indigenous class' and 'by eclipsing the growth of sources of wage labour power' (Cowen, NCCHP: 13). The evident sympathy of international capital should not be surprising given its recognition that either organised labour or, more especially, unemployed or poor landless people, may be politically destabilising and hence threaten longer term interests (Feder, 1977: 56-78). In some cases, this has led to demands by international capital for 'land reform' (Halliday, 1979: 26-27) and 'redistribution', while in other cases, the existing social formations are more hospitable to this advanced Narodism and its international development packages of 'appropriate technology' and 'nonformal education'. While at one level these packages stymie the development of capital and the socialisation of labour, at another they alter the value of labour power and reduce the most glaring contradictions of Narodism.[20]

Tanzania is quite hospitable to Narodism in a certain sense, because even prior to the massive re-entry of international capital, the material base of the ruling class led to its adopting policies which effectively acted both to curtail the development of a bourgeoisie and a proletariat and to base state accumulation on a landed middle peasantry. However, as Cowen has argued in another case, 'the *preponderance* of the middle peasantry has been *secured* by the action of international capital at the economic level. . .' (Cowen, NCCHP: 5; my emphasis). Ironically, then, international capital in Tanzania cannot be accused of having turned Tanzania away from its 'socialist' path towards capitalism. Tanzania has already embarked on the capitalist road. Instead, international capital has bolstered the existing petit-bourgeois capitalism by entering with capital of a different form and period. This has effectively worked further to expand household production, and thereby to perpetuate the bureaucratic bourgeoisie and its efforts to forestall a competitive capitalist class.[21] If international capital is to be correctly accused, it cannot be for having created a class of kulaks, but rather for helping temporarily to cement Narodism, which Lenin noted 'stands for levelling out the peasantry and is "regressive" because it desires to keep capital within those medieval forms that combine exploitation with scattered, technically backward production and with personal pressure on the producer' (Lenin, I: 485). The fact that international capital can to some degree transform the value of labour power and rationalise commodity relations (by raising food prices, grain storage projects, etc.) does not mean that the middle peasantry can be secured indefinitely. The middle peasantry is, after all, a fragile petit-bourgeois class within the confines of capitalism itself. Efforts to solidify the middle peasantry and curtail the extremes of bourgeoisie and proletariat cannot surmount the law of value, which in turn generates contradictions that point to the inherent instability of the middle peasantry as a class and the logical impossibility of its indefinite perpetuation. Furthermore, in the face of developing commodity production, it would be only realistic to view the middle peasantry as a trapped proletariat in the face of one mode of production and totally inappropriate to see it as a pre-capitalist formation. This is a continuation of the arguments put forward by Cowen and Banaji (1977), who maintain that where the state subjects household commodity producers to quality and quantity controls and supervises their labour, producer prices are equivalent to wages and the household producers themselves become wage labour equivalents. However, as both Lenin and Marx noted on numerous occasions, there are clear and significant differences between a trapped equivalent and labour power as 'free' commodity (*Capital*, I: 169).

Conclusion

Narodism stifles class formation and gives birth to a repressive state. It cannot be the vehicle for a transition to socialism, and no such process of transition is occurring in Tanzania. Narodism in that country has instead been the vehicle for pauperisation both at the economic and political level.

Economically, Narodism has led to stagnation and starvation. By now there should be no mistake concerning causes. The recent war with Uganda and the impending drought have simply tipped the scale on an inherently precarious system which was doomed from its conception. The logical contradictions of Narodism have matured and can only become starker amidst the developing commoditisation of the economy. Here, socialism has not triumphed over capitalism. Nor is the Tanzanian system preferable to more ostensible and advanced types of capitalism. In Tanzania one is only viewing capitalism in its 'least developed' and 'worst' form (Lenin, I: 436), capitalism 'containing greater relics of medieval, semi-feudal forms of capital and nothing more' (Lenin, I: 380). In addition, it is false that the Tanzanian way provides for a greater degree of internal 'self-reliance' and autonomy from international capital. The economic stagnation induced by Narodism has actually increased Tanzania's dependence on external forces, verbiage to the contrary notwithstanding.

Politically, the results of Narodism are equally chilling. With the extraction of relative surplus value precluded under this system, compulsion is the only way the State can squeeze greater surpluses from its poor and demoralised peasantry. This necessitates an increasingly repressive political and administrative system, which in turn reduces the opportunities for popular expression and political participation. It is no accident that one working-class area in Dar es Salaam is commonly called 'Soweto' and that Tanzania's Special Branch is nervously referred to as 'Savak'. Furthermore, Tanzania's 'small is beautiful' Narodnik underpinnings have other undesirable political results as well. Class differentiation has been stifled. The State still holds legal title to the land, wage labour in the countryside is either frowned upon or actively prohibited, and the middle peasantry has been perpetuated through the enforcement of minimum acreage requirements and restrictions on its freedom of movement. There is no reason to applaud this 'victory' of the small peasant enterprise over big capital. Exploitation continues, but with fewer avenues of regress for the exploited. A backward parasitic capital continues to oppress poor and middle peasants; their produce is often shortweighed, they do not receive prices for their commodities which cover the full costs of their reproduction, and they are thereby forced to overwork and underconsume. Politically, the legal perpetuation of the middle peasantry has effectively reduced the socialisation of labour and thereby increased the authority of the State. Peasants cannot legally organise against the capital which exploits them on a daily basis because formally speaking they are not wage labour. Hence, they are reduced to subverting the State individually at the point of production and exchange. Such action creates periodic crises for the State as agricultural commodities are the mainstay of the economy and the principal source of foreign exchange. However, this repressive state and these crises do not in themselves provide the basis for revolutionary action or for a transition to socialism. In a country with little history of organised mass political struggle in either the colonial or the post-colonial period, Narodism has effectively cemented political as well as economic backwardness. Elsewhere in Africa, this sort of economic stagnation and political repression have paved the way for military intervention rather than for progressive change.

Under these circumstances, there is no point in speaking of socialism or the transition to socialism in Tanzania. To use the word 'socialism' here is to empty it of all content. Furthermore, to invoke the euphemism of the 'transition to socialism' and to analyse the existing situation in terms of setbacks and difficulties, incorrectly assumes that the process is still going on and that socialism in Tanzania is still on the agenda. Given the existing material and class forces and the implantation of Narodism, this was never the case. In addition, it would only be possible to speak of such a process if one moved from the world of dialectical materialism into the realm of voluntarism. It is more difficult to say exactly what is on the agenda in

Tanzania. One of the principal forces at work remains shrouded in mystery. The ruling class itself is awkwardly termed and poorly understood; it continues to mouth 'socialist' rhetoric and the ideology of Narodism has become its legitimator. Beyond this it is more difficult to describe this class or to understand its divisions and tendencies. The repressive state apparatus itself makes it impossible to determine whether this class is simply enriching itself, engaging in a process of capitalist accumulation, or something else altogether.

The broader question of what is to be done in circumstances where commodity relations have been poorly developed historically, where the productive forces are backward, and where the social relations have themselves been stifled is disturbing indeed. However, one thing is clear. Revolutionary situations have not emerged by mystifying the present or by supporting Narodnik social formations. Any further mystification concerning Tanzania's Narodism can only support its ruling classes against its popular classes. Certainly, these illusions have helped to attract the outside funds and liberal support which have buffered the contradictions of this inherently unstable system and have solidified its ruling class. In this sense, it is no different from many other systems. However, elsewhere Narodism is not embraced as socialism and self-styled 'leftist' analysis has not become the ideological enemy of the popular classes.

NOTES

1. See Lenin, DCR, Vols. I-II, IV-VI.
2. Cowen's discussions concerning the expansion of middle-peasant household production in Kenya and the role of international capital in buttressing this expansion critique—the populist notion that the effect of this intervention is to support accumulation by a domestic bourgeoisie. Although some of my findings differ from Cowen's, his writings have been an inspiration.
3. In his discussions of Kenya, Cowen argues that international capital enters as finance industrial capital with a consequent propensity to extract by relative surplus value in contrast to the estate merchant capital of a previous era which extracted by absolute surplus value. Cowen demonstrates that while estate capital sought to maintain producer prices, international capital attempted to raise producer prices as part of a more general attempt to raise the value of labour. As such, he maintains in contrast to populist writers, no instance of pauperisation resulted. Cowen, D.C.; 1977.
4. There is a need for a study of the relationship between the kulaks and the bureaucratic class which took over at independence. Since there is little solid evidence on this point, one must rest with the generalisations that exist at present.
5. Tanganyika was a German colony until the end of WWI, when it became a British Protectorate under the League of Nations. How much or whether its status as a Protectorate influenced Britain's policy here is an open question.
6. Clark, pp. 30-34.
7. Clearly proletarianisation was not uniform in Kenya.
8. The nascent big bourgeoisie in Kenya could be said to have been fighting the colonial state's Narodism in trying to better indigenous accumulation in refusing

to give title deeds to the few.

9. Use of the term 'bureaucratic bourgeoisie' has been criticised. See Saul, von Freyhold, Nabudere. Tanzania's ruling class is in fact awkwardly termed and poorly understood. While one can describe the negative historical conditions which prevented the rise of a strong capitalist class taking control of the State, it is more difficult to discuss this class in positive terms. In general, it appears in the literature as a faceless class. To understand more about it, the following questions need to be investigated: a) what are the historical and material roots of this class and what was its role and relationship to the nationalist movement; b) what is and has been its relationship to rural capitalists; c) is this class using its salaries and perks simply to enrich itself or to transform itself into a class of capitalists; d) who controls the 50 per cent of the economy which has been in private hands since the Arusha Declaration of 1967.

10. In many respects, the colonial state could be said to have done the dirty work for Kenya's big bourgeoisie. First, it separated the producers from the means of production by alienating land. Second, it smashed 'Mau Mau' and made it impossible for the landless to regain that land. Third, it loaned the Kenyan ruling class the money to buy out British settlers and thereby gave this class the proper excuse to create a land market and sell the land rather than redistribute it to the landless.

11. This is a history that awaits further research, especially that concerning the relationship between the bureaucratic bourgeoisie and the kulaks.

12. Marx noted, 'A greater number of labourers working at the same time (or if you will in the same field of labour) in order to produce the same sort of commodity under the mastership of one capitalist, constitutes both historically and logically the starting point of capitalist production. . . With regard to the mode of production itself, manufacture in its strict meaning is hardly to be distinguished in its earlier phases from the handicraft trades of the guilds other than by the greater number of workmen simultaneously employed by one and the same individual capital' (Marx, *Capital*, I: 322).

13. The food crisis coincided with a drought. However, the legacies of an earlier period of Narodism meant that there were no reserves and the process of villagisation disrupted existing patterns of production. The actual process of villagisation has been discussed more extensively by Boesen, Coulson, Fortmann, Raikes, Tabari, von Freyhold.

14. Prior to 1971, Tanzania had been a 'net exporter' of food. Between 1973-1975, 500,000 tons of maize was exported, foreign exchange reserves were exhausted and the balance of payments deficit increased threefold by 1974 (Lofchie, pp. 453-55).

15. Coulson (1977) has shown that most of the agricultural advice given peasants from the colonial period up to the present has been incorrect, including the question of whether inputs should be used at all on certain types of land and, if so, what types.

16. The World Bank and the Marketing Research Bureau have pushed for an increase in food prices and devised plans for a grain storage project. A continuous production for exchange can only be assured if the peasantry is not prey to famines in the face of natural disasters. Higher producer prices encourage the production of food crops for exchange, while storage facilities insure the retention of buffer stocks and increase the likelihood that over time food commodities will be circulated for exchange in the rural areas.

17. In Tanzania, one could not argue tht pauperisation is averted by the intervention of international capital. It is true that through its greater rationalisation and expansion of commodity relations it can attenuate the very worst contradictions

of middle-peasant household production, including starvation; nevertheless, limited to household labour, overwork and underconsumption are conspicuous features of middle-peasant household production even following this intervention, in part because of the class which controls the State, in part because of the inherent contradictions of Narodism both in its backward and 'advanced' forms.

18. A genuine transformation would involve transforming the productive forces beyond improved inputs.

19. For example, the World Bank is supporting the development of a programme for village management and a number of other international agencies are supporting other programmes to 'deconcentrate' state authority to the village level (Boesen, N.D.). Furthermore, deductions for inputs received on credit remain high and the general approach to recouping credit, both by state and international agencies, is to put more pressure on the producer at the same time that he increasingly receives less for what he produces.

20. The most glaring contradiction is starvation.

21. As Cowen notes in another case, 'It is not the indigenous bourgeoisie which has been created by the interventions of international capital. Rather that the formation of the indigenous bourgeoisie in the countryside has been deflected by phases of expansion of household production where the expansion has been directly set in motion by the intervention of international capital' (Cowen, NCCHP: 2).

REFERENCES

Awiti, Adhu, 'Economic Differentiation in Ismani, Irigna Region: A critical Assessment of Peasants' Response to the Ujamaa Vijini Programmes', University of Dar es Salaam, Economic Research Bureau Seminar Paper, 1972.

Banaji, Jairus, 'Modes of Production in A Materialist Conception of History', *Capital and Class*, 3 (August 1977), 1-44.

Bernstein, Henry, 'Tanzania' in *New African Yearbook 1980*, London, 1980.

Bienen, Henry, *Party Transformation and Economic Development*, Princeton, 1969.

Boesen, Jannik, 'Tanzania: From Ujamaa to Villagization', unpublished paper, Department of Economics, University of Dar es Salaam, n.d.

Brett, E.A., *Colonialism and Underdevelopment in East Africa: The Politics of Economic Change, 1919-39*, London, 1973.

Bryceson, Deborah Fahy, 'Peasant Food Production and Food Supply in Relation to the Historical Development of Commodity Production in Pre-Colonial and Colonial Tanganyika', Bureau of Resources Assessment and Land Use Planning (BRALU), the University of Dar es Salaam, May 1978.

Clark, W. Edmund, *Socialist Development and Public Investment in Tanzania, 1964-73*, Toronto, 1978.

Cliffe, Lionel, *et. al.*, *Rural Cooperation in Tanzania*, Dar es Salaam, 1975.

Coulson, Andrew, ed., *African Socialism in Practice: The Tanzanian Experience*, London, 1979.

Coulson, Andrew, 'Agricultural Policies in Mainland Tanzania', *Review of African Political Economy*, 10 (1977), 74-100.

Coulson, Andrew, 'Peasants and Bureaucrats', *Review of African Political Economy*, 3 (1975), 53-58.

Cowen, M.P., 'Notes on Capital Class and Household Production', (NCCHP), unpublished paper, n.d.

Cowen, M.P., 'On Household Production in the Countryside', Section III of Michael Cowen and Karibu Kinyanjui, 'Some Problems of Income Distribution in Kenya', Nairobi, I.D.S., 1977.

De Vries, J.L., Fortmann, and A.C. Sharma, 'A Study of Ujamaa Villages in Iringa Region', unpublished paper, Department of Rural Economy and Extension, Faculty of Agriculture and Forestry, University of Dar es Salaam, December, 1974.

Feder, Ernest, 'Capitalism's Last Ditch Effort to Save Underdeveloped Agriculture', *Journal of Contemporary Asia*, 7, 1 (1977), 56-78.

Fortmann, L.P., 'An Evaluation of the Progress of the National Maize Project at the End of One Cropping Season in Morogoro and Arusha', unpublished paper, USAID. Tanzania, November 1976.

Fortmann, L.P., 'The Road to Maendeleo: Issues Involved in Tanzanian Village Development', unpublished paper, September 18, 1978 (b).

Fortmann, L.P., 'Ujamaa Villages: Tanzania's Experience with Agrarian Socialism', prepared for COPAC/FAO, unpublished paper, February 1978 (c).

Halliday, Fred, *Iran*, London, 1979.

Hyden, Goran, *Political Development in Rural Tanzania*, Lund, Sweden, 1968.

Hyden, Goran, 'The Resilience of the Peasant Mode of Production: The Case of Tanzania', unpublished paper, University of California, Berkeley, 1978.

Iliffe, John, *Agricultural Change in Modern Tanganyika*, Historical Association of Tanzania, Paper No. 10, Nairobi, 1971.

Iliffe, John, *A Modern History of Tanganyika*, Cambridge, (UK), 1979.

Kjekshus, Helge, *Ecology Control and Economic Development in East African History: The Case of Tanganyika 1850-1950*, London, 1977.

Lenin, V.I., *The Development of Capitalism in Russia*, Moscow, 1974.

Lenin, V.I., *Collected Works, I-IV* (1893-1901), Moscow, 1972.

Lofchie, Michael F., 'Agrarian Crisis and Economic Liberalization in Tanzania', *Journal of Modern African Studies*, 16, 3 (1978), 451-474.

Maeda, Dr. J.H.J., 'Managing the Ujamaa Village Development in Tanzania: An Assessment of the Implementation of the Rural Ujamaa Policy', Sixteenth Inter-African Public Administration and Management Seminar on 'Managing Rural Development', Banjul, the Gambia, November 28-December 3, 1977.

Maguire, Andrew, *Towards Uhuru in Tanzania*, Cambridge, 1969.

Mandel, Ernest, ed., *Karl Marx, Capital, Vol. I*, New York, 1977.

Marx, Karl, *Capital, Vols. I & III*, New York, 1967.

Mantango, R.R., 'The Role of Agencies for Rural Development in Tanzania: A Case Study of the Lushoto Integrated Development Project', Economic Research Paper 76.3, University of Dar es Salaam, March 1976.

Mbilinyi, Marjorie, 'Peasants' Education in Tanzania', Paper No. 12, The 12th Annual Social Science Conference of East African Universities—1976, University of Dar es Salaam, December 20-22, 1976.

Mbilinyi, Marjorie, 'The Transition to Capitalism in Rural Tanzania', Economic Research Bureau paper 74.7. University of Dar es Salaam, November 1974.

McHenry, Dean E. Jr., 'A Report, Communal Agircultural Production in Ujamaa Villages', unpublished paper, Department of Political Science, University of

Dar es Salaam, 197? (subsequently published in *African Studies Review*, December 1977, pp. 43-59; pagination from original paper).

Mihyo, 'The Struggle for Workers' Control in Tanzania', *Review of African Political Economy*, 4 (1975), 62-84.

Mwapachu, Juma Volter, 'Operation Planned Villages in Rural Tanzania: A Revolutionary Strategy for Development', *The African Review*, 6 (1976), 1-16.

Nabudere, D. Wadada, 'Imperialism, State, Class and Race', a critique of Shivji's *Class Struggles in Tanzania, Maji Maji*, 27 (1976), 1-22.

Njonjo, Apollo, 'The Africanization of the 'White-Highlands': A Study in Agrarian Class Struggle in Kenya, 1950-1979. PhD thesis, Princeton University, 1977.

Nsari, K., 'Tanzania: Neo-Colonialism and the Struggle for National Liberation', *Review of African Political Economy*, 4 (1975), 109-118.

Nyerere, Julius. K., *Freedom and Socialism*, Dar es Salaam, 1968.

Nyerere, Julius K., *Freedom and Unity*, Dar es Salaam, 1966.

Operation Songeza, n.d.

Pratt, Cranford, *The Critical Phase in Tanzania, 1945-1968*, Toronto, 1976.

Proctor, J.H., ed., *Building Ujamaa Villages in Tanzania*, Dar es Salaam, 1971; articles by Musoke, Bakula, Ntirukigwa, Daraja, Mashauri, Mboya.

Raikes, P.C., 'Ujamaa and Rural Socialism', *Review of African Political Economy*, 3 (1975), 33-52.

Raikes, P.C., 'Rural Differentiation and Class Formation in Tanzania', *Journal of Peasant Studies*, 5, 3 (1978), 285-325

Raikes, P.C., *State and Agriculture in Tanzania*, unpublished manuscript, forthcoming.

Rweyemamu, J.F., 'Some Aspects of the Turner Report', Economic Research Bureau Paper 69.20, Dar es Salaam, University College, 1969.

Saul, John, *The State and Revolution in Eastern Africa*, New York, 1979.

Saul, John, 'The State in Post-Colonial Societies: Tanzania', *The Socialist Register*, London, 1974, 349-372.

Shivji, Issa G., *Class Struggles in Tanzania*, New York, 1976.

Swainson, Nicola, 'The Rise of a National Bourgeoisie in Kenya', *Review of African Political Economy*, 8 (1977), 39-55.

Tabari, Ayoub, 'Review of *Freedom and Development* by Julius K. Nyerere', in *Review of African Political Economy*, 3 (1975), 89-96.

von Freyhold, Michaela, 'The Post Colonial State and its Tanzania Version', *Review of African Political Economy*, 8 (1977), 75-89.

von Freyhold, Michaela, *Ujamaa Villages in Tanzania*, New York, 1979.

UNDP, *Country Programme for the United Republic of Tanzania: UNDP Assistance Requested by the Government of the United Republic of Tanzania for the Period 1978-1981*.

Widstrand, Carl Gosta, *Co-operative and Rural Development in East Africa*, Uppsala, 1970.

BEYOND RELATIVE AUTONOMY:
STATE MANAGERS AS HISTORICAL SUBJECTS*

Fred Block

Neo-Marxist analyses of the state and politics now centre on the vexed question of the 'specificity of the political'. What is the degree to which politics and the state have independent determining effects on historical outcomes? Can the state or the people who direct the state apparatus act as historical subjects? The questions are critical because without a clear set of answers, it is impossible to develop a consistent theory of the state.

In an interview done only months before his death, Nicos Poulantzas insisted that these questions had been answered through the idea of the relative autonomy of the state. Poulantzas' remarks are worth quoting at length:

> Interviewer: Much of your writing has been directed towards questions of the state and of politics, based upon the concept of 'relative autonomy'. What is your assessment of the capacity of a theory based on a concept of 'relative autonomy' to grapple with the problems of the specificity of the state and politics?
>
> Poulantzas: I will answer this question very simply because we could discuss it for years. It is very simple. One must know whether one remains within a Marxist framework or not; and if one does, one accepts the determinant role of the economic in the very complex sense; not the determination of forces of production but of relations of production and the social division of labour. In this sense, if we remain within this conceptual framework, I think that the most that one can do for the specificity of politics is what I have done. I am sorry to have to speak like that.
>
> I am not absolutely sure myself that I am right to be Marxist; one is never sure. But if one is Marxist, the determinant role of relations of production, in the very complex sense, must mean something; and if it does, one can only speak of 'relative autonomy'—this is the only solution. There is, of course, another solution, which is not to speak of the determinant role of the economic at all. The conceptual framework of Marxism has to do with this very annoying thing which is called 'relations of production' and the determinant role of relations of production. If we abandon it then, of course, we can speak of the autonomy of politics and of other types of relations between politics and economics.[1]

Poulantzas' comments constitute a direct challenge to those in the Neo-Marxist tradition who would argue for greater recognition of the

*This paper has grown out of discussions with Karl Klare, Theda Skocpol, Larry Hirschhorn, Margaret Somers and David Plotke.

specificity of the state and politics than is possible within the relative autonomy formulation.[2] The challenge does not rest ultimately on a dogmatic assertion about what is and what is not Marxism. Rather, implicit in Poulantzas' formulation is the warning that those who proceed beyond the relative autonomy formulation risk losing what is most valuable in Marxism—the analytic power of the framework. The clear danger is slipping into a form of theorising in which everything influences everything else, so that it becomes impossible to grasp the basic dynamics of a particular social formation.

The present paper is intended as a provisional attempt to take up this challenge. My argument is that the relative autonomy formulation is too limiting and that it is possible to construct an alternative framework that goes further in recognising the specificity of the state, while still acknowledging the 'determinant role of relations of production'. In a brief essay, I can only outline such an alternative formulation, but I hope to demonstrate its analytic power by comparing the interpretations of the present conjuncture that flow from the two competing frameworks.

The Limits of Relative Autonomy

The major thrust of recent Marxist work on the capitalist state has been to view the state, 'as a system of political domination with specific effects on the class struggle'.[3] The relative autonomy formulation has played an important role in this development by making clear that the state is not subject to direct and immediate control by the capitalist class, but that it has a degree of autonomy from such control. This insight makes clear that not all state actions can be explained as responses to the interests of particular fractions of the capitalist class, but rather many actions can be understood as flowing from the state's function as the *'factor of cohesion'* in the social formation.[4] Yet in fulfilling these functions, the state is acting in the interests of the capitalist class as a whole—hence the autonomy of the state is relative and limited.

The central problem with this formulation is the difficulty of specifying the limits of 'relative autonomy'. The phrase suggests that if the state managers were to exceed certain limits, the capitalist class—or factions thereof—would act to bring the state back into line. But such disciplinary action would appear to depend on the degree of consciousness, consensus, and political capacity of the capitalist class or its most important fractions. But if the argument is formulated in this way, it is possible to imagine historical circumstances in which capitalists are unable to keep the state from achieving full autonomy. Alternatively, if the argument is that there are structural limits on the degree of state autonomy, then it should be possible to identify concrete structural mechanisms that prevent the state from exceeding its normal authority. Thus far, there has been little said about what those structural mechanisms might be.

Another important problem is that the relative autonomy formulation preserves the tendency in orthodox Marxism to explain all *major* state initiatives as the products of specific class interests. Hence, theorists of relative autonomy, no less than earlier Marxist theorists, explain Roosevelt's New Deal or Hitler's policies as reflections of specific class interests. This approach requires locating the relevant fraction of capital whose policies were being pursued even when there is little historical evidence that such fractions existed.[5] The result is such anomalies as the claim that both the National Socialist regime and the German Federal Republic were rooted in German heavy industry and finance capital.

These difficulties suggest that the relative autonomy formulations might not be, as Poulantzas suggests, the final destination of the Marxist theory of the state. It appears rather as a cosmetic modification of Marxism's tendency to reduce state power to class power. This reduction does not occur in the relative autonomy formulation as quickly as it does in orthodox Marxist formulations that centre on the state as executive committee of the ruling class. But the reduction does ultimately occur because state power is still conceived as entirely a product of class relations. In Poulantzas' phrase, the state is the 'condensation of class relations'.[6] A condensation cannot exercise power.

An Alternative View: State Power in a Class Context

The starting point of an alternative formulation is the acknowledgement that state power is *sui generis*, not reducible to class power. As Weber insisted, the heart of that power is the monopoly over the means of violence, which is the basis on which the managers of the state apparatus are able to force compliance with their wishes. But the exercise of state power occurs within particular class contexts,[7] which shape and limit the exercise of that power. These class contexts in turn are the products of particular relations of production. To put it in other terms—each social formation determines the particular ways in which state power will be exercised within that society and social formations will vary in the degree to which the exercise of state power is constrained by class power.[8]

This formulation assumes that state managers[9] collectively are self-interested maximisers, interested in maximising their power, prestige, and wealth. But any set of political institutions will set limits on the kind of maximisation normally pursued. For example, within a parliamentary system, where control of the executive branch alternates between two parties, it is generally foolish for a particular group of state managers to take excessive actions to preserve their power in the short term if these actions might jeopardise their party's future chances for electoral victory. In short, state managers will tend to maximise within particular political 'rules of the game'. Beyond these rules lie particular patterns of class relations that reinforce the limits on state managers' pursuit of their collective self-interest. Yet it must be stressed that all of these limits are contingent and not absolute. Within particular historical circumstances, state managers might pursue their self-interest in ways that violate both the existing political rules and the normal constraints of class relations.

This possibility means that state managers pose a potential threat to other classes, particularly those classes that control substantial resources. The possibility exists that state managers, to improve their own position, will seek to expropriate, or at the least, place severe restrictions on the property of dominant classes. This threat is the root of the emphasis in bourgeois ideology on the need to prevent the emergence of a Leviathan state that swallows civil society. Yet since the bourgeoisie or other propertied classes cannot survive without a state, those classes have little choice but to seek a *modus vivendi* with the state managers. In social formations dominated by the capitalist mode of production, the dominant historical pattern has been the development of a *modus vivendi* that is highly favourable to the owners of capital. Not only have state managers been generally restrained from attacking the property rights of capitalists, but the exercise of state power has largely been used in ways that strengthen the capitalist accumulation process. This *modus vivendi* is rooted in the class context created by capitalism.[10]

The Capitalist Context
One key dimension of the context is capitalism's existence as a world-system. One need not accept all of Wallerstein's formulations to acknowledge that capitalism operates on a world scale. The components of this world system are a world market and a competitive state system. Although the competitive state system predated the rise of capitalism, it became a critical component of the global workings of capitalism. The self-interest of state managers, particularly within the more developed nations of the capitalist world system,[11] leads directly to a concern with their nation's relative standing within the world economy and state system. Both military defeat and declining international competitiveness raise the spectre of fewer resources available internally and effective challenges by outside or inside forces to the state manager's control over the state apparatus. These dangers can be reduced if state managers pursue actions to strengthen the accumulation process. An expanding economy provides the resources for an effective military and the means to buy off potential challenges for state power.

The pressures of the competitive state system also give state managers an additional impetus to reduce internal conflicts, even when those do not pose an immediate threat to state power. If significant groupings in the society such as racial, ethnic, national or class groups are strongly discontented, they create possibilities for an internal 'fifth column' for a rival power or, at the least, of non-cooperation in the event of war, significantly weakening the nation's military posture. While pressure to conciliate such groups increases with the likelihood of war, the pressure is present at other times since war is a constant possibility within a competitive state system. [12]

These aspects of the international context interact with a number of key aspects of the domestic class context in shaping the exercise of state power. The first and most important of these domestic factors is the reality of capitalist control over the investment process. State managers are dependent upon maintenance of rates of investment that will assure a high level of economic activity. As noted above, economic strength is a critical component of military preparedness. Further, declining rates of economic activity make it more difficult for state managers to finance the state budget. Finally, declining rates of economic activity tend to lead to increasing discontent and political attacks on the existing order. Hence, state managers have a strong interest in persuading businesses—both domestic and foreign—to invest at rates that will assure high levels of economic activity. Further, there is a strong disincentive against taking actions that will damage business confidence and lead to an investment slowdown. [13]

The second internal contextual factor is the disproportionate control of the capitalist class over wealth of all types. This means that capitalists tend to own the most effective means of persuasion such as the mass media, and the capitalists, more than any other group, have the resources to bribe state managers. This can occur through simple pay-offs, through promises of lucrative jobs after individuals leave political office, and through the bankrolling of election campaigns. The weight of these factors can be attenuated through state control over certain mass media, state financing of elections, and strict codes of ethics. Yet the basic pattern of disproportionate control of resources by a single class remains. [14]

A third factor is that the capitalist mode of production generates a set of interrelated contradictions. The operation of a market economy, as Polanyi insisted, [15] if left to its own devices would destroy society, as capitalists in search of profits would deplete both the labour force and the physical environment. Further, a market economy creates periodic economic crises, resulting from the 'anarchy of production'. These contradictions threaten social dislocation and social rebellion, so that state managers are impelled to act to regulate the market both to protect society and to protect their own rule. Yet in regulating the market, state managers act to save capitalism from itself, reforming and modifying the system in ways that tend to increase its viability.

When these contextual elements are taken together, one can see how the exercise of state power has generally served the needs of the capitalist accumulation process. On the one hand, state managers are reluctant to disrupt the accumulation process, but on the other hand, they face pressures to intervene to ameliorate the economic and social strains that capitalism produces.[16] Yet it must be emphasised that these interventions still involve conflict between capitalists and state managers. In order to conciliate subordinate social groups, protect society from the market, prevent severe economic crises, and maintain national defences, state managers have had to pursue policies that impinge on the property rights of the capitalist class. Taxation and various forms of state regulation represent challenges to capitalist property rights, and have often been perceived as such. The consequence is that many of the state actions that have served to strengthen capitalism have been opposed by large sections of the capitalist class because they are seen as threats to class privilege and as steps towards the Leviathan state.

One can even speak of a modal process of social reform, where state managers extend their regulation of the market or their provision of services when faced with pressures from subordinate groups or the threat of social disorganisation. Such actions are often opposed by many capitalists, but once the reforms are institutionalised, they are used by state managers in ways that contribute to the accumulation process and to the maintenance of social control.[17] Hence, for example, the extension of educational opportunities might result from working-class pressure, but the expanded schools are used to prepare pliant workers and good citizens.

But given the power held by capitalists, such reforms are ordinarily likely to occur only at the margins of the system. If state managers pursue policies that large sections of the capitalist class see as posing serious challenges to their property rights, the results are likely to be a collapse of domestic and international business confidence, leading to high levels of unemployment and an international payments crisis. Even when motivated by a desire to break with the capitalist mode of production, state managers are likely to respond to such a collapse of business confidence by retreating from their proposals for reform.

Exceptional Periods: War, Depression, Reconstruction
There are, however, certain historical periods in which the capitalist context changes, allowing state managers more freedom of action in relation to capitalists. In the twentieth century, periods of war, depression, and post-war reconstruction have been marked by the use of various forms of economic controls that tend to weaken the links between a national economy and the world market. With such controls in place, the loss of international business confidence ceases to be as critical an element because the controls impede the flight of capital. At the same time, the role of domestic business confidence also declines significantly. In depressions, when economic activity has already been sharply reduced, the threat of a further loss of business confidence loses its urgency since the negative consequences are already present. In periods of war-time and

of post-war reconstruction, the business threat is less compelling for the opposite reason—fuelled by government efforts or by pent-up demand—the economy is so strong that business has little freedom to withhold investment. There is also an ideological dimension, particularly during war-time, because the withholding of investment would appear unpatriotic.

It is hardly surprising therefore, that such periods have seen the most dramatic qualitative growth in state activity and the most serious efforts to rationalise capitalism. State managers take advantage of the changes in the structural context to expand their own power and to pursue policies that they perceive as necessary to strengthen the nation's position in the world system and to preserve internal order. Yet even in these circumstances, the capitalist context continues to place certain limits on the exercise of state power. First, state managers still depend upon the capacity of capitalists to produce an economic surplus from the direct producers. Second, such exceptional periods are generally of limited duration and state managers know that they will soon return to their earlier dependence on capitalist cooperation. In depression periods, for example, if state managers succeed in restoring reasonable levels of business activity, they are vulnerable to capitalist pressure, since another economic downturn would be likely to have devastating political consequences. Third, capitalists do retain other weapons, such as their control over the media and often over an opposition party, and these weapons place further constraints on state managers' freedom of action.

But there has been at least one historical case where state managers have taken advantage of the dynamics of an exceptional period to free themselves of constraints imposed by the capitalists. This was the case in Nazi Germany after 1936.[18] Depression conditions and the system of exchange controls imposed during the Mark crisis in 1931 gave Hitler a good deal of freedom of action in the period from 1933 to 1936. He used this freedom to destroy the parliamentary system and to increase vastly the state's role in the economy. Given the seriousness of the social and economic crisis, these actions were generally accepted, if not applauded, by German capitalists. However, the manner in which the Nazi economic programmes were implemented placed German capitalists in a position of growing dependence on the National Socialist regime. Because of the vastly expanded economic role of the state, capitalist firms depended on the state for government contracts, for access to raw materials, and for export and import permits. In the years after 1936, the Nazis used this dependence to discourage capitalist resistance while pursuing policies that were no longer in the interests of German capital. An investment strike became impossible because too many of the major firms feared that non-cooperation with the regime would lead to severe economic penalties. Furthermore, the authoritarian nature of the regime stripped capitalists of their normal access to the media or opposition parties, and since even the capitalists lived in fear of the Gestapo, there was no effective capitalist response.

To be sure, the capitalists generally remained in control of their property, and many profited handsomely from such services of the Nazi regime as the provision of slave labour for their factories. Nevertheless, the capitalists had been reduced to the role of highly paid functionaries of a state whose direction they did not control. They had little leverage to resist the orders that came from the state about the direction of their own firms, and they could not halt the regime's irrational march towards self-destruction.

The Tipping Point, Late Capitalism, and the Left

This interpretation of the Nazi experience suggests the idea that the growth of the state's role in the economy can reach a tipping point past which capitalists lose their capacity to resist further state intervention, leading ultimately to the Leviathan state. Obviously, where parliamentary forms still exist, the capitalists will have more room to manoeuvre, but if the state's economic weapons are powerful enough, they can be used to discourage a variety of different forms of resistance including legal political opposition. The essence of the tipping point is that increased state intervention in the economy means that state managers will be making decisions with serious consequences for the profitability of most of the major firms. Through withholding licences or contracts or credit or a variety of other regulatory or legal actions, the state managers can threaten key firms with retaliation if they withhold cooperation with other government policies. If these threats work, and the state managers are able to augment their economic powers even further, then at the next stage, the costs of resistance by capitalists will be even higher, and ultimately, state managers would succeed in depriving capitalists of the freedom to withhold investment, so that they become, as in the Nazi period, mere functionaries.

While this tipping point has not yet been reached in any of the developed capitalist nations, a number of developments have brought it closer. Most obviously, the expansion in the state's regulatory role and in the state's purchases of goods and services have drastically increased its leverage.[19] Moreover, the concentration of capital—to the point that a few hundred firms control the vast majority of capital investment—increases the vulnerability of capital, since there is a high likelihood that most of those firms can be seriously hurt by a hostile state. This vulnerability is suggested by a number of recent developments in the United States. The Nixon administration, at a number of junctures, threatened or did use its regulatory and legal powers to punish corporate opponents and to gain campaign contributions from otherwise reluctant firms. More recently, the Carter administration sought to back up its 'voluntary' programme of wage and price controls by denying contracts to offending firms. While these incidents fall far short of the systematic use of state economic power to assure capitalist compliance, they do suggest that these powers represent a growing temptation for state managers.

While the socialist left has generally supported or acquiesced in the growth of state regulatory powers *vis-à-vis* capital, the left can take little comfort from the prospect that the tipping point might soon be reached. One problem is that there is little prospect that the left could take advantage of the tipping point as a means to launch a transition to socialism. In fact, the closeness of the tipping point makes the parliamentary road to socialism even more problematic than it was previously. Nevertheless, a variant of the tipping point argument has been used to defend the practicality of the electoral road to socialism, most recently in reference to the strategy of the Communist-Socialist alliance in France in the period in which an electoral victory seemed imminent. The argument was that because of the enormous powers of the French state including a large nationalised sector and a strong tradition of economic controls, a left government would have the means to counter effectively the inevitable capitalist offensive against the new government. By using this power effectively, the new government would block capital flight and keep investment at some reasonable levels during a transition period in which popular support was gradually rallied for additional series of reforms that would ultimately end with the expropriation of the remaining centres of private capital.[20]

The flaw in this argument is that the tipping point mechanism can only work in a situation where capital is caught off guard because it is dealing with a group of state managers who appear committed to the maintenance of private property. As long as businesses have some advance warning that they face a threat—as they would with the election of a left government— they will be able to launch a capital strike and an outflow of capital. Not even the most draconian controls can be assured of restoring economic stability once such a capitalist offensive has begun, and the chances are great that the resort to such draconian controls would fatally weaken the electoral base of a parliamentary left regime. Since the prospect of a left electoral victory in France occurred in a period when capital was already preoccupied with the tipping point, it was a certainty that the new regime would have had no breathing space at all before the capitalist offensive began.

Another problem for the left is that the scenarios in which the state passes the tipping point all suggest the emergence of a dangerously authoritarian regime. The point is that such a regime, whatever its rhetoric, would still depend heavily on the capacity of the capitalists to control the labour force, since continuity in production would remain essential. Yet through its fusion of economic and political power, this state capitalist regime would have far more formidable weapons for destroying labour and political resistance than exist in liberal capitalism. State managers, with relatively little difficulty, could deprive dissidents of a livelihood providing a powerful disincentive against political action. Furthermore, since parliamentary forms and civil liberties would no longer serve vital needs of the capitalist class, their elimination would encounter less resistance.

Moreover, the authoritarian outcome is made more likely by the prospect that such a regime would be unable to solve the underlying problems of the capitalist economy. To be sure, there might be an initial period in which controls are effective and the elimination of certain forms of waste could strengthen the economy. But soon the familiar problems that plague Soviet planners would emerge as a source of contradiction. Once one has relegated to secondary importance the forms of accounting based on corporate profits, how does one make the basic decisions about what to produce, how much to produce, how to produce, and so on? Further, because the contradictions of the late capitalist economy require fundamental forms of reorganisation of energy resources, of land use, of transportation patterns, and so forth, what are the chances that state planners will choose optimal directions for restructuring? The strong commitment of state planners in both East and West to nuclear energy is an indicator of how easy it is to make the wrong choices, even in a situation where private interests are a negligible consideration. But since wrong choices can be very costly, the likelihood is that problems of slow growth and inflation will persist, forcing the state capitalist regime in a more repressive direction.[21]

Analysing the Present Conjuncture

While the tipping point argument raises the spectre of authoritarian state capitalism, it also points in a more hopeful direction. To see this direction requires a further analysis of the present conjuncture of state-capital relations. This can best be done through a critique of the analyses that flow from the relative autonomy framework.

Theorists of the relative autonomy framework tend to view the present period as one in which there is a drift towards corporatism and more authoritarian forms of rule. It is generally accepted that a capitalist offensive began in the early seventies throughout the developed capitalist world that was designed to erode working-class living standards by reducing wage gains, increasing 'normal' levels of unemployment, and cutting state provided services. In this view, capital, faced with mounting economic difficulties, has chosen to sacrifice a part of the state's legitimacy in order to make changes that would strengthen accumulation. Theorists of relative autonomy acknowledge, in short, that some of that autonomy has been temporarily abandoned, as capitalists have reverted to more direct forms of control over the state in order to use the state as a weapon in a more intense period of class conflict.[22]

While this account has a good deal of plausibility, especially in regard to the state's role in labour relations, it fails to penetrate beneath the level of appearances. Its major single flaw is its failure to account for the absence of corporatist institutional innovations. One would expect, if this analysis were correct, to see forms like the NRA of the early New Deal in which corporations and government worked together to limit inflationary pressures. But instead of such institutional innovations, we see such anomalous behaviour as the American corporate elite opposing the corporatist government bail out of Chrysler as an interference with the free market. The latter incident makes little sense within the perspective of a drift towards corporatism.

The underlying problem with this argument is its failure to recognise that the core of the capitalist offensive has been an attack on the state itself. Capitalists realised that with the mounting problems of stagflation, there would be powerful pressures for a further extension of the state's role in the economy. But they also realised that such an increase in state power might well push the state past the tipping point, depriving them of their leverage over the state managers. To prevent this outcome, an offensive was launched to blame state intervention for the economy's difficulties and to propose reductions in taxes, state spending, and government regulation as the solutions to stagflation. At the same time, efforts were redoubled to use business channels of influence on the political system to block expanded state regulation and to pressure for a rollback of certain forms of state activity.[23] Of course, the capitalist offensive has also been characterised by attempts to use state power to weaken the bargaining power of the union movement.

This offensive has been remarkably successful in reversing a drift towards more *dirigiste* economic policies and in bringing conservative politicians to power, but it suffers from a major weakness—the lack of a coherent solution to the problems of stagflation. The recycling of traditional free market ideology with its emphasis on monetary restraint and balanced budgets was more a useful ideology to attack the state than a serious set of policy proposals. It is hardly surprising, therefore, that the efforts to implement those proposals have proven ineffective. It is hardly worth repeating the explanations of why such policies cannot succeed; suffice it to say, that the solutions to the underlying problems that generate stagflation require serious forms of restructuring, including direct challenges to some of the major corporate actors in the 'free market'.

Yet if 'free market' solutions do not work, the basic contradiction that generated the capitalist offensive remains. As long as stagflation persists, the danger is acute that opportunistic state managers, under pressure from subordinate groups, will attempt to resolve the economy's problems with dramatic increases in the state's role, including the imposition of controls over wages, prices, credit allocation, and investment. Capitalists must maintain constant vigilance to prevent this outcome; they must maintain at a high level their efforts to use channels of persuasion and bribery to keep state managers in line. And they must also be careful to avoid inadvertently giving state managers more leverage over them. This is the reason why there have been few corporatist innovations, since such forms of corporate-government cooperation require, at the very least, a surrender of vital information to government officials.[24]

My argument is that under the surface of recent corporate successes in shaping state policies lies a sharpening contradiction between the interests of capital and the fundamental interests of state managers. While this contradiction has thus far been contained, the continuation of economic difficulties is likely to bring it to the surface. The reasons for this are clear from the earlier discussions of the pressures on state managers. Stagflation undermines a nation's position in the world market and in the competitive state system because it makes high levels of defence spending politically and economically more problematic. Furthermore, stagflation threatens to weaken the political base of any particular administration and it undermines the legitimacy of the entire political regime. This means that it is increasingly in the interests of state managers to attempt to solve the problems of stagflation through a further extension of state power. Even without any grand design to pass the tipping point, state managers will be pulled by objective economic circumstances to pursue more statist policies.

Capitalists will continue to attempt to counter this pull through the use of various forms of persuasion and by the threat to withhold investment. But it is reasonable to expect that over time, as the political costs of inaction by state managers rise, and the 'free market' solutions become discredited through failure, the contradictions will surface in the form of more direct conflict between state managers and capitalists. One possibility might be that state managers take advantage of a sharp economic downturn to impose certain types of economic controls when capital's threat to withhold investment is less potent, and that capitalists will respond with other types of economic sabotage such as the creation of artifical shortages. Yet because the two parties to the conflict are relatively evenly matched, it is unlikely that a clear resolution would be reached quickly. State managers are unlikely in the short term to pass the tipping point, nor are capitalists likely to succeed in persuading state managers to abandon their interventionist ambitions. It is more likely that there will be a prolonged period of conflict, attenuated only by the fact that there remain certain areas in which the antagonists still need to cooperate. Yet as the conflict intensifies, even shared interests will not suffice to heal the divisions.

While the notion of an underlying contradiction between capitalists and state managers appears counter-intuitive in the present period, it is already implicit in recent discussions of the internationalisation of capital and of the fiscal crisis of the state. The process of global optimisation of profits by international corporations creates serious problems for the 'home' countries of those firms. The most obvious problem centres on the export of jobs to other parts of the world, leaving structural unemployment in what had been the industrial heartlands of the developed nations. Similarly, the pattern of collusion between the international oil majors and the OPEC nations forces the developed nations to adjust to rapidly rising oil prices, at a time when the power of oil firms had suppressed energy alternatives. In each case, it is state managers who are forced to handle the resulting problems, as short-term political problems that threaten their own political base, and as larger structural problems that weaken the entire political economy.[25]

Similarly, the fiscal crisis of the state thesis also suggests growing strains between capitalists and state managers. In O'Connor's framework,[26] there is mounting pressure for increased state expenditures to maintain the military, to manage the surplus populations, and to provide forms of social investment necessary for continuing capital accumulation. Under optimal circumstances, these expenditures could be financed by the state taking a constant share of a growing economic pie. Yet in late capitalism, this proves impossible, since the pie is expanding too slowly. The state can only cover its expenses by expanding its percentage share of total resources. But this leads, in turn, to inflation, as both workers and capitalists attempt to avoid any reduction in their shares of the total economic product. It also leads, as we have seen, to efforts to reduce the inflationary pressures by restricting state expenditures. The point is that state managers are caught in a contradictory position. On the one hand, they have the responsibility to carry out those state expenditures that are necessary to make a capitalist economy work, but on the other hand, that economy does not generate the economic growth needed to finance those expenditures. This contradictory position is bound to produce strains between capitalists and state managers.

Conclusion

To assess the meaning of a contradiction between state managers and capitalists, an historical analogy is useful. In her recent study of the French, Chinese, and Russian revolutions, Theda Skocpol argues that those revolutions grew out of a structural crisis in the old regime—a conflict between the pressures that the international state system placed on state managers and the limited productiveness of the existing system of agricultural social relations.[27] The problem, in brief, was that state managers needed expanded revenues to defend their nation's position in the state system, but there were structural obstacles to any significant increase in agricultural revenues. State efforts to raise more money through increased taxes generated fierce resistance from the dominant landed classes who saw this as a fundamental threat to their own privileges. The resulting political conflict between the state apparatus and the landed classes produced political paralysis and a breakdown in the machinery of social control. As a result, other social groups were able to mobilise and carry out a revolution against the old state apparatus and the old landed classes.

An analogous structural crisis emerges in late capitalism. Neither the state nor capital are willing or able to carry out the forms of re-organisation needed to release new productive forces that could overcome the economy's weaknesses. Instead, the contradictions and conflicts between capitalists and state managers grow deeper as neither statist nor 'free market' solutions are capable of solving the underlying problems. The result is likely to be political paralysis and an accelerating erosion of bourgeois ideological hegemony. In the context of deepening state-capital conflicts, new opportunities would exist for oppositional social forces determined to eliminate the oppressive power of both capital and the state. Hence, we might well be at the beginning of a period in which the contradictions between state and capital dramatically shift the balance of forces in favour of those who envision an emancipatory form of socialism. Yet circumstances will not by themselves create a new society, and the failure to seize this possible opportunity redoubles the likelihood of new forms of barbarism.

NOTES

1. The remarks are from an interview with Poulantzas by Stuart Hall and Alan Hunt that was published in *Marxism Today*, July 1979, and reprinted in *Socialist Review*, 48, November-December 1979. The quoted passage is on page 67.
2. The seriousness of the challenge derives from Poulantzas' own enormous contribution to the revival of Marxist theorising on the state.
3. Bob Jessop, 'Recent Theories of the Capitalist State', *Cambridge Journal of Economics*, 1977, p. 356.
4. *Ibid.*, p. 355.
5. Mouzelis criticises Poulantzas' interpretation of the 1967 military coup in Greece along precisely these lines. See Nicos Mouzelis, 'Capitalism and Dictatorship in Post-war Greece', *New Left Review* 96, March-April 1976.
6. The condensation notion is elaborated in Nicos Poulantzas, *State, Power, Socialism*, New Left Books/Shocken, New York, 1978.
7. For purposes of this paper, I am using the term 'class' to mean social groups that have a common relation, direct or mediated, to the means of production. Since class does not exhaust the forms of structured inequality in human society, referring only to class involves some simplification.
8. In the Asiatic Mode of Production and in contemporary state socialist societies, the degree to which state power is unconstrained is particularly high. Yet even in these instances, there are social groups that can place limits on the exercise of state power. For a recent discussion that argues that Marx and Engels recognised the autonomy of the state in the Asiatic Mode of Production but had trouble reconciling it with the rest of their theory, see Alvin Gouldner, *The Two*

Marxisms, Seabury, New York, 1980.

    It should also be noted that the thrust of my argument is consistent with the famous passage in the *Grundrisse:* 'In all forms of society there is one specific kind of production which predominates over the rest, whose relations thus assign rank and influence to the others. It is a general illumination which bathes all the other colours and modifies their particularity. It is a particular ether which determines the specific gravity of every being which has materialised within it.' Karl Marx, *Grundrisse,* Vintage, New York, 1973, pp. 106-107. Yet it must be acknowledged that much of Marx's work is not consistent with this particular passage.

9. State managers are those at the peak of the executive and legislative branches of the state apparatus. Sometimes occupants of these positions are on loan from capitalist firms, but they operate in a situation that tends to be dominated by people for whom politics is a vocation, whether advancement comes through pursuit of elective or appointive offices. It is my hypothesis that such temporary state managers tend to adapt to the ways of thinking appropriate to their new occupational situation, just as a corporate executive would alter his or her views in accordance with a shift from one type of firm to another.

10. This *modus vivendi* explains the historical power of the Marxist formulations that see the state as an executive committee of the bourgeoisie. The problem, however, comes in those periods in which the *modus vivendi* breaks down or is strained.

11. This qualification is necessary because one option for state managers in less developed nations has been to serve as the clients of more powerful nations. In this case, their nation's standing in the world system is irrelevant; what is more important is the standing of the regime of which they are clients.

12. This dynamic has played an important role in the extension of citizenship rights through the 19th and early 20th centuries.

13. This argument is made at greater length in Fred Block, 'The Ruling Class Does Not Rule', *Socialist Revolution* 33, May-June 1977, and in Charles Lindblom, *Politics and Markets,* Basic, New York, 1977.

14. On this point, see Ralph Miliband, *The State in Capitalist Society,* Basic, New York, 1969.

15. Karl Polanyi, *The Great Transformation,* Beacon, Boston, 1957. While Polanyi lacks an explicit theory of the state, his book is an important source for my argument.

16. I do not mean to exaggerate the insight and understanding that state managers bring to these tasks. Their understanding of the overall situation tends to be limited, and their actions tend to be crisis oriented. This is not surprising since they are necessarily preoccupied with short-term problems of maintaining their political position.

17. For a useful case study, see Karl Klare, 'Judicial Deradicalization of the Wagner Act and the Origins of Modern Legal Consciousness', 62 *Minnesota Law Review* 265, (1978).

18. I am following here the argument of Mihaly Vajda, *Fascism as a Mass Movement,* Allison & Busby, London, 1976.

19. One is reminded here of Marx's description of the French state in the Brumaire where he is stressing the state's freedom of action: 'It is immediately obvious that in a country like France, where the executive power commands an army of officials numbering more than half a million individuals and therefore constantly maintains an immense mass of interests and livelihoods in the most absolute dependence; where the state enmeshes, controls, regulates, superintends and tutors civil society from its most comprehensive manifestations of life down to

its most insignificant stirrings, from its most general modes of being to the private existence of individuals, where through the most extraordinary centralization this parasitic body acquires a ubiquity, an omniscience, a capacity for accelerated mobility and an elasticity which finds a counterpart only in the helpless dependence, in the loose shapelessness of the actual body politic—it is obvious that in such a country the National Assembly forfeits all real influence when it loses command of the ministerial posts. . .' Karl Marx, *The Eighteenth Brumaire of Louis Bonaparte*, International Publishers, New York, 1963, pp. 61-62.

20. For a longer discussion of the limits of Eurocommunist strategies, see Fred Block, 'The Stalemate of European Capitalism: Eurocommunism and the Postwar Order', *Socialist Review* 43, January-February 1979.

21. This argument rests on an analysis of the economic crisis of late capitalism in Fred Block and Larry Hirschhorn, *Theory and Society*, VII, May-June 1979. I am also drawing on discussions of the contradictions of centralised planning in Lindblom, *Politics and Markets*, and Radovan Richta, et. al., *Civilization at the Crossroads*, International Arts and Sciences Press, White Plains, N.Y., 1969.

22. Such views are expressed in Poulantzas, *State, Power, Socialism*; Ernest Mandel, *Late Capitalism*, New Left Books, London, 1975, Bob Jessop, 'Capitalism and Democracy: The Best Possible Political Shell', in Gary Littlejohn, et. al., eds., *Power and the State*, St. Martin's, New York, 1978, and in a number of American writings that centre on the role of the Trilateral Commission that are collected in Holly Sklar, ed., *Trilaterialism*, South End Press, Boston, forthcoming.

23. Alan Wolfe noted in an unpublished paper that just as Marxists have developed an extremely sophisticated theory of the state, capitalists have reverted to crude instrumentalism. Yet this is only a part of the story.

24. A recent illustration of this was intense corporate resistance in the United States to efforts by the Federal Trade Commission to obtain profit information by product line.

25. This is also Polanyi's theme in *The Great Transformation* that I have sought to extend into the post-war period in *The Origins of International Economic Disorder*, University of California Press, Berkeley, 1977.

26. James O'Connor, *The Fiscal Crisis of the State*, St. Martin's, New York, 1973.

27. Theda Skocpol, *States and Social Revolutions*, Cambridge University Press, Cambridge, 1979. This brief summary of her argument applies most completely to the French Revolution.

THE STATE AND THE ECONOMY: SOME THEORETICAL PROBLEMS

Laurence Harris

The relation between the state and the economy is the central issue for all who try to understand the upheavals of the past decade and a half.[1] Even the most academic economic theorist, building mathematical models on monetarist assumptions, has it as a central problem (at least implicitly). Marxists address the problem without Marx himself having formulated a concept of the relation. His writings on the capitalist economy and on the state are, on the whole, separate. In *Capital* and *Theories of Surplus Value* we have the basic elements of the economy and economic ideologies but the references to the role of the state, however suggestive, do not constitute a concept of the state—a political economy in the strong sense. And writings such as *The Eighteenth Brumaire* which take the state as their object say almost nothing directly about the economy.

Thus Marx did not develop an analysis of the relationship, in either direction, between the state and the economy. On the one hand, he did not present a developed theory of the manner in which capital accumulation affects the form of the state. Instead, in key passages he established a general framework for treating the issue in terms of a relation between the superstructure and an ultimately determinant base, but the enigmatic nature of these passages has stimulated a modern controversy which has revealed precisely that because the concept of that relation is undeveloped it is far from robust.[2] On the other hand, Marx also did not give an adequate analysis of the manner in which the capitalist state regulates, intervenes in, or is integrally involved in the economy. Instead, his study of the Factory Acts and the 1844 Bank Charter Act and his comments on state employees within the productive/unproductive labour taxonomy, are isolated passages which do not yield a general concept to the reader. In consequence, when the present generation of Marxist theorists face up to contemporary problems like the nature of corporatism, the development and contradictions of the welfare state, the nature of Keynesianism and Monetarism, or the state's role in production, in the reproduction of the labour force, and in the control of credit, they have no well-developed concepts from which to start.

The past decade has witnessed a burgeoning of books, articles, conferences and debates on the problem that Marx had left for later work, the interconnections between the state and capital accumulation. The

243

contributions can be classified into two main groups: those such as Altvater and Yaffe[3] who argue that it is possible to derive the concept of the capitalist state and its relation to the economy in terms of the functions that it 'has to' perform for capital, and those such as Holloway and Picciotto who adopt a less functionalist approach. The latter argue that contradictions in state policy are associated with the fact that the capitalist state has to act in a context of class struggle where capital accumulation is predicated upon victories in the struggle rather than being an automaton which simply sweeps all before it. All this work has held out an exciting prospect for, since it could not utilise well-developed Marxian concepts, it had to develop such concepts anew. This was a refreshing contrast with much work in other areas which was content merely to repeat the basic concepts handed down by Marx. Unfortunately, however, the enterprise has so far been a failure. In this paper I explain this conclusion and discuss the directions that should be taken to overcome the problem.[4]

I am going to focus on one aspect of Marxist work on the state/economy relation: the area sometimes known as The Political Economy of the Welfare State. A book of that title by Ian Gough and two other recent books, by Norman Ginsburg and CSE State Group respectively,[5] are representative of the state of thinking on the subject and I shall use them to illustrate my argument. Concentrating on the political economy of the welfare state rather than other aspects of the relation between the state and economy does, moreover, correspond to developments in the real world; current political and economic policy force the state-run welfare system (rather than, say, industrial policy) to the forefront crystallising the difficulties that relations between the state and the economy experience. Expenditure cuts, monetarism and the changes in the welfare state with which they are associated are subjects that even non-Marxists would expect Marxist theory to be able to analyse better than orthodox economics or political science if for no other reason than that Marxism is not confined by narrow disciplinary boundaries.

It is indeed, the case that it has yielded some valuable insights and has established a groundwork on which more fruitful theories may be developed. But the theory has failed in two senses, first, it provides no basis for a socialist policy toward the welfare state; the 'anti-cuts campaigns' that have developed have been weak and in the absence of an alternative policy, have achieved their limited successes only in particular fights for particular services (a local hospital, for example) and those successes themselves are rare enough. Second, the theory has failed in an epistemological sense. Each writer has attempted to overcome the polarisation between theories of structure and theories of action, but the attempt is abortive. Action theories of society base their explanations upon the activities of distinct subjects, individuals, interest groups or classes acting in pursuit of definite objectives. A Marxian variant of action theory would be an explanation of the welfare state which relies upon the consciously organised struggles of the working class and bourgeois class in its creation; with each conceived as a 'class for itself' the proletariat has demands and the bourgeoisie has needs, and these have come together in particular ways to produce the welfare state. Structure theories, on the other hand, explain social phenomena such as the welfare state by the anonymous forces of the social system without reference to the conscious actions of classes or other agents. Such theories rely upon a specification of the functions that the welfare state performs for the cohesion and reproduction of the capitalist system without considering the agency through which the welfare state is established; class conflict is admitted as part of the capitalist system but it is the needs of the system itself rather than the conscious actions of classes that bring about social changes like the establishment of the welfare state. The action/structure dichotomy has marked orthodox work in all the social sciences, and Marxist theory claims to overcome it. The recent Marxist work on the state and the economy, however, fails to do so.

This failure is related to the wider methodological confusion current in Marxist theory just as the first failure is related to the confusion in socialist policy. I shall return to these themes later in the article. First, I lay the groundwork by focussing on two questions. How have Marxist theories of the welfare state's political economy explained its existence and its development over recent decades? And how do they analyse the attacks on it that have become qualitatively of a new order since 1976?

Explaining the Existence of the Welfare State
In writing of the welfare state, it is common to be less than precise about the definition of the object. I shall not attempt to depart from that tradition, but assume that in Britain we are broadly concerned with the non-marketed services provided to individuals by institutions of the state since World War II. They include services produced by the state such as education, social work and health care and also redistribution of income through mechanisms like pensions and supplementary benefits. They did not arise from nowhere after the war, but the post-war government did systematise the state, charitable, and friendly-society provision of such services that had existed, thereby creating the coherent whole that we understand as the welfare state. In explaining it Marxists have to answer two distinct questions: why have such services been expanded, systematised and entrenched since the war, and why have they been provided through the state rather than the private sector. The answers that Marxist theory so far provides for the first question are now commonplace but, nevertheless, problematic; the second question, however, is virtually unanswered.

Let us start with the first question. Why has British capitalism since the war seen an expansion of education, health and other welfare services and rises in pensions and other forms of income which do not directly derive from employment? Why, to use Gough's phrase, has there been such expansion in these areas which 'modify the reproduction of labour power and. . . maintain the non-working population'? The answers from Marxist writers are of two kinds: welfare services have expanded because they satisfy the needs of capital or because labour has demanded them. Contemporary writers put forward both explanations as complementary, but there are differences in emphasis. The CSE state group and Ginsburg argue that ultimately the welfare system in Britain has been shaped by the needs of capital. The books of each start with theoretical introductory chapters relating the growth of the welfare state to the .two-sided class conflict that accompanies the accumulation of capital. But their main chapters are concerned with the specific historical analysis of particular aspects of the welfare state's expenditure and in each case those analyses virtually reduce the explanations to an argument that the system grew, and grew in particular ways, because it accorded with the needs of one side in the class conflict, the needs of capital. In Ginsburg's analysis of the development of British housing and social security systems, for example, he argues that 'the working class through the organs of the trade union movement and the Labour Party has exerted very little "real" as opposed to "formal" control over the shape of welfare policy'. Gough, by contrast, takes as his recurrent theme the interaction of both sides of class struggle, capital's needs and labour's demands. His book is a wide ranging survey of concrete developments in the welfare state and of relevant aspects in Marxist economic theory and political theory. In it sentences such as the following play a central role: there are 'two factors of importance in explaining the growth of the welfare state: the degree of class conflict, and, especially the strength and form of working class struggle, and the ability of the capitalist state to formulate and implement policies to secure the long term reproduction of capitalist social relations'.

To the extent, however, that all three writers recognise that *both* labour and capital had an interest in the development of the welfare services in Britain (while at the same time conflicting over the ways in which those services should be organised) they are uncontroversial. The benefits to the working class of welfare services do not require elaboration although it is undoubtedly the case that their particular forms have disadvantages as well as yielding benefits. What of the benefits for capital or for the social system which is the condition of capital's existence? Gough sees welfare services as important to the reproduction of capitalist social relations primarily through their effect upon the reproduction of labour power; they ensure the existence of a labour force which is educated, healthy and housed enough to meet capital's requirements. Income maintenance programmes under the welfare state (redundancy payments, social security and others) ensure that when Marx's reserve army of labour is expanded in crises and in periods when capital is restructured, it is managed and maintained without decimation of the labour force which capital is holding in reserve. Moreover, because capital is dynamic it generates changes in social conditions which produce new needs of capital for welfare services. Gough, for example, identifies proletarianisation as a trend generating a need for social security payments and the changing division of labour as the basis of the need for education policy.

No Marxist worth his or her salt would deny that the post-war development of welfare systems has benefitted both labour and capital; nor, surely, would any orthodox writer. To that extent the theoretical framework built around the couple 'capital's needs/labour's demands' and used, with different emphases, by CSE, Ginsburg and Gough, has a definite appeal. But even at this point where we are examining only the question of why welfare systems develop (without looking at the problem of why they are the responsibility of the state) severe problems with that framework become apparent. The primary problem is that to say that both labour and capital benefit from welfare services is not the same as *explaining why* those services have developed at a particular stage of capitalism. This underlying problem has several aspects and corollaries. One is that it is a specific example of the problems of explaining social change which, in a broader context, underlie the dichotomy between action theories and theories of structure. I take up this problem later. Another is that it leaves as unexplained puzzles aspects of the welfare services which appear to be inefficient and disadvantageous from the point of view of both labour and capital. Consider one example of this inefficiency. Radical work in the area of health policy has redefined ill health as, in part, something that is produced by the capitalist economy and yet it is clear that capital, like labour, benefits from the existence of health services for workers. But why should either capital or labour make do with health services that concentrate upon curing individuals using advanced techniques, when in many instances preventive medicine in mass campaigns together with curbs on the effects of industrial activity would be more 'cost-effective' for capital as a whole? The needs of capital or labour's demands either by themselves or in combination cannot account for such facts.[6] This weakness arises partly from the framework's neglect of competition between different sections of capital (and within the working class). I discuss this in a different context below, but here it is sufficient to note that it is an example of the difficulty that the framework has in explaining why things develop as they do. Another indication of the same problem is that the framework by itself cannot explain why welfare systems differ markedly between countries, as instanced by, for example, the international differences in housing policy that Ginsburg quotes (*op. cit.*, p. 136).

One way in which to characterise the inadequacy of the theoretical framework employed by recent writers for explaining why the welfare services have developed at this stage of capitalism is to note that there is a tendency for it to be used in a teleological manner. In other words, there is a tendency toward a historical analysis which, instead of explaining developments, looks back from the present and assumes that everything that has happened in the path to the present had to happen; in teleological writings all developments have a historical necessity to them which is evidenced by the fact that they happened and did bring us to the present. This tendency results from the weakness of the 'capital's needs/ labour's demands' approach; if it is not adequate for explaining why welfare systems have developed in particular ways there is a temptation for those who use it to do so simply by looking back from the present and judging that everything there is so because of capital's needs or labour's demands. To avoid such teleology the 'needs of capital/demands of labour' approach would at least have to be used in such a way that it can demonstrate that particular policies happened because there was no alternative or because the particular needs of capital and demands of labour would have had to be different if alternative policies were to have ensued. The books by Ginsburg, Gough and the CSE State Group do go some way to overcoming such teleology by providing detailed historical studies of some areas of welfare policy; while Ginsburg examines the historical development of housing and social security the CSE book has (all too short) chapters on education, housing, social security, social work and health. But historical studies by themselves are insufficient for if their underlying problematic is one of 'capital's needs/labour's demands', they can reinforce a simple teleology by interpreting historical information in a way which suggests that the balance of needs and demands was always inevitably right for the policies that happened.

The teleology that can result from careless use of the 'capital's needs/ labour's demands' framework however, can happen with many frameworks applied to historical problems. Associated with it in the present case is the danger of the framework collapsing so that in the hands of some writers (such as the CSE State Group or Ginsburg) it is effectively dropped and all that is emphasised are the needs of capital, while in the hands of others such as Dorothy Thompson what is emphasised is that the welfare state is a victory for working class values.[7] With other writers there is a danger not of ignoring one side or the other in the framework, but of combining both in a purely eclectic manner. Saville,[8] for example, is a writer whom Gough criticises on the grounds of eclecticism, for writers like him stress: 'both aspects of the welfare state but leave open the way in which they are related'. Gough's intention is to avoid such eclecticism, to look at: 'the effect of class conflict on welfare policies, at the way in which the state represents the interests of capital and at the interrelation between these two sets of forces'.[9]

But despite these good intentions Gough fails to elucidate these inter-relations. He sets out the brief facts of the growth of working-class parties and follows this by noting only that there is another side to things because 'there *are* imperatives created by the capitalist industrialisation process' so that we have 'to explain how the long-term interests of the capitalist class are formulated and enacted'. Gough's failure to avoid eclecticism arises because there is no framework in which to analyse a hierarchial relation-ship; to avoid eclecticism it is necessary to be able to say that capital's needs or labour's demands are related to each other in particular ways, either one being more important than the other because it determines it or because a third set of factors determines each of these in definite ways. I shall argue that writers in the 'capital's needs/labour's demands' frame-work are unable to avoid either such eclecticism or an arbitrary insistence on the primacy of one side or the other, and this is for a basic reason: their concepts of the state and the economy are unduly limited so that the manner in which these needs and demands are conceived is inevitably restricted to one where they have no determinate hierarchical relation to each other except an arbitrary one.

There are, therefore, weaknesses in the answers that Marxist theory has so far provided to the question of why welfare services have grown. Answers to the distinct but related question of why all these services have in Britain been developed through *state* provision equally suffer from significant weaknesses. The question is why the state should have undertaken the *production* of welfare services. This is distinct from the problem of why it is concerned with redistributing wealth but the two are related; why should the state produce welfare services instead of providing the means for people to buy them themselves? Why should the education, health and housing of the labour force not have been provided entirely through the operations of the market with private schooling, private doctors and hospitals, and private landlords and home ownership? If both capital and labour benefit from these services why does capital not provide them in response to labour's desire to purchase them? Marxist answers are closely allied to the general Marxist theory of the capitalist state, and within that area there is a division over the relative emphasis upon the needs of capital and class conflict over labour's demands respectively.[10] The 'capital-logic' school best represented by Altvater and Yaffe argues that the capitalist state's functions are directly connected to, are derived from and can be deduced from the requirements of capital itself. By contrast, Holloway and Picciotto and others, while not denying the need of capital for a state which has a direct economic role, have developed a conceptual structure which allows them to argue that the political actions of the working class (and bourgeoisie) mediate, in important ways, the relation-ship between the state and the economy. The Holloway and Picciotto view finds expression in the CSE State Group's book on the welfare state, whereas the capital-logic approach is the basis of Ginsburg's work. He quotes Altvater approvingly on capital's need for a state providing such 'necessities' as welfare services since capital:

> requires at its base a special institution which is not subject to its limitations as capital, one whose transactions are not determined by the necessity of producing surplus value, one which is *in this sense,* a special institution 'alongside and outside bourgeois society' and one which at the same time provides, on the undisputed basis of capital itself, the immanent necessities that capital neglects.[11]

The problem with Ginsburg's explanation of why the capitalist state has the responsibilities that it does have is that it leaves unanswered (and unasked) the question of why capital itself neglects these necessities, why welfare services are not provided by private capital. And this problem exists in the Holloway and Picciotto approach, too, as it must for any approach that in any way relates the state to capital's needs: If capital needs it, why does it not provide welfare services? If it could make a profit from them why not produce them for sale? The problem's historical relevance is highlighted by the fact that capitalist countries other than Britain have relied upon private capital to provide many welfare services. The United States and Japan provide clear examples, with the latter being renowned for the system by which the large corporations provide complete welfare services for their employees. Those countries provide some benchmark by which we can judge common views on why British capital relied upon state provision. One common view is that capital could not provide adequate resources for the development of welfare services but if applied to capital as a whole, this is clearly an inadequate response; to the extent that the state's revenue is drawn from surplus value, the welfare services are effectively financed by capital. Nor is there any reason to believe that individual firms cannot mobilise the resources. Private firms in the USA and elsewhere do get the resources to produce welfare services such as health as commodities for sale and private education, equally, is produced for sale. Moreover, if it is argued that firms cannot afford the resources to finance *free* social services to their own employees, the comprehensive schemes provided by the large Japanese corporations are counter-examples. A more sustainable view is that individual firms cannot provide free welfare services to secure the health and quality of their labour force because they would lose the value of their investment in the workforce when they shed labour in the processes of crises and redundancies that accompany capitalist accumulation; the competition of capitals (as one argument of the capital-logic school goes) necessitates the state acting on behalf of all capital. This view appears to find a counter-example in the welfare systems the large Japanese corporations provide for their own employees but, in fact, they are the exception that proves the rule. For the specific feature of the Japanese economy is that the large corporations rely upon a system of sub-contracting by which production processes are farmed out to a myriad of small firms without welfare systems. In times of crisis the large corporations retain their labour forces and compel redundancies in the small sub-contractors, so that the value of their own expenditure on welfare services is preserved. Thus it does appear that as long as crises are the concomitant of capitalist accumulation, provision of free welfare services by all private firms is impossible. No universal coverage is possible on that basis, but it is possible with state provision. This explanation of *state* provision rests upon competition between individual firms, but current work does not examine that competition and its effect on the welfare state. Indeed, concentration upon the needs of capital (as a whole) and labour's demands discourages it.

The universality of welfare services is important for another reason, too, in explaining the state's activities according to one school of thought. This is the school that emphasises the welfare state's function as a means of social control. Can the explanation of the existence of state rather than private provision lie in the fact that the education, health and other welfare systems under the control of the state act to discipline and condition the labour force, to reinforce individualism and the values of capitalism (a role which the state has taken on as the changes in the family have weakened its former functions in the reproduction of labour power?). The role of the state in reinforcing the ideology and values of capital and weakening the potential for class organisation has been emphasised by many writers, such as George and Wilding, and is reaffirmed by Gough, Ginsburg and the CSE State Group. As the latter writes:

> when we speak of the role of the state in the reproduction of capital, we must remember that we are speaking not simply of performing certain material functions for capitalist industry but of reproducing a certain form of social relations. More simply: what makes the state a capitalist state is not so much what it does as the way in which it does it. For example, any society would have to educate workers for industrial production: what is particular about capitalist education is that it reinforces the atomisation on which class domination is based under capitalism.[12]

Whatever the value of this type of analysis—and studies of the ways in which the welfare services are organised are a welcome feature of recent studies—it cannot provide an explanation of why the state runs the welfare services. A private educational or health system, for example, would undoubtedly reinforce the centrality of the market at least as well as a welfare state system outside the market. The studies by Gough, Ginsburg and the CSE State Group (particularly the latter two) do provide a further body of evidence that the organisation of the welfare state does reinforce social control and its recent re-organisations strengthen that function. But it does not follow that its ability to perform this control is the reason for state provision of welfare services; the evidence fits well with the view that whatever the cause of the state's involvement in welfare provisions, the form of the welfare state has been subject to social pressures pushing it in a direction where its social control and ideological functions are brought to the fore.

Nevertheless, whatever the merits of explanations of the state's role in terms of the need for social control or the need to by-pass the competition between capitals the underlying question remains. Why was the British state drawn into the production of services instead of simply re-distributing income to guarantee that all classes can afford privately produced services? Why were labour's demands and capital's needs not resolved through a tax-credit system or a system of negative taxes of the form proposed by Friedman instead of by the establishment of the National Health Service, municipal housing and so on? If we are to explain the welfare *state* that is what we have to explain, but the Marxist theory of the state and the economy has not succeeded in doing so.

Explaining the Attacks on the Welfare State

If Marxist theory has not been able to provide an adequate explanation of the existence of state production of welfare services, its greatest test has come with the attacks on the welfare state that Labour and Conservative governments have pushed forward since 1976. Since the welfare state's existence has been explained by its congruence with capital's needs and labour's demands, how can the state's threats to it be explained? Have capital's needs or labour's demands declined? There have been three types of answer. One concentrates upon ideology, the Tories' attempt precisely to alter labour's demands by stimulating the ideology of the market and anti-statism, but I shall not consider it here, for it is a major subject in its own right and cannot be adequately covered in the present context. Another takes the view that the welfare state and the long boom of post-war capitalism were preconditions for each other, and with the end of the latter the former inevitably came into question; and the third argues that the development of the welfare state contained its own contradictions which have come to fruition in the cuts.

The connection between the welfare state and the long boom is unclear but widely believed to exist. The end of the long boom is seen to produce the necessity both for cuts in welfare state expenditure and for a drastic reorganisation of the welfare services. Asking why this reorganisation is taking place the CSE State Group answers: 'quite simply because the old patterns could not be maintained, because capital is in crisis'.[13] In Gough's analysis, the connection between the boom, its end and the welfare state are more explicit. Since a growing national product 'permits all groups to gain a larger slice' the long boom provides the 'material base for reformism and the welfare state'. Thus, if 'the long boom of post-war capitalism and the golden age of the welfare state share a common origin, so they may share a common fate'. But simply to postulate a connection between the boom and the growth of the welfare state is not a sufficient explanation of either, nor of the attacks on state expenditure at the end of the boom. (Moreover, it assumes that the long boom was unproblematic whereas in fact it was punctuated by several economic disturbances and threats to the development of state expenditure.)

The third approach appears to be superior. It does not merely put the long boom and the welfare state side by side and suggest that they are linked so that the end of one spells the crisis of the other. It goes a step further and considers how that crisis arose, and it argues that the long boom and the development of the welfare state themselves generated contradictions which could only be resolved by the traumatic end to the boom and the harsh attacks on the welfare state that we have witnessed. In particular the long boom itself has, according to Gough, caused a fall in profitability and this has forced capital to reconsider whether it can continue to afford the cost of the welfare state or whether it can achieve its 'needs' without high levels of government expenditure—without, that is, the welfare state. The idea that the long boom and the welfare state generated contradictions which made inevitable a crisis temporarily to resolve them plays a central role in Gough's analysis and it has a clear Marxist lineage since it hinges on the dialectics of change. It is a point which is central to Yaffe's 'capital-logic' analysis of the crisis but Gough's explanation of the underlying contradiction is different from his.[14]

For Gough the central contradiction is the militancy of the labour force. It first gave rise to a 'settlement' between a powerful working class and the bourgeoisie as they emerged from the Second World War and then grew as a result of the settlement until it threatened the basis of the arrangement itself. According to Gough this settlement included the construction of the welfare state and a commitment to state intervention to maintain full employment and growth and it did in fact succeed in producing that result, the long boom. But the boom itself stimulated further labour militancy which, by pushing up wages, ate into the profits of capital. Falling profitability, according to this thesis, brought high rates of accumulation—the boom—to an end. It also had a direct impact upon capital's attitudes to the welfare state. Since state provision of welfare services on a universal basis is ultimately financed out of taxation it does, within Marxist political economy, reduce the amount of surplus value that is available for appropriation by private capital, and that element is perpetually in conflict with the fact that the welfare system yields indirect benefits which satisfy 'capital's needs'. When profitability falls, the cost of the welfare state overrides the benefits in the calculations of capital and stimulates a political movement, Thatcherism (or perhaps it should be called Healeyism), to reduce the costs of the welfare state. The thesis is appealing, but it does suffer from several problems. Although there was undoubtedly a significant fall of profitability during the post-war boom it is not likely that it resulted from trade union militancy pushing up wages. Apart from the doctrinal dispute that has raged for a decade over the issue of whether high wages cause low profits (and as a result of which it is clear that Marx did not attribute low profits to this cause)[15] there is the fact that high rates of wage rises occurred in the years after the sharp rise in unemployment after 1967. Increases in wage militancy became noticeable and severe after the long boom's end had arrived, rather than during the years of high employment. Nevertheless, whether or not Gough is right to ascribe falling profitability to wage militancy stimulated by full employment, it is undoubtedly the case that falling profits have stimulated the attack by capital upon the financing of the welfare state. What remains unexplained is why the 1940s have been different from the 1970s. Why should a combination of labour militancy and precarious profits in the former period lead to a willingness by capital to build a settlement with the welfare state as its cornerstone, whereas in the latter period militancy and low profits have stimulated an attack on the welfare state? That, surely, is the type of question that we would expect a theory of the state and economy to be able to answer, and it is highly pertinent to the formulation of alternative policies. But it is a mark of the theory's weakness at present that it has provided no answer.

The closest that Gough comes to explaining the circumstances of the attack on the welfare state is an exposition of the prescient thesis put forward for the United States by James O'Connor in *The Fiscal Crisis of the State*. The crisis in the accumulation of capital intensifies the general momentum for increasing state expenditure but at the same time the sources of revenue to finance it are restricted. Taxes on the working class or capital, borrowing and the creation of money are all unable to act as the source of new funds to finance the expansion. Each form of fund raising has undesirable consequences or meets resistance in one way or another so ultimately the only option is to restrict the growth of state expenditure. The picture painted is intuitively appealing for it appears to correspond to the financial problems posed in 1974/75 in Britain. The rise in state expenditure as private accumulation contracted caused a rise in the Public Sector Borrowing Requirement to levels that were unheard of in the City and did present real problems of financing. How could the state borrow the large amounts of money without pushing interest rates too high?

If this contradiction (or what Gough calls the 'Catch-22 situation' in which a hypothetical Chancellor of the Exchequer finds himself) is what accounts for the attacks on the welfare state, then it deserves to be analysed fully. However, it has not been and concentration on the simple framework of capital's needs/labour's demands appears to prevent such an analysis. The way in which that framework hinders analysis is related to the fact that it encourages a concentration upon the actions of different classes and groups rather than the structural forces that affect the fiscal crisis. In the remainder of this essay I discuss that contention further.

Problems in Structure/Action Dichotomy

The framework in which all Marxist writers on the welfare state now work is one of trying to avoid each of two extremes. On the one hand there is the functionalism of the view that the welfare state exists because the capitalist system's structure requires the functions that it performs; on the other hand, there is the action theory perspective of the view that its origins, development and limits arise from class conflict. The CSE State Group, Ginsburg and Gough in their own ways are all conscious of the need to avoid these extremes, and Marxism appears to offer the way to do so by treating the system and class conflict as an integrated whole rather than polar opposites. As Gough writes:

> In other words, the dichotomy between these two basic approaches to under-standing the welfare state. . . can be overcome within Marxist political economy. It has the merit over pluralist theories of social policy in situating the 'conflict' within an ongoing mode of production, and it has the merit over functionalist theories of social policy in relating the socio-economic 'system' (its structure and its development through time) to the class conflict which is an integral feature of it. Of course, it does not simply sit these two theories side by side: both elements are developed within a completely different theoretical framework.

None of the writers on the welfare state, however, justify this claim.

To start with, there is a serious confusion over the nature of the dichotomy between structure and action. It is confused with the dichotomy between capital's needs and labour's demands since 'capital's needs' are seen as expressing the requirements of the structure or mode of production. In fact, however, it has quite a different status. The 'capital's needs/labour's demands' framework concerns only class conflict, action theory. The dichotomy between capital and labour is relevant only for asking and attempting to answer questions like 'is the welfare state a victory won by the working class in struggle against the bourgeoisie; or is it constructed by the bourgeoisie in its own interests or is it both in differing degrees?' These are questions about the *actions* of the different classes; questions about the anonymous effects of the structure are of an entirely different nature, as I explained earlier, but the framework of capital's needs/labour's demands is only relevant to the former. What is important here is that the capital's needs/labour's demands dichotomy is quite distinct from the structure/action one and focuses only on the action part. The central question of the structure/action dichotomy is whether the welfare state is shaped by class struggle (action theory) or through structure forces other than the conflicts of classes, anonymous system forces which guarantee that the welfare state exists in a way which is functional to the reproduction of the system. Marxist theory does have a way of moving beyond the structure/action dichotomy with that type of central question, but it is not attainable by focussing on the different dichotomy of capital's needs/labour's demands and it is itself enmeshed in controversy.

Marxist theory overcomes the dichotomy between structure and action in the following way. At a high level of abstraction, the mode of production is the structure and it has its own laws of development. In other words, it has a history which is produced by the working of anonymous system forces. On the basis of it, and as a condition for its existence, there exist classes which act and through their action modify and make concrete the history of the structure. Thus the structure (mode of production) and the agents of action (classes) are inextricably bound together rather than being dichotomised. Marxist analysis of historical phenomena such as the relation between the state and the economy has, therefore, the basis for moving beyond a concentration upon either the structure or the actions of classes, but by using the capital's needs/labour's demands framework, in its current condition it is forced to concentrate on the latter alone. That is one problem with the capital's needs/labour's demands framework; it neglects the structure. A second problem is that it does not even permit a robust analysis in terms of action theory itself.

Let me begin with the question of why the action theory that is inadvertently practised by current Marxist writers is weak even in its own terms. It will assist in the subsequent discussion of how structural analysis may be conducted. The problem with an action theory that focuses on the needs and demands of capital and labour is that it is at a high level of abstraction. In more concrete historical analysis it is necessary to take into account finer divisions of social groups—fractions of classes, for example. Capital is not homogeneous but is divided into fractions, primarily financial capital, merchants' capital and industrial capital. Even though these may be bound together in particular ways (as financial and industrial capital are in the category of finance capital) they have distinct interests and effects. Similarly, the working class may be divided into distinct fractions (as theorists have attempted to do with concepts like the aristocracy of labour). To analyse the actions of different agents in an explanation of British history, it is at least necessary to take into account the behaviour of these different fractions as well as the interests of capital and labour as wholes. In several traditions, it is common to do such work. Marxist studies of the labour process and technical change, for example, do take into account the actions of distinct fractions of the working class and their trade union organisations.[17] And studies of British financial policy do take into account the distinct actions of financial capital (the City) and industrial capital.[18] However, the theories of the welfare state and the general Marxist theories of the state that I have surveyed here neglect these fractions and are concerned only with the actions of capital as a whole and labour as a whole. This is a regrettable weakness and two examples indicate why. Historically the establishment of the welfare state in Britain was not seen as an unalloyed victory for the working class as a whole; those well-organised groups with established friendly societies had different attitudes toward the development from other workers. And the attacks on the welfare state have been orchestrated by City interests in quite a different, more powerful, way from the influence exerted by industrial capital. Thus, an adequate historical explanation of the development of the welfare state along action theory lines requires a developed treatment of the different fractions of capital and labour.

If Marxist theory is to move beyond action theory alone and provide a complementary structural explanation in terms of the anonymous system forces exerted by the mode of production a different problem arises. How can we conceive of these structural forces? It is one thing to say that the welfare state performs certain functions for the structure at certain times and that cuts in it perform a function at other times, but it is another thing to explain *how* the structure causes this useful apparatus to arise. Apart from the conscious or organised actions of the classes and fractions of classes, are there anonymous structural forces that have any concrete, empirical relevance? I think that the 'laws of demand and supply' so often quoted by right-wing politicians to justify their policies do, in fact, act as anonymous system forces giving effect to the structure's influence.[19] In other words, the markets for labour, commodities and finance do impose their own constraints upon the development of the economy, the state and other aspects of society, and they would do so in an anonymous way even if trade unions, employers, traders and bankers did not play any organised political role on those markets. Take the influence of the market for finance upon the policies of the state.

The Labour Government in 1976 was forced to impose major cuts upon state expenditure. Against the expectations of many it actually succeeded in reducing the ratio of state expenditure to Gross National Product. The circumstances that forced the government's hand were market forces and although they were intertwined with the actions of definite agents (such as the intervention of the International Monetary Fund which was triggered by market events) these forces had an effect of their own. As was described in the 'fiscal crisis of the state' thesis, the government found itself in 1975 and 1976 in a position where it had to borrow unprecedented amounts of money. The difficulties of doing so without paying very high interest rates and without disrupting the flow of finance to industry were instrumental in causing the government to cut back its expenditure in order to cut its borrowing requirement. The way the financial markets operate, their 'laws of demand and supply' dictate that if the state has a high borrowing requirement usually it can only meet it without paying higher interest or disrupting the financial flow if it creates more money, or, in other words, increases the money supply. With the expectation of money supply rising in 1976 there was a 'knock-on' effect upon the market for foreign exchange for these factors caused an outflow of money which led to an extremely sharp fall in the exchange rate. That was another market phenomenon that affected government policy and determined the government to cut state expenditure in order to cut its borrowing and its effect upon the money supply.

The argument is, then, that the study of the state and economy requires two developments that have so far been absent. One is that within action theory, it is necessary to take account of distinct fractions of capital and labour. The other, and the more important one, is that it is necessary to develop the concept of structural forces and that to do so we have to come to grips with the operation of market forces and the way they influence the state and the economy. Without an analysis of structural forces operating through markets, there is a strong tendency for writers to concentrate on purely political mechanisms within the state and assume that the economy can only affect policy through such political mechanisms. Gough, Ginsburg and the CSE State Group are, for example, concerned only with such political questions as the role of the Labour Party, and of an ill-defined 'class conscious political directorate' within the state machine. There is one exception to this. When Gough discusses the 'fiscal crisis of the state' he does present the Chancellor's 'Catch-22 situation' in the context of problems like the difficulty of borrowing money and the problems of the money supply, but because his earlier discussion of the economy does not encompass the distinct fractions of capital, a concept of how markets work, or any analysis of money, he is forced to mention such problems briefly, with errors, and pass on. For a Labour Government which is constrained by such problems, however, it may appear that they cannot be despatched briefly but are a danger to a reform programme as strong as the politically conscious activities of the representatives of capital. It is interesting to see the distinction between action theory and a theory of the structure in the minds of Labour politicians themselves. Foreign exchange crises which affect government policy are open to different interpretations. In the mid-1960s Harold Wilson blamed them for blowing his government 'off-course' and saw in them the hand of the Gnomes of Zurich; his theory of the relation between the state and the economy was clearly the 'action' variant. In the mid-1970s, by contrast, Denis Healey clearly based his policy on the view that the anonymous forces of the money market and foreign exchange market set definite limits to what is possible; the laws of supply and demand have a political effect. It is pertinent to ask what the left wing's policies are or should be based upon: an awareness of the danger of right-wing actions by gnomes, a respect for the 'laws of supply and demand', or a third view which encompasses both.

My argument that concepts of class and concepts of market forces have to be further developed if the theory of the state and the economy is to progress is an argument that both the concept of the economy and that of the state require elaboration if their relation is to be theorised adequately. In arguing that a strengthening of the concept of the economy is necessary, I am not suggesting that market forces are all that matters, that we should commit the error of concentrating upon structure instead of action, but, instead, that without analysing them no study of the state and economy's relations can succeed in the task of integrating structure with action. Regrettably, however, such a programme cannot avoid its own problems. One is that market forces are themselves borne by agents who are not political eunuchs; a run on the pound when a Labour government looks leftward is not independent of the political positions of market operators, but such events are nevertheless distinct from organised political action and are, in any case, relatively rare and insignificant in comparison to the everyday pressures of market forces upon government finances. A second is that while it is illustrative and convenient to picture the financial system as placing constraints upon the state and forcing cuts and reorganisations in the welfare state it is equally important to be able to examine how structural conditions in the markets were particularly favourable to the development of the welfare state in the immediate post-war period. A third is that the concept of the state, as well as that of the economy, has to be developed further if the influence of the structure and the action of its agents is to be adequately understood in the relation between state and economy.

In developing the concept of the state it has first to be recognised that the state is not only a political body but also has a significant economic aspect. Its branches are themselves economic agents enmeshed in market forces. As an employer the state's branches have to buy labour-power in the labour market; they have to buy other commodities and in the case of nationalised industries sell them; and they have to borrow money. Although the state may carry great weight in these markets for labour, commodities and finance they remain markets whose operations are thoroughly conditioned by the capitalist system and, accordingly, the state's branches' situation as economic agents is the channel through which the effects of the structure make themselves felt. Secondly, in order to complement a theory of structural forces with a theory of the organised actions of distinct classes it is necessary to develop the concept of the state in other directions too. In this context the present concept of the state is severely limited by its concentration upon the nation state as if it were a well defined unitary structure. Writers such as Gough do look at its relations with other nation states, thereby avoiding a too narrow focus on Britain alone, but that in no way avoids the idea that 'the state' is 'the nation state'. If Marxist theory were to continue to make this identification it would be difficult to account for important interventions which have affected the development of the welfare state. For example, the interventions of the International Monetary Fund in British policy at different conjunctures like 1968 and 1976 (conjunctures where in relation to these actions by agents, the structural influence of financial market forces in the foreign exchanges were especially important) can only be treated as the appearance of a deus ex machina if our concept of the state is the same as the nation state. For with such a perspective we can have no analytical concept of the IMF (is it a bank, a central bank, a political elite for the whole capitalist world or something else). To have such a concept it is necessary to think of the state as more than the nation state. I think it should be conceived as a hierarchical structure of state institutions, only one set of which are those encompassed by the idea of the nation state. At one level in the hierarchy we have to place international state institutions such as the IMF, the organs of the EEC, the Bank for International Settlements, and NATO. At a different level we have to place the institutions of 'the local state' of towns and regions. With such a hierarchical concept of the state it is possible to analyse the relations between the actions of agents in its different parts, the manner in which organised class forces in one part affect the others, and how market forces affect each part of the structure.

Conclusion

At the start of this article I stated that weaknesses in the analysis of the welfare state are related to epistemological problems and also parallel the inadequacy of the labour movement's response to 'the cuts' and recent governments' strategies for reorganising welfare services. A large part of that response has focussed upon particular cuts—actions to protest at the closure of this hospital, that nursery and so on—and it has generally failed. I am not one who thinks that theory always necessarily yields strong lessons for practice or that the types of things that follow from the arguments in this paper are in any sense new. Nevertheless, it is useful to draw them out. One is that protests about particular cuts are necessarily weakened by the fact that the branch of the state immediately responsible is only one part of a hierarchical structure so that particular campaigns only have a future if they are integrated with, at least, a national programme. Another is that such a wider programme has to place the question of welfare services in the context of the relation between the state and the economy as a whole. If economic market forces are an important structural force within which the actions and policies of different classes are constrained, a political campaign around the subject of the welfare services will not succeed if those structural forces maintain their constraints. Thus, policies to develop the welfare services should be placed in the context of a break in the links between market forces and the state. This, of course, is the general thrust of the Alternative Economic Strategy[20] with its perspective on foreign exchange controls, nationalisation of financial institutions and planned reflation; the reflation and the building of a new expanded system of welfare services is there conceived as possible only to the extent that nationalisation, controls, and planning loosen the influence on the state of structural, market forces.

NOTES

1. I am grateful to Marjorie Mayo, Ben Fine, Ron Smith, Sonja Ruehl and Linda McDowell for helpful comments upon an earlier draft and to the editors of the *Socialist Register* for valuable suggestions.
2. Major texts in this controversy are, among others, L. Althusser, *For Marx*, (London, 1969); N. Poulantzas, *Political Power and Social Class*, (London, 1973) and A. Cutler, B. Hindess, P. Hirst and A. Hussain, *Marx's Capital and Capitalism Today* Vols. 1 and 2, (London, 1977, 1978).
3. E. Altvater, 'Some problems of state interventionism', *Kapitalistate*, 1 and 2, 1973; D. Yaffe, 'The Marxian theory of crisis, capital and the state', *Economy and Society* Vol. 2, no. 2, 1973.
4. Examples of recent work are in John Holloway and Sol Picciotto, *State and Capital*, (London, Edward Arnold, 1978), Ernest Mandel, *Late Capitalism*, (London, NLB, 1975), James O'Connor, *The Fiscal Crisis of the State*, (New York, 1973), Ben Fine and Laurence Harris, *Rereading Capital*, (Macmillan, London, 1979), Leo Panitch, 'The Development of Corporatism in Liberal Democracies', *Comparative Political Studies*, Vol. 10, no. 1, April 1977, Bob Jessup, 'Recent Theories of the Capitalist State', *Cambridge Journal of Economics* Vol. 1, no. 4, December 1977 and Suzanne de Brunhoff, *The State, Capital and Economic Policy*, (London, 1978). Of course it is not true that recent work on the relationship between the state and the economy is the first by Marxists. Writers such as Hilferding and Lenin were notable earlier theorists, but recent writers are effectively the first to tackle the problem in the context of the stage of capitalism known as State Monopoly Capitalism with its Welfare State, Keynesianism and credit policies.
5. Ian Gough, *The Political Economy of the Welfare State*, (London, Macmillan, 1979), Norman Ginsburg, *Class Capital and Social Policy*, (London, Macmillan, 1979), CSE State Group, *Struggle over the State*, (CSE Books, London, 1979).
6. This is not to suggest that preventive medicine as such is necessarily 'a good thing'. As is noted in Lesley Doyal, *The Political Economy of Health*, (London, Pluto, 1979), pp. 211-212 preventive medicine itself can be adopted and promulgated in such a way as to emphasise the individual's failure rather than the social determinants of disease.
7. Dorothy Thompson, 'Discussion: The Welfare State', *New Reasoner* no. 4, 1958, pp. 127-8.
8. John Saville, 'The Welfare State: An Historical Approach', *New Reasoner* no. 3, Winter 1957/8.
9. I. Gough, *op. cit.*, p. 57.
10. Neoclassical economic theory, too, has developed theories of market failure and that school of thought can demonstrate the restrictive nature of the assumptions that have to be satisfied if markets were to work optimally. Their failure to be

set up or work satisfactorily leads some neoclassical economists to argue for the existence of state provision (in contexts such as the US medicare programme). In the present article, however, I concentrate upon Marxist analyses which are based upon the concepts of classes rather than individuals.

11. N. Ginsburg, *op. cit.*, p. 28.
12. CSE State Group, *op. cit.*, p. 18.
13. CSE State Group, *op. cit.*, p. 3.
14. In 'The Crisis of Profitability: A Critique of the Glyn-Sutcliffe Thesis', New Left Review 80, July/August 1973, Yaffe criticised Gough's explanation when it was put forward by A. Glyn and B. Sutcliffe, *British Capitalism, Workers and the Profit Squeeze.*
15. These debates are surveyed in B. Fine and L. Harris, *Rereading Capital,* (London, 1979).
16. I. Gough, *op. cit.*, p. 46. Ben Fine and I also argue in *Rereading Capital* that class struggle and concepts of a structural determination are integrated in Marxist theory, but I think that we, as much as the authors discussed here, fail to present a satisfying integration. Instead we leave open the question of how class struggle and structural forces have an effect.
17. See, for example, the symposium by B. Elbaum, W. Lazonick, F. Wilkinson and J. Zeitlin in *Cambridge Journal of Economics,* Vol. 3, no. 3, 1979.
18. Two examples are F. Longstreth, 'The City, Industry and The State' in C. Crouch (ed.), *State and Economy in Contemporary Capitalism,* (London, 1979) and J. Coakley and L. Harris, 'The City, Industry and the Foreign Exchanges: Theory and Evidence', mimeo. Both these articles examine only the action theory aspects of the division between financial capital and industrial capital and neglect structural forces.
19. The disingenuous element in such politicians' reference to these laws is in the implication that they are immutable and cannot be tampered with.
20. A statement of some major aspects of the Alternative Economic Strategy is given by London CSE Group, 'Crisis, the Labour Movement and the Alternative Economic Strategy, in *Capital and Class,* no. 8, 1979.

ON BEING A MARXIST: A HUNGARIAN VIEW

György Bence and János Kis

*Introduction**
*The following text represents one of the first major fruits of the revival
of* samizdat *activity and democratic opposition in Hungary since the late
1970s. The text originally appeared in 1978 as part of a collection entitled*
Marx in the Fourth Decade, *which together with* Profile *(a collection of
essays which had been rejected by official publications produced around
the same time) marked the first effort at* samizdat *publication in Hungary.
The editor, András Kovács, circulated a questionnaire on present attitudes
towards Marxism among a loose circle of friends who in the 1960s had
been caught up in the 'renaissance of Marxism' in Hungary, an independent
current of Marxist thinking which based itself on a revival of interest in the
early work of Lukács, and whose ideas bore certain affinities to those of
both the Western New Left and Czechoslovak democratic socialism. The
contributors were asked to consider both their personal relationship to
Marxism and its wider contemporary significance. As the editor's letter
began, 'The thinking of the great majority of our generation was determined
in some form or other by Marxism'.*

> *Those who regarded themselves as Marxists or those who took up a standpoint
> consciously against Marxism both felt that they knew precisely what they
> rejected and why. Today the situation has changed. This has led me to put to you
> the question: 'What in your view is Marxism and what is your attitude to it?'*

*The second main question was, 'How far is or is not Marxism appropriate
in Eastern Europe today?' The recipients of the questionnaire were asked
in addition whether they believed Marxism to be of continued relevance for
the left in the West and in the Third World, even if they no longer regarded
it as such for Eastern Europe.*

*The questionnaire was answered by 21 people, whose current occupations
range from philosophers and social scientists to literary critics and even
theologians, and their replies encompass a diversity of intellectual and
political positions. So far as can be judged from the summaries of the
volume and the excepts which have appeared in English, the bulk of the*

---

*This introduction was written by friends of the authors in Britain.

contributors (with certain conspicuous exceptions), are united in their conviction that the 1960s strategy of promoting reform from above through a revival of true Marxist thinking has proved illusory, and that this development throws into question the claims of Marxism to provide either a framework for theoretical analysis or a guide to practical political action in contemporary Eastern European societies.[1]

The authors of the present text, György Bence (b. 1941) and János Kis (b. 1943) were trained as professional Marxist philosophers in Budapest. As they explain in the third section of their essay, Bence and Kis were deeply influenced in the early 1960s by the lectures of György Markus on the history of philosophy. Given the predominant influence of Lukács in Budapest Marxist thinking, Markus and following him Bence and Kis gradually drew closer to that grouping of Lukács' former students known in the West as the 'Budapest' or 'Lukács School', and came themselves to form a third generation of Lukács' students. The Budapest School is defined in this essay as consisting of the philosophers Agnes Heller, Ferenc Feher, and Mihaily Vajda, in association with the sociologists Maria Markus and András Hegedüs (pre-1956 Prime Minister of Hungary) though others might draw its boundaries more widely.[2] *Its principal contribution to the 'renaissance of Marxism' in Hungary was its effort to develop Marxist theory in the direction of a 'philosophy of praxis'.*[3]

Both the older and younger wings of the Budapest School were united in their open opposition to the Soviet invasion of Czechoslovakia, but came to differ in their interpretation of its significance for their own intellectual and political positions. While most of the older members of the School continued their efforts to ground a critique of existing socialism in an abstract conception of the human essence, Bence and Kis, together with Markus, embarked in the early 70s on a lengthy critique of the model of a communist economy contained in Marx's Capital *(forthcoming from Allison and Busby). As a nervous response to the development of any type of independent Marxist thinking, the Party shut the door of public life on both generations of Lukács' students; in 1973, two years after Lukács' death, Bence and Kis were dismissed from their academic jobs and prohibited for a time from publishing in Hungary, along with both Markuses, Heller, Feher, Vajda, and Hegedüs.*

Between 1974 and 1976, Bence and Kis wrote a series of essays attempting to develop a novel theoretical analysis of Soviet-type societies as sui generis *forms of class society which are neither socialist, capitalist, nor transitional between the two. These were published in English in 1977 under the pseudonym Marc Rakovski as the volume* Towards an East European Marxism *(Allison and Busby, London, 1977).*[4] *With the temporary emigration in 1976 of the older figures of the Budapest School,*[5] *(including Markus), Bence and Kis were left as the only major representatives in Hungary of this oppositional Marxism which had been associated with Lukács, and from 1975 they began to play a central role in the emerging democratic opposition, in which they were the main figures belonging to this highly theoretical Marxist tradition. The present text itself served as a bridge between Marxists and non-Marxists involved in the emerging democratic opposition. In 1977 the two authors participated in a letter of solidarity with Charter 77 in Czechoslovakia, signed by 34 Hungarian intellectuals; in autumn 1979, they, together with János Kenedi, sent a special letter of protest to Kadar about the trials of Charter 77 activists, as part of a wider campaign against the Prague trials which resulted in a petition signed by 250 people. As a consequence of their role in this protest, official harrassment against them has been stepped up, and they have been deprived of the opportunities for free-lance editorial work by which they have supported themselves since 1973.*

*   *   *

At the end of 1977, one of our friends, András Kovács, circulated a detailed questionnaire on the present state of Marxism. He planned to collect the answers into a volume, later to be published in manuscript form. This is how the collection entitled *Marx in the Fourth Decade* was produced and became, along with the volume *Profile* (edited by János Kenedi), one of the first major undertakings of the newly-emerging Hungarian *samizdat*.

The addressees of the questionnaire belonged roughly to the same generation, constituting a loose intellectual circle, of young academics, philosophers, economists etc. and literary critics, who at the end of the sixties had been caught by the wave of the 'renaissance of Marxism' as it was somewhat pretentiously called at that time. The allusion of the 'fourth decade' in the title thus stands both for the age of the contributors and the length of time a Soviet-type society had been established in Hungary. Due to the nature of the group addressed by Kovács, the individual questions themselves had a rather narrow academic focus. We therefore decided to ignore the concrete questions, to concentrate only on the most general and at the same time the most personal points of András Kovács' questionnaire: 'What is your understanding of the term Marxism and what it your own present position vis-à-vis Marxism?' Or, in our more personal interpretation of the question: 'If you were a Marxist in the past are you still a Marxist today and if you either were or are a Marxist, what does Marxism mean to you?' Of all the questions in the circular, only the last had real relevance for us: 'Can you give reasons which, in your opinion, make Marxism particularly relevant or irrelevant for contemporary Eastern Europe?' The second and third part of our contribution constitutes our answer to this question while the first part will serve as an introduction.

Despite our attempt to use an entire first section to introduce the core of our answer, on many points our reply turned out to be comprehensible only to the 'initiated'. In 1977 these groups that now form the Hungarian democratic opposition—former 'renaissance' Marxists, critical sociologists and economists, underground artists, socially-aware architects, writers who are unable to reconcile themselves to our national grievances, dissident priests and their followers—had only begun to notice each other's existence. Thus our audience was then more or less confined to those of our generation who, like us, started off from Marxism. It was they whom we tried to convince that—contrary to what we had previously maintained—Marxism is not a necessary precondition for participation in oppositional politics in Eastern Europe.

What we had been suggesting to our friends at home, was in fact already the situation in some other countries of Eastern Europe. The Polish ex-revisionists were the ones to travel furthest, greatly influencing our personal development as well. However, we could not simply follow them in everything they did; not only because the Hungarian democratic opposition was in a much more primitive state than the Polish one. The Polish ex-revisionists went as far as a total refusal of Marxism. Such ideas as theirs are not unknown in the West: they have much in common with the language of the so-called New Philosophers of Paris. Of course, unlike the latter who only followed the changing atmosphere of French intellectual *salons,* the Poles tried to face the bitter experience of the official anti-semitic campaign directed against them. They reasoned that it was by no means an accident that the persecution of Jewish (and non-Jewish) intelligentsia should take place precisely in a country whose official ideology is Marxism. For them, Marxism doesn't recognise any absolute moral values, in other words it denies that the individual has inalienable rights, which ought not to be sacrificed for any practical reason whatsoever.

We have not arrived at such conclusions. We think that the relationship of Marxism and ethics is somewhat more complex. At the same time, we are too much imbued with historical materialism to ascribe the behaviour of large groups of people, which is the *summa* of myriad factors, to such entities as the regime's declared ideology. So, we do not believe that a Marxist who wants to join the new opposition must at once deny Marxism. What we do maintain is that he no longer needs it and is quite unlikely to derive any relevant theoretical or political guidance from it.

This position is somewhat unusual in Eastern Europe, and is most likely a peculiarly Hungarian one. But it is not altogether improbable that there may be some people in Western Europe who have undergone a similar development. There are certain signs to support this, and some of our friends visiting us from the West seemed to understand our position; without their encouragement we would never have thought of reviving this discussion. This is why we risk publishing an unchanged *samizdat* text originally addressed to a rather confined circle. Alterations have been made only in a few cases where the original wording seemed unclear. We have also omitted a few personal remarks concerning events known only to a very small number of people even in Hungary.

May 1980

Within the Tradition

Ever since Marxism became Marxism, the most usual definitions of this particular *ism* have been designed to undercut other *ists*. In cases where the definition was not derived from an opposition between different sorts of Marxisms, then the tactic was to restrict the *ism* to the sole genuine Marxist one of its current interpretations. Even sophisticated historical accounts are always organised around some great historical juxtaposition.

The kind of teleological historiography which considers the historical Marxist tradition as the prehistory of the one and only true theoretical and political system, would of course not admit the existence of any such competitions. The development of Marxism is a unitary process, and oppositions can only arise between the one genuine Marxism and its falsification or abnegations. A quite absurd, but nonetheless logical implication of this sort of history is the well-known distinction even in the works of Marx himself, between Marxist and pre- or non-Marxist components. So perhaps it is necessary to state the simple truism that Marxism as an *ism* came into existence only with the appearance of the first independent thinkers and political figures who conceived their own activity as the continuation of a specific tradition founded by Marx.

The activity of Engels after 1883 is a borderline case. The difficulty is not to decide whether Marx and Engels had exactly the same *Weltanschauung* or not. This is a problem for those studying the Sacred History of Marxism, as is the question 'when did Marx become a Marxist?' Sticking to historical common sense we must categorically reject such approaches. The examination of the actual divergences and similarities is a task for the textual critic and the biographer. But whatever conclusions unbiassed research may come to in the future, the fact still remains that they were too close to each other for us to say that Engels was simply following some tradition set out in the works of Marx. He was continuing their common project. Even when his own later contributions lacked textual precedents in the works of Marx, Engels still believed that he had merely expanded, applied and systematised their common method and theory. Whenever he did in fact contradict something Marx had said, this always concerned some specific historical or political case, without leading him even to raise the question of a possible discontinuity within the tradition. He did not visualise this problem even in the polemical battles waged to win over the emerging social democratic workers' movement. He saw himself as merely explaining Marxism and nothing else. Marx's first disciples and adversaries were not even acquainted with the most essential texts. Whenever someone came into personal contact with the 'master', his impressions were always determined by the specific character of the occasion. Engels was, therefore, continually drawn into polemics. His argument usually developed into a positive explanation of a kind which may be called, in the original sense of the word, 'vulgarisation'. This is how he arrived at those philosophical reflections which later played such an important role in the disputes on the nature of what constituted orthodox Marxism.

It must be kept in mind that philosophising for Engels meant something quite different from what later Marxism understood as 'philosophy'. For it was not so much the foundation of socio-economic thought but its extension and elaboration. Engels was forced to deal with it because his antagonists pushed the debate onto the terrain of philosophy and he was obliged to follow them there. For him, Marx's work was principally a socio-economic theory and its political application and nothing more. Marxist theory was still seen as a coherent unity, or at least so it appeared to Engels. It was only later that different interpretations of the main socio-economic and political theses emerged, necessitating the selection of the genuine orthodoxy which was only possible by raising the level of discussion to a higher plane of abstraction. Engels could only see that certain adherents to Marxism misunderstood or oversimplified his and Marx's work: that is, he could not see different traditions, differences in kind. The differences for him were merely nuances. He himself used the term 'Marxism' in theoretical contexts only ironically, citing Marx's famous dictum: 'All I know is that I am certainly not a Marxist!'—to rebuke over-zealous disciples.

Of course, the issue is not about terminological conventions. While in the 1860s and 70s only individual Marxian and Engelsian propositions exerted an influence on a few representatives of the various socialist movements, by the 80s some socialists had self-consciously rejected their own former theoretical and political positions and replaced them with a wholesale acceptance of the teachings of Marx and Engels as a comprehensive general system. This was the real birth of the Marxist tradition. However, the relationship of these first Marxists to the tradition was hardly any clearer than that of Engels himself. For Kautsky, the young Bernstein or Plekhanov, Marxism was something fixed, an inheritable tradition, but in such a way that the continuity of the tradition also appeared as given. When they modified or applied Marxist principles to a new problem they never asked themselves whether the relationship between their new results and the general theoretical basis of Marxism could be in some sense problematic.

The turning point in this respect came only in the late 90s, precipitated by Bernstein's revisionism. But it was not simply due to the fact that Bernstein openly criticised certain propositions of Marx, or that he even dismissed some of them. Others had done this before him. Even his criticism of the most important political predictions could not constitute real change. That was certainly new, but it could only be considered a decisive change in the tradition if orthodoxy wished to define the tradition by the very propositions Bernstein had attacked. Let us bear in mind that these propositions were similarly criticised by non-Marxists too, but neither their nor Bernstein's criticism really managed to alter the conviction of significant numbers of socialists. There were hardly any who had agreed with Bernstein on everything. The real novelty lay in Bernstein's self-conscious attempt to define the alternatives open for the development and improvement of Marxist theory. If a Marxian proposition was to be rejected, then either there was something wrong with the foundations of the theory or with the way it was used. If the problem was the foundations then one had to discard the whole edifice of Marxism. If on the other hand there were implicit inconsistencies which could be eliminated, the theory as a whole would remain valid, even if extensive modifications were made. Or, to quote Bernstein, the proposition to be modified 'could fall without shaking the foundations in the least'. The essence of Marxism is its general view of history, its method of historical analysis, which was not applied consistently even by Marx himself. We may, therefore, reject propositions regarded by Marx himself as fundamental and still remain Marxists as long as we stick to the general interpretation of the world.

But the abstract general propositions to which Bernstein tried to tie the continuity of the tradition were not accepted with approval by contemporary Marxists. They did, however, have to face the contradictions that Bernstein had revealed. Even for orthodox Marxists the system could not remain the organically developing and unproblematic whole as before. They, too, had to accept the distinction between the essential and the non-essential elements of the tradition; and for them, too, what was really essential was the method, and the general interpretation of history. However, what was, at first, only a conceptual distinction soon became a real divide. It turned out that an ever-growing number of things had to be rejected in the name of a common unifying method, and likewise more and more unprecedented propositions crept into the system, sheltering behind the appeal to method. Eventually, it was Lukács who seriously concluded that one could remain a pure orthodox Marxist even if every single proposition of Marx was proved to be false. ('What is Orthodox Marxism' in *History and Class Consciousness*, Merlin, London, 1971.) The seriousness—or frivolity rather—is quite clear if we care to think about it and realise that none of the orthodox Marxists ever really accepted this view. Orthodoxies came to include various lists of systematic propositions, some of which were no longer reconcilable. What was orthodox to one was revisionist to another, what was Marxist for one was no longer so for the other.

In the light of all this what use is it to speak of a Marxist tradition? By the early 1920s numerous irreconcilable Marxisms had developed and, on the basis of some abstract philosophical-methodological construction, each set itself up as the sole legitimate heir to Marx's legacy. We can hardly avoid the feeling that somehow they still belong to a common tradition. It is, however, very likely that this is an illusion. Perhaps we imagine this unity because they and others all make a point of their being Marxists. However, after reading Wittgenstein, we cannot let ourselves be so easily carried away by the logic, 'there must be something in common, or they wouldn't be called. . .' Wittgenstein writes in the *Investigations*, '*look and see* whether there is anything common to all. . .' And we don't have to strain our eyes very much. What, if anything, could be common to the Marxist philosophy of nature, which concentrates on attacking the Copenhagen interpretation of quantum mechanics and the historical theory organised around the thesis of a class struggle between rich and poor countries. Both proclaim themselves, quite aggressively, as Marxist. If we compare these two theories with the texts of Marx and Engels separately, we might find chains of resemblance that have some links in common; but we would soon come across some links in the respective chains which have nothing whatsoever in common. In such cases Wittgenstein speaks about 'a family resemblance'. Now, if all the different Marxisms are related to one another only by a mere family resemblance, then we can only talk about a Marxist tradition in the most trivial, that is in a purely genealogical sense.

Perhaps we could find more continuity if we defined the terms 'theory', 'proposition', 'philosophy' etc. more precisely. Recent research into the history of science uses an elaborate conceptual scheme to describe ramified theoretical traditions in a common, single, significant scientific initiative; and by applying this scheme one can describe such traditions as genuine historical processes, as opposed to teleological constructions, recurrent histories which are always written from the point of view of the current, accepted theories. Transcending the one-sidedness of all modern Marxism, it would be possible to construct a 'paradigm', a core of the Marxian 'research programme', and then the further development of the tradition could be characterised as 'puzzle-solving' within the paradigm, or as a series of 'problem-shifts' designed to cope with anomalies. The conceptual schemes elaborated by Kuhn and Lakatos have proved quite productive in various areas of the history of science and become so popular that it will surely not take long before they are applied to the history of Marxism too. Yet we did not believe that we should look in this direction for a solution to our problem. The historical picture that could be drawn with the help of such a methodological device would still describe only a segment of the tradition (taken now in the broadest possible sense of the word); it would be restricted, just as the prehistories constructed by the different orthodoxies themselves, to defining one 'main line' of 'genuine' Marxism. The only difference would be its more historical character, because according to the new method this main line would be defined genetically starting from the origins rather than from a contemporary version of Marxism. However productive the conceptual scheme of the new history of science may be, there is still something in the Marxist tradition which would elude the conceptual net of these methodologies. The problem is neither simply that the Marxian 'paradigm' is associated with a *Weltanschauung,* nor that the Marxian 'programme' involves tasks of social praxis. The methodologies mentioned could cope with this. What they cannot possibly grasp is that the *Weltanschauung* of Marxism and its socio-political programme are of a particularly political character, that is that it is defined in relation to a framework of rival social classes; the debate between the theories is intimately linked to the struggle for power. And perhaps this is what one should regard as the common link which holds the whole tradition together.

Can this be true? Don't we see even greater contradictions within the tradition when we take political struggles into account? We must remember, however, that there are not only various 'Marxisms' fighting each other, but there is also a conflict between Marxist and non-Marxist theories, ideologies and political forces. C. Wright Mills' observation in *The Marxists* (Penguin, Harmondsworth, 1963) may be of some help here. He explains that the successive theories within the Marxist tradition are linked neither by too much similarity of content, nor by methodological structure, but by their specific function of co-ordinating the political aims of Marxian socialism with the proletariat, the assumed agent of their realisation. The tradition is continuous as long as this co-ordination can be verified. But, according to Mills, this verification became doubtful in modern industrial societies. This doesn't mean that some parts of the theories that evolved within the tradition cannot be further developed, but the outcome of such a development will no longer be Marxism. For us, the significance of Mills' characterisation is where he contrasts Marxism with another tradition, that of liberalism, which, according to him, has also disintegrated like Marxism. Less of the original aims and pure theoretical framework of liberalism survived, but at the outset, this tradition too was organised around specific political aims and had elaborated a distinctive philosophy and system of values to match them. It entailed its own economics and sociology, and the whole tradition also addressed itself to a specific social class. Mills calls both liberalism and Marxism 'the great traditions'. Perhaps he thought that there were no other traditions so well articulated, so thoroughly developed in all respects, or perhaps only these two were relevant for him in the context of his book. Anyhow, other such traditions can easily be listed although there are some in which certain elements of the structure are indeed not so well elaborated, e.g. the romantic-conservative tradition, the romantic-anarchist tradition and the bureaucratic-technocratic tradition which only evolved later on.

We can grasp the first phase in the history of the Marxist tradition by relating it to other relevant traditions. In his study, *La diffusione del marxismo*, (Studii Storici, vol. xv, no 2, 1974) E.J. Hobsbawm demonstrates that between 1890 and 1905 the real demarcation line was not between revisionism and the various orthodox Marxisms, but rather between the romantic-anarchist tradition and the Marxist tradition as a whole. Up until 1905, the boundaries of Marxism were open towards the liberal tradition, and if one were attempting to draw a sharp line between the liberal tradition and Marxism, precious little would remain of what is specifically Marxist, apart from the particular individual theories of a few early orthodox Marxists. The lopsidedness of the first historical phase in the development of Marxism has had lasting effects ever since. Even half a century was not enough for the great bulk of the tradition to absorb such ideas as industrial democracy and self-management. Apart from the constraints of sheer practical considerations, this doctrinal onesidedness itself also played a part in the developing convergence between the Marxist and bureaucratic-technocratic traditions. However, after 1905, the stress was increasingly placed on the opposition to the bourgeois pole of the ideological spectrum. The demarcation line between the most significant Marxist factions was increasingly drawn according to their attitudes towards the liberal tradition and the way they theorised this attitude. So from then on, the boundaries of Marxism became finely drawn on both sides and even if one doesn't seek a definition on more than purely theoretical grounds, there is already a danger of being drawn into similar restricted vistas as if one sought to define the boundaries simply on the basis of established orthodoxy.

But what if we considered the *content* of the tradition more or less as a changing variable? Couldn't the sole principle of circumscription be that each of the significant, genealogically descended factions claims to establish a great tradition, independent of the other great traditions, and challenging at least one of them? This would certainly widen the scope. The romantic-conservative tradition is irrelevant here, provided that there were no new appearances of 'feudal socialism' as described in the *Communist Manifesto*; however, opposition to conservatism has no significance even in that case, since Marxism has no specific message in this respect. On the other hand, we can easily imagine a type of Marxism which is closed towards the romantic-anarchist and the bureaucratic-technocratic tradition but open towards the liberal tradition; or a Marxism which is closed towards the liberal and the bureaucratic-technocratic tradition but open to the romantic-anarchist tradition.

But even so, what do we do with those factions that are far from claiming the role of a great theoretical-political tradition? Ever since the emergence of the Marxist mass parties that have an independent educational and research apparatus, theoretical work has been mostly confined to specialists. This has been even more the case since Marxism became the official ideology of states. Moreover, since at least the 1920s, the number of those factions that represent some minority or directly oppositional point of view, but which, however, intend to stay within party limits or within the scientific and cultural institutions of the state, has been on the increase. These factions are characterised by the way that they conceal or only indirectly articulate the political consequences of their theories, with the centre of their activities being shifted to topics removed from politics. We only refer to one example not well known in our country, namely that the extremely abstract orthodoxy of the Althusserian school represents an oppositional political attitude; for a general description of such phenomena see Perry Anderson's *Considerations on Western Marxism* (NLB, London, 1976). This difficulty with those factions which try to conceal some relevant political distinctions, however, can be overcome if we define their relationship to the great tradition more loosely.

If one's conviction is that the only possible method for political mediation between theory and the class is to influence the ideology of the Communist Party or that of the state, then it is correct to conclude that abandoning politics will be useful to reconnect politics and theory in the long run. And if our definition is loosened even further, we can trade a nostalgia for the role of a great tradition even among such Marxist groupings which operate independently of any Marxist organisations. Let us take some of the most recent cases. A significant portion of the student generation participating in the New Left movements of the sixties while withdrawing into academic life has not wholly abandoned its radicalism. By the seventies their efforts had considerably altered the relationship of the academic sciences to Marxism. Whereas before, Marxism could exert a considerable influence only in the French and Italian scientific communities, we now see strong Marxist minorities developing in all fields of social science in West Germany and even in Britain and the USA, where there has been an absence of any major Marxist traditions. And if we distinguish between those scholars who utilise elements of the Marxist tradition without however proclaiming themselves Marxists and those who in fact consider themselves Marxists, then we'll see that it is exactly political engagement that the latter group stresses with the emphasis on the continuation of the tradition. The political character of such a gesture is all the more conspicuous in the case of those scholars who, although claiming to be Marxists, borrow no more from the tradition than their non-Marxist colleagues. The English and American historians claiming to be Marxists are no closer to historical materialism than, say, the adherents of the *Annales* school; most of the English and American Marxist economists are just as far from accepting the main propositions of *Capital* as those left-wing Keynesians or Sraffa-followers who are socialists but do not consider themselves Marxists. It is also quite revealing that the most aggressive representatives of the two rival tendencies of Anglo-Saxon anthropology, namely, cultural materialism and structural anthropology, both turn to Marx for 'ammunition'.

Thus, we can see that if we interpret the intention to develop a great tradition widely enough, we may eventually find some unity in the Marxist tradition taken in a broader sense. But is there any practical significance to such unity? Hasn't the connection as construed above become so loose that it no longer plays a role in any of the theoretical debates and political clashes? True, the different Marxisms, particularly the committed followers of this or that orthodoxy, do not seem to care that the theory their opponents are trying to elaborate is quite similar to their own, both in form and function. Nor is it probable that such a loose conception of the tradition would be sufficient to define the topic of relatively impartial historical research which transcends the limits of the current orthodoxies. Historical scholarship using new source material should necessarily concentrate on narrow segments of the tradition. On the other hand, syntheses based mainly on the analysis of select 'classics' and secondary literature usually require a more precisely defined similarity of content than this conception permits. The unity, represented by this thin thread interweaving the whole tradition, becomes visible only at such crucial moments when even the slightest continuity of a greater branch of the tradition is interrupted. And this is what happened with the Marxisms of the Soviet Union and Eastern Europe in the late 60s and the early 70s.

Great Marxist schools have often suffered defeat at the same time as crises in the socialist and communist movements. Many large groups of Marxists have broken with the tradition at such turning points. Theory was often deprived of its orientative function within organisations proclaiming Marxist ideology; theory in such cases became restricted to demonstrating some political continuity. But the defeats of social-democratic orthodoxy have, in turn, strengthened the positions of revisionism and communist orthodoxies; the defeat of communist orthodoxy brought about the emergence of New Left Marxism and a characteristically Third World Marxism. Let us think of the situation in Germany at the turn of the century: Marxism then became rather a burden to the social-democratic leadership and keeping up the continuity became a matter of pragmatic considerations. But in the meanwhile, Marxism still represented a whole tradition in its continuity for Kautsky and Rosa Luxemburg. A similar opposition was reproduced between Stalinists and Trotskyists—though, for one side, on a lower level of consciousness. Marxism for Marchais probably means no more than an alibi, while for Althusser the defence of orthodoxy is a question of principle. (Let us remember that it was because Marchais rejected the objectives of the proletarian dictatorship that

Althusser stepped openly into opposition.) But up till the late 60s and early 70s, the defeat of one tendency within Marxism always strengthened the position of others in turn, and the theory could never completely lose its political significance, even within organisations whose concern for the continuity of the tradition was a mere formality, because for the specialists of Marxism within those organisations it was more than a formality. But in the Soviet Union and in the Soviet-type societies of Eastern Europe things took a different turn.

The defeat of the reformist or dissident tendencies, claiming to represent 'genuine' Marxism, 'genuine' Leninism or the 'renaissance' of Marxism, promoted the partial or total suppression of those ideologists within official Marxism, who tried to exert a conservative influence on the political leadership in the name of some orthodoxy. Official Marxism retreated into education and became almost neutral in politics; the ideological decoration of political decisions became all the more formal. From time to time the big stick of orthodoxy strikes against certain political, economic or cultural phenomena considered harmful. However, even in these cases it is not the ideologists who take the initiative. The same is also true of the polemics between the political leaders of different countries or between the power groupings in individual countries.

Reformist or dissident Marxism has suffered a political defeat while official Marxism has abandoned its claim to the great tradition. But this in itself would not preclude the possibility that at least some representatives of the defeated tendencies might keep up the continuity by their individual efforts. What we intend to show in the next part of our paper is why this did not come about. (We wrote this paper .before Bahro's book appeared. It is difficult to judge what direction East-German Marxist opposition has taken. But it is quite certain that they have no influence on other countries in Eastern Europe. (1980)). But before discussing this, we should like to complete the above characterisation of official Marxism, because it may seem to the reader that we have overestimated the practical-political significance of Marxism in the earlier phases of development of Soviet-type societies and attributed too great an importance to the independence and initiative of its specialists, while we run to the other extreme when talking about contemporary Marxism.

It would be a great mistake to think that Marxist theory had ever played a crucial role in the making of important political decisions. But in an age when all political decisions were articulated in terms of Marxist theory, it was extremely difficult to keep apart from the ideology. The evolution of reformist and dissident Marxisms demonstrates how deep the conviction was—especially among the intelligentsia—that the elimination of mass terror and the democratisation of the system would become possible precisely by the criticism of Stalinist ideology and by getting the ideas of 'genuine' Marxism recognised as the official ideology. The defeat of these tendencies was not only the result of the radicalism of their demands. It was also due to the recognition by more and more of the intelligentsia that the system can make concessions more easily if it chooses de-ideologisation, and that official Marxism has to retain its political functions as long as there exists a dissident Marxism too.

But there are appearances showing that the de-ideologisation has not been completed and some indications that it is not even on its way. Official Marxism appears to be very much alive. The study of Marxism is imposed on ever-growing circles, the number of specialists and of scholarly publications is on the increase and, in the long run, the quality is also improving. Inertia alone cannot account for such an increase and improvement; even if we consider that the emphasis on the continuity of the tradition serves as a symbol of the inviolable unity of the power structure, we still remain in the dark. There is a genuine development in official Marxism which, however, doesn't contradict our general analysis, but is a result of special circumstances. Paradoxically, the specialists of official ideology also enjoy the benefits of the general de-ideologisation of scientific life. Since the elimination of dissident Marxism there is a greater freedom to experiment with a modernisation of official Marxism. Today's official ideology is just as far from the system of doctrines of the Stalin era, as are other non-official or dissident tendencies, the only difference being that this distance does not result in any kind of political opposition. What is more, in Hungary and in Poland the content of the eliminated dissident Marxisms has been partly incorporated into official Marxism but, of course, it has been deprived of its critical overtones, serving instead as an open apologetics; the anthropology and the philosophy of values based on Marx's early writings, which seemed to have compromised itself, has now been restored in teaching and publications. This development has been further promoted by the fact that in politically consolidated countries where there are no confrontations—consequently there is no need to take sides—and where the slogans of the Party are not to be uttered outside formal occasions, some kind of medium is needed for communication so that political loyalty transcending mere conformism may be manifested. Official Marxism, more and more vague as to its political content, but still acting as the special ideology of the system, serves as such a medium.

After the Break

Trends holding 'genuine' Marxism to be on their side have mostly criticised official Marxism on issues quite distant from politics. Most of the debates centred around quite abstract doctrinal questions: are there alternatives in history; is there an Asiatic mode of production; is the concept of alienation an Hegelian remnant in the young Marx; is there a dialectics of nature; is it possible to define the concept of matter in Marxist philosophy? But even the most abstract debates had some political significance since it was the conviction of the neo-Marxists that these confrontations would result in the emergence of a renewed, 'creative' Marxism, with a capacity to influence political decisions. That the 'renaissance' of Marxism was able to arouse a part of the scientific community and a part of the general public was mainly due to this very expectation and not to the generally not too high theoretical standards. This explains why when the authorities banned discussions, making it evident that political leaders were not interested in the advice Marxism could offer, the trends opposed to the official ideology lost not only the opportunity for public discussions, but also their very basis of existence. Having had silence imposed on it, the whole movement vanished rapidly.

Most adherents of the movement have, openly or tacitly, abandoned Marxism. A small minority has joined the official specialists of Marxist ideology. Together with the more intelligent official ideologists, they constitute the group which is trying to bring the textbooks up to date. Finally there has been another and even smaller minority which quit the official culture and took the path of marginalisation.

Since the late 60s, official culture has ceased to retain its monopoly in Eastern Europe. In some of these countries the non-official forms of communication have become customary, and in others, efforts have been made toward the same end. Works banned by the censor and works that had never been submitted to the state-controlled publishers began to circulate. This literature in some countries creates a whole system of non-official communication, a parallel culture; bulky volumes and periodicals appear, disputes flare up, different ideological tendencies become crystallised. Political ideologies, practical programmes and tactical conceptions are formulated and sometimes even political movements—though embryonic—are born. These movements are usually organised to achieve special and concrete aims. They do not have an exclusive ideology and they do not seek the support of any particular class. Participation in these movements fluctuates. Often the same people participate in different movements. The lifetime of such a movement is usually rather short. Doubt often arises whether such movements are able to advance their causes towards the desired ends. But one thing is certain, these movements are in fact able to create some consensus as to a certain minimum of social and political aims. It was exactly such a minimal consensus which made the civil rights movements of the recent past possible.

In short, Marxists who remained in opposition are not doomed to silence. They may participate in ideological discussions outside the channels of official communication. They may publicly reflect on their position; they may reconsider their relationship to official Marxism; they may determine their place among the representatives of different dissident ideologies. Then why not allow that it will be they who will succeed in recreating the Marxist tradition? Indeed, only they, if anybody, have the chance.

But it isn't as simple as that. Marginalised Marxists can take up once more the themes of the political core of the great Marxist tradition, but it is not at all certain that an independent theoretical tradition can be developed around this. Let us consider our misgivings on this score.

The early 1960s had seen the enthusiasm of the 'renaissance' of Marxism. More and more layers of Marx's thought were revealed under the rubble of crumbling Stalinism. The influence of the Communist thinkers of the 1920s began to be felt and their predecessor, i.e. Rosa Luxemburg, was also rediscovered. The Frankfurt School was taken up as an heir to their ideas; it was considered as a school which developed further the perspectives opened up by the Western Marxism of the twenties. Justice was given to the French left-wing existentialists. The growth theories of early Soviet economists, Oscar Lange's model of a socialist market economy, and many other things already half-forgotten were busily studied. It seemed that the Marxist tradition was never more alive than in those years. But if we take a look as to how this enormous material was moulded, the picture becomes rather deficient. The theoretical development of the 60s was fatally one-sided. Certain parts of the tradition were taken up and further developed in their full scope, while others suffered great curtailments. Thus, when the administrative ban imposed on the trends and schools polemicising with the official ideology made problematic the continuity of the tradition, what in fact really came to be problematic was whether there was anything worthwhile to continue.

Tendencies claiming to represent 'genuine' Marxism had a clear practical programme and a quite developed philosophical conception. Though not elaborated in detail, the programme aimed at a general democratisation and said the economy should be loosened, the Party and the mass organisations ought to act as organs of social control over the bureaucracy. This programme of 'democratic socialism' was matched by a philosophical theory, that of praxis philosophy. Praxis philosophy was the most organically-developing and mature part of 'renaissance' Marxism. It formulated an anthropology, a philosophy of history, an epistemology and a philosophy of values. The system made up of all these carried a clear—though not always explicit—critical message.

No such theory was elaborated in the field of economics. One group of Marxist economists was preoccupied with working out formal growth theories to improve the planning of the national economy. Others attempted to criticise the institutional system of the bureaucratic planned economy, but their criticism was restricted to the aspects of micro-economic efficiency. The furthest any criticism went was to attempt to reveal the consequences of over centralisation in cyclical fluctuations and in the slowing down of macro-economic growth rates. These criticisms were, however, never synthesised into an explanatory theory of the Soviet-type economies; non-Marxist economists, neglecting ideological questions, had already reached much further in elaborating comprehensive theories.

Marxist sociology remained even less developed. In some fields the development consisted merely of acquiring the methods of modern sociology. Some development could be observed in a few special areas, as for example in rural sociology. But aside from these, only two attempts deserve mention here. One was the effort of some Marxist scholars to elaborate a critical theory of the existing institutions, i.e. of the bureaucracy. These efforts were, however, limited to an application of the commonplaces of the sociology of organisations. Attempts to provide a description of the social structure proved somewhat more productive. It was finally demonstrated that the stratification of Soviet-type societies cannot be derived from the traditional concept of classes, which is based on property relations. Attempts were also made to define the different strata, but these were restricted to determining the appropriate categories of social statistics. No one has gone as far as to identify and to examine sociologically the real classes behind the statistical categories, to name those functional groups of society that are actually separated from each other by the frequency and pattern of interaction, that possess a distinct class consciousness and represent distinct or even mutually-exclusive interests in respect of macro-economic and macro-sociological changes. Furthermore, no one thought of making predictions as to the changes of class relations, owing to the lack of a theory of economic development of Soviet-type societies.

The uneven development of philosophy, economics and sociology was not the only problem. None of the tendencies belonging to the 'renaissance' of Marxism was able to synthesise the results of the different fields. And since the programme of 'democratic socialism' did indeed allow two divergent interpretations, a democratic and a technocratic one, it could thus happen that while the philosophy of praxis was undoubtedly committed to the democratic interpretation, the research in social statistics was openly bound to the technocratic conception. (See P. Machonin's account of the survey made in 1967 by the Sociological Institute of the Czechoslovak Academy: 'Social Stratification in Contemporary Czechoslovakia', in *American Journal of Sociology,* vol. lxxv, no. 5, 1969.) The collision between the Yugoslav philosophy of praxis and the advocates of market socialism brought into the open the fact that philosophy and economics may come into conflict with one another.

But the critical weakness of the whole 'renaissance' was its inability to designate the social addressee of 'genuine' Marxism. Or, to be more precise, this was not even attempted. The majority accepted—following uncritically some lines of tradition—that the theory was still exclusively connected with the working class, and then substituted, mostly unconsciously, the party leadership or some enlightened faction of it for the working class. Those who were looking to social groups other than the working class made similar substitutions too. When the dialogue with the political leadership was interrupted, the whole theoretical construction collapsed at once. Owing to the lack of a dynamic socio-economic theory, it was impossible to predict which social forces would back the desired reforms in the long run. Together with the programme, the philosophy connected with it also became irrelevant. It became clear that the reason why philosophy occupied the most important place in the whole 'renaissance' was not because it could explain the characteristics of Soviet-type societies better than economics or sociology. While sociologists and economists were unable to provide a description of the regularities of the system, philosophers simply skipped over it. Their philosophy of praxis derived the concept of an ideal society from the general idea of a 'human being'. The resulting criteria of evaluation were just as applicable to all societies as to none. The illusion that these criteria were especially relevant to Eastern-European societies was created by the tacit, and sometimes not so tacit, assumption that the historical mission of these societies, as socialist ones, is the realisation of the 'human being'. The moment this metaphysical thread was broken, it became clear that the praxis philosophy has no special relevance to Eastern-European societies.

The 'renaissance' did not convey a tradition to be continued to dissident Marxists outside the official institutions. The most it was able to hand down were some fragments of a tradition. And in itself, this wouldn't have been fatal. The boundaries of a Marxist tradition would have become sufficiently clear, even without a thoroughly elaborated theoretical apparatus, provided that at least some of the other dissident ideologies claimed the role of a great tradition. If, for example, liberalism as a tradition were well rooted in these circles, then it would be quite easy to tell who belonged to the Marxist and who to the liberal tradition. But although liberals may be found within the Soviet and Eastern-European opposition, their liberalism hardly represents more than a political programme. Russian ideologies rooted in the romantic-conservative tradition are the only ones which possess a specific philosophy and a characteristic conception of society. Their philosophy is aggressively idealistic; the particular dignity of man is determined by the fact that man, as a citizen of the world of spiritual values, can overcome his needs rooted in the material world. This opposition appears in their criticism of the modern world order: secular mass societies—both Eastern and Western that is—have destroyed all spiritual values; they set material interests free from the tight hold of traditional morals and, in the arrangement they have thus established, material interests turn men against one another. The practical conceptions of these Russian conservatives follow consistently from their philosophical idealism: the materialistic world order cannot be defeated with the means and tools of materialism; political conflicts can only modify the relations between different social groups, but the world can only be saved and uplifted from the state of general disorder by the moral regeneration of individuals. Philosophical idealism, social traditionalism and the rejection of political activity are all incompatible with Marxism. But they are also incompatible with the liberal and the technocratic tradition. It is not only Marxism that is opposed to the conservative tradition, but all of the modern secular ideologies.

True, Russian conservatives primarily polemicise against Marxism. But if we take a closer look, we'll see that the dividing line between conservatism and Marxism is not continuous either. There is an upper and a lower limit to this opposition. The lower limit corresponds to the general preconditions of oppositional activity. The articulation of oppositionist ideologies is necessarily connected to some minimum movement-like activity. The technical and institutional requirements of communication are not given; with the creation of public thinking, the channels to reach the public also have to be developed. This in turn presupposes the cooperation and solidarity of people—a cooperation that is very loose and a solidarity that is very abstract, but both genuine. We are not thinking of the fact that it is widely considered to be indecent to press the contradictions between the different trends to the very extremes. Manners and tactical considerations hardly influence the clashes between conservatives and their opponents. Certain accusations by Solzhenitsyn and Shafarevits oddly resemble in tone the ideological campaigns of the period between the 30s and the 50s. However, every oppositionist owes a certain amount of commitment to these principles of cooperation and solidarity as none can avoid the responsibility for defending the legal means of communication. No oppositionist ideology can exist without including the demand for freedom of expression in its political programme. Legality, the rule of law, is a common demand of all oppositionist tendencies. (It is not difficult to show that the few exceptions not only manifest an ideological anomaly, but that they are anomalous in their sociological situation too.)

The upper limit of ideological differentiation is set by the present state of the movements operating through non-official forms of communication. Even the most highly organised movements are extremely fragile. They set out their practical objectives on an *ad hoc* basis; they do not have long-range strategies which would demand exclusive engagement with a certain ideology, and which would definitely point to a certain part of the population—class or group—which is driven to their support by its specific interests. The first organisation that was formed to protect the members of a definite class is the Polish Workers Defence Committee; but although the committee was intended to protect the workers, there is no indication that it would be a committee of the workers.

It is hardly predictable whether the Soviet and Eastern European dissident movements will reach a higher level of ideological differentiation in the near future, or whether they are going to stagnate at their present level, or even fall back into a more amorphous state. It is probable that the development will vary according to the different countries. But as long as they are unable to reach a higher level of differentiation, the ideologies whirling around these movements cannot clearly be distinguished as to their sociological addressee and programme.

All oppositionist ideologies are characterised by their possession of a minimum of common objectives on the one hand and by their lack of a proper class support on the other. The differences among them can be drawn only within these limits, considering that even in this range there is further overlapping of the programmes. The re-establishment of an independent Marxist tradition is impossible under these circumstances. Marxism doesn't offer a specific conception of Eastern-European economy and society; it doesn't point to any specific class to realise its objectives; and, moreover, it doesn't have a monopoly over any specific programme. This situation is without precedent in the history of Marxism. That is why we are forced to put the question crudely: is it at all possible to be a Marxist here? What use is there to articulate those social efforts that are exerted outside official institutions in terms of Marxism, if no specific consequences follow from the employment of the Marxist conceptual scheme? Wouldn't it be enough if there were as many ideologies as there are distinguishable types of practical programmes?

For a first approach, one might say that the multiplication of ideologies may be of advantage sociologically even if logically it seems useless. The more ideologies there are to a practical programme, the more followers it will be likely to attract. According to this reasoning then, dissident Marxism is simply addressed to those people who are more inclined to accept the objectives of the opposition if they are articulated by Marxist concepts than in terms of some other ideology. But if it is only this that gives sense to the continuation of Marxism, then—although it is not impossible to be a dissident Marxist—it is altogether not too attractive.

There is an element of truth in the above statement, but if we take a second look, we will find it a bit rash on the whole. That there is no mutual and definite correlation between oppositionist ideologies and programmes doesn't mean that every ideology plays the same role with respect to every programme. We have to examine what role Marxism might play in the individual cases.

Luckily, we do not have to take each individual case into consideration. We may neglect those programmes that are incompatible with all of the existing Marxisms, and those that have no significance to any of the Marxists. The rest can be classified into a few main types. We define these types according to two criteria. First, we differentiate between legalists and liberals according to their conception of the political structure..

Legalists are those who would like to put the existing political structure on a legal foundation, and liberals are all those who want to change the political structure itself. And, according to our second criterion, legalists and liberals belong to the same group as opposed to radical reformists. The group made up of legalists and liberals have in common that they start out from specific objectives that are deduced from normative presuppositions. Radical reformists, on the other hand, concentrate on the social and political conditions for the establishment and development of an independent oppositional movement in Soviet-type societies. Legalism has spread primarily in the Russian underground; outside the Soviet Union we only know of Marxist legalists. Liberalism has spread in all of those Eastern-European countries where dissident movements exist at all. Radical reformism is a Polish phenomenon; it came about as a result of the actions taken by the intelligentsia against the modification of the Constitution, and by the workers' demonstrations against the price rises, and finally by the experience of the movement for the defence of the imprisoned workers.

Not all of those who aim at the stabilisation and expansion of human and civil rights can be considered legalists. Almost every oppositionist ideology could be considered legalist in this sense of the word. We are rather using the term to designate those ideologies that restrict themselves to this common minimum on principle. Their argument is always based on the shortcomings of Western parliamentary democracy, although they don't always agree as to the nature of these shortcomings. Russian conservative nationalism is the most characteristically legalist ideology. It is based on the conviction that parliamentary systems are too democratic: they let the material interests of the masses dominate over moral values, thus leading society towards a moral and political disaster. Russia should rather be governed by a strong, authoritarian government whose authority is derived from moral support, and which is based on strict legal foundations. Another characteristically legalist ideology was elaborated by Marxists symphathetic towards legalism although, curiously enough, these are the most frequently attacked opponents of conservatism. They also reject the western system of representation, but on different grounds, namely because in their eyes this system isn't democratic enough. Parliamentarism—as in most socialist theories—means no more to them than merely formal democracy, and, opposed to parliamentarism, they uphold the idea of a genuine, all-pervading democracy. The reason for their not wanting to change the institutional structure of Soviet society is that they find the structure a suitable basis for the realisation of a higher level democracy by way of its further democratisation. Seemingly this conception is identical to the idea of 'democratic socialism' but there is a great difference. In the beginning the representatives of 'democratic socialism' were by no means legalists. Their democracy was not to be developed by the strict observation of the letter of the law, by strict adherence to legal forms. The idea of legalism only appeared in their political thinking as they were increasingly marginalised. But from then on it was to become more and more central: the less they speak about 'the reconstruction of the Leninist norms of the Party' the more they emphasise the importance of the freedom of the press, of the independence of the judiciary and of the abolition of laws contradictory to human rights.

But the transformation of 'democratic socialism' into 'legalist socialism' presents an unexpected problem: the dividing line between dissident Marxism and dissident liberalism, which was perfectly clear before this, has now become faint. If 'democratic socialism' goes so far as to demand a formal legal system, on what grounds then, does it reject the other institutions that the dissident liberals call for?

There is an inconsistency here, one which is not only pointed out by outside criticism, but which is quite manifest in itself. If we look at Roy Medvedev's *Socialist Democracy* written in the early 70s, we will see that he is rather undecided as to the problem of the multi-party system and other related institutions. He is not at all enthusiastic about a future in which the political institutions of the Soviet state would be based on rival parties, but neither does he have any fundamental objections to it. He tries to break out of this circle by concluding that the multi-party system should indeed be allowed in socialism since by the time genuine socialist democracy comes into being, non-socialist parties will lose their influence and power anyway.... We don't in fact get to know what this democratic socialism will look like, as his specifications point to a kind of limited liberalism at the most. (R.A. Medvedev: *De la démocratie socialiste.* Paris 1972, p. 139.) However, a few years later, when Medvedev had already had to face Solzhenitsyn's antidemocratic legalism, he reacted to it by defending the multi-party system by all means. (R.A. Medvedev: 'Was erwartet uns?' in A.R. Dutschke and M. Wilke ed. *Die Sowjetunion, Solschenizyn und die westliche Linke,* Reinbek bei Hamburg 1975.)

'Democratic socialism' is swaying somewhere in the no man's land between legalism and liberalism. It may bend in both directions but it cannot be carried consistently to either end; it goes too far for the one, and doesn't go far enough for the other. For this reason Marxism cannot play a significant role among rival ideologies in providing a conceptual scheme either for the legalist or for the liberal political programme. But providing a conceptual apparatus is not the only possible function of Marxism in respect of legalism and liberalism. Marxism as a philosophy may function as a source of values to justify the ends either of legalism or of liberalism. The philosophy of praxis of the 60s had elaborated a system of values bound to the traditions of classical humanism; and although we do not know of any attempt to develop the political applications of praxis philosophy, there are still signs showing that this value system has penetrated into the political thinking of the opposition. (See the open letter of the Czech writer, Vaclav Havel, addressed to the president of the Czechoslovak Republic; Encounter XLV. no. 3, 1975.)

It is beyond doubt that Marxist philosophy exerts at least an indirect influence on legalist and liberal thinking. But let us not overestimate the possible influence of this kind of philosophy. The reason is easy to find: praxis philosophy derives its values from a rather optimistic anthropology. The conception that man is a free, conscious and universal being, who is only held back from the absolute realisation of these abilities by the historically developed circumstances, was very much adequate to the atmosphere of the 60s. But the isolated opposition of the 70s cannot derive too much hope from this anthropological optimism. If the opposition cherishes any hope at all, it is rather on the existentialist philosophic concept of man that it relies: man can be manipulated, moreover, he needs to be manipulated in his everyday life, but still, he is able to break off from the *Dasein* of manipulation with some kind of a last, desperate effort.

With respect to radical reformism the possibilities and limitations of Marxism are of a totally different nature. Radical reformism doesn't offer a political programme in the strict sense of the word; it merely expounds some tactical conceptions. Or, to put it more precisely, it restricts itself to tactical questions that are not derived from the need for a different system taking the place of the present one. The assumption here is that social aims, worth fighting for in Eastern Europe, are those that can be realised without resulting in a crisis of power; anything else leads to the fabrication of utopias or straight to catastrophe. The alternative of reform or revolution is not a valid one in Eastern Europe; the sensible choice is between two kinds of reformism. The reformists of the 50s and the 60s, the 'old evolutionists', wanted to promote their cause 'from the inside', by enlightening and convincing the political leadership. 'Neo-evolutionism', to use the term suggested by the Polish historian, Adam Michnik, in a lecture in September 1976 in Paris, tries to draw the lesson from the failure of this tactical conception. Michnik concludes that internal criticism is not capable of influencing the leadership effectively: it is exposed to conjunctural changes of power and, in the long run, it is bound to give up its critical content. Serious and lasting pressure on the government can only be exerted by independent social movements. From this it follows that it is not enough for political realism to make sure that its aims can be reconciled with the continuing existence of the present power system. It also has to see that each demand be supported by social forces adequate to the size of the demand. Significant reforms can only be realised with the support of significant forces. But, on the other hand, the independent social movements are not only tools in the tactics of radical reformism. The autonomous self-organisation of society is an end in itself. The more organised society is the less the strength of the ruling power, the closer is the time ripe for the changing of the system itself too. And so, according to Michnik, the chances of neo-evolutionism lie in the hands of the working class.

Radical reformism is also supported by people known as Marxists, just as legalism and liberalism are (see Jacek Kuron's interview in *Le Monde*, 19 January 1977). However as yet we only know of personal sympathies. Marxism as a theory has, so far, failed to add anything to radical reformism. And it is certain that those parts of the theory that had been incorporated into legalism and liberalism are in no ways useful to radical reformism. This movement has nothing whatsoever to do with 'democratic socialism' or with the philosophy of praxis: it does not set final aims and thus has no need of an ideological apparatus to articulate its programme, with the help of a philosophical value system. What it may need instead, is a dynamic socio-economic theory. It may need such a theory, if it moves within a wide enough time-horizon. If radical reformism means no more than a short term tactical conception then it does not pre-suppose more knowledge about the conduct of social classes than it is already given in everyday experience. But if it really stands for 'evolutionism' and if the movements aiming at possible reforms can only produce significant results in the very long run, then we have to be able to predict changes in the class structure, at least to the extent that social sciences are at all able to predict such changes.

This task is not alien to Marxism. One branch of the Marxist tradition is closely related to this long range interpretation of radical reformism: the task of theoretical thinking is not to provide the world with aims and goals; theory is rather to help to predict which social classes are likely to support the different aims and goals, as well as their chances of success. Something of this kind was achieved by Marx in *Capital*, Rosa Luxemburg in the *Accumulation of Capital*, the Russian Marxists of the 90s, Struve, Lenin and Tugan-Baranovski in their polemic writings addressed to the Narodniks, Trotsky in his analysis of the economic and social conditions of the first Russian revolution. . .

Lots of analogies and heuristic principles can be deduced from this tradition. On the other hand, many things have to be wiped out in order to apply these fertile analogies and heuristic principles. Marxism has not been able to elaborate an applicable theory of Soviet-type societies; either before or during Stalinism, or after its dissolution. And this is only one obstacle, not at all the greatest. More damaging are those elements of Marxism that can in no way be reconciled with such an undertaking: the threefold typology of historical societies/traditional societies—capitalism—socialism, the opposition of capitalist market economy and socialist planned economy, the definition of classes through property relationship etc.

Radical reformism offers important research tasks for Marxists, but if they reconsider these tasks they will be shocked to see that practically nothing of direct utility can be drawn from the Marxist tradition. They can't even cherish the illusion that they have any advantage compared with those social scientists who start out from a different background. The position of Marxists who adhere to liberalism and legalism is somewhat better; they may continue with the political and philosophical apparatus on the fringe of the Eastern European Marxist tradition. The question in their case is whether there is any point in this continuation. To be a Marxist, it seems, is very problematic in any case.

For Us

In the beginning we saw nothing of these problems, although we had called ourselves Marxists ever since we had any philosophical conception. The first phase of our Marxist career is of no interest here; luckily, it only lingers on in the memories of our childhood friends. It was quite a ridiculous nonsense and a bit shameful too. Thanks to the circumstances it did not have any serious effect, since in the sixties, the ideological fury of individuals, the ideological rages of students could no longer do serious harm as in the 1950s. Partly to bring some excuses and partly to characterise that era, let us just remind the reader of one thing. We had been adherents of György Lukács, making no secret of our sympathies, which were by no means forbidden at that time. But neither was it forbidden to attack Lukács politically, on the basis of his conduct in 1956. Many aestheticians and critics grabbed this opportunity to legitimise those branches of modern art which had been attacked by Lukács. We considered this, quite rightly, a challenge. We tried to prove that Lukács's aesthetics is the genuine and only possible Marxist aesthetics. Our enemies acted in bad faith, making use of Lukács's bad official reputation. We, on the other hand, were narrow-minded enough not to see that in this case, by having taken Lukács's side, we took the side of Stalinist conservatism. Both parties thought themselves awfully brave. They, because they attacked Marxist dogmas, and we, because we defended something that was not absolutely official.

We had never been run of the mill little Stalinists, as the above conflict shows. The fact that Lukács exerted such an influence on us was strongly determined by the political events of 1956, by the inner emigration of Lukács. But actually it was the works of Lukács written between the 1930s and the 1950s that determined our thinking, and this did not allow a systematic criticism of Stalinism and official Marxism at that time. But in the middle of the 60s things cleared up, or at least this was what we thought. We came to read Lukács's recent political statements, the *Letter to Alberto Carocci* (1962), the paper *On the debate between China and the Soviet Union* (1963) and his first paper on Solzhenitsyn (1964). From then on, we received actual guidance from Lukács on really decisive political issues as well. We became acquainted with the *Aesthetics*, which appeared in 1963. From it we could derive a concept of history which could be opposed to the official dogmas on almost every point—even the naturalist epistemology constituting the core of dialectical materialism appeared to us in a historical context. This enabled us to get to understand the 'young' Lukács and in no time we were already on the point of totally negating dialectical materialism. Finally it was also at this very point that a group of Lukács's students began to form what they first called the Lukács School, and which later came to be known as the Budapest School. We lined up with this group, and, with this, we seemingly found our proper place among the ideological tendencies of the evolving reform period.

But it was not through the founders, nor even through Lukács that we came into contact with the Budapest School. We had no contact with the members of this group in our first student years because they were not allowed to teach in the universities following 1956. We had been students of György Márkus. Whatever has happened since, we still feel grateful to have had him as our first professor. Márkus had studied in Moscow, and the information we got from him, we couldn't have got from Lukács, nor even from his students. In the Soviet Union, Márkus came into contact with the future leaders of the school of the sixties. Thus it was he who recommended to us the writings of Ilyenkov, Davidov and Gajdenko.[6] He was also familiar with the Polish neo-Marxists who had been of much greater significance, and through him we knew not only of Kolakowski, but of Fritzhand and Baczko as well, even if this knowledge was second-hand. All this, however, we could have found out on our own sooner or later. In the long run it was much more important that Márkus provided us with information on the new Soviet and Polish efforts in the philosophy of science that were taking up traditions completely unknown to us. We could finally breathe fresh air, having digested the *Dialectics of Nature* and the *Philosophical Notebooks* after, let us admit, the stale Hegelianism of Lukács. We started to study the classics of the Vienna Circle, some recent English and American works, psychology and linguistics. We considered Márkus unique, someone above all other Hungarian philosophers. Yet, when around 1965, Márkus started to move closer to the evolving Budapest School, it did not take us by surprise. The rapprochement seemed natural to us. The path Márkus took led him to the anthropology of the young Marx, similarly to the Soviet and Polish neo-Marxists, and to Lukács's students. The fact that thus, we too were drawn closer to the students of Lukács could not have bothered us, since we considered ourselves as followers of Lukács. So with Márkus's lead, we began to feel ourselves belonging to the Lukács School.

The Budapest School represented a very specific local variant of the 'renaissance of Marxism'. Up to the point where we can trace the activity of its leaders, it was continuously determined by specifically Hungarian circumstances, and by Lukács's person. Up to the early seventies the political conceptions of Fehér, Heller and Márkus never transcended 'democratic socialism at least as far as their writings go. (The only one to go beyond that limit had been András Hegedüs who worked out one of the most comprehensive conceptions of old evolutionism. He, however, was not a member of the school, although he often worked together with Lukács's students.) The reason for this was most probably the fact that the illusions about 'socialist democracy' were much more stubborn in Hungary than in any of the neighbouring countries. Even to the present day there has been no political or cultural tendency which would have clearly distinguished itself from the officially acknowledged and controlled system of communication; no one has ever come to expound the legalist version of 'democratic socialism'. This can partly be explained by the historical effect of Lukács's attitude towards the communist movement. He stubbornly and almost irrationally insisted on staying within the bounds of the Party.

Now, if we attempt to give a philosophical characterisation of the Budapest School, the local colours are harder to see. Common to the entire school are the praxis philosophy and its value system based on Marxist anthropology. The fact that the textual basis of such an anthropology has been elaborated most thoroughly by Márkus among all Marxists of the period, and that Heller was able to give such a concrete content to the 'generic being of man' nearly ending up in moralising, should be seen as personal achievements rather than local characteristics. What is to be seen as a local speciality is epistemological conservatism on the one hand and provincialism on the other. This is indeed a hard judgement. To mitigate it, let us make it clear that when we say conservatism we are not thinking of the pejorative denotation of the word, and when we say provincialism, we should immediately point to such exceptions as Márkus's entire oeuvre and Vajda's experiments to break through to a Marxist phenomenology.[7]

Anyway, our principal aim is not to mitigate, but to explain our characterisation. Let us start by recalling the well known fact that around the 1930s Lukács was converted to dialectical materialism in all great philosophical questions. He came to refine his position later on, especially in the middle fifties; several thoughts from his first Marxist period are incorporated in the *Aesthetics* and in the *Ontology*. But for him there was no way back to the pragmatist type of epistemological idealism. Consequently it was impossible for him to join in with those Western, Polish, Yugoslav and Czechoslovak neo-Marxist tendencies that started out partly from his very works written in his early period, and that were then advancing towards a special version of pragmatism. As far as we can see, Lukács's above stand determined how far his students were able to go in this respect. Their conservatism resulted in an *a priori* isolation, which might deserve our respect, had it only meant a mere acceptance of the consequences drawn from such a philosophical background. But the fact is that the Budapest School in no way reflected the diverse development of neo-Marxism, nor did it enter into theoretical debates with the more and more diverging tendencies. This is precisely what we mean when we say it was provincial. It is by no mere chance that neither in the East nor in the West did the Budapest School really provoke serious reactions; in modern Marxist literature this period is rather marked by Polish, Yugoslav and Czech achievements.

On political questions our thinking was no clearer than was that of the older members of the school. There was only one thing that disturbed us unlike others. The party leadership strove to make of Lukács a kind of quasi-official ideologist once more. With this they succeeded through a skillful compromise *à la Hongroise:* neither Lukács nor his students were to withdraw anything they had said or done up till then, but, in turn the Party leadership censored their views and endorsed only those parts of their teaching which did not touch upon the more sensitive nerve-ends of Marxist state ideology. And on top of this, everybody acted as if the views held by the school had always been part of the official ideology. We were not the least happy about these developments, but neither did we raise our voice in opposition. Although to a different extent, the new situation provided advantages to us all. It would be hypocrisy on our part to deny that these advantages impressed us. But then, we had a more elevated motive for not coming out into the open. At this point, we, like the rest of the school, held that it is only through and within the official circles that one is able to achieve anything. We accepted the bonds tying old evolutionism to the Party, to academic life and to official publications and we projected this conviction on the school itself. Only after the death of Lukács were we able to break out from this double bondage. And even then, it was rather by force that we managed to break off; first we were excommunicated from the school by its founders, and soon, together with Hegedüs and four others we were plainly shown, as it were, the door of scientific life.

In theoretical questions we were, from the very outset, somewhat independent, always ready to play cheeky jokes on older Lukácsists. The conservatism of the Budapest School made it possible for us to follow our leanings towards scientism. Had we been among philosophers of a genuinely modern theory of praxis, we would have been diagnosed to show an extremely severe manifestation of alienation, that of seeking self-complacency in scientific objectivism. We considered ourselves to be very learned and we continued our zealous hunts into areas of ill fame for a genuine praxis philosopher, trying our hand in economic theory, economic history and in the history of technology. So even when writing on matters of common interest to the entire Budapest School, our products already turned out to be somewhat unusual. Our paper on 'everyday life' is a good example of how we used to work. To start with, we gave it the title: 'Language in the Theory of Everyday Life'. Not to speak of the footnotes parading enormous erudition, in which, however, we referred only to Márkus from among our teachers. Those who were familiar with Heller's book on *Everyday Life* could clearly denote our impertinence.[8]

Anyway, it was not scientism that made the real difference. In Heller's concept, the 'particularity' of everyday life is opposed to universality as such, and this opposition is undoubtedly a normative one. When one of our friends, an electro-technician by profession, made an attempt to transcend his science-mindedness, and set out to read Heller's bulky book, he had to admit that, in his words: 'Having read a hundred pages of the book, I was still unable to grasp what it was about, when at once it suddenly struck me that Heller says it is not right to be selfish.' We, on the other hand, were trying to elaborate a general sociological theory of 'everyday life' that was to be not only void of any such moralising, but which lacked any political implications whatsoever. So it was not at all by accident that, apart from a few of the initiated, no one really heard about us while Heller was even read by electro-technicians, and her audience was growing parallel to her new habit of employing the terms elaborated in her book with an open socio-critical tendency. The message of her articles published in literary journals was understood by all: in Eastern European socialism, the revolution of everyday life is only to come in the future. . .

Our revulsion from mere moralising did not, of course, neutralise our passion for politics. But by our natural inclinations towards scientism, we were driven to look for appropriate political ideas in the fashionable New Left sociological theories. When we began to import Mallet and Gorz, we not only felt ourselves great scholars, but we were sure we had acted as great radicals. It did not occur to us that the most pressing of all deficiencies in the Hungary of the sixties might not be the satisfaction of 'the qualitatively superior needs of the new working class'. This was the price for not being provincial, because indeed, always reading the latest Western journals, we always knew ahead of everybody else what the *dernier cri* had been in the left-wing journals of Paris, Berkeley and Frankfurt.

This was the state we were in when, in 1970-1972 we wrote a book together with Márkus: *How is a Critical Economy Possible?* (We usually refer to the book as 'Überhaupt', which is a reduction of its 'transcendental main question', because, of course, we were going to have one: Wie ist eine kritische Ökonomie überhaupt möglich?) Our theoretical aim was to liberate Marxian economics or the 'critique of political economy', i.e. critical economics, from the model of a socialist system based on the labour theory of value. We wanted to keep up the continuity of the Marxist tradition by means of something similar to a methodological construction dealt with in the first part of this paper: it is not only through a labour theory of value that Marx's intention can be realised, moreover, in Marx's work itself, the realisation is actually controversial to the intention. Our argument was the following: Marx criticised capitalism by means of contrasting it with the communist planned economy based on the direct calculation of labour values. But such an economic system is possible only if a society is ready to restrict the free development of needs and thus the sovereignty of its individual members. . .

The theoretical argument in fact had a definite political tendency. *Capital* belonged to the ideological arsenal of the conservative opposition to economic reforms. What we intended to do was to win over the arsenal of critical economy to the side of the reformers, openly giving voice to our hopes that we might thus attract those reformist economists back to Marxism, who, at that :ime, were increasingly abandoning it. Yet, although we were becoming engaged in a definitely local debate, we carefully avoided connecting our criticism of the Marxian model of a socialist economic system to Soviet and Eastern European experiences. We thought it wiser to keep the argument on a strictly theoretical level, and if necessary, bring it into connection with the economic history of capitalism, but that only. Throughout the entire book there is not one hint that there is human life to the East of Elbe, and that something significant had happened in Saint Petersburg in 1917. And this was not simply prudence on our part; we rather considered our deliberate oversight as a kind of daring allusion. We intended to suggest that the Marxian concept of socialism is something totally different from what the term socialism normally means in Eastern Europe. But why then, did we want to connect our undertaking to the efforts of the reformers? And why did we attempt a somewhat pedantic criticism of the model of a socialist economy as seen in *Capital,* rather than giving a criticism of Soviet-type economies? Evidently, because we failed to examine and carry our standpoint to either logical end.

The arguments in our book were quite traditional, only they were directed against a Marx turned upside down. This inversion was not at all unjustified, and as an interpretation of Marx it contained a few original thoughts. The opposition of capitalist and socialist economy is in fact there in *Capital,* though latently, and perhaps it is not unnecessary to show that this opposition is based on a very specific conception of socialist economy. The question of the direction in which one should look to find out about Marx's basic intentions is less relevant to us today, because we are no longer interested in keeping up the continuity of the tradition with some similar construction. What is more important now is to see that while we were searching for the remaining element of critical economy, we failed to notice the one which is inherent in it, and which, perhaps, is worth developing. We failed to notice that Marx has also provided a dynamic theory, and connected the development of the economic system to the developments in the class structure. . .

The mistake we made was not only a theoretical blunder, it followed directly from our political narrow-mindedness. We were naive in thinking that the reformist economists were in desperate need of our critical weapons. On the contrary, they would instead have been quite embarrassed by our unwanted help, out of fear that we would provoke the official specialists of political economy into defensive action. And it was an even greater naivety to think that we—being pronouncedly Marxists as it were—should line up with the protagonists of the reform in any case. The greatest naivety of all was to think that people would be so interested in our demonstration that the Soviet-type economic system differed from the ideal of a communist economy, and that this difference might in any way be significant in a criticism of these societies. Our deliberately neglecting to analyse our society, intended as a covert allusion to our conviction that these societies do not live up to the socialist ideal, eventually almost turned our work into an apology of the system we meant to criticise. Our silence might have been read as if we accepted that our society was in fact the realisation of the socialist ideal, (at least to a limited degree), and that the task for its socialist critics is to show what is still missing from the full realisation of the ideal.

We thus have to consider it as our special personal luck that the appropriate committee of the Hungarian Socialist Workers Party dealing with 'the prevention of creative ideological thinking' found our book worthy of official condemnation. And we felt it an honour to have been condemned, along with other members of the school, in the very same party decision as András Hegedüs, who went much further politically than we did at that time. The party resolution was followed by administrative steps. Scholars named in the resolution no longer had a place in the official scholarly life. As for us two, we no longer had our place in the Budapest School either. Following the death of Lukács in 1971, we had to face the ambiguity of our situation. Politicians in charge of cultural life had a real interest in Lukács as his prestige supported their legitimacy, they did not however, tolerate his pupils. Yet we were aware of the fact that their intention to keep up the appearance of due reverence could secure our position for a limited period. Realising all this, we had to ask ourselves: what had the compromise provided us with? We decided to make up a questionnaire similar to the one we are answering at the moment, the subject of which had been our attitude to 'Lukácsism'. It was on that occasion that we first formulated those problems with which we have been preoccupied ever since. However, the older members of the school still hoped that the *status quo* could be kept. They were embarrassed by our initiative, not lacking a certain amount of aggressiveness. They probably saw our effort to dwell on hitherto concealed problems as a betrayal of political solidarity. Their embarrassment grew to an extent where our break became unavoidable. Except for Hegedüs, we had broken with all those named in the party resolution which expelled us all from our jobs. And although we remained in contact with Hegedüs, we came to realise the significance of his ideas only later when we had already formed our own conception, different from his as well.[9]

In spite of the burdens of the semi-intellectual wage labour we have been driven to do since 1973,[10] we have constantly been feeling the liberating effect of our new situation. We became free of the restrictions of academic life, of the censorship of official publications and we are no longer compelled to watch over the unity of the school. But in the beginning, our newly-gained independence seemed somewhat empty.

We knew what we wanted: first of all to understand our situation. And as true-born Marxists injected with the concept of totality from our early childhood, this meant to understand the social system we had been living in. We knew that the conceptual framework of Marxism used for characterising whole societies would not take us very far. We abandoned questions like the number of possible social formations, whether there were five or more, and whether there were some that developed only in Asia, Africa or the Antartic. In Paris or in London it might seem crucial to decide whether Soviet-type societies constitute a particular social 'formation', or they are no more than particular 'systems', or only 'transitions' between different systems. For if viewed from the inside, they very much look distinct systems. And on a human scale they seem to be lasting, which means they should have mechanisms for self-reproduction. We thus tried to look for these mechanisms, and, as Marxists, we first tried to reconstruct the model of the economic system so as to be able to proceed to the definition of classes and the description of their dynamism. . .

We have no space here to describe our findings in this area. (We are referring to a collection of papers, *Towards an East European Marxism* (Allison and Busby, London, 1977), published under the pseudonym, Marc Rakovski. Our authorship was not yet disclosed at the time of writing the above text and that is why our allusions here are rather vague—1980.) What we want to emphasise is that while looking for the answers it became less and less clear what it means for us to be Marxists. We were looking for classes whose dynamism would lead to socialism, and we were unable to locate them. The fact that socialist movements did not exist, not even in embryonic form, would not have discouraged us. For Marxism has an old—even if only vaguely tested—recipe for such situations. If we could have supposed that the existing tendencies or movements would, in the near future, undergo such a differentiation that the evolution of socialist movements would follow, we could have turned to the old Marxist recipe. But there seemed to have been no ground for such a hypothesis. We had to content ourselves with stating rather empty formulas such as: the observable decentralisation of the economic system, the changes in the consumer habits of the working class or the evolution of an intellectual counter-culture might create more favourable conditions if, at a point, the cause of socialism would seem timely. But why would it become timely? We had no answer to this question.

We would have been much better off, if we could have ascribed the fact that the class which—according to the theoretical tradition—should strive for a socialist transformation does everything but this, if we could ascribe this fact to some fearful force such as indoctrination or manipulation. In that case we could have become some sort of Marcuses of the Balkans. Our Marxism would have been a negative, but politically meaningful, Marxism as well. But to place ourselves on such ground would have meant that we should have condemned the aspirations of the majority as fully negative. We would have played the role of a new-left tourist who feels desperate upon seeing that the workers have enough to eat and, alas, some can even afford a car. We felt no affinity with such a role. And following Gdansk and Radom, and especially after the creation of the Workers Defence Committee, we had to admit that we could not aspire to anything more or different than radical reformism does.

But at this point the political content of our Marxism and our relation to the great tradition became extremely problematic. For up till then, even if we thought that our Marxism had been politically empty, we could maintain that after a due analysis we would arrive at an appropriate political view. But now, after finding a truly substantial political stance, we realised that it does not imply anything we could see as especially belonging to Marxist thought. And we had to realise that our viewpoint can, from now on, be considered Marxist only in a genealogical sense.

But this is no reason for denying our ancestors. We reached radical reformism coming from Marxism. Our method and the results of our social investigation contain as much of the tradition as that of others who still consider themselves Marxists. In this sense we are Marxists. Yet we do not count on drawing the sympathies of others who, in some sense, are also Marxists, with this mere fact. But nor do we have to be afraid of scaring anybody off by our ancestry.

Postscript

We find it necessary to mention that while writing our answer, we often had in mind E.P. Thompson's 'Open Letter to Leszek Kolakowski' in R. Miliband and J. Saville *Socialist Register 1973*.

Thompson defines four different versions of Marxism. (1) Marxism as a system of ideas—this is the generally accepted version. (2) Marxism as a method—we have dealt with this in the first part of our paper. (3) Marxism as a heritage—this is something close to what we have termed tradition in the genealogical sense. Thompson accuses those who conceive of the tradition in this way of intellectual consumerism: As if the entire human culture were a great supermarket, where each author could choose according to his preferences; one likes this, the other likes that, you only have to pay with a footnote. . . (4) Marxism as a tradition. This differs from the previous versions in three respects: (a) The intellectual earnestness of the relation to the tradition: one has to fight one's battle with the heritage, and although one is not compelled to redefine the content of the whole tradition for oneself one must indeed set out a place in it for oneself. (b) Most Marxisms imply strong political engagements which, however, can be identical in case of theoretically different Marxisms. (c) The Marxist tradition is continuous and alive in a number of disciplines throughout generations; the tradition to which the historian Thompson belongs is such a tradition.

We have to content ourselves with something which is closest to Marxism taken in the sense of the third point. Beyond this, perhaps we might claim also to have fought a battle with the heritage. But as to the other two points, first, we have been unable to find a political stance that can be characterised as specifically Marxist, and second, there is no living Marxist tradition present in any of the disciplines we know anything of in Eastern Europe.

Leszek Kolakowski, the addressee of Thompson's letter, can in none of the above senses consider himself a Marxist. The reasons are mostly of content, and these we have no place to discuss here. There is only one point we would want to repeat from the answer to Kolakowski ('My Correct Views on Everything' in *Socialist Register 1974)*, that has great weight coming from the greatest figure of one-time Eastern European revisionism: 'What was called "revisionism" in the peoples' democracies has practically died out (with the exception perhaps of Yugoslavia) and this means that neither the young nor the old think about their situation in terms of "true socialism" and "true Marxism" any more.'

Budapest, April 1977.

NOTES TO INTRODUCTION

1. A detailed summary of the contents of the volume was published in *Index on Censorship* 6/1978 by a Hungarian writing under the name Balazs Rab; *Index* 2/78 and 4/78 contain additional articles on *Profile* and the emergence of Hungarian *samizdat*. Abridged excerpts from several of the essays in this volume, including the present one, have appeared in English in F. Silnitsky, L. Silnitsky, and K. Reyman, eds., *Communism and Eastern Europe*, Harvester, Brighton, 1979, and in French in the anthology of Hungarian samizdat *Opposition = 1.0%* (edited by Bence and Kis and introduced by Miklos Haraszti), Paris, Seuil, 1979.

2. For a wider interpretation of the Budapest School, see Ivan Selenyi, 'Notes on the Budapest School', *Critique* 8, Summer 1977.

3. Major works by members of the Budapest School in English include: the

anthology . *The Humanisation of Socialism: Writings of the Budapest School*, Allison and Busby, London, 1076; Agnes Heller, *The Theory of Need in Marx*, Allison and Busby, London, ?; András Hegedüs, *Socialism and Bureaucracy*, Allison and Busby, London, 1976; Mihaily Vajda, *Fascism as a Mass Movement*, Allison and Busby, London, 1972; and György Markus, 'Debates and Trends in Marxist Philosophy', in Silnitsky *et al., op. cit.*

4. A different version of chapter 1 of this book appeared in *Capital and Class* 1 (1977).

5. Feher and Heller now live in Sydney, and Heller teaches at La Trobe University; Markus teachers in Melbourne.

NOTES TO TEXT
(authors notes are included in the text)

6. Ilytenkov, Davidov and his wife Gajdenko were the major younger philosophers emerging from the short-lived post-20th Congress Soviet theoretical revival. Ilyenkov's important book on the dialectic in Marx's *Capital* was only published in Russian. Yuri Davidov's influential book on alienation, *Work and Liberty* and Gajdenko's study of Heidegger were published in Hungarian translation by the publishing house of the Hungarian Party. Fritzhand and Baczko are Polish philosophers; the former published a book in 1961 entitled *Man, Humanism, and Moralism*, and the latter a study of Rousseau.

7. Before writing *Fascism as a Mass Movement*, Vajda did his doctoral work on Husserl's phenomenology and published two works in Hungarian, *Science in Brackets* (Budapest, 1968) and *On the Borderline between Myth and Reason* (Budapest, 1969). On the problem of the provincialism of the Budapest School, see Agnes Heller's own account of the same developments in her interview in *Telos* (1979), 'Moral Philosophy in Eastern Europe'.

8. Agnes Heller, *The Every-day Life* (Budapest, 1970). The acknowledgements listed Bence and Kis as ones who helped the author with advice and criticism. Bence and Kis' own study was published in a highly prestigious and esoteric Hungarian academic publication, *Studies in General Linguistics*, vol. 7 (1970).

9. There was a famous open clash between Hegedüs and Bence-Kis on the question of the desirability of a multi-party system in Hungary in 1977 (in which Bence-Kis defended a pluralist position) which was turned into a samizdat publication. Hegedüs' contribution was published in Ken Coates and F. Singleton, eds., *The Just Society*, Spokesman, Nottingham, 1977. Bence and Kis' critical answer exists only in Hungarian.

10. For an autobiographically inspired description of this situation see Rakovski, *Towards an East European Marxism*, ch. 3 on the 'sub-intelligentsia'.

ONE WORLD OR THREE?
A CRITIQUE OF THE WORLD-SYSTEM
THEORY OF IMMANUEL WALLERSTEIN*

Peter Worsley

Our thinking about the process of development has been fundamentally changed in recent years by the emergence of world-system theory, notably in the writings of André Gunder Frank, Immanuel Wallerstein and Samir Amin. It is with the thought of the first two, and primarily Wallerstein, that I shall be concerned here. All of us stand deeply in their debt, not only for the clarity with which they have presented their theoretical frameworks, but also for the serious documentation they have adduced from the historical record. One has only to contrast, for example, the impressionistic account of the 'creation of the world' that I sketched in the first chapter of my book, *The Third World,* in 1964, to see what a step forward their work represents in terms of theoretical rigour and empirical research. [1]

World-system theory was initially generated in reaction to 'dualistic' notions which informed most of the development theory of the period following World War II. The most important theoretical statement of the dualist approach was Arthur Lewis' *The Theory of Economic Growth* (Allen and Unwin, London, 1955), for which he has been awarded a Nobel Prize. But in terms of its influence upon government policy, the Economic Commission for Latin America (ECLA) achieved much more than did Lewis' abortive venture into planning in Africa and elsewhere. The basic assumption was that the economies of the backward countries could be divided into a modern and a traditional sector respectively. The task of 'modernisation' then consists, it was argued, in shifting resources from the latter to the former; the strategy advocated that of import-substitution.

The debate that followed was a highly political encounter, the riposte of the world-system theorists being aimed, on the one hand, at this advocacy of capitalist modernisation, and on the other, at another set of 'dualists', the Communist Parties which were advocating a policy of allying with the 'national' bourgeoisies against both the reactionary, allegedly 'feudal' landowning oligarchies at home and their new allies, the foreign multinational corporations abroad. As against both ECLA and the Communists, the world-system critique argued that there were not two

*This paper was prepared for a Conference in Berlin in September 1979 organised by the Institut für Vergleichende Sozialforschung.

distinct economic sectors, but that both were merely parts of a wider whole: the world capitalist economic system. The landowners, then, were not 'feudal', but an agro-exporting bourgeoisie, and had been for centuries. Nor were the industrial bourgeoisie any more 'national' or progressive. They would never provide principled opposition to foreign capital because they themselves were only junior partners in an alliance with foreign multinational corporations. Between them, they controlled the State, which acted as the bridge between foreign and local capital, mobilised capital and controlled labour. In this alliance, it was the multinational corporation which was predominant. Being capital-intensive, the industrial sector, under their aegis, would be unable to absorb the growing population, much of it displaced from the countryside by the penetration of capitalism into agriculture. Those who did find employment would be subjected to intensified exploitation, while those who resisted could expect the ultimate in repression to be unleashed against them—State terror.[2]

In wider historical terms, world-system theorists carried out detailed analyses of the process by which capitalism had implanted itself across the globe: its growth and maturation in Europe, and its subsequent expansion abroad. From the sixteenth century onwards, they argued, the world had become a *system*. From thenceforth, what happened to the silver-mines of Peru and Mexico, the textile-industry in India, or the gold-mines in South Africa would have direct and fateful consequences for Madrid and Lancashire, and even for Poland and Portugal—and vice-versa. Whole states would be destroyed; others invented; pre-existing polities fused together and their economies similarly transformed. Burma was to become, in Furnivall's phrase, a 'factory without chimneys'; Java a 'vast coffee estate';[3] Egypt a cotton plantation.

So convincing seemed this model, especially since its prophecies seemed to have been borne out by events, that it came to dominate the thinking of an entire generation seeking for an intellectual alternative to the then dominant functionalist, diffusionist and evolutionist schools of 'modernisation' theory largely developed in the USA, and a political alternative to capitalist growth-strategies and Communist dogma respectively. Here, the turning-point—which Foster-Carter has termed a 'classic paradigm-shift'[4]— was the devastating critique by Frank of *The Sociology of Development and the Underdevelopment of Sociology,* published in 1967.[5]

True, there were those who asked how we could speak of a capitalist *world*-system, when the expansion of Europe only began in the sixteenth century and was not finally completed until the nineteenth. To them, Wallerstein replied that a 'world-system' doesn't have to be *world-wide* at all; merely to operate at a level 'larger than any juridically-defined political unit'.[6] In his first volume (there are three more to come), he was attempting the initial task of charting the emergence and maturation of capitalism within the core of this system, Western Europe, and the subsequent extension of its trading activity across the globe during the mercantilist phase of capitalism in the sixteenth century.

But there were also those who felt uneasy about the notion that the world had become *capitalist* so early. They noted the persistence of pre-capitalist relations in colonial zones, and the use of the term 'capitalist' to describe what many would have simply called 'trade'. Nor did the colonies seem particularly capitalist in terms of the ways in which goods were produced or in terms of their political institutions. Moving to the present, it seemed difficult to reconcile the notion of a single world-system—which, for shorthand, I shall dub the 'monistic' approach—with the notion that there is not just one world, but three—or more.

Hence when people were asked how they reconciled these two different models, they were often taken aback. Until recently, the question was not often asked. Most of us operated not only with both monistic and 'pluralistic' models at one and the same time, but with *more than one version of the pluralist model.* I wish to argue here that this is a perfectly defensible heuristic procedure, not mere eclecticism or sloppy-minded empiricism, and a far more adequate response to the complexity of the real world than that provided by world-system theory. Like Foster-Carter, however, I have no desire whatsoever to engage in 'sectarian' denunciations of world-system theorists, insofar as I share with them certain fundamental assumptions: that all countries now form part of a world international order in which a handful of those countries which industrialised early have the capacity to keep the rest 'dependent'.

World-system theorists themselves, equally, do not simply insist that there is a world-system, *tout court.* But they start from the assumption that the world is the only meaningful framework within which the history of any particular country or group can be understood, and as Herbert Spencer classically observed in the nineteenth century, what distinguishes a system from a mere assemblage or congeries is not simply that a system is made up of parts, but that the relations between the parts *are themselves systematic* in such a way that changes in one part have effects on the other parts of the system. (We will take up later the question of the *degree* of systematicity, or, to put it another way, the degree of autonomy of the parts.)

So, the system-theorists say, we must abandon the view that the world is composed of so many nation-states, each with 'separate parallel histories', for 'societies' are merely 'parts of a whole reflecting that whole' and it is this whole—'one capitalist economic system with different sectors performing different functions'—that must therefore be taken as the basic logical and historical-sociological framework within which the 'society' can then be located. 'A state', he rightly observes, 'no more has a mode of production than does a firm. The concept "mode of production" describes an *economy,* the boundaries of which are. . . an empirical question.' In the case of the capitalist mode of production, its boundaries are world-wide.[7] 'To understand the internal class-contradiction and political struggles of a particular state, we must first situate it in the world-economy. And that economy is 'a single capitalist world-economy, which had emerged historically since the sixteenth century and which still exists today'.[8]

The parts within this whole, then, are determined by an international division of labour which allots 'tasks' as between the industrialised 'core' countries and those on the periphery: an international division of labour which is not just a functional division, but also a relationship of exploitation.

The core countries are those which began by successfully developing 'a complex variety of economic activities—mass-market industries. . ., international and local commerce in the hands of an indigenous bourgeoisie, and relatively advanced forms of agriculture. . . with a high component of yeoman-owned land'. The peripheral countries became monocultural economies, specialising in cash crops produced by coerced labour; and the semi-peripheral countries were those that went downhill, *de*industrialising and losing their former core status. In these latter, the forms of labour are typically intermediate between 'the freedom of the lease system and the coercion of slavery and serfdom. . ., for the most part, sharecropping'.[9]

Now pluralists equally accept that the three or more worlds they identify are not economically, politically or culturally sealed off from each other, but form part of an over-arching world-order. But this world-order is not a capitalist world-order. Within it, there is a capitalist *sector,* which is still the most powerful sector. Within that capitalist sector, there are two distinct sub-sectors: the developed, industrial countries and the dependent, agrarian ones. But the world is no longer a capitalist world, whatever may have been the case in the past. Rather, the capitalist 'world', like the other 'worlds', has *another* major system-alternative and rival, communism. Hence the system as a whole is *neither capitalist nor communist,* but a system of oppositions based on two major polarities: developed v. under-developed, and capitalist v. communist. The world is constituted by the alliances and antagonisms between these sets of countries. Each set has as its main unit 'the country' (nation-state), though each country is especially influenced by the most powerful members of the set, the Superpowers, and, because of 'unequal development' between its component zones, is not internally homogeneous either. Hence these cross-cutting pairs of polarities result logically in four boxes—four 'worlds', not three. Much of the confusion in the literature comes from trying to squeeze four types of country into three boxes and from the equally mystifying 'linear' procedure of merely listing countries according to indicators of levels of development.[10]

For world-system theory, there is only *one* world, divided into three components (completely different from the three 'worlds' discussed above): the core, peripheral, and semi-peripheral countries. Communist societies, though they have special characteristics of their own which set them off from capitalist countries, are not a set of countries *different in kind* from capitalist ones. Hence the communist 'world', in this model, is decomposed, and its component countries also treated variously as core, peripheral, or semi-peripheral.

The Growth of the World-System

The differences between monists and pluralists, then, arise at all levels and at all points: over the conceptualisation of the whole; over the conceptualisation of the parts; and over the nature of the relationship between the parts and the whole.

The point of departure is the assumption on the part of the monists that the world-system is a *capitalist* world-system. For myself, *per contra,* though I accept that the world did indeed only come into being as a single social system only during the period beginning with European mercantilist expansion and ending with modern imperialism, it did so as a system in which production for the market was conducted on the basis of non-capitalist relations, for the hallmark of mercantilist colonialism was the establishment of a mode of production in which forms of coerced labour persisted or were introduced which depended upon the direct use of force, and in particular upon the power of the State, which intervened directly in both constructing and operating the economy.

I would have liked to have called this the 'colonial' mode of production, had this term not been preempted (indeed invented) by Alavi and used in a different sense.[11] Alavi calls the initial, 'political' phase of colonialism that I am describing 'pre-capitalist'. Since this is a negative or residual designation—and to avoid confusion—I will call it, rather, 'mercantilist'. It is later displaced, at points in time that varied from the late eighteenth century for India to the Independence period for Latin America—by a dependent capitalism that he labels the 'colonial' mode of production. In his discussion of India, Alavi shows clearly the centrality of the political coercion of labour in the 'mercantilist' phase:

> 'the social relations of production were reconstituted on the basis of ownership of the land that was *conferred. . . under the authority of the colonial state,* the state of the metropolitan bourgeoisie. The landlords no longer exercised direct coercive force over the peasant. Their class power was now articulated through, and by, the colonial state'.[12]

'The landlord became landowner' (p. 24) and the conformity of the producer was ensured by one of the East India Company's servants, 'a man with a cane who would watch over the weaver and beat him "to quicken his deliceries".'

Panikkar painted a similar picture for Java, twenty years ago:

It was a silent but far-reaching revolution that the plantation-system introduced. . .
Previously the Dutch had only been merchants buying the spices and rice. . . and
selling them at a profit. True, they used their powers to establish a monopoly, but
beyond this the trading activities did not interfere with the life of the people. But
the change over into a plantation economy involved the actual exploitation of
labour, a control of the economic activity of the population and an effective
supervision. . . in fact "estate management" over a whole country. The island of
Java became a plantation of the Dutch United East India Company. . . The
relations between the sovereign [the Company PW]. . . and its subjects were in
substance those of planter and coolie, in which the former was not merely the
employer of labour, but also the authority vested with the rights of life and
death. . . A whole people was. . . converted by the exercise of sovereignty into a
nation of estate coolies, with their own natural aristocracy reduced to the
position of foremen and superintendents. (Panikkar, *loc. cit.*)

After this initial period of colonial transformation through the
exercise of the direct political power of the East India Company, for
example, the Industrial Revolution in Europe stimulated a second-stage
transformation of the colonies. Now, Alavi emphasises, 'the peasant
was. . . driven to work for the landowner', not by 'direct [i.e. "extra-
economic" PW] coercion', but by economic necessity—the threat of
starvation.[13] By the late eighteenth century, then, the 'freedom' of the
dispossessed—*capitalist* relations—was being substituted for the political
compulsions of the mercantilist phase. Nevertheless, the new phase of
capitalism was still 'colonial', he insists, in that 'the colonial economy. . . is
only completed via the imperialist centre' and because it has been
thenceforward 'distorted', since 'surplus value is realised only by and
through the imperialist capital accumulation'.[14]

Today, the dependent economies originally implanted by political
force can continue to work according to the logic of the world capitalist
market, because they have become capitalist in their internal constitution;
not merely because they are articulated to a world capitalist market. Yet
political force is still needed because the dichotomy between the
capitalism of the centre and the capitalism of the periphery creates new
contradictions. The first of these is that the world was not simply
integrated by imperialism. It was divided at the same time, between several
major imperialist powers. The second was the resistance and counter-
attack provoked in the colonised countries. And the third was the decisive
breach in a capitalist world-system that had only very recently become
established: the Bolshevik seizure of power in 1917.

Today, despite increasing differences between socialist states, then, the
'principal contradiction' that has developed since then has been the
polarisation of the world as between two different kinds of social system,
the capitalist and the socialist respectively. World-system theorists, how-

ever, discount this difference as subsidiary, if not an illusion. For them, the fundamental divisions are those of core, periphery and semi-periphery. To my mind, this simply ignores the qualitative differences not only in the way communist countries organise their economies, but also the distinctive features of the entire political and cultural life of those societies.

The discounting of these differences of social system is not peculiar to world-system theorists. Various non-Marxist 'Third Worldists', for example, in a spirit of 'a plague on both your houses', most explicitly and militantly expressed during the Bandung era of 'non-alignment', contrast their backwardness with the technological and economic levels obtaining in both the capitalist and the communist industrialised societies.

For Wallerstein, Russia possesses a productive system in which 'private ownership is irrelevant',[15] a negative formulation which he amplifies elsewhere more positively: the communist state is merely a 'collective capitalist firm so long as it remains a participant in the market of the capitalist world-economy' (ibid., pp. 68-9). Since there can only be one world-system at global level, and since existentially that system is a capitalist one, 'there are today no socialist systems in the world-economy' (ibid., p. 35), and the USSR is merely a 'core power in a capitalist world-economy' (ibid., p. 33, Wallerstein's italics).

This treatment of what to me is the central division in the world derives from a methodological assumption that capitalism is a system in which 'production is for exchange, that is. . . determined by its profitability on a market'.[16] In my view, this mistakenly locates the defining properties of capitalism in exchange and not in the relations that govern the way commodities are produced: in trade rather than in production.[17] A 'capitalist' system for Wallerstein is merely one in which the producer receives less than he produces. All then, are 'objectively proletarian', even peasants: 'Africans working on the land in the rural areas should be thought of as "peasants" who are members of the "working class", that is who sell their labour-power even when they are technically self-employed cash-crop farmers'. (CWE, p. 176).

Slaves, too, are 'proletarians'. In the literal, etymological sense the proletariat are those who have nothing but their children. Historically, they didn't even necessarily labour much, but were supported by State handouts—the panes that were coupled with circenses. But the term has come to be used to refer to those who produce (labour) but own no means of production. Because they work for those who do own these means they 'yield part of the value they have created to others'. Of course, there are variations in the amount yielded—all or part—and the forms which the surplus takes. 'Proletarian', in this sense, simply means any exploited producer. Wallerstein distinguishes eight varieties of proletarians, only one of which meets the classical model, and instances the wage-worker, the 'petty producer' (or 'middle peasant'), the tenant farmer, the sharecropper, the peon and the slave.

Rather than 'clarify' the phenomenon of exploitation (p. 290), what he acknowledges to be 'great differences between the various forms of labour'—the modes of social control entailed; the legitimating ideologies; the relative extent of reliance on force, persuasion, etc.—are reduced to a lowest common property: exploitation-in-general. The analogue, at system level, would be simply to treat capitalism, feudalism, slavery, etc. as variants of class society. Undoubtedly they are, but the analytical problems we face require going beyond this level of abstraction to the specific properties of each *type* of social relationship and institution.

Finally, I consider the model over-deterministic. It rightly emphasises the impressive historical power of capitalism, which swept all existing political and economic competitors before it. But at the level of conceptualisation, it depends upon 'the teleological assertion. . . that things at a certain place and time *had to be* a certain way *in order to* bring about later states of development. . . [that Wallerstein's] model of the world capitalist economy required and predicts'.[18] And at the level of implications for social action, it is a picture of a world *so* determined by capitalism, and particularly by those who control the core capitalist states, that it leads logically to fatalism and resignation, for it becomes difficult to see how any part of such a tightly-knit system can possibly break away. Indeed, movements which purport to do so, or already to have done so, are, we are told, either deluding themselves or those who believe in them, or both. But I say 'logically' because there is, happily, a contradiction between this 'managerialist perspective' and the 'metaphysical pathos' implicit in it, on the one hand, and the recognition that since the parts always stand in conflictful relationships, exploited classes and countries have always struggled to improve their position *vis-à-vis* the core countries and at times even tried to break out of the system altogether. Frank and Wallerstein not only recognise this, but laud it. Nevertheless, the model they use does not accord with their political stance.

For it is a model which emphasises the capacity of the ruling classes to manipulate the system, and others in it, as they wish, whilst underplaying resistance to their domination. 'The system', at times, is as endowed with a logic, power and even quasi-personality as it is in that other major variant of Marxist system-theory, Althusserianism.[19] But systems do not take decisions. Ruling classes do. They try to run the system in their own interests. In this, overall, they succeed—by definition, otherwise they wouldn't continue to rule. But those they rule also try to maximise their interests. Such models therefore underestimate agency, especially resistance to domination. In the colonial context, they also underestimate the role of the 'collaborators'—those who possess or develop *local* political power and who use it actively to assist the colonisers, firstly, in establishing colonial institutions and then in participating in their operation as junior partners.

Of course, primary resistance did not prevent the onward sweep of capitalism and its final consolidation. In the dialectic of opposition between rulers and ruled, the rulers of the core countries had their way. But the triumph was long in the making, and the hegemony of capitalism has been a very uneven process along the way, in different zones, at different times, and with differing degrees of penetration and success.

The spread of capitalism is also discontinuous, not linear. The operations of mercantile traders; the establishment of colonies with predominantly non-capitalist production-systems; then of capitalist relations; the final integration of the world under capitalism; and the replacement of colonial political institutions by independent states constitute its main phases. Wallerstein has indicated that he distinguishes four phases in the development of world capitalism. So far, he has dealt in detail only with the epoch in which mercantilist trade and the implantation of colonies began. Yet even these represent two distinct kinds of economic activity, not some generalised, linear diffusion of something called 'capitalism'.

The two systems are respectively typified by Portugal-in-Asia, on the one hand, where trade was conducted via the (to modern ears, oddly-named) 'factories'—fortified and other trading-centres, where indigenous products were purchased, not produced—and the Spanish pattern in the Americas, on the other hand, where colonies were established *ab initio*, though run on quite non-capitalist lines.

In the mercantilist phase, trade usually involved a contract between State and private merchant venturers commonly granted a monopoly. Where they encountered strong polities with developed economies—as in early nineteenth century China—they were obliged to stick to peaceful forms of trading. Where it was possible and necessary to use superior military force, this was freely done—by Cortes and Pizarro in the Americas, and by the Portuguese in a series of military campaigns which culminated in the repulse of the Egyptian fleet at Diú in 1509. Hence the 'mercantilism', which may seem to some redolent of pacific exchange between buyer and seller freely interacting in the security of the market-place, in reality routinely involved the use of force, with or without the direct backing of the State, in order to open markets and drive out rivals. Further, what Weber called 'booty capitalism' and ordinary people 'piracy' were normal ways of acquiring commodities which were 'ready-made', either through seizing stores of goods by main force or by compelling others to produce them. The gamut ran from attacks on treasure fleets to the despoliation of pre-colonial population centres or of settlements established by other colonial powers. Its most dramatic expression was the enforced delivery of Inca gold to the Spanish conquerors: the 'ransom' of Atahualpa.

Further, much 'trade' took the form of what both Wallerstein and I have called 'hunting-and-collecting' (or 'gathering')—albeit with a more advanced technical equipment than the Bushmen or the Australian aborigines possessed (guns instead of spears) or, more accurately, indirect hunting-and-collecting—forcing others to collect what Nature provided: sandalwood in Melanesia, bird-of-paradise feathers in New Guinea, *pau-de-Brasil* in the Amazon, and, above all, men in Africa—rather than 'production' in the sense of transforming raw materials by human industry. Whether collection or production, the process Marx looked at in terms of its consequences for capital formation and labelled 'primitive accumulation' (note: *'primitive'*, not just 'primary'), depended, of course, on the actual amassing of commodities, including gold and silver, which were at first only commodities, and only capital *in posse*. Before they could become capital, they had to be both produced and sold. But the ways in which they were accumulated had little to do with capitalist ways of *producing*. Rather, it depended upon the exercise of political power.

'Booty capitalism' and hunting-and-collecting did not necessarily call for the establishment of colonies at all, though these were, in fact, commonly established at the outset. Within the colonised areas, in both towns and countryside, new forms of production soon emerged, though collecting continued in the Brazilian Amazon, for instance, for rubber and wild chestnuts into this century. The transformation of production, however, was not just an *economic* transformation, for economies do not exist 'in themselves'. It depended, rather, upon the radical re-working of entire cultural orders, sometimes via incorporating or adapting aspects of existing structures, at other times smashing them and replacing them with quite novel institutions, the most striking instance in the New World being the dismantling of the central machinery of the Inca and Aztec states while retaining something of the lower structural levels. But the new institutions included novel forms of agricultural enterprise— the encomienda, the hacienda, the slave-population, etc.

In this process, the State—both that of the metropolis and the local apparatus—played a key role, providing the *sine qua non*: the backing of force which paved the way and which guaranteed the viability of the whole system. The establishment of colonies, therefore, was a process of *political* economy, not a 'purely economic' process governed by the play of the market. It entailed the construction, not just of systems of production, but of government and taxation; a total racist social order; and a strong machinery of ideological control in order to suppress existing cultural values and institutions where these could not be accommodated to the new order, and, where necessary or feasible, replacing them by imported ideologies, especially Christianity, and the institutions—the Church and the religious orders—with which to enforce them.

The whole colonial order, then, is hypothecated upon the forceful construction of socio-cultural categories which were institutionalised and built into the structure of State and civil society. The fundamental components of the edifice were certainly classes, in terms of their respective roles in a division of labour and system of exploitation. But they were classes in which membership was ascribed by birth and descent and sanctioned by law and custom. They were, in fact, *estates*, brought into being and maintained in being by the exercise of colonial power. Before, there had not been any such thing as 'the Bantu', or 'the African', 'the Indian' (Indian Indian or Amerindian). As Bonfil has insisted,[20] the category 'Indian' is a colonial category. For Indian labour to be exploited, the Indian had first of all to be created as a legally-exploitable category: *economic* exploitation had to be *socially* institutionalised. And since his status was defined according to physical criteria; it was to stimulate an obsession with the genetic[21] and with ethnic identity. But the consequences were not only availability for economic exploitation. Membership of an estate, as distinct from membership of a class, determined the whole of one's social being. It determined, for instance, whom one might and whom one might not marry; whether one was allowed to leave one's natal village or whether one was forced to; whether one came under a different legal code from townsmen; a totality of rights and duties, codified as civil status.[22]

The divergence in the trajectories of the two Iberian empires reflects the qualitative differences in the kinds of colonial economies they developed. For the Portuguese in Asia, despite their forceful irruption onto the market, their economic role remained restricted to the niche formerly occupied by Arab and other traders, but in which they now articulated Asia not only with Europe, but also with the New World through the exchange of bullion for spices. Yet however great their military power, this trade was not part of the *European* world-system, as Wallerstein acknowledges, but of another zone outside Europe: what he calls an 'external arena'. Within this arena, the volume and value of trade with Europe was not as significant for Asia as it was for Europe, and only centuries later, with the growth of European demand for raw materials after the Industrial Revolution, did the capitalist mode of production become directly implanted.[23]

On the margins of the world-system, in a country like Ecuador, though early in the nineteenth century landowners and merchants might take power from the metropolis and create an independent state under their control, not until just before World War I would the now-dominant coastal agro-exporting commercial bourgeoisie take power from the 'feudal' Sierran hacienda-owners after the Liberal victory in the lengthy Civil Wars; not until the inter-War period were beginnings made on 'bourgeois' political and economic institutions: a Central Bank and a modern bureaucratic machinery; not until after World War II was the 'administrative revolution' completed under Galo Plaza; and not until the military revolution-from-above were the new industrial bourgeoisie put into power. And not until the capital—without which modern capitalist development would remain merely an abstract idea—actually arrived in the oil-bonanza of 1972 could Land Reform begin, as landowners were assisted by the State to turn their haciendas into capitalist estates, and unfree labour was replaced by wage-labour.

The 'rational kernel' of dualist theory is that pre-capitalist labour-relations, based on extra-economic coercion, and the persistence of a formally autonomous 'peasantry' tied to the haciendas (a system constructed under colonialism), did in fact continue for so long. To the mass of the population, it has been said, the arrival of Independence a century and a half earlier, only meant the 'ultimo día del despotismo y primero de lo mismo', as a cynical popular saying of the time put it.[24] Capitalist relations in agriculture grew only with painful slowness in the Sierra. Real political power was local power: that of the landowners on their estates. They had little need of the State, for they were the State, and the effective formal central State in any case had little to offer. But once exporting became dominant, the new owners of the plantations had to take over and modernise the State. To do so necessitated civil war with the older landowning class.

The persistence of non-capitalist relations has been the central fact of life for over three centuries in such countries. But this has not been the case universally. Because of the lateness of the penetration of European capitalism in other parts of the globe, when it did penetrate it did so, not as mercantilism, but in its most modern form. Hence the rapidity and thoroughness of the process Alavi describes as the implementation of the 'colonial mode of production' in India in the late eighteenth and early nineteenth centuries.

Even so, as I pointed out fifteen years ago,[25] the consolidation of the entire world-edifice as a completed system has been of very *short* duration: no more than the very few decades between the final scramble for Africa which only began in the 1880s and the Russian Revolution of 1917. And even then Japan, Ethiopia, Afghanistan and Thailand preserved their independence; and China, Turkey and Persia were only 'semi'-colonies.

The process that led up to this final consolidation certainly did begin in the sixteenth century. But it was not unambiguously a capitalist process, firstly, because the early leading countries were themselves feudal societies; secondly, because what they implanted was based upon pre-capitalist, unfree labour. Hence accounts of colonialism which present it as the story of 'capitalism', without qualification, are profoundly unhistorical. Not only do they underplay the non-capitalist dimensions; they also underplay the quite distinctive kinds of capitalism and the phases of its development.

The model is also a one-way model in that it discounts the consequences for colonialism of the profound differences in the nature of the *pre-capitalist* societies and cultures the colonisers encountered. The social space that became the colonial world was inhabited by many different kinds of society, each possessing a variety of institutions and cultural codes which can only residually be labelled 'pre-capitalist', since this merely tells us, negatively, what they were *not,* not what they were. In fact, there were many different *kinds* of society, which differed from each other and not only from capitalism: acephalous bands and bureaucratic empires, to name but two extremes, and the differences of cultural logic, of social structure, of sheer scale of organisation were to impose themselves on colonial institutions, too, since those responsible for constructing colonial political institutions had to come to terms with them. As Frank has reminded us, criticising Rostow's concept of 'the traditional', some areas were emptied of their exiguous populations by wiping them out and subsequently repopulating them with immigrants, as in Argentina, Australia or North America, giving rise to a quite distinct set of countries from those with large pre-colonial populations.[26]

The legacy of the pre-colonial heritage tends to get neglected if we concentrate on only one side of the colonial question: the undoubted success of capitalism in imposing its cultural logic upon what it was to turn into the 'periphery' and upon the people it was to turn into 'natives'. So does the resistance offered to invasion and continued after defeat. Even if in the encounter between colonisers and colonised, the power of the colonisers was superior, their victims never ceased to try and maximise their own interests.

But as various writers have shown, e.g. Ranger for Africa, resistance was not the only form of reaction to conquest. There were also those who went along with the conquerors from the beginning—the allies of Cortes and Pizarro, for instance. Left-wing and liberal scholars have tended to tackle the important task of chronicling the story of *resistance,* rescuing from the obscurity of the archives the record of piecemeal, small-scale resistance by hunting-and-collecting bands; reminding us of the creation of new forms of organisation among peoples lacking centralised political institutions: the Araucanian military reorganisation that enabled them to fight off the Spanish and the Chilean State for 300 years; the prophets who emerged to mobilise peoples like the Nuer, or the more dramatic and public victories over British armies by the Ashanti, the Zulu and the Afghans.

But reaction to conquest also included despair, resignation, fatalism and defeatism. Further, there were many individuals and groups who collaborated with the new authorities and who manipulated new institutions to their own advantage in ways both left-wing and liberal writers do not approve of: the *comprador,* the collaborating chief, the feudal lord, even the enterprising peasant who became a capitalist farmer, and so on. The colonised, then, whether they resisted or collaborated, were not simply inert objects pushed around by some impersonal 'logic of the system', or, more concretely, by government and settler.

It is also important not to over-emphasise the continuity of capitalist expansion. It was in fact discontinuous politically, involving successive re-organisations of political relations between centre and periphery of which the most important, politically, were the initial establishment of direct colonies and their subsequent emergence as new, independent, nation-states. The crucial economic transition was the shift from trade with the centre in goods produced along non-capitalist lines to production based on wage labour. In the core countries themselves, the crucial watersheds were the industrial revolutions which occurred at different times at different rates in different countries, when the feudal agrarian pre-eminence of landowning classes was replaced by the new bourgeoisies. The process was not simply one of political transformation *following* economic differentiation, and the consequent struggle between old and new classes for supremacy. Rather, the development of the economy depended upon the *prior* conquest of political power, which then afforded opportunity for economic entrepreneurs to innovate and expand.[27]

But in the colonies, no such economic transformation occurred. And it was the political power of the metropolis that doomed their economies thenceforth to underdevelopment in the interests of London and Madrid. Even with the establishment of political independence, they remained obdurately economically dependent states, restricted to the role of suppliers of primary commodities to the metropoli and, except where the needs of the core countries called for capitalist innovation (plantations, mines, etc.), non-capitalist in their production systems. Pre-capitalist patterns of obligation to render dues in kind or in labour continued right up to our own times in the Andes, for instance, and outright slavery persisted in Brazil until 90 years ago (not to mention the southern states of the USA). To say this, as Laclau remarks, 'does not necessarily involve maintaining a dualist thesis'—that 'no connections exist between the "modern" and the. . . "traditional" sector'—for 'the modernity of one sector is a function of the backwardness of the other'. Rather, it entails distinguishing between an 'economic system' which involves 'mutual relations between different sectors of the economy' but in which the 'constitutive elements' may be different 'modes of production'.[28] Pro-duction along capitalist lines, in response to metropolitan industrialisation, and particularly in sectors devoted to exports, became widespread even in the colonial period, in some parts, as mines and plantations were developed ultimately on the basis of wage labour and not forced labour, and as wage labour was increasingly used to produce cash crops for the world-market and handicrafts for the internal market. But the stranglehold exercised by the world-system was not absolute. Some colonies did make the breakthrough not only to political independence, but also to a thoroughly capitalistic economy, notably the 'first new nation'. It *was* therefore possible for some to escape from dependence. Further, how some countries became core countries, others regressed to semi-peripheral status, and yet others climbed to semi-peripheral or even core status is often well described by Wallerstein. *Why* they did so is less well explained by his model, except, as we shall see, in sub-sociological terms, where technology, geography, etc. seem to function as the *deus ex machina*. The reasons why have rather to be sought in the variability of the relations between economic, political and other social orders, their interplay and relative autonomy, and cannot be explained by models which over-emphasise the all-determining nature of 'the economic'.

The metropolitan stranglehold normally, however, proved decisive. And it led to a special kind of capitalist production: a *colonial* mode, in which State power was deployed initially to induce the production of commodities wanted by Europe. That State power might later be wielded by local landowners and merchants, rather than by agents of Madrid or London, but production still depended upon the direct coercion of labour to produce, in forms ranging from slavery to serfdom, from debt-peonage to indentured labour. Even manufacturing, as in the *obrajes,* depended upon compulsory obligations to deliver, backed by extremes in violence. The State too, intervened in the form of taxes which had to be paid in cash rather than, as with traditional tribute, in kind or in labour, and in greater amounts. Cash could only be obtained by working in mines or on plantations, or factories, or by selling agricultural and handicraft products on the market. 'Extra-economic' sanctions then were the norm until very recently in most parts of the globe; the cash-nexus the exception.

These differences in modes of controlling labour are fully recognised in Wallerstein's schema. That labour was normally coerced in the periphery is central to his model. The differences between slavery, serfdom, wage labour or indentured labour, however, are all forms, for him, of *capitalist* labour relations, dictated by the different *technical* needs of different products, e.g. different kinds of crops. *Per contra,* I am arguing that capitalist relations of production based on wage labour—which requires the dispossession ('freeing') of the producer from the means of production— are a late development, and that slavery, serfdom and unfree, coerced labour in general are not modes of capitalist *production* at all. The beginnings of the implantation of those relations could not occur until the centre itself had been transformed along capitalist lines. Only then did the parcelling-out of the world get completed; only then did the capitalist organisation of production get under way, though only a very little of this was in manufacturing. In this process, it was inevitably the leading industrial countries which also became the leading colonial powers. That general process of capitalist expansion is therefore highly uneven and occurs chronologically at quite different times in quite different parts of the world, due to a double determination: the nature of the colonising core country, and the nature of the zone being colonised; not as something 'allotted' by some reified functionalist 'logic' of a system.

It may be objected that all this dispute about the definition of capitalism in terms of production as against capitalism in terms of the market is simply a matter of arbitrary definition. But the importance of making these distinctions, and the greater heuristic power of the latter kind of definition become evident when we face the problem of why it was that colonial expansion was initially pioneered by countries which were by no means the farthest advanced along the road to industrialisation, to wit, Spain and Portugal (the latter so marginal in the capitalist development of Europe that Anderson, in his magisterial survey of the transition from feudalism to capitalism, country by country, includes many backward states—Austria, Russia and Poland for instance—but omits Portugal, which plays a leading part in Wallerstein's model).[29] The 'deep' reason for this difference is that Anderson's model is *overly* Eurocentric, scarcely alluding to colonialism as a significant factor in European capitalist development. To this, Wallerstein's model is a healthy corrective.

But the reason why capitalism failed to get implanted in the colonies, does, in the end, have to be sought in Europe. It lies in the success of some countries, not in developing *trade,* but in transforming their systems of production along capitalist lines. Capitalism reorganises all the factors of production—land, labour and capital—in such a way as to build in a dynamic of expansion. Other systems—merchant guild-production, feudalism in agriculture—restricted productivity and production in the interests not only of monopolising economic opportunities through the prevention of competition, but also because these economic advantages depended upon and underpinned an interlocking system of political and social relations. Only with the removal of these social constraints could expansion on the dramatic scale of the Industrial Revolution begin. From thenceforth, the capitalist firm would plough back profits so as to enable it to maintain its competitive edge in a market where all others were doing the same.

Such a system emerged in Holland and then in England, and it was the latter that was to become the leading modern imperialist power. The reason why capitalist production relations were so belated in becoming implanted in South America now becomes clearer: not simply because that part of the world was allotted a peripheral role in the world-system but because the countries which did that allotting, however politically absolute, were themselves backward in terms of capitalist economic development. It is this, then, that is at the root of the world-historic failure of Spain to maintain herself as the leading colonial power, culminating in her successive bankruptcies in 1557, 1575, 1596, 1607, 1627, 1647, 1653 and 1680, by which time, 'two thirds of the silver of the treasure-fleet went straight to foreigners without even entering Spain'.[30]

The failure was not due to the unsuitability of her political institutions—the structure and size of the Empire ('Spain was an empire when what was needed. . . was a medium-sized state')[31]—for competing in a world-system of trade. What was needed, rather, was the centralisation and modernisation of the internal market along capitalist lines (something impeded by an economy in which the Mesta was pre-eminent).

Spain, Wallerstein tells us, 'did not have the energy to create a large bureaucracy in the Americas because of limited resources, human and financial'.[32]

But despite the 'slowness' of the Spanish bureaucracy, it can scarcely be described as 'no indigenous state authority at all' (ibid., p. 31). It was capable, for instance, of suppressing settler revolt effectively on at least two occasions in sixteenth century Peru, despite problems of distance. And it certainly tried to regulate everything from Madrid. Indeed, Elliott remarks that 'no states were more governed in the sixteenth century than those of the King of Spain'.[33]

The Spanish colonial service was probably no thinner on the ground than, say, the British in Nigeria or the Australian in New Guinea early in this century. But in the end even the local bureaucrats and even the Church—consider Hidalgo and Morelos—and the humanist-liberal religious orders shared with landowners and merchants (to whom many were related anyway) resentment of Spanish control. Quite early, they were able to obstruct Madrid's efforts to protect the Indians against the settlers. The bureaucrats' defiance was beautifully expressed in the formula 'Obedezco pero no ejecuto' (I obey, but do not execute [Imperial directives])'. In the end, it was Spain which lacked the muscle to discipline them. As for the Portuguese, in the sixteenth century 'the most impressive fact. . . is the remarkable manner in which the fleets in the East were kept reinforced by the Portuguese home government. Armada followed armada in unending succession. . . Even in the most difficult of circumstances they could therefore hold out'.[34]

The financial failure can certainly not be attributed to lack of capital, for the annual treasure-fleet at times brought back as much as a quarter of Spain's annual revenues, between 1503 and 1660 'enough to triple the existing silver resources of Europe, and to increase its gold supplies by one-fifth'.[35] Capital was available, but was not invested in promoting capitalism. Eventually, much of the annual bullion supply had to be used to pay off debts to the more advanced capitalist countries, notably England. The reasons for the loss of leadership by Spain and Portugal, then, are to be found primarily in terms of their backward metropolitan economies, their failure to develop capitalism in the homelands, vis-à-vis more dynamic core countries, and the parallel attempt to maintain mercantilist forms of control over colonies that themselves were developing indigenous export-agriculture, mining and sizeable internal markets.

Otherwise, it becomes logically difficult to explain why, given Wallerstein's belief that 'slight edge' can turn into a 'large disparity', Spain fell behind at all. Logically, too, given the notion that the centre determines the periphery, it is in *Spain* that we should look for the causes of the debility of the Spanish Empire. Spain and Portugal did not fail in America and the East; they failed in Iberia.

*   *   *

The World Today

Let us turn now to the implications of this kind of model for understanding the world of today. If the world constitutes a system, what kind of system is it? How systematic is it? What, in other words, is the nature and relationship of the parts?

We have seen that the colonial mode of production did not prove, as Marx thought it would, to be a re-run of capitalism back in Europe. Rather than the whole world being made over in the image of metropolitan capitalist development, the colonies became a dependent, distinct sector within the capitalist world-system, allowed or forced to stagnate or even regress at some times and in some places—to 'underdevelop'; at others, to be forcibly and intensively transformed—but always in the interests of the 'mother' country.

The triumph of capitalism on a world scale, however, seemed to presage the displacement of pre-capitalist, including colonial-mercantalist modes of production, and the ultimate fulfilment of Marx's prophecy, as coerced labour began to be displaced by wage labour in textile factories, mines and plantations in the nineteenth century. But the dependence of the colonies did in fact persist, still determined by the political and economic supremacy of the core countries. To the pioneer thinkers who tried—from very different theoretical positions—to make sense of the process of imperialist consolidation as it was happening around them, like Hobson and Lenin, it was the triumph of imperialism that was the most immediately striking fact, and especially the pre-eminence of the leading industrial power, Britain. Yet central to their analyses were the built-in conflicts *between* rival empires, which offered some leeway for the colonised to play one off against the other. These theorists did note the protracted primary resistance offered to the armies of imperialism. But such resistance seemed doomed. Nevertheless, they themselves did not accept that victory. Hobson, a classic liberal, shared with Spencer, Hobhouse and others a fierce objection to the 'extra-economic' establishment of colonies in the first place, since this ran counter to *laissez faire* dogma, according to which economic development should properly be left to the entrepreneur and the market. It was not the proper function of the State to create colonies, even less to intervene so as to foster the development of mines and plantations, to turn the peasantry into cash-crop producers for the world market, and to force a proportion of them to provide labour for those mines and plantations. Resistance to this 'political' capitalism was the last shining intervention of Liberalism upon the world-scene. It took the form, in Britain, of principled opposition to the Boer War. But it was a limited critique from within capitalism that was soon to be eclipsed by a challenge to capitalism's very existence.

As Marx was fond of quoting, 'the owl of Minerva only flies at dusk'. For no sooner were these accounts of the completion of capitalist mastery of the globe written than the first major defection from that system occurred, in 1917, together with the first major stirrings within the colonised world of a new kind of future-oriented rejection of imperialism in China and India. Hence after the white-hot experience of those few years which saw the establishment of a Bolshevik regime in Russia, and the new growth of nationalism in the colonies, Lenin, whose *Imperialism*, written in 1916, had charted the irresistible expansion and ultimate hegemony of capitalism as a world-system, was, within a few years, predicting that world revolution would triumph, not in the heartlands of imperialism, as Marxists had hitherto asserted, but in what we now call the Third World.

Since that time, one-third of humanity has come to constitute a world-alternative to capitalism, dedicated, indeed, to 'burying' capitalism. Hence for most of us, the distinction between 'capitalism' and 'communism' is the first pluralist distinction with which we commonly operate. The second is the distinction between the core countries of the capitalist world and the exploited segment of that world. The assumptions underlying these two polarities, however, are quite different, implicit rather than explicit, and sometimes contradictory. Further, they cross-cut each other.

What is usually taken for granted is not so much the mere number of 'worlds' identified as the nature of the underlying rationale which generates the typology itself as well as the component worlds. The first dichotomy has as its main criterion differences in 'social system' or 'ideology'; the second, differences in levels or kinds of technological development (e.g. in Marxist versions, 'levels of development of the productive forces'). These are usually measured in terms of production, productivity, output, etc., using 'indicators' such as GNP per head, income, etc.

In the former, the differences of social system usually identified—and rightly so—are those between capitalist and socialist (or communist, according to taste) societies respectively. For Pierre Jalée, for instance, the world is 'sliced into two' in this way.[36] But those who think in terms of technology/production divide the world into 'agrarian' and 'industrialised' or into 'rich' and 'poor', rather than capitalist and communist. Note that Marxists are to be found in both camps, Jalée adhering to the ideological model; Frank and Wallerstein to models in which level and form of development (underdeveloped/developed) is more significant than social system or ideology.

Technology/output models are also characteristic of circles far removed politically from Frank and Wallerstein, notably the 'aid lobby', which embraces a wide liberal spectrum of Christians, non-Marxist socialists, pacifists and humanists who see differences between capitalist and socialist countries as insignificant in comparison with their respective statuses as either developed or underdeveloped countries. These are not, we should note, what are often called, for shorthand, 'class' models—based on differences between capitalism and socialism.

The most important specimen of this class of theory, surprisingly, is the Chinese world-model, which sees the First World as constituted by the Superpowers; the Second World by a set of technologically developed intermediate countries; and the large Third World (which includes China)— the majority of mankind—the backward countries. This model thereby conflates the USA *and* the USSR together (though pride of place in the hierarchy of enemies of mankind is now given to the latter); puts Hungary and Switzerland in the same bed; and makes no distinction between Haiti and Cuba. All this, of course, has implications for policy: China finds it perfectly acceptable to ally herself with Mrs. Bandaranaike, with General Zia or with Chancellor Schmidt, or with 'feudal' or military allies, whilst at the same time directing its fiercest fire at the largest and pioneer communist power.

To explain the apparent paradox of Chinese 'convergence' with technological (non-class) models, we have to turn to the ways in which they are located within wider systems of values. For the aid lobby, the implications are, firstly, that what is needed is 'aid' or 'development'; ideology and social system are secondary, if not irrelevant, or even barriers to growth; secondly, that the poorest and/or the non-aligned need/deserve it most. The Chinese, of course, don't accept *that*. Though they see themselves as a poor country, potentially leading the mass of humanity, the Third World, against the two super-imperialisms (First and Second Worlds), to do this they have to defend and promote socialism, of which their country is the only uncorrupted exemplar.

Yet socialism, as Wallerstein rightly insists, is based upon the nation-state. As a world economic system, on the other hand, socialism, he claims, does not exist. Yet he never examines the considerable degree of interdependence and trade within COMECON, or the pattern of aid to countries like Cuba and Viet Nam. If he did, there would seem no logical reason, according to his own criteria, for refusing the communist trade bloc the title of a 'world system'. Nor—because his model is one in which 'the economic' is abstracted and given causal priority—does he consider the persisting political and military dependence of the communist world, China apart, on the USSR.

This refusal of the status of world-system to the communist world is, in fact perfectly consistent with his neo-Trotskyist world-view. Capitalism is, for him, a system of production for profit on the market; socialism, in principle, a system of production collectively organised, at world level, for the satisfaction of human wants. This is an implicit criticism of those socialists who think that internationalism (and equality) have to be deferred until the effective majority of nation-states go socialist, and the 'forces of production' then become fully developed. As against that scenario, pragmatists reply that socialism can only be developed within nation-states at present, and that even if this falls short of the ideal, it is the only practicable 'transition'. To that riposte the world-system theorists retort that the 'transition' will be permanent if *inter*national economic planning between socialist states does not begin, however cautiously, now.

However, basically all can agree that the current reality is not internationalism: not even 'socialism in one country'—true when there was only *one* socialist state, but not now, when there are many 'socialisms in one country'. Hence the distinguishing feature of all these socialist states today is their fierce nationalism, however much it may be discounted in the formal ideology of 'proletarian *inter*nationalism', but as characteristic of socialist states today as it was of the capitalist countries during their internal consolidation and mobilisation for development, whether from the absolutist period onwards, or in the nation-building of Third World countries today.

State socialism, in the absence of world revolution, is, then, national socialism, oriented, internally, to consolidation and mobilisation for development, and, externally, to the defence of the nation, not to cooperation with other like-minded countries to coordinate their economies through collective decision-making.

Unequal development has left them, too, with a heritage of disparities, commonly culturally consolidated as national and ethnic superiority and inferiority, which make for potential conflicts, especially between advanced and backward countries, above all, between the Superpowers and the rest. Hence, not only do socialist states not 'converge' with capitalist ones; they increasingly—'polycentrically'—diverge from each other.[37]

In the development of the USSR, that country, endowed with abundant human and natural resources, was able to opt for a policy of largely autarkic development. Such an option is impossible for the smaller communist states that have emerged subsequently. Hence only China has had a similar endowment which permitted her to found her economic development, too, on thirteen years of virtual autarky, and only China has had the resources to stand up to the Soviet Union. The rest, especially micro-countries with a legacy of monocultural economies like Cuba, are forced into a new dependence, as the Chinese rightly point out, on the communist Superpower, as are those countries where newly-victorious Marxist regimes have inherited a devastated economy (Angola, Mozambique, Viet Nam, Cambodia). Since the establishment of communist power has everywhere been *both* a struggle to establish a new kind of social system *and* a *national* liberation struggle, nationalism is at flash-point in precisely those countries that have just—proudly and paid in blood—established their communist regimes. It is between them that actual war has broken out.

In the last resort, then, the socialist state is not only a state, but a nation-state. Like *any* state, it resorts to force in defence of its interests if necessary. The phenomenon unthinkable to the pioneers of Marxism—of actual war between socialist states—was naturally delayed until after World War II, before when a plurality of socialist states to have war between did not exist, but the first near miss did not take long— Yugoslavia's defiance of the Cominform, followed by actual invasion of Hungary and Czechoslovakia (leaving aside 'internal war' in East Germany and Poland). Socialist countries, living in a world-system of nation-states, have, therefore, to distinguish, politically, between their friends and their enemies (and those in between), and geo-politically, between those zones on their borders, remote countries and intermediate zones. It is this logic that informs Chinese foreign policy, and which explains their formal convergence with technologistic models of the world.

The two modes of 'slicing' the world, then, ideological and technological, can be diagrammatically and ideal-typically represented as follows (only the more important or typical countries being shown):

	Superpower	Developed	Underdeveloped
communist	USSR	Eastern Europe, North Korea	China
			Vietnam, Cuba, Mozambique, Angola
capitalist	USA	EEC and other Western European countries, Japan, Australia, South Africa	rest of capitalist world

Ideological models read across the rows, treating all communist and capitalist countries as falling into one or other of two great opposed 'camps'.

Technical-economic models read down the columns, separating industrial-ised countries, whether capitalist or communist, from agrarian. (China is separated by dots from the rest of the Third World, for those who wish to distinguish her for either sheer size or ideological heterodoxy.) But since both polarities reflect real properties of the world, all models in actual use inevitably combine elements of both. Analytically, two bipolar models, in any case, cross-cut each other so as to yield not *three* worlds, but four. This was not so serious when only two countries, China and Cuba, awkardly aligned themselves with the 'non-aligned' capitalist Third World. Now that there are many under-developed communist countries, that box becomes more important. Now we have both industrialised communist states and underdeveloped ones. I have already mentioned the dire consequences of trying to squeeze four worlds into three boxes. Four, because communist countries, merely by virtue of being communist, are not thereby necessarily either industrialised or agrarian, though historically, nearly all (East Germany and Czechoslovakia apart) began as agrarian societies, and backward ones at that. Leaving aside the capitalist 'newly-industrialising countries' (NICs), it has been the historic role and achievement of communism to have carried out the industrialisation which capitalism had previously refused and continues to refuse to the majority of Third World countries. The whole of Eastern Europe (except Albania), plus North Korea, is now industrialised, as UN agencies now recognise. But the newer communisms remain agrarian and underdeveloped.

A framework based on bipolar extremes by definition excludes anything between those extremes, and forces them into one or other of the polar Procrustean extremities. This is not so problematic for the capitalist/communist polarity, but awkward for those important inter-mediate countries ('semi-peripheral', in Wallerstein's terminology), which are 'newly-industrialising': Brazil, Mexico, Taiwan, Singapore and Hong Kong and for the 'capital-surplus' oil countries. I freely acknowledge the limitations of the schema. No diagram can encompass reality, and if this one has limitations, it is still heuristically more useful, because it is more differentiated than overly-monistic world-system models. A model of double oppositions, too, avoids the infinite multiplication of 'worlds' which otherwise tends to ensue.[38]

Hence the two cross-cutting axes in the above diagram generate four logical *and real* boxes: capitalist-industrial; capitalist-dependent (under-developed/agrarian); communist-industrialised; and communist-agrarian.

The use of such categories, of course, implies a rejection of any model of the world-system which postulates merely one dominant world-system, one 'world'. Lest anyone object that such taxonomies are mere scholasticism, I would remind them that the world is complex, and that schematically forcing simplicity upon it 'by fiat' is dangerous, for ideas are real in their consequences and bad ones can lead to ineffective and mistaken behaviour in the real world, as the above discussion of Chinese foreign policy shows. Most inhabitants of the globe recognise that these are *not* mere academic abstractions but real differences in the nature of the world around them, the stuff of their lives, and therefore find the categories meaningful. To them, differences between capitalism and socialism or between developed and underdeveloped are not just verbal games, but significant realities. For those who, like refugees and migrants, have actually lived under more than one of these systems, say, the three million who fled the German Democratic Republic or the twelve million migrant workers from the peripheral Mediterranean countries working in Western Europe, the proposition that they are living within a world-system is something they would readily recognise and endorse. But they have also moved because the differences between the four worlds were real to them.

The Turkish migrant is experiencing the logic of the capitalist world: the difference between development and underdevelopment—as have millions who constitute 'cheap labour' and have sought out its opposite—capital—either by going where the capital is—to 'runaway' zones and richer countries—or who have been sought out by capital in their own countries. The East German refugees, too, were reacting to the pull of superior development. But they were reacting even more to the second polarity: differences of social system.

At the risk, therefore, of boring Turkish migrants and East German refugees, and because world-system theory accords so much more importance to level of development rather than differences of social system, we now need to explain the nature of the parts of the world system: their *internal* constitution.

The First World consists of those advanced capitalist countries (with a few thoroughly capitalistic satellites closely dependent upon their markets for the export of primary products: Australia, New Zealand, Canada, in part, Denmark), in all of which the fundamental institutions of private ownership of the means of production and the operation of the economy according to the logic of market competition persist, but are now combined with heavy State intervention in the economy; in the political sphere, with parliamentary and institutional pluralism (separation of powers and legitimate opposition); and socially, with a developed Welfare State, all of which qualify the primary ideology and practice of competitive possessive individualism.

The Second World cannot be treated simply as a component or set of components of the capitalist world-system. 'Genotypically, stratification in Soviet society is significantly different from stratification in the West', because it is 'subject to political regulation' in which the central goal of the leadership is 'a future Communist society' . . . characterised by a high level of social welfare, and indeed eventually by private affluence, while still under the undisputed dominance of the Party'.[39] Many labels have been used to describe the specificity of these social systems (and, I insist, *social* systems, not just economic): 'socialist', 'communist', 'state socialist', 'state communist', 'deformed workers' states', 'social imperialism', and so on. (I restrict myself to Marxist usages since it is with Marxist theoreticians that we are here debating.) Now it does matter what label we use, for labelling implies not only a cognitive statement, but also an evaluative one about the nature of the social system in question. Such statements are also 'real in their consequences'. But even those who use different labels can probably agree on at least certain central characteristics of those societies.

Economically, the means of production are not privately owned, and the economy is planned. Politically, they are run by an all-powerful Party, entry to which is determined not by ascription or wealth, but by meritocratic performance. Conformity to the official ideology and value-system is of course, a *sine qua non* in that performance, and its role becomes ever more important as monopoly of the means of opinion-formation and communication increasingly replaces terror as the decisive instrumentality of social control.

Both these worlds, as the Chinese insist, are dominated by a Super-power—with decreasing effectiveness.

The Third World consists of a sub-set of underdeveloped capitalist countries, which, in Robin Jenkins' mordant formula, are 'owned, run and underdeveloped by the First World'.[40] The main political forms in these countries have been variants of demagogic populism, on the one hand, and repressive authoritarian right-wing regimes on the other, both strongly monocentric. Culturally, apart from such important trans-societal, but not universal 'world'-religions such as Islam, Christianity, Buddhism and Hinduism, they only share a common experience of imperialism and the pervasive influence of capitalist consumerist values.

The Second World, then, is distinct in *kind* from the First World. It is not, *pace* world-system theory, simply a part of the capitalist world-system, but a social system of a different order which constitutes a rival and an alternative to capitalism. Of course, this social system is no longer a disciplined bloc, as it was under Stalin. It is now 'polycentric', and the two largest communist powers are at each others' throats. The smaller ones, as we have seen, depend heavily upon the USSR, but also resist the pressures coming both from that Superpower and the pressures of their fellow-communist regimes.

The most fundamental differences, however, exist between the two social systems. The antagonisms between nation-states are either epiphenomenal 'spin-offs' of these more fundamental conflicts, or historical legacies of unequal development. The 'principal contradiction', then, should not be obscured either because of *rapprochement* or because communist powers can have capitalist allies. That the Soviet Union once allied itself with the leading capitalist countries against the Nazi invasion (and the obverse—that the capitalist powers allied themselves with, to them, unspeakable communists) does not make either any the less communist or capitalist.

It is with no desire whatsoever to revive the Cold War, therefore, that one must point out that between the two social systems there is a built-in antagonism. That they have long entered into more positive relationships—'co-existence' in the Soviet case; olive-branches all round in the Chinese drive to isolate the USSR—should not blind us to the extremely limited, situational, and provisional nature of these 'reconciliations'. There would be no poverty on earth today if all the proportion of world output now going into the primary conflict—the capitalist/communist arms-race—were not as great as the proportion devoted to productive investment. Hence, despite real *détente,* despite polycentrist tendencies within both worlds, the Chinese formula 'contending and colluding' to represent the nature of the 'class collaboration' is exaggerated—too even-handed and conspiratorial— for it is still *contending* that predominates.

All that has happened—but it is a big 'all'—is that under the threat of mutual nuclear annihilation, co-existence (a very *negative* formula, meaning agreement not to wipe each other out) has led to the replacement of a previous readiness to contemplate the unthinkable—in the American case, 'roll-back'—in favour of more limited confrontations, preferably fought by proxy. These still include hot wars and ideological battles. In the space created by this limitation upon the freedom of manoeuvre of the Superpowers, especially their freedom to resort to the ultimate 'deterrent', smaller countries have been able to exploit the partial power-vacuum, above all Viet Nam. Hence co-existence is primarily an outcome of military considerations, a facet of international relations left out of so many models. Trade between the capitalist and communist worlds is in any case very limited, and involves no basic reformation of relationships. Indeed, as we saw, what is striking about both Soviet and Chinese development has been not their dependent position within a world-capitalist economic system, but their independent, for a long time quite *autarkic* development 'in one country'.

The world-system, as a system of trade, still plays a minor part in communist development. It is the capitalist countries that dominate world trade, the USA consuming at least a third of the world's scarce resources. Moreover, at a time of world inflation, and in an epoch of trans-national corporations, we are only too aware of the inter-connectedness of the world economy and of the power of the institutions that dominate the capitalist economy thereby also to influence profoundly what happens in the non-capitalist world. To the extent that foreign trade forms a part of the total Soviet economy, the world-system model is correct: capitalist domination of the world market does have serious consequences for the *internal* economy of socialist countries to the extent that they even have internal 'hard currency' markets for the privileged. And for all, privileged or otherwise, living standards in Irkutsk and Harbin *are* to that extent determined by decisions taken in Washington and London, by the necessity to sell food and other commodities on the world market, and by the nuclear and space arms-races which impoverish the masses everywhere. World military expenditure is now roughly equivalent to the entire income in cash and in kind of the poorest half of the world's population.[41]

In world-system theory, it is the universal processes that are emphasised, and rightly so. Nor do differences of social system pass unnoticed. But they occupy a quite different place within their models. Whether a country is capitalist or communist, for them, is not of first importance. What is important is whether or not they are core, peripheral or semi-peripheral countries: the position they are allotted in a 'hierarchy of occupational tasks' (*MWS*, p. 350).

Thus Wallerstein, as we have seen, follows the earlier Marxist and later Trotskyist tradition of dismissing 'socialism in one country' as a 'logical and actual impossibility', since socialism can only, in this view, be instituted on the basis of egalitarian, collectivistic political and economic decision-making *between* countries, which would eventually necessitate world-government. But, Wallerstein observes 'world-government does not exist' (*ibid.*, p. 348); therefore, logically, neither does socialism. There are not even 'socialist economies', only 'socialist movements controlling certain state machineries'. Hence, the claim that they are socialist 'needs to be treated with circumspection' (p. 351). 'It is', he declares, 'merely a variant of classic mercantilism' (*CWE*, p. 90); the communist state merely, as we saw above, a 'collective capitalist firm' because 'it remains a participant in the market of the capitalist world-economy' (*ibid.*, pp. 68-9).

This theory shares the common view that whatever it is, it isn't socialism, or the cognate view that it may have begun as such, but went wrong somewhere along the line. In my view, this is an idealist, stipulative defining-away of the problems of socialist construction, for the fact of the matter is that these countries are organised on quite different lines from capitalist societies in every institutional sphere and it is these internal arrangements that constitute their distinctive character. The crucial defining property is that they are 'command economies', based on collectivistic production and oriented to an ethic of 'social' distribution, an alternative world-system in which both the ends and the politically monistic means are based on an interpretation of *Marxism*, not of laissez-faire economic theory or bourgeois-democratic constitutional theory. Hence the notion that they are not 'really' *pure* Marxist states ('deformed') and that the human costs of using these means—including twenty-five million dead—cannot be charged against socialism constitutes both a philosophical sophism and a political evasion, an evasion that commonly takes the form of the argument that 'socialism (like Christianity) hasn't even been tried yet'. These are, however, states constituted precisely upon a 'reading'—not the only one possible—of Marx.

*　　　*　　　*

The Disintegration of the Third World

Models of three worlds were a response to the emergence of a whole series of newly-independent countries, largely in Africa, in the 1960s, which, although still economically dependent upon the metropoli—like their predecessors in Latin America—were so conditioned by the recency of the colonial experience that they came together to form a loose grouping of 'non-aligned' powers, anxious both to complete decolonisation, at home and abroad, and not to lose their newly-found independence: to steer their way between the Scylla of Washington and the Charybdis of Moscow in a world in which Cold War in the core countries was matched by very hot war in a series of confrontations in the shatter-zones between the two geographical blocs. These wars were often fought indirectly, and on the territory of Third World countries.

Internally, 'non-alignment' was paralleled by a rhetoric of populism[42] — usually, it was to turn out, *only* a rhetoric, institutionalised in the form of the single mass party and an official ideology, and tricked out with a mythology of direct rapport between Leader and people or Party and people, the reality of which, despite its emphasis on the poor (the *descamisados,* etc.) was an updated version of the traditional system of vertical links of patronage for those individuals and groups which toed the Party line. Nor were the agricultural and industrial bourgeoisies deprived of their power. But the masses were mobilised, and became a force on the political scene. Further, one or two industrialising countries, notably Argentina under Perón, did possess the economic wherewithal with which the rhetoric of populism could be turned into actuality, via income-redistribution in favour of the working class (or favoured segments of it) and via the political involvement of the working class, especially the trade unions, in public life for the first time, albeit in the form of incorporation as a segment of the single party. But since the working class could not be made to confine its demands within these limits, rising militancy began to threaten profits and stability to such an extent that a counter-offensive by the ruling class became inevitable, and took the form of military repression—and the end of practical populism.

Not only has internal populism disappeared, but also the expression of it at the international level, between States. Since the Bandung epoch, the Third World has disintegrated as an international power-grouping. The 'non-aligned' group is now 'non-aligned' only in the most Pickwickian of senses. Weakened in numbers and activity, it no longer possesses credibility. This weakness is the outward manifestation of the failure of the ideology which provided it with a social content and dynamic—the 'third way' which would be neither communist nor capitalist. The Third World has increasingly become a hollow shell, and it is precisely the centre which has been eroded away most, as one country after the other has gravitated to one or other of the polar alternatives in the world social system in their search for a development strategy.

Most, naturally, have opted for a fierce commitment to the most powerful system, that of capitalism. In a few cases, communist regimes have won out. Since the very blocs they have become attached to have themselves become less totalising the fear of domination has thereby diminished. The Second World has been shattered by the challenge of China, in Western Europe by the rise of various kinds of Eurocommunism, by unorthodoxies within Eastern Europe and by national conflicts in South-East Asia between communist states. True the economic strength of the USSR has ensured that most new mini-communist states (Cuba, Viet Nam, Mozambique, Angola) are forced into dependence upon the communist Superpower. Only a country which, like the USA and the USSR, is virtually a continent, China, has been able—whatever its poverty—to develop independently of Soviet (or American) aid, despite the extra burden created by military confrontation with the USSR.

Following its world-historic defeat in Viet Nam, the other Superpower has been unable to retain its authority even over its most closely-controlled satellites—in Iran and Nicaragua, to take only the latest instances.

The political disintegration of the Third World has been accompanied by economic disintegration also. The two processes, it should be noted, are not neatly related in some one-to-one way. The growing economic power of the oil-producing countries, and their challenge to the hegemony of the First World, does *not* result in their identification with the major system-alternative to capitalism. Rather, since there is no effective working class in Saudi Arabia or Kuwait, and what there is is composed of immigrants, and now that populism is no longer on the cards, they have usually expressed their rejection of Western political and cultural hegemony via a reassertion of pre-colonial identities, suitably updated. Thus, the 'traditions' of Islam—in which *sunna* (custom) and *hadith* (narrative statements of the usages set by Mohammed himself) have always been sources of legitimation second only to the Koran,[43] are appealed to and reinterpreted both by radical internationalists like Gadafy, and by the Ayatollah Khomeini, who purports to find Koranic justification for the quite un-traditional overthrow of monarchy and its replacement by priestly rule.

But the rise of the OPEC countries has also had particularly fateful consequences for the unity of the former Third World. Unity, of course, is always relative and situational, depending upon the issue and the occasion: one's allies in one situation may be, in the extreme, one's enemies in another. The non-industrialised countries, even the richer ones, do still act in concert as an economic pressure-group at UNCTAD meetings, both *vis-à-vis* the First World, and—one should note—also *vis-à-vis* the industrialised countries of the Second World, since these, between them, dominate world trade. But they have been able to achieve virtually nothing, and in other contexts, the '77' (actually over 120) evince no such solidarity. Above all, rising oil-prices hit the agrarian Third World even more disastrously than they damage the industrial West.

Finally, the solidarity of the '77' is fractured by the fact that some of them have actually made the 'take-off' to industrialisation, as Marx originally predicted. So committed are left-wing thinkers to the notion that underdevelopment is created and maintained in perpetuity (a notion not shared by Wallerstein, who notes the replacement of former core countries, down-graded to semi-peripheral status, and the similar graduation of some former peripheral countries to semi-peripheral status), that it is only slowly and painfully that most of them have begun to recognise one of the major transformations of our time: the rise to industrial status of the ex-colonial NICs, albeit often on the basis of technologies that the 'North' has largely left behind. Hong Kong is now number 9 in world trade, Brazil produces 11½ million tons of steel per annum, and Mexico City is bigger than London. It is not satisfactory, therefore, simply to go on parroting the term 'underdevelopment' when, as Booth puts it, 'the end product' may be either 'the sertão or Venezuela'.[44]

These are not economic 'miracles'. They have depended upon the severe political repression of working-class demand, both economic demand and every other kind of demand. Hong Kong is juridically still a colony, and South Korea and Taiwan have been described by Jon Halliday as 'semi-militarised societies', the abundant military force being directed at their own working class and not just at China and North Korea. In the Mexican case, following a popular revolution seventy years ago which cost the life of every tenth person, cooption has had to take different, more skilful forms of political incorporation not only of the working class but of any other alternative power-centre to the dominant Party. Brazil, then, and, say, Bhutan, Burundi, or Bolivia, are worlds apart, no longer part of the same Third World, dependent as both still are on the capitalist core countries. The difference has been wryly expressed in V.S. Naipaul's designation of the Caribbean as 'the Third World of the Third World'.

*   *   *

Economy and Society

We noted above that the phases of development in the colonial world reflected the changes going on in the metropoli, where the growth in power of the absolute monarchy signified an increased security for internal trade, a consolidation sealed by the development of a national culture: the invention of a new history, tradition and identity. But the new bourgeoisies were still only islands within predominantly feudal agrarian systems, and were not strong enough to take over the State for another century and a half after the political Revolution in England, and machinofacture was only to become dominant another century after that. Ruling classes themselves, moreover, are long in the making. Their coherence is therefore itself problematic and changing, and the 'fit' between political institutions and economic systems has never been one-to-one. As Hill has remarked: 'The absolute monarchy was a different form of feudal monarchy from the feudal-estates monarchy which preceded it; but the ruling class remained the same, just as a republic, a constitutional monarchy and a fascist dictatorship can all be forms of the rule of the bourgeoisie.'[45]

In the transformation of the economy along capitalist lines, the two crucial mobilisations are the mobilisation (accumulation) of capital and the making of a working class. In world-system models, the domination firstly of the core-zone, then of the rest of the world, is the crucial mechanism in the genesis of the capital that fuels the industrialisation process. Nationalist versions of the general model of course emphasise the crucial contribution represented by the exploitation of their particular country: Caribbean and African writers emphasise 'how Europe underdeveloped' those countries via the triangular trade, sugar plantations and slavery; Indian historians the looting of India by the eighteenth-century nabobs and its deindustrialisation; sinologists the trade in opium and tea, and so on. But the general thrust is clear. Wallerstein cites Marx's pronouncement that the emergence of modern capitalism could be said to date 'from the creation in the sixteenth century of a world-embracing commerce and a world-embracing market',[46] and again:

> Direct slavery is just as much a pivot of bourgeois industry as machinery, credits, etc. Without slavery you have no cotton, without cotton no modern industry. It is slavery that gave the colonies their value; it is the colonies that created world trade, and it is world trade that is the pre-condition of large-scale industry.[47]

The contribution of colonial primitive accumulation is easy to exaggerate, even the vast wealth pouring in from the Indies: 'Less than a quarter of the Spanish King's revenues came from remittances of American silver.'[48]

By 1700, 'colonial trade... amounted to 15 per cent of [British] commerce [and] by 1775 to as much as a fifth'.[49] By the middle of the nineteenth century, 'between £200 and £300 million of British capital investment—a quarter in the USA, almost a fifth in Latin America—brought back dividends and orders from all parts of the world'.[50] [The British] industrial economy grew out of commerce and especially... commerce with the underdeveloped world'.[51]

But it is not the relative importance of the internal market, or the European market, as against the rest of the world, that is really the issue. Rather, it was the use of capital in such a way that 'for the first time in human history, the shackles were taken off the productive power of human society, which henceforth became capable of the constant, rapid and up to the present limitless multiplication of men, goods and services'.[52] For that to happen, political revolution had first to occur; not only the act of seizing State power, but also the remaking of the State. 'The most decisive single event in the whole of British history', Hill has remarked, was 'the destruction of the royal bureaucracy in 1640-41'—over a hundred years before the climax of the Industrial Revolution.[53]

The distinction between the 'external' and 'internal' generation of capital soon becomes metaphysical, in any case, once profits repatriated from India and invested in British industry, after the initial investment, become 'internal'. Whatever the significance of external trade and overseas profits, it is ultimately the transformation of the mode of production *at home* that was decisive. In the mercantilist period, absolutist centralisation and cultural integration, the ending of what Anderson has termed 'parcellised sovereignty', reflect the initial importance of the internal economy, rather than the external market. And the external trade that mattered then was in Europe. Only very much later did the world outside Europe become more important.

Hence the explanation of how it was that certain countries successively acquired and lost the leading 'edge' remains crucial. In Wallerstein's system, Brenner has argued, 'technological advance and innovation function as a deus ex machina', particularly the 'quantitative... expansion of the division of labour which makes possible *specialisation*'[54]—specialisation, that is, in terms of organising labour 'best suited for particular types of production' (*MWS*, p. 87). 'Free labour is the form of labour control used for skilled work in core countries... coerced labour... for less skilled work in peripheral areas. The combination thereof is the essence of capitalism' (*MWS*, p. 127). But there is a tendency to resort to other kinds of pre-sociological explanation as well: to geography—'natural geography... posed fewer obstacles' to a centralising monarchy in England than elsewhere (p. 231); 'with sugar went slavery' (p. 43); Portugal, 'because of its geography', had to expand overseas (p. 47); and to demographic explanations: 'demography played the critical role' in explaining why 'labour was contractual in northwest Europe and coerced in eastern Europe' (p. 112).

But as Hill remarks, 'geography provides conditions "without which"; it does not offer a causal explanation of why. . .'[55] This is not to dismiss altogether the importance of location, climate etc. in understanding why some areas are better-favoured for certain kinds of production, particularly agriculture, than others. But the tendency is to accept these kinds of explanations at the expense of explanations in terms of social institutions or cultural orientations. Brenner emphasises the absence of emphasis upon new modes of class relationships that permitted the readier growth of capitalism in England than elsewhere, 'the already favourable social-productive or class relations, marked by the dissolution both of serfdom and entrenched peasant property' (*ibid.*, p. 76). Macfarlane has now suggested a whole range of other predisposing factors in Britain.[56] None of these are restricted to geography or technology, but facilitate the growth of kinds of social relations that ultimately generated a pressure for the more strictly political changes that writers like Wallerstein and Anderson, following in Weber's footsteps, rightly emphasise: the monopolisation of force by the monarch (standing armies), the creation of an effective national system of taxation, of an efficient bureaucracy, the imposition of a hegemonic national culture, etc.

The growth of both trade and production stimulated by these changes in political and social institutions, the growth of market-security, security of transport, contracts, weights and measures, coinage, etc., has been amply documented by historians. But this was not the kind of capitalism which was to usher in the Industrial Revolution. Rather, mercantilist capitalist production-systems, through monopolistic merchant and artisanal guilds, not only controlled commerce, but also restricted it, inhibiting the free play of the market and the innovator at home just as much as it was to do later in the colonies. Hence, in Marx's remark cited by Brenner, 'commerce. . . is incapable by itself of promoting and explaining the transition from one mode of production to another'.[57] The rise of *modern* capitalism had to await the formation of an entrepreneurial bourgeoisie oriented to expansion, and not just to rural-urban trade but to innovation in production and especially in manufacturing. It was to be a very long time before they became strong enough to challenge the absolutist State and the entire range of social institutions that supported it, from the Church to the system of feudal obligations. These class struggles, which ended in political revolution, are obscured if we direct our attention primarily to the outside world in looking for an explanation as to why it was that capitalism first took off in certain Western European countries.

The transition to capitalism, as Weber insisted, involves more than changes within the polity and the economy. It involves correlative changes in the entire system of social institutions and cultural orientations, of which Weber's discussion of the relationship between Protestantism and capitalism is the best-known instance. That insight has been revived recently in Macfarlane's powerfully-argued and documented charting of individualism as an economic, familial, and legal phenomenon many centuries *before* the triumph of the bourgeoisie. (His account of feudalism—omitting the feudal lord—is much less impressive.) The growth of capitalism in England, then, may well be as much due to the presence of *non*-economic institutions and values favourable to capitalist production and enterprise and not simply to economic and political structures *per se* because, in the phrase Weber was fond of quoting, the former had an 'elective affinity' with the latter. This is not to say that either *caused* the other. It is interesting to observe, therefore, that after an impeccable Marxist beginning, in treating the transition from feudalism to capitalism in terms of modes of production and social formations, Anderson goes on to emphasise the correlative importance of two 'cultural' institutions: the Roman Catholic Church—'extraordinary' in its persistence, 'indispensable' as a bridge between Antiquity and the Middle Ages; and the revival of Roman law, adapted so as to strengthen 'the idea of absolute private property in land' and 'the concentration of aristocratic class power in a centralised State apparatus'.[58]

'The economy', of course, is an analytical abstraction which in reality never exists 'in itself'. It is the observer who, by analytical 'fiat', compartmentalises social behaviour and dubs this or that aspect of it respectively 'political', 'economic', 'psychological', and so on. In the eighteenth century that process of decomposition had not gone so far, and was not yet built into the thought-system of the pioneer social scientists, including Marx. In various ways, they tried to retain the notion of the *interdependence* of ways of producing and consuming with other social and cultural institutions and values, whether by using 'political economy' in a way that was coterminous with 'social science', or by distinguishing between the State and 'civil society', the latter *including* the economy.

Yet that enlightened perspective was on the way out: classical bourgeois economics was soon not only to abstract 'the economic', but also to make it *determinant*. Capitalism was rational, it argued, insofar as it was governed by 'purely' economic principles of supply and demand, articulated only by the market. Everything else—the totality of 'non-economic' institutions and values—ought not to influence the economy: to allow it to do so was 'irrational'.

Marx was just as mystified, at times, in swallowing this aspect of laissez faire ideology which, as Sahlins has put it, 'installs one. . . cultural logic as the definition of everyone's material necessity'.[59] So have generations of subsequent Marxists.

As against the myth of the 'nightwatchman state', Wallerstein is correct in arguing that

no free market has ever existed, or could have existed within a capitalist world-

economy. The hypothetical free market is an intellectual construct which serves
the same intellectual function as frictionless movement, as a standard from which
to measure the degree of deviation (*CWE*, p. 149).

> Far from being a system of free competition of all sellers, it is a system in which
> competition becomes relatively free only when the economic advantage of upper
> strata is so clear-cut that the unconstrained operation of the market serves
> effectively to reinforce the existing system of stratification (*ibid*., p. 16).

But this is still too absolute and ahistoric a statement, for the state does
not always intervene or play the same role. The absolutist State did
arrogate power to itself, turning 'landlord' into 'landowner'. It intervened
powerfully to assist the birth of the new industrial order. The State then let
the bourgeoisie—'the economy'—have their head in the lengthy epoch 'before
the socialists'. And in the colonies, the new 'landowners' were able to turn
to what Alavi calls 'economic coercion' in lieu of direct State intervention
in the management of the economy.

The relationship between polity and economy is thus historically
variable. But there are important differences in modes and degrees of
coercion, which Wallerstein's model recognises, but at times departs from,
as in the formula that the producer who receives less than he produces is
'objectively' a 'proletarian'. In this model, all exploitation becomes
capitalist exploitation, as long as it is oriented to profit on the market.
Feudalism, slavery, bureaucratic despotism, capitalism simply dissolve into
a generalised exploitative 'class society'.

A dialectical historiography and sociology, however, has to treat the
relationship between 'the economy' and 'the rest' as problematic, not as if
it were absolute and self-evident. Thus, it is just not true that 'the basic
linkage' between the 'parts' of the mercantilist world-system was
'economic' (*MWS*, p. 15), for Wallerstein has immediately to qualify this
by adding 'although this was reinforced to some degree by cultural links
and eventually by political arrangements'.[60] What he actually shows in his
excellent analysis of Portugal-in-Asia (pp. 317-344) is that trade depended
upon the military capacity to force open markets and that the establishment of colonies was the initial act—a political one—by Spain, not some
post-economic ('eventual') reinforcement.

Wallerstein, at other times, adopts a resolutely political-economy
position:

> Not only is the capitalist system not properly described as a system of free
> enterprise today, but there never was a moment in history when this was a
> reasonable descriptive label. The capitalist system is and always has been one of
> state interference with the 'freedom' of the market in the interests of some and
> against the interests of others. (*CWE*, p. 121).

This is excellently put, though it needs to be pushed even further. For we have all been victims of reductionist materialism, a classically bourgeois conception antithetical to a *dialectical* social science. Some twenty years ago, Denis Wrong argued that modern social science was afflicted with an 'over-socialised' conception of man.[61] Today, we are tempted by 'over-integrated' conceptions of society and of world-society. As Gouldner has insisted, Parsonian functionalism formulated a model of 'the social system' which accorded too little autonomy to the constituent sub-systems.[62] So today there are 'systems' Marxisms which are equally over-integrated, the most formalised of which in the West has been Althusserianism, and in the communist world, Soviet functionalist Marxism.

It is true that economic requirements impose a logic of necessity upon society: people must eat and produce, and society has to be 'provisioned', in Sahlins' term, via technical and social apparatuses they have inherited for such purposes. But this necessity does not 'determine' what is produced, how the technical division of labour is distributed, what kinds of things become valued, the nature of wants, whether things become commodities, the ends to which production is devoted, the distribution of consumption and ownership. These are not, somehow, inherent in the mode of production, certainly if this is conceived of—as all too often it is—mainly in terms of the logic of the 'labour process', for these things are never just aspects of a mode of production, but always a mode of production *and appropriation,* and further, of the range of social and cultural systems in which these are embedded.

Capitalism, like any other social system, is faced with trying to impose its cultural logic on the whole range of institutions inherited from the past. It need not do so absolutely, making everything anew, only at decisive points. Nor is it always *able* to uproot or transform everything: it has to come to terms with deeply-entrenched structures and values, 'reworking' the old so as to be at least minimally consistent with the requirements of the new. These include not only the socio-cultural legacy inherited from the *immediate* past, since societies typically embody a number of coexistent and conflicting modes of production and institutions which persist across whole epochs: 'Rather than presenting. . . a cumulative chronology, in which one phase succeeds and supersedes the next. . . the course towards capitalism reveals a *remanence* of the legacy of one mode of production within an epoch *dominated* by another. . .'[63]

In the colonies, equally, modern colonial capitalism was stamped with the legacy not only of the immediate past epoch—that of mercantilist capitalism—but of the precolonial heritages that preceded it.

What is produced and who gets what, then, are culturally and not just economically determined. The crassest forms of reductionist materialism, we might note, are not those of Marxists, but of non-Marxist technological determinists and anthropological 'materialists'. And some Marxists have, at last, become aware of the concept of culture.

The myth of the 'nightwatchman' state has now been definitively exploded by Foster's analysis of the crucial role played by the State in England's Industrial Revolution. Moreover, despite his retention of 'base/superstructure' language, he has also demonstrated that the Industrial Revolution entailed, certainly economic and political class struggle, but also total confrontation of class *cultures* in every sphere of life, from schools to friendly societies, pubs and churches:[64] the enclosure of the land through parliamentary legislation; the dispossession of those who worked it; the making of a working-class; the deportation of their leaders to England's Siberia, Australia, when they resisted; the counter-terror and espionage visited upon trade unions and popular organisations; in general, the removal of a proto-revolutionary threat in an England that saw cotton operatives drilling nightly on the moors outside the mill-towns, and in which there were more troops quartered on the population than were used to defeat Napoleon in the Peninsular War; the mounting of a concerted campaign to undermine the independent political and social institutions built up by the working class, from churches to pubs; and the provision of charitable relief for some at least. In all this, the State played a central role. Within thirty years the threat of revolution had been removed.

Nevertheless, it is not ever thus: the extent and manner of state intervention have still to be taken as problematic, as matters for empirical historical investigation, for ruling classes are not often or always obliged to mount that kind of cultural counter-offensive. These relationships between polity, economy and the rest of the social order varied from epoch to epoch, just as they vary from society to society. They cannot be reduced to some schematic formula about '*the* role of *the* state' under capitalism, when, as we have seen, 'capitalism' underwent successive transformations. What proved distinctive about capitalism in the end, however, was its built-in drive toward infinity, (a drive which is today evoking the counter-philosophy of 'limits to growth'). This dynamic is equally typical of state socialism, devoted as it is to the raising of living-standards as its primary goal, a contrast most vividly seen when contrasted with those societies which possess what Sahlins had called 'Zen economies' or those he labels the 'original affluent societies',[65] those peoples who produce individually and appropriate socially.

Capitalism, then, is not protocypical of human society. It is the most developed form of class society based on private property in the means of production. To understand it, the concepts of 'elective affinity' and of 'culture' would seem more adequate than over-integrated base/superstructure or world-system models. For these always require running repairs, leading to casuistical distinctions between the 'determining' and the 'determinant'; about 'the economic' only being 'determinant' in the last instance', 'juridico-political' and 'ideological' 'superstructures', and the rest of it.

Rather than 'economies' or systems which appear to determine human development independently of human agency, we might get back to the humanistic ('Promethean') notion Marx inherited from the Enlightenment: that people 'make their own history'—even if not 'under circumstances chosen by themselves, but... given and transmitted from the past'.

Althusser, on the other hand, tells us that history is 'a process without a subject'. For Marx, despite Althusser, there *was* a subject: a human, social agency: 'The history of hitherto existing societies is the history of *class struggles*'. But only 'hitherto'. Engels, referring to pre-class societies, ended his own *Origin of the Family* by quoting from the conlcuding lines of Morgan's *Ancient Society*: 'A mere property career is not the final destiny of mankind... The next higher plane of society... will be a revival, in a higher form, of the liberty, equality, and fraternity of the ancient gentes'.

Hence a truly human society would not reduce people to the role either of producers or consumers, but allow them to enter the 'realm of freedom', which, as Marx put it, begins 'only where labour which is determined by necessity and mundane considerations ceases...; in the nature of things... beyond the sphere of actual material production.'

NOTES

1. Weidenfeld and Nicolson, London (revised 1967).
2. A good account of the debate is provided by Philip J. O'Brien in his 'A Critique of Latin American Theories of Dependency', *Beyond the Sociology of Development: economy and society in Latin America and Africa*, (eds. Ivar Oxaal, Tony Barnett and David Booth), Routledge and Kegan Paul, London, 1975, pp. 7-27. See also the article 'André Gunder Frank: an introduction and appreciation', by David Booth, in the same volume (pp. 50-85).
3. K.M. Panikkar, *Asia and Western Dominance: a survey of the Vasco da Gama epoch of Asian history 1498-1945*, Allen and Unwin, London, 1954, p. 88.
4. Aidan Foster-Carter, 'Marxism versus Dependency Theory? A Polemic', *Occasional Papers in Sociology*, No. 8, Leeds University, p. 13.
5. Originally in *Catalyst*, University of Buffalo; republished in *Latin America: Underdevelopment or Revolution*, Monthly Review Press, New York, 1969, pp. 21-94.
6. *The Modern World-System: capitalist agriculture and the origins of the European world-economy in the sixteenth century*, Academic Press, New York, 1974, p. 15 (hereinafter '*MWS*').
7. Immanuel Wallerstein, *The Capitalist World-Economy* (hereinafter '*CWE*'), Cambridge University Press, 1979, p. 220, (Wallerstein's italics). This is not the second volume in Wallerstein's tetralogy, but a separate volume of collected essays.
8. *CWE*, pp. 68 and 53.
9. *Op. cit.*, p. 38.
10. I discuss some typical instances in my 'How Many Worlds?', *Third World Quarterly*, Vol. 1, No. 2, 1979, pp. 100-107.
11. 'India and the Colonial Mode of Production', *Socialist Register* 1975, (eds.), R. Miliband and John Saville, Merlin Press, London, 1975, pp. 160-197.
12. 'The Structure of Colonial Social Formations', (for publication); my italics.

13. 'The Structure of Colonial Social Formations', pp. 21, 22.

14. 'India and the Colonial Mode of Production', p. 192.

15. *CWE*, p. 34.

16. *CWE*, p. 159. Though elsewhere in *CWE* capitalism is characterised not in terms of the market, but as a system oriented to 'endless accumulation' (p. 272); 'the only mode of production in which the *maximisation* of surplus creation is rewarded *per se*' (p. 285, his italics).

17. A line of criticism first developed by Ernesto Laclau in his 'Feudalism and Capitalism in Latin America', *New Left Review*, 67, 1977, pp. 19-38, and by Robert Brenner in his 'The Origins of Capitalist Development: a critique of neo-Smithian Marxism', *New Left Review*, 104, 1977, pp. 25-92. My intellectual debt to both of them will be obvious in these pages.

18. Theda Skopcol, 'Wallerstein's World Capitalist System: a theoretical and historical critique', *American Journal of Sociology*, Vol. 32, No. 5, p. 1088 (my italics).

19. On which see the definitive philippic by E.P. Thompson, *The Poverty of Theory*, Merlin, London, 1978, pp. 193-397. The resort of 'system-maintenance' arguments, and *ad hoc* 'repairs' where the historical evidence does not support the model; and the replacement of one inadequate form of 'outmoded theoretical category' by another (i.e. 'system' in its functionalist version) are noted by Skopcol (pp. 1088-9), since 'national system' has merely been displaced by 'world system'.

20. Guillermo Bonfil Batalla, 'El Concepto de Indio en América: una categoría de la situación colonial', *Anales de Antropología*, Vol. IX, Medico City, 1972, pp. 105-124.

21. Gonzalo Aguirre Beltrán, *La Población Negra de México: estudio etno-histórico*, Fondo de Cultura Económica, Mexico City, 1976, Part III, 'Premisas Biológicas', p. 153-194.

22. Excellently described by Gerald T. Robinson for the Russian peasantry, in *Rural Russia Under the Old Regime: a history of the landlord-peasant world and a prologue to the peasant revolution of 1917*, Macmillan, New York, 1932.

23. See J.C. van Leur, *Indonesian Trade and Society: essays in Asian social and economic history*, W. Van Hoeve, The Hague, 1955: 'Western trade was always a one-sided movement of goods... in that costly merchandise was exchanged for coin and certain metals in ingot'. [Asian] handicrafts 'never left any important place for European craft goods. And European factory products found no admittance in Asia before the advent of... mass production of consumer goods in Western Europe', (p. 281).

24. Agustín Cueva, *El Proceso de Dominación Política en Ecuador*, Solitierra, Quito, 1977, p. 7.

25. *The Third World*, p. 15.

26. See Darcy Ribeiro, 'The Cultural-Historical Configurations of the American Peoples', *Current Anthropology*, Vol. II, No. 4-5, 1970, pp. 403-434.

27. This disjunction between economic and political power is important, in particular, for Wallerstein's 'attempts to equate the strong core state and the absolute monarchy... for the strongest states were not always in the core... in fact, equally strong or stronger states can grow up in the periphery...' (Skopcol, p. 1086). She instances the relative weakness of governments in seventeenth century England and Netherlands, 'the center of the nascent capitalist commercial economy'. By contrast, Sweden, Prussia and Spain were much more absolutist.

28. *Op. cit.*, pp. 31, 33.

29. Perry Anderson, *Lineages of the Absolutist State*, New Left Books, London,

1974, and the companion *Passages from Antiquity to Feudalism* (also 1974). A more sustained comparison of Anderson's work would require an examination of his use of the country (Spain, France, England, etc.) as his unit of analysis in *Lineages*, within a framework, established in *Passages*, of modes of production and a typology of 'social formations', themselves set against the legacy of Antiquity and a division of Europe into 'West' and 'East'. The contrast with Wallerstein's framework is self-evident. Nevertheless, and 'curiously enough for a theory that sets out to de-emphasise the nation-state' (Skopcol, p. 1080), the main unit of analysis in the latter work remains the nation-state or the colony. To explain the emergence of these centralised polities would require analysis of the formation of the internal market, not of foreign trade.

30. J.H. Elliott, *Imperial Spain 1496-1716*, Penguin, Harmondsworth, 1970.

31. *MWS*, p. 179.

32. *MWS*, p. 187.

33. Elliott, *op. cit.*, p. 177. The elaborate system of Councils, *audiencias, corregidores, oidores, visitas generales*, and *residencias*, is well-described in John L. Phelan's *The Kingdom of Quito in the Seventeenth Century*, University of Wisconsin Press, 1967.

34. Panikkar, *op. cit.*, p. 35.

35. Elliott, *op. cit.*, p. 183.

36. 'The Pillage of the Third World', *Monthly Review Press*, New York, 1968, Chap. 2.

37. See the incisive critique of 'convergence' theory by John H. Goldthorpe, 'Social Stratification in Industrial Society', in *The Development of Industrial Societies*, Sociological Review Monograph, No. 8, Keele, 1964, pp. 97-122.

38. As in the case of Woolf-Philips' 'linear' model, or J.E. Goldthorpe's use of no less than nine major different categories of 'poor countries' (see my 'How Many Worlds?', p. 102-6.

39. John H. Goldthorpe, *op. cit.*, pp. 110, 112, 113.

40. *Exploitation: the world power-structure and the inequality of nations*, Macgibbon and Kee, London, 1970, p. 18.

41. Richard Jolly, 'Why the poor still bite on bullets', *Guardian*, London, 8/5/78.

42. See Chapter 4 of *The Third World*; the further debate in G. Ionescu and E. Gellner (eds.), *Populism: its meanings and national characteristics*, Weidenfeld and Nicolson, 1969; and the introduction to the Brazilian edition of *The Third World*, (in press).

43. See H.A.R. Gibb, *Mohammedanism: an historical survey*, Oxford University Press, London, 1962, Chapter 5.

44. In Oxaal, Barnett and Booth (eds.), *op. cit.*, p. 77. Hence 'dependence' is a more powerful concept term than 'underdevelopment', for colonialism entailed both massive innovation and transformation and the utilisation of older institutions for new ends in new ways. Old or new, both contributed to the formation of dependent economies even after formal political independence. 'Underdevelopment', however, is acceptable if it is used—as it often is—to signify peripheral status in the world economy.

45. Christopher Hill, 'A Comment', in *The Transition from Feudalism to Capitalism*, New Left Books, 1976, p. 121.

46. From *Capital*, Vol. 1, Chapter 4, cited in *MWS*, p. 77.

47. From *The Poverty of Philosophy*, cited in *CWE*, p. 147.

48. Elliott, *op. cit.*, p. 147.

49. E.J. Hobsbawm, *Industry and Empire*, Penguin, Harmondsworth, London, 1969, p. 53.

50. E.J. Hobsbawm, *The Age of Revolution 1789-1848*, Mentor, London, 1964,

p. 72.

51. *Industry and Empire*, p. 54.

52. *Age of Revolution*, p. 45.

53. Christopher Hill, *Reformation to Industrial Revolution*, Penguin, Harmondsworth, London, 1969, p. 98.

54. *Op. cit.*, p. 57, Brenner's italics. For example: 'What products are exchanged in this "unequal exchange" are a function of world technology' (*CWE*, p. 71). I have not emphasised the implications of the functionalist language: of 'tasks', 'allotted', 'functions', 'hierarchies' and so forth: but this could be done.

55. Hill, *op. cit.*, p. 82.

56. Alan Macfarlane, *The Origins of English Individualism: the family, property and social transition*, Blackwell, Oxford, 1978.

57. From *Capital*, Vol. III.

58. Anderson, *Passages*, pp. 131-7; *Lineages*, pp. 24-9.

59. 'Anthropology and Two Marxisms: problems of historical materialism', Chapter 3, *Culture and Practical Reason*, Aldine, Chicago, 1976, p. 165.

60. On p. 77 of *MWS*, sixteenth century capitalism is defined as the 'dominant mode of *social* organisation of the economy' (my italics), but the implications of the word 'social' are not theoretically spelled out, other than in the chapter on 'statism'.

61. 'The Over-socialised Conception of Man in Modern Sociology', *American Sociological Review*, Vol. 26, No. 2, 1961, pp. 183-93.

62. Alvin W. Gouldner, *The Coming Crisis of Western Sociology*, Heinemann, London, 1971, pp. 215-6.

63. Anderson, *Lineages*, p. 421.

64. *Class Struggle in the Industrial Revolution: early industrial capitalism in three English towns*, Weidenfeld and Nicolson, London, 1974.

65. Marshall Sahlins, *Stone Age Economics*, Aldine, Chicago, 1972.

51. *Industry and Empire*, p. 54.
52. *Age of Revolution*, p. 45.
53. Christopher Hill, *Reformation to Industrial Revolution*, Penguin, Harmondsworth, London, 1969, p. 98.
54. Op. cit., p. 57. Brenner's italics. For example: 'What products are exchanged in this "unequal exchange," are a function of world technology' (CWF, p. 71) ... have not emphasised the implications of the functionalist language of 'tasks allotted', 'functions', 'hierarchies', and so forth; but this could be done.
55. Hill op. cit., p. 82.
56. Alan Macfarlane, *The Origins of English Individualism: the family, property and social transition*, Blackwell, Oxford 1978.
57. ... *Capital*, Vol. III.
58. Anderson, *Passages*, pp. 131-3 ... pp. 20-2.
59. *Anthropology and Two Marxisms: problems of historical materialism*, Chapter 3, *Culture and Practical Reason*, Aldine, Chicago, 1976, p. 165.
60. On p. 77 of MWS, sixteenth century capitalism is defined as the 'dominant mode of social organisation of the economy' (my italics), but the implications of the word 'social' are not theoretically spelled out other than in the shape of nations.
61. The Over-socialised Conception of Man in Modern Sociology, *American Sociological Review*, Vol. 26, No. 2, 1961, pp. 183-93.
62. Alvin W. Gouldner, *The Coming Crisis of Western Sociology*, Heinemann, London, 1971, pp. 215-6.
63. Anderson, *Lineages*, p. 421.
64. Class Struggle in the Industrial Revolution: early industrial capitalism in three English towns, Weidenfeld and Nicolson, London, 1974.
65. Marshall Sahlins, *Stone Age Economics*, Aldine, Chicago, 1972.